YALE AGRARIAN STUDIES SERIES
JAMES C. SCOTT, SERIES EDITOR

THE AGRARIAN STUDIES SERIES AT YALE UNIVERSITY PRESS seeks to publish outstanding and original interdisciplinary work on agriculture and rural society—for any period, in any location. Works of daring that question existing paradigms and fill abstract categories with the lived experience of rural people are especially encouraged.

—*James C. Scott, Series Editor*

James C. Scott, *Seeing Like a State: How Certain Schemes to Improve the Human Condition Have Failed*
Steve Striffler, *Chicken: The Dangerous Transformation of America's Favorite Food*
James C. Scott, *The Art of Not Being Governed: An Anarchist History of Upland Southeast Asia*
Timothy Pachirat, *Every Twelve Seconds: Industrialized Slaughter and the Politics of Sight*
James C. Scott, *Against the Grain: A Deep History of the Earliest States*
Loka Ashwood, *For-Profit Democracy: Why the Government Is Losing the Trust of Rural America*
Jonah Steinberg, *A Garland of Bones: Child Runaways in India*
Hannah Holleman, *Dust Bowls of Empire: Imperialism, Environmental Politics, and the Injustice of "Green" Capitalism*
Johnhenry Gonzalez, *Maroon Nation: A History of Revolutionary Haiti*
Christian C. Lentz, *Contested Territory: Điện Biên Phủ and the Making of Northwest Vietnam*
Dan Allosso, *Peppermint Kings: A Rural American History*
Jamie Kreiner, *Legions of Pigs in the Early Medieval West*
Christian Lund, *Nine-Tenths of the Law: Enduring Dispossession in Indonesia*
Shaila Seshia Galvin, *Becoming Organic: Nature and Agriculture in the Indian Himalaya*
Michael Dove, *Bitter Shade: The Ecological Challenge of Human Consciousness*
Japhy Wilson, *Reality of Dreams: Post-Neoliberal Utopias in the Ecuadorian Amazon*
Aniket Aga, *Genetically Modified Democracy: Transgenic Crops in Contemporary India*
Ruth Mostern, *The Yellow River: A Natural and Unnatural History*
Brian Lander, *The King's Harvest: A Political Ecology of China from the First Farmers to the First Empire*
Jo Guldi, *The Long Land War: The Global Struggle for Occupancy Rights*
Andrew S. Mathews, *Trees Are Shape Shifters: How Cultivation, Climate Change, and Disaster Create Landscapes*
Francesca Bray, Barbara Hahn, John Bosco Lourdusamy, and Tiago Saraive, *Moving Crops and the Scales of History*

For a complete list of titles in the Yale Agrarian Studies Series, visit yalebooks.com/agrarian.

Trees Are Shape Shifters

How Cultivation, Climate Change, and Disaster Create Landscapes

ANDREW S. MATHEWS

Yale
UNIVERSITY PRESS
NEW HAVEN AND LONDON

Published with assistance from the foundation established in memory of
Calvin Chapin of the Class of 1788, Yale College.

Yale University Press books may be purchased in quantity for educational, business, or promotional use. For information, please e-mail sales.press@yale.edu (U.S. office) or sales@yaleup.co.uk (U.K. office).

Set in Electra type by Westchester Publishing Services.
Printed in the United States of America.

Library of Congress Control Number: 2021951702
ISBN 978-0-300-26038-0 (hardcover)
ISBN 978-0-300-26037-3 (paper)

A catalogue record for this book is available from the British Library.

10 9 8 7 6 5 4 3 2 1

To Kaia, Elias, Taddeo, and Tara

CONTENTS

Preface and Acknowledgments ix

Introduction 1

ONE
Sensing the Invisible:
Plant Form and Landscape Transformation 13

Interlude I. Plant Morphology Leads to Geomorphology 33

TWO
From Plant Morphologies to Landscape Structures 42

THREE
Fast and Slow Disasters:
Plant Disease, Forest Fires, and Climate Change 73

Interlude II. Pine Cultivation and Pine as an Agent of Landscape Transformation 101

FOUR
Plant Morphology, Geomorphology, and Weather 109

FIVE
Biogeomorphological Politics 126

SIX
From Landscape Histories to Climate Models 150

SEVEN
From Climate Change to Biomass Energy 178

Interlude III. Airscapes 199

EIGHT
Landscapes and Energy Politics 203

EPILOGUE
Trees Are Shape Shifters 223

Appendix 1. Ecology and Climate of the Monte Pisano 231

Appendix 2. Equations as Stories 233

Appendix 3. List of Organizations 235

Glossary 237

Notes 241

References 269

Index 293

PREFACE AND ACKNOWLEDGMENTS

As a child in the 1970s, I encountered an Italian landscape and rural society that were changing rapidly. Returning to Tuscany every summer, I thought of this world as stable and more or less eternal. As a teenager and college student, I began to notice change. Abandoned farmhouses were converted into holiday cottages. An industrial wine estate ripped out thousands of hectares of small farms to plant kilometers of grape vines. I was happy to get summer jobs picking grapes, an arduous and often boring job in the heat of summer, but doing so was also a way to spend days outdoors. By the time I went to graduate school, first to study forestry and then anthropology, I had learned that change has been a constant feature of the Italian landscape. Over the past several thousand years, peasant farmers constantly tinkered with the plants, animals, and soils that they depended upon. The results of their labors were olive terraces, carefully tended woodlands, grazed mountain pastures, and chestnut groves. This was an agrosilvopastoral landscape of extraordinary beauty that required constant care. I learned tiny fragments of their knowledge from these peasants through conversations and working in fields and when staying with my Aunt Beatrice Cazac, who shares my profound respect for them. That world is now largely gone.

This book bears witness to the knowledge of the peasant cultivators who built this landscape, and explores how this history continues to affect the world we now live in, as we struggle to confront climate change, forest fires, and plant disease epidemics. To protect their privacy, I have used pseudonyms for most of the elderly peasants and for the farmers and loggers whom I talked to. For the same reason, I have used pseudonyms for most of the officials, activists, biomass entrepreneurs, and scientists with whom I talked, except for a few who were public figures or who have read and commented on the chapters in which they appear. Thank you all for your kindness and patience.

When I started to think about research in Italy, I was moving from over fifteen years of research and writing on Mexico to a country in which I had partly grown up, but with a scholarly literature with which I was unfamiliar. Although I am not a historian, this book builds on a deep reservoir of Italian scholarship on rural and environmental history. Wherever I can, I have cited English-language works, but there is much that is only available in Italian. I have done my best to point toward key debates in this scholarship, but this is only a beginning. I hope that my Italian readers will forgive the gaps in my knowledge, while accepting this work not only as history, but as something different: an ethnographic historical ecology and natural history that also engages with contemporary environmental politics.

Research and writing depend on friendships. This is all the more true of transdisciplinary projects like this one, which depend so much on the help and patience of others. I have been lucky in my colleagues and in the collaborators and friends whom I met along the way. In Italy, Diego Moreno and Roberta Cevasco generously introduced me to the world of Italian historical ecology, and Pietro Piussi taught me about forest history. Sergio Nelli and Valentina Simonetti introduced me to the extraordinary riches of the Archivio di Stato di Lucca, and the director of the archive, Simone Sartini, supported a workshop on the Monte Pisano in 2018. Marco Armiero shared difficult-to-locate Italian language materials, and Roberta Biasillo advised me on how to find a critical image archive. Francesco Roma Marzio and Alessandra Sani helped me with botanical fieldwork. My collaborator Fabio Malfatti, of the Centro Ricerche EtnoAntropologiche, accompanied me in interviews with farmers and officials in 2015, 2016, and 2019. His deep knowledge of Italian anthropology and rural life has helped and challenged me. Our shared fieldwork and our conversations about what we learned together have been true collaboration. The maps in this book are the product of his skill and imagination. In Lucca, many people helped me. My thanks to Paola Meschi, Aurora Chiesa, and Enrico Chiesa, who loved the rural landscape but did not live to see this book published. My thanks also to Massimo Giambastiani, Alessandra del Chiaro, Giuseppe del Chiaro, Angelo Frati, and the Museo del Castagno at Colognora. Try to visit this gem if you can! My thanks also to Ivo Poli for his introduction to the world of chestnut cultivators, to Gabriele Casazza, and to Fabio Casella, who opened up my eyes to the world of litter raking on the Monte Pisano. Massimiliano Grava generously shared historical land-use data, and Andrea Bertacchi shared botanical maps; the combination of this data provided the basis for the maps in chapter 3. I have also drawn extensively on the work of the local historian Giovanni Massoni, whose history of the valley of Vorno covers much more than I can.

In this book, I have tried to combine my training in forestry and anthropology with my lifelong practice of walking, looking at, and thinking about the relationships between people, trees, and landscapes. At first it seemed impossible to bring together such disparate forms of noticing. Forest walks and conversations with my colleague Anna Tsing helped me be bolder. Listening to Donna Haraway in action helped me imagine how ecology and anthropology could talk to each other. The research and writing of this book emerged in parallel with "Slow Seminar" conversations with the Aarhus University Research on the Anthropocene project, led by Anna Tsing and Nils Bubandt, including several visits to Aarhus to share early fragments. At Aarhus University, conversations with biologist Peter Funch inspired me to experiment with tree drawings as evidence. Natasha Myers helped me think about plants; Heather Swanson was a source of enthusiasm and questions; and Elaine Gan advised and encouraged my drawing efforts and my use of images and diagrams. This work has also benefited from conversations with audiences at Oslo University, including Rune Flicke, Knut Nustad, and Cecilia Salinas. At Oslo, Marianne Lien and John Law invited me to present portions of this work at the Center for Advanced Study on Arctic Domestication at the Norwegian Academy of Sciences and Letters in 2015 and 2016. Their ideas and questions, as well as conversations with Diane Gifford-Gonzalez and Annemarie Mol, have stayed with me.

Parts of chapters 3 and 6 have been presented to audiences at the University of California Davis, and at workshops at Bennington College and the University of Chicago. At Davis, my particular thanks go to James Smith; at Chicago, to Julie Chu, Michael Fisch, and Jun Mizukawa; and at Bennington, to David Bond, Andrea Ballestero, and Joe Masco. I have also benefited from insightful comments and criticisms from the infrastructure reading group with Michael Fisch, Julie Chu, Eleana Kim, and Jun Mizukawa. Portions of this work were presented at workshops at the University of Calgary, at Berkeley, and at the Yale MacMillan Center Program in Agrarian Studies. I thank all my interlocutors for their questions and for their kindness.

The Department of Anthropology at the University of California Santa Cruz, where I work, is a wonderful place to expand my imagination and to experiment with writing. I am grateful for the generosity of my colleagues and students. I learned to think about secularity from Susan Harding and Mayanthi Fernando, to try to figure out what the big questions are from Mark Anderson, and from walks with Jerry Zee. I am indebted to my colleagues in a UC Humanities Institute research cluster on the Anthropocene: Mayanthi Fernando, Jennifer Derr, and Kristina Lyons. Many graduate students have engaged with versions of my thinking, including Zac Caple, Colin Hoag, Daniel Schniedewind, Rob Davenport, Eda Tarak, Jon Nyquist, Emily Reisman, Lachlan Summers, Gillian Bogart, and Lizzy Hare.

Scholarship takes time and money. This book is based on fieldwork carried out in Italy in 2013–2014 and in the summers of 2015 and 2016. I was supported in this research by a sabbatical from my position in the Department of Anthropology at the University of California Santa Cruz, and by grants from the Division of Social Sciences and the Committee on Research. A critical return visit in the spring of 2019 was supported by a grant from the Garden and Landscape Studies program of Dumbarton Oaks. Time to write this book was made possible by a sabbatical leave in fall 2018, and by an Executive Vice Chancellor's Fellowship in 2019–2020. I am grateful for their support and for that of my department chair, Nancy Chen, and to Melissa Caldwell, who helped organize teaching leaves at critical moments.

Versions of some of the ideas in this book have emerged in other places. Chapters 2 and 3 contain material that was published in *Cultural Anthro-*

pology 33, no. 3 (August 2018): 386–414, and as "Ghostly Forms and Forest Histories" in *Arts of Living on a Damaged Planet: Ghosts and Monsters of the Anthropocene*, ed. Anna Lowenhaupt Tsing, Heather Anne Swanson, Elaine Gan, and Nils Bubandt, University of Minnesota Press, 2017, G145–156.

At Yale University Press, I have benefited from the wise advice and encouragement of my editor, Jean Thomson Black, who supported me in incorporating the many images that are a central argument of this book. My thanks also to Elizabeth Sylvia and Amanda Gerstenfeld, to Kate Davis for inspired copyediting, and to the rest of the production team at Yale University Press. Anonymous reviewers helped me strengthen my arguments. My mistakes are, of course, all my own.

Last but not least, my thanks to my family, who make my work possible. My father, Christopher Mathews, read and responded to the complete manuscript; my mother, Marianne Mathews, suggested that I base myself in Lucca in the first place; and my brother, Benjamin Mathews, has discussed land care in Italy with me for many years. Thank you to my in-laws, Sven and Barbara Huseby, for their support and conversation throughout this project. My sons, Elias and Taddeo, put up with an unfamiliar school system and a strange language during the year we lived in Italy. Finally, as always, my love and thanks to Kaia, my companion in this and other adventures.

Trees Are Shape Shifters

Introduction

Forest fires have become a recurring feature of life where I live in Northern California. In the summer of 2020, raging wildfires forced us to evacuate for several days. We were lucky. Hundreds of people lost their homes in the Santa Cruz Mountains and elsewhere across the state. Dramatic pictures of the Golden Gate Bridge beneath an apocalyptic yellow sky circulated around the world. Smoke kept us indoors for days, running homemade air filters full tilt, and wearing masks whenever we went outdoors. The act of breathing left a sour taste in our mouths, as fragments of charred leaves and ash rained from the sky. Even when fires do not come so close as they did in 2020, this taste of smoke has become a predictable reminder of disaster tens or hundreds of kilometers away. In 2018, the Camp fire burned out the town of Paradise, killing eighty-five people, destroying over eighteen thousand structures, and doing over $16 billion in damage. As I write in 2021, the Dixie fire has burned over 388,000 hectares, and this is only the largest of many. The power company, PG&E, whose electricity line had sparked off the Camp fire, subsequently declared bankruptcy. The hot and dry Santa Ana winds that blow off the mountains in the fall encounter overgrown landscapes and aging power lines. Power is cut off when the wind blows, and we cook our dinners by the light of battery-powered lamps. How should we think of such fires and of who is responsible? Were these fires caused by high winds, by climate change that made forests dry and flammable, by insect epidemics that killed trees, or by a neglectful power company? Perhaps fire risks were increased by building houses in landscapes that had formerly experienced burning by Indigenous people, followed by a century of fire suppression by federal and state governments?[1] In the wake of the 2020 fires, interest in prescribed burning and fuel reduction has increased across the state, and historic and contemporary Indigenous land-care practices are discussed ever more widely. What difference, if any, does it make to daily life once you know that a particular disaster is somehow linked to that nebulous creature "climate change"? Might you prefer to think about the predicament of the plants or animals that you encounter in your daily life, or the history of the landscape in which you live and work?

We often learn about climate change through newspaper stories wherein scientists tell us that their computer models show that a particular hurricane, fire, or flood was partially due to climate change. Today, for example, the newspaper told me that climate scientists attributed 30–50 percent of a twenty-year megadrought in the US Southwest to climate change. Climate change modelers tell us of the projected increase in average global temperatures. We read that an increase of 1°C, small as this sounds, would be bad, and that 2°C would be worse. Often we see colorful global climate anomaly maps, with swaths of frightening-looking red and orange warning us which regions will be worst affected. Such maps do not tell us who will suffer the unequally distributed impacts of climate change, which are affected by wealth, race, and class. Average temperatures and global climate maps do little to help us make sense of our daily lives, beyond adding to a distant sense of malaise. Scientists define climate as the long-term average of weather over a considerable space and time. This mathematical construct may inspire the newspaper stories that make me feel uneasily, that climate is changing, but it does little to help me make sense of my daily life. As anthropologist Tim Ingold points out, we live in a world of weather, of wind and rain. I experience weather when I take my children to school, when I notice how the flowers in my tiny garden grow, when I go for a walk and look at clouds moving across the sky. When I look at the smoke-laden sky, I think more of fires than of climate change. When I cannot water my garden because of drought restrictions, I think about water and wilting plants and not about climate. It is not that I lack a sense of climate, however. As geographer Mike Hulme points out, people everywhere have models of what counts as normal weather and what is strange, bizarre, and unnatural.[2] My sense of surprise at an early summer rain depends upon a commonsense model of climate that is more relevant to me than scientific accounts of changing global or regional climate. Like most people, I am concerned with the plants, soils, and weather processes that I encounter in my daily life.

We live in a profoundly human-transformed world. Ecosystem processes all over the planet have been so profoundly affected by human activities that many scholars are calling this era the Anthropocene.[3] As with climate change, the Anthropocene is a difficult concept to imagine. We read of the accumulation of plastic in the bodies of marine animals, of the disappearance of bees, of red tides in coastal waters. The derangement of biogeochemical cycles spreads beyond carbon to the water cycle, the phosphorus cycle, and the nitrogen cycle. The *longue durée* of plant domestication, and the histories of fossil-fueled capitalism and of empire and nuclear testing are involved in the Anthropocene. These histories call on us to connect our experiences with long-term processes. As with climate change, thinking about the Anthropocene elicits a sense of loss, a malaise that is hard to reconcile with the routines of daily life. How then can we link the scales of human experience with large-scale phenomena such as climate change, or the very long-term histories of racism, capitalism, and empire that have brought us here? How can we link geological and biogeochemical processes with the scales of human experience and politics? In order to answer some of these questions, I take you to the ancient human-modified landscapes and unstable sedimentary soils of Central Italy. Rather than starting from the planetary scale of global environmental change, however, I look at how people encounter plants and soils, diseases, and weather, in a world that has been changing for a long time. People in this landscape have learned to live with environmental change by attending to the traces of the past in the present. Traces of disaster and care are recorded in the shapes of trees and landscapes, bringing the Anthropocene of mid-twentieth-century agricultural abandonment into twenty-first-century climate change politics.

The enchantingly beautiful Italian landscape is an ideal place to learn what environmental politics looks like in a human-transformed world. In Italy and around the Mediterranean, almost every stone, every tree, and every hillside shows traces of human activities. Coastlines have been shaped by histories of swamp drainage and land reclamation; hillsides have been reshaped by terracing systems; mountain pastures by grazing and fire.[4] Ecosystems are full of plants and animals that have come here from other parts of the world. Plants, animals, and the shape of the landscape record traces of human activities, continually raising questions of human responsibility and care. In such places it is impossible to imagine nature outside of history. The Anthropocene is not so much a new discovery here as the latest iteration of a long-standing dilemma of bringing human and natural histories into present-day politics. The climate change crisis is certainly a concern, but so too are the ongoing impacts of other disasters and the need to care for other processes, from plant growth to soil movement.

The profoundly human-transformed landscapes of Italy and of the Mediterranean more broadly are harbingers of the experiences that all of us are likely to face. People around the world experience climate change and the Anthropocene through encounters with fires, heat waves, and floods that affect daily life. Addressing these disasters will call upon us to think about the human and natural histories of the landscapes we live in. People living in coastal cities facing sea level rise must reckon with the histories of dam building, groundwater pumping, and river diversion that have caused land subsidence. People living in forest landscapes that are being ravaged by droughts caused by climate change will also have to think about histories of human settlement and about international trade that has brought invasive insect pests and pathogens. In settler colonial societies such as the United States and Australia, it was possible to imagine that nature was somehow outside of history and society. Anthropogenic Italian landscapes remind us that humans have long had relationships of care and responsibility with landscapes that they have changed, something that Indigenous people never forgot. If, very broadly, North American environmentalists have tried to protect the environment by excluding people from nature, people in Italy have often tried to bring people *into* nature in order to care for it better.[5] Environmental historians and historical ecologists in the United States have long argued for attention to human-modified landscapes, but it is only recently that their insights have come to affect conservation policies. The urge to separate nature from people is baked deeply into institutions, laws, regulations, and popular culture. American conservationists who see the conservation of pristine wilderness as no longer sufficient, and who emphasize the importance of urban and working landscapes, are traveling a path that people in Italy have followed for a long time. My story of human-tended landscapes in Italy finds echoes in these debates.

Histories of disaster and care are embedded in the morphologies of plants and landscapes, if we can only learn to notice them. Outside my office window on the campus of the University of California Santa Cruz, a coastal redwood (*Sequoia sempervirens*) sheds a welcome shade on hot days. The form of this tree—its morphology—helps me imagine its biography. Sometime in the early twentieth century this tree was cut down and shoots resprouted from the stump. Over time the tree allocated more resources to some shoots than to others, and the number of stems gradually diminished. A century later four towering twenty-five-meter trunks remain, forming a tight circle around the original tree stump. This morphology is an echo of the predatory logging that cut down ancient trees as fuel for the limestone kilns at the base of campus. Plant morphology records a trace of the violence of the early-twentieth-century frontier economy through which this tree helped build San Francisco. Between the sixteenth century and the present, colonial genocide and natural resource extraction devastated Indigenous societies and transformed landscapes that Indigenous people had tended for millennia.[6] The traces of this violence and of these economic transformations are visible in the morphologies of long-lived beings, the ancient redwood trees and the younger coastal live oaks (*Quercus agrifolia*) that have grown on into the era of climate change. As immobile organisms with an extraordinary capacity for changing shape in response to light, water, nutrients, fire, and logging, the bodily forms of long-lived plants make visible the past in the present. The morphologies of individual plants can change our sense of the structure and history of entire landscapes. Regional histories of fire, of disease and conquest, of industrialization and land abandonment can give us better reasons to act than global climate change models can.

Global environmental change is present in our daily surroundings wherever we are. I chose to start with an ordinary Italian landscape, much like any other. I began by walking from my back door in Lucca to the crest of the nearest mountain range and down the other side. People and plants care a lot about weather, water, and soil. Walking across a mountain range can teach you a lot about the ways that people have made a living in any landscape. Walking, looking, and wondering, I tried to move slowly enough to notice the shapes of trees and landforms. I took time to talk to people who lived and worked in this landscape and who could teach me to make sense of what I was seeing. The landscape I chose, the Monte Pisano between the cities of Lucca and Pisa in Central Italy (figure 1), is both special and ordinary. It is special because by walking and by looking, by talking to farmers and by visiting archives, I have learned to see this landscape as the site of dramatic encounters between fast-moving fires, catastrophic plant disease epidemics, and changing human societies. It is ordinary because this landscape resembles other mountain landscapes across the Mediterranean and around the world. Every landscape has its own dramatic histories of social and environmental encounter, and every landscape can change how we think about global environmental change. I have learned some of these histories of disaster and change by combining interviews, oral histories, maps, landscape walks, and more. This intentional use of multiple methods and lines of evidence is a feature of the flourishing interdisciplinary field of historical ecology.[7] These eclectic histories can expand our imagination of pasts and futures.

Like many cities in Italy and around the Mediterranean, the cities of Lucca and Pisa are located on coastal floodplains, near unruly rivers that flow down from young and unstable mountains. The plate tectonics that lifted the Apennine mountains from the seabed between sixty-five million and three million years ago have revealed unstable former marine clays, shales, and sandstones. These unstable landscapes are given to landslides and earthquakes. The River Arno and River Serchio bring sand and mud down from the mountains, sometimes jumping their banks and changing course after heavy floods.[8] The nearby Apuan Alps are composed of harder limestones and marbles and are more stable. Nevertheless, here too, wildly variable Mediterranean rainfall regimes and dramatic increases in precipitation with altitude mean that floods are a perennial risk to people who live in valleys and floodplains. While these landscapes are unique, they are similar to

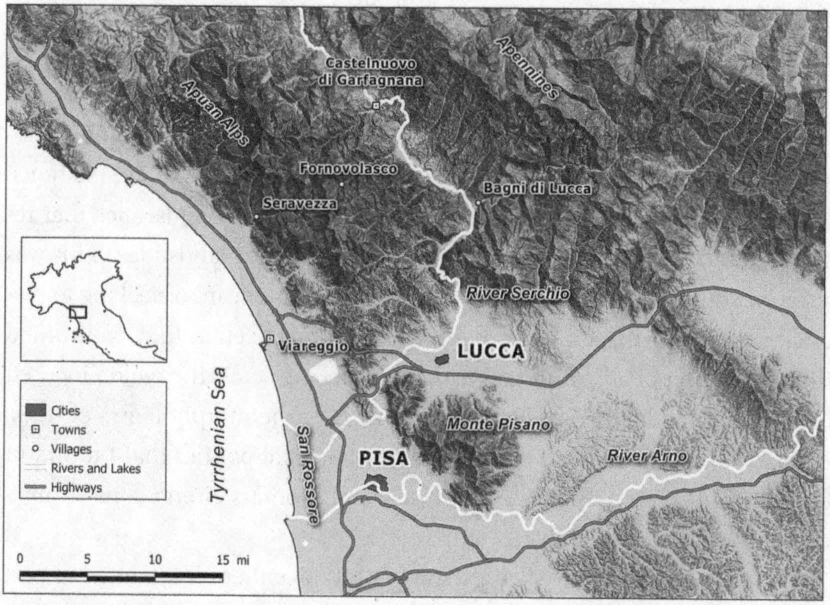

Figure 1. Regional map of Lucca and Pisa. (Map used by permission of Fabio Malfatti)

other landscapes around the Mediterranean, where mountains are almost always in sight of the sea and where unstable marine clays and schists render landscapes unstable.

It was by walking, looking, and wondering in the Monte Pisano that I learned to notice evidence of long-term relationships between plants, people, soils, and weather in Italian landscapes. Through encounters with peasant cultivators and cultivated chestnut trees, I learned to appreciate the capacity of long-lived trees to entice humans into caring for them. Peasants cared for long-lived trees by noticing and responding to plant morphology. By walking and wondering, I learned to see the terracing and drainage systems that cover large parts of this landscape, and I began to see these biogeomorphologies as human responses to the desires of plants. Plant morphologies told me of histories of encounter between people, fires, and diseases, pulling me outside the present and making me wonder about the histories of disaster that had left traces in this landscape. I learned to appreciate the landscape structures of fire-blasted pine forest as an echo of disease epidemics that had faded from living memory but which had left traces in the archive. As we shall see, most of the time, climate change was a fugitive and secondary presence, flitting in and out of conversation but with little purchase on practical action. Rather than focusing on climate as a problem of warming atmospheres and changing weather, people talked of plant/soil/climate relations. People were aware of living in unstable and fire-prone landscapes that responded to intense weather events through floods and landslides. This was a way of connecting the atmospheric and the subterranean, of seeking to reconcile plant growth, soil movement, and weather. Even as they confronted the new disaster of climate change, ordinary people across the region focused on maintaining landscape stability by caring for the morphologies of trees, riverbanks, and hillsides. The biogeomorphological politics that I found in the Monte Pisano helped me make sense of biomass energy and climate change politics across Italy.

Plants are extraordinary beings. Many of us take them for granted as part of the background of daily life. It takes time to notice their wild inventiveness and adaptability. Unlike animals, plants have their digestive organs on the outside of their bodies. Leaves and roots are the location of nutrient absorption, the equivalent of stomachs for animals. Rather than running around the landscape as we animals do, plants stay in place, sensing and responding to the world. Plants do not have the luxury of running away from predators or of chasing prey, as animals do. Plants endure fires, diseases, predators, and lack of nutrients, with little capacity for immediate escape. Faced with these challenges, plants have become adept at sensing danger and opportunity. Plants are shape shifters that can engage in metamorphoses that humans can only dream of. Plants can shed limbs or leaves that are no longer useful, they can grow toward water and light, they can resprout from tree stumps or from tiny seeds scattered across fire-blasted landscapes. Plants can form alliances with plants, animals, or fungi, and they can share nutrients through root grafts and symbiotic mycorrhizal fungi. Plants challenge our assumptions about individuality and competition.[9] The shape-shifting capacities of plants tell me of the histories of particular places and of entire landscapes. Plants change the shapes of the stories that I tell about the world.

The rootedness of plants, their insistence on staying in place, means that plant morphologies record biographies of encounter. Humans, fires, diseases, weather, soils, plants, and animals can all leave traces in plant morphologies. Long-lived trees, in particular, can be witnesses to history. Through their capacity to live for centuries, trees can entice people into caring for processes that stretch beyond human lifetimes. Through their affinity for deep soils and moisture, short-lived domesticated plants have also persuaded humans to reshape landscapes, from cornfields in Iowa to wheat fields in Tuscany. The gardens, agricultural fields, and the terracing and drainage systems that surround us are the visible consequences of human love, dependency, and exploitation of plants. Much of the time we fail to notice what a plant-centered world we live in. Learning to notice plant ingenuity requires us to slow down, to walk, look, and wonder, to realize that what we took for granted is much stranger than we had imagined. The botanist Francis Hallé points out that one way to slow down and notice the strangeness of plants is through drawings of plant form: "It is as if we were visiting a distant planet and encountered a form of extraterrestrial life with which we share no language—a form of life based upon principles not our own. If we wish to understand this creature, it is best not to rush."[10]

Plant morphology was the clue that led me to notice morphologies not only of trees, but of soils and drainage systems and then of a distinctive form of human biogeomorphological politics through which people in Italy confront climate change. Noticing plants drew me into noticing other processes, the slow movement of soils across terraces, the rapid movement of floodwaters and mudflows down hillsides. As with plants, diagrams and drawings are the best way to slow down and notice choreographies of plant/soil/water assemblages across Mediterranean landscapes. I am inspired by the drawings and diagrams of Oliver Rackham. The terracing and drainage systems that cover much of the Italian landscape have received only episodic and passing attention from officials, scientists, and literati.[11] These choreographies are the result of a largely invisible biogeomorphological politics that has reshaped the landscape over the past millennia. To make sense of this politics, you have to learn to see biogeomorphological diagrams emerging from the messiness of the world.

You can read this book as a more-or-less-ordinary anthropology or history book, moving from beginning to end and looking for key arguments in the text. I encourage you to try reading in another way also. In a series of interludes across this book, I have offered you drawings and photographs of plants, diagrams of landscape structures, of biogeomorphological choreographies, and of atmospheres. These interludes are morphological arguments that ask you to think with your senses. These are not just illustrations to be hastily passed by as you search for the point of the argument. These diagrams and photographs *are* the argument. They do not work like ordinary arguments that use narrative or imagery, argument, and evidence. I use these interludes to try to show you a way of linking sensory experience and wondering with the specificity of relationships between particular beings. These diagrams are simplifications that emerged from my encounters with plants, soils, and people at specific places and times. These drawings, both my own and those of my gifted collaborator Hannah Caisse, reflect an effort to draw diagrams out of a particular moment of encounter.

When I link diagrams to photographs, I do so to show you how diagrams reflect choices, a deliberate selection of which aspects of a messy world needed highlighting. If I see a tree as bearing histories of disease, I draw it one way; if I wish to show firewood cutting, I draw it another way. A drawing is partial, it is one way of noticing the world, and it makes it possible to imagine other relationships as being worthy of consideration. I invite you to give these morphological arguments a chance to transform your senses, to hesitate and reflect upon the landscapes you live in. You might try moving first through the interludes and then through the text. You might skim chapters and look for drawings or photographs that provoke or perplex you. You might even go for a walk and try to notice the morphologies and diagrammatic simplifications that emerge for you from the shapes of trees, roads, bridges, hillsides, atmospheres, and drainage systems. Your own sensory responses to the world might shift if you allow yourself to entertain, for a few moments, the morphological arguments I set before you. You might see city streets or suburban neighborhoods differently. You might notice the slow and sly transformations of trees and landforms around you. Only you can figure out the morphologies and landscape structures that matter where you live and work.

If you are an anthropologist or a historian, you might have to work hard to avoid the native habits of our disciplines, which invite us to respond to arguments with written arguments of our own. You might use a diagram or a drawing to formulate your response to the diagrams that I offer you.

Biologists and ecologists largely abandoned morphological analysis in the twentieth century. Morphology could tell you about the biographies of individual organisms, and it could help you make sense of evolution, but in its specificity and uniqueness it seemed to lack the capacity to support more-general stories about ecological relations. The natural sciences, including ecology, focused on quantification, largely sidelining historical and morphological thinking.[12] Morphological evidence does not have to remain at the level of individual organisms, however. The shapes of fire-scarred trees on the Monte Pisano led me to the landscape patterns of forest fires and the histories of pastoralism, agricultural abandonment, and industrialization that have reshaped landscapes across the Mediterranean. Morphologies can be linked to larger-scale landscape patterns and to the regional histories that brought these structures into being.[13] Morphological analysis can bring disparate temporalities into the same frame, from soil formation and forest fires to urban housing politics.

This book is about the details of our encounters with landscapes, but it is also about our capacity to project our imagination from these details in order to tell larger-scale stories. In moving from the details of human encounters with plants and soils to larger-scale landscape structures, I argue for the importance of what might seem unimportant details. Plant and landscape morphologies bring the past into the present, they bear witness to disaster, and they bring humans into projects of long-term care. Around the world, scientists and activists and policymakers have tried to persuade ordinary people of the urgency of climate change. Such approaches assume that ordinary people do not have their own ideas about climate and that a shared understanding of climate is necessary for effective climate change policies.[14] Climate change policy in Italy encounters popular knowledge rather than ignorance. Vernacular models of climate/landscape/plant assemblages have inspired largely invisible forms of landscape care and of biogeomorphological politics that have transformed climate change policy in Italy.

ONE

Sensing the Invisible

Plant Form and Landscape Transformation

How do plants come to be political? How do they come to appeal to human imaginations, to inspire changed cultivation practices, landscape transformations, and diverse forms of social life and politics? To answer these questions, we need to pay attention not only to the legal, social, and discursive effects of plants, but also to how they respond to encounters with other beings, from humans to fires and diseases. The best way to notice the power of plants in our daily lives is to attend to plant morphology and the shape of landscape itself. By attending to plant form we can learn to notice landscape politics in a different and unexpected way. Let us consider how a particular plant, the sweet chestnut, *Castanea sativa*, responds to human cultivation practices of grafting, pruning, and terrace building. In the Apennine landscapes of Central Italy, chestnut was formerly a subsistence food crop for millions of people. Because of its economic importance, early modern Italian states taxed, regulated, and recorded the smallholder chestnut groves that were the basis of peasant agriculture in the middle hills.[1] This bureaucratic history provides a way of following plant care and landscape transformation over the past few hundred years. By moving between present-day cultivation practices and historic literary accounts and legal codes, we can learn how peasant farmers have attended to plant and landscape forms over the *longue durée*. By noticing and caring for the morphologies of plants that they cared about, peasant cultivators in Italy became attuned to the sensory responses of these plants to their environments. Plant responses inspired peasants to reshape and replumb the landscape, engaging in a mundane and largely invisible biogeomorphological politics.

Plant morphology records the responses of plants to their environment. Because plants do not walk around, their movement is recorded in their growth patterns, as they respond with exquisitely attuned senses to their surroundings. Plant morphology is a kind of biography of where plants have been and where they are going and of what kinds of other beings they have encountered along the way. Plants are strange beings that may appear to many of us to grow so slowly that they seem to barely change at all. If you pay attention, however, you will notice how plants unfurl new leaves in a few hours, and trees and shrubs change shape dramatically over years. There is a long tradition in Western philosophy and social theory of thinking of plants as passive.[2] This is not something that farmers have ever believed in. Farmers and gardeners, from Italy to California, know that plants are sensitive, responsive, and ultimately puzzling and mysterious. By watching plants closely, humans have learned to notice how they grow toward nutrients, light, and water and how they recoil from dry and poor soils. The morphologies of trees record their biographies of encounters with fire, cutting, pruning, and diseases, experienced years or decades in the past. In Italy, peasant cultivators have become attuned to the lives of plants through their interests in the taste of seeds and fruits, the colors and textures of bark, the architecture of fruit trees.

Peasant and farmer knowledge and response to plant form are an informal biogeomorphological politics that is part of the background of daily life for most literati, both in the past and in the present. Across the Mediterranean, caring for plant forms has given rise to collective projects of building terracing and drainage systems that transform landscapes. Archaeologists have found evidence of terracing in Liguria, in Central Italy, from around 1000 BCE, but literary accounts and legal documents record only indirect evidence of terracing from the classical period until the Middle Ages. It is only in the sixteenth century that we see a flowering of agronomical treatises in which terracing systems and various kinds of complex polycultures of trees, vines, and grains are explicitly mentioned. The plant/soil/water politics of peasant landscape shaping took place with relatively little attention from elites. Recognizing the power of peasant practices of attending to the responsiveness of plants and soils is a decolonizing practice that draws our attention to work that has been largely ignored.[3]

Over the past two millennia, across the Mediterranean, peasant farmers built drainage and terracing systems to sustain the health of the plants they cared about and depended upon. Chestnut and other tree crops directed the attention of cultivators to largely invisible processes of soil formation and to the dangers of flooding and erosion that would denude roots and prevent plants from flourishing. This history of tree/soil/water care has reshaped the imaginative and material landscapes of Italy and of other Mediterranean hill landscapes, with continuing consequences for official and popular responses to climate change. Through their ability to sense soil fertility and water movement, plants have drawn human attention to largely invisible processes. This capacity of long-lived trees to act as proxies for invisible processes is suggestive of how we might be able to confront global environmental change, including climate change. Plants can act as sentinels for the invisible flows of carbon from the atmosphere, even as people continue to understand trees as beings who stabilize hillsides. Historic interactions between people, plants, and soils have large-scale consequences for the form of landscapes and for how people in Italy make sense of contemporary environmental politics, including climate change. Let us turn therefore to the history and present relations of one particularly charismatic tree crop, the sweet chestnut. Although now in decline, this tree tells us why people in Italy continue to see tending forests as a way of stabilizing hillsides and regulating rivers.

Cultivating a Charismatic Tree

This story begins with the slightly sweet and floury taste of roast chestnuts. For most Europeans and Americans, chestnut is a food that is eaten only a few times a year, perhaps as stuffing for roast turkey, perhaps as roast chestnuts purchased from a street stall, or perhaps (to my taste much too sweet) as *marrons glacés* in a holiday gift. In figure 2 you can see the difference between larger and sweeter cultivated chestnuts and the smaller but perfectly edible wild fruits. Peasant farmers have always paid attention to particularly

Figure 2. Wild (left) and cultivated (right) chestnut varieties, Lucca, 2013. (Author photograph)

desirable chestnut trees that they encountered in forests or on their neighbors' land. Cuttings from trees that produced particularly large or tasty fruits could be grafted onto a wild rootstock. Chestnut trees are, therefore, both domestic and wild, united by an uneasy graft union.

It may come as somewhat of a surprise that chestnuts were formerly a staple food crop that sustained millions of people across the Mediterranean. Chestnut cultivation has an ancient history, and chestnut is a major food crop in China, Korea, and Japan.[4] In Italy alone, over eight hundred thousand hectares of cultivated chestnut groves supported hundreds of thousands of smallholder farmers in 1800, and abundant medieval and early modern documents record legislation, charters, and legal protections encouraging chestnut cultivation. In Europe, chestnut was likely restricted to glacial refugia in the high Apennines of Italy, eastern Turkey, and the Balkans, and only began to become more widespread as a result of human cultivation in the first century CE. Chestnut is not particularly effective at spreading across

Figure 3. Chestnut grove near Fosciandora, Lucca, 2013. (Author photograph)

the landscape on its own accord, and human assistance was required to move chestnut beyond these narrow refugia. Too many animals like to eat chestnuts, and the fruits are too heavy to fall far from their parent tree. During the late antique and early medieval periods, humans planted chestnuts in hill and mountain areas across the Mediterranean, wherever the right combinations of moist well-drained soils with sufficient summer rain were available. By the year 1000, cultivated chestnut trees had become a prominent feature of the landscape, including particularly in the foothills of the Alps and in the Apennine mountains that stretch from Central to Southern Italy. Chestnuts were desirable for peasant farmers because of their versatility and the moderate labor required for cultivation. Chestnut could provide food or construction timber from groves (*selve*), poles (*vernacchiaia*), or firewood from a coppice (*ceduo*).

Look closely at the image of the chestnut grove in figure 3, and let me try to persuade you that this is a strange sight. This is a well-maintained *selva* in the high Apennines, about twenty-five kilometers north of Lucca, at nearly eight hundred meters above sea level. The trees are well spaced out to favor fruit production, and are perhaps two hundred years old (they are sixty to eighty centimeters in diameter). In looking at this picture, you should imagine the continuous hard work of generations of peasant farmers. These trees' responses to human care have left a record in their morphology. None of these trees have shoots (suckers, *polloni*) at the base, which means that someone has cut them back quite recently. Without this continuous work of cutting, the shoots that emerge from the wild rootstock (*portainnesto*) will draw nutrients away from the grafted main stem, which will gradually lose vigor and die. The crown of the tree just to the right of center has been cut out. This required someone to climb a ladder and carry out a dangerous and laborious job of tree pruning. This kind of work needs to be done perhaps every twenty or thirty years. The low stone walls, known as *lunette,* retain soil around the roots of some of the trees. Terracing structures are a testimony to centuries of collective geomorphological work by peasant farmers, although present-day farmers no longer do this work. Finally, the orchard is clear and relatively grassy. This requires the work of sheep or goats to graze the grasses, but also of a farmer to rake up leaves and burrs. In the past the leaves might have been used for stable bedding, which could be combined with animal waste and made into fertilizer (*letame*) for spreading across fields. At present, in this area, leaves are usually burned, leaving patches of black mineralized soil. What cannot be easily seen in this picture are the graft scars, the material echo of a long-ago moment when a peasant farmer grafted a desired domestic scion (*marza*) onto a wild rootstock. So too, what remains invisible is the existence of different names for the numerous cultivated varieties and for the different parts of these trees.[5] Such names are more easily made visible by a diagram or drawing than by a photograph.

From the mid-nineteenth century, and increasingly rapidly since the 1950s, a combination of pathogen epidemics and the abandonment of agriculture by peasant farmers have caused a dramatic decline in chestnut cultivation. Water-powered industrialization, taking off in the nineteenth century, began to pull peasant farmers into paper and textile mills in steep mountain valleys. After World War II, many hill farmers abandoned their land for jobs in pharmaceutical, paper, and other factories. Ruined chestnut groves have produced a landscape that is haunted by memories and traces of human cultivation. Across Italy about 8 percent of forest is still officially classified as chestnut forest, but only about a tenth of this, some sixty-eight thousand hectares, is still cultivated.[6] Most chestnut groves are in ruins; former groves have changed form to become firewood forests. In many places chestnut has been replaced by other species.

In Italy, as in many parts of the world, millennia of agricultural, pastoral, and forest management practices by peasants and Indigenous people have produced an infrastructure of cultivated and abandoned forests, of terracing and drainage systems. This infrastructure is material, linguistic, and imaginative. Collective understandings of tree and landscape form and of what forest protection is supposed to achieve inform popular expectations as to how the Italian state should confront climate change. Before we come to look at contemporary politics, however, we need to look more closely at the contact zones between people, plants, and soils, where cultivators interpret the gestures of plants toward soil, water, and disease.[7]

Learning to Recognize a Good *Marza*

One morning in February of 2014 I visited the Uccelliera, a farm near the city of Lucca, where Giuseppe del Chiaro continued to practice the arts of grafting and growing fruit chestnuts. In this area, on the lower slopes of the Monte Pisano, chestnut cultivation has almost entirely disappeared over the past century. Giuseppe cultivated a particularly prized variety known as Marrone di Pozzuolo on former olive terraces. He was eighty-five years old when I met him and his daughter Alessandra, but he was a ball of energy. Whenever the weather was good he was out on the land with a pruning knife in hand, too busy to talk to visitors for long. Too much was going on, and shaping trees was a passion. Walking with him I learned to notice the potential shapes that trees and plants might take. Giuseppe reminded me that trees move by means of their capacity to change form. Through his attention to plant form and to the responsiveness of plants to pruning and grafting, Giuseppe came to be involved with chestnut trees, olives, and vines. This was a process of attunement, of coming to be affected by plants, of wishing to change and live with plants. These affective, sensory experiences gave rise to an acute interest in plants and to the morphologies and linguistic terms that Giuseppe and farmers like him were interested in.[8]

From Giuseppe, I learned how grafting worked. In so doing, I came to be more involved with plants. I learned to sense the world differently, to notice graft scars, and to become more alert to differences in plant forms, to the colors and textures of bark and buds. In the following section, Massimo, a biologist; Giuseppe, a peasant; and his daughter Alessandra try to teach me how to recognize a stem that would be a good scion.

> *Massimo*: Here it is, no! [He gestured that I was looking at the wrong branch.] This branch here if you have to take scions, in theory you take it home, maybe even this one here, but . . . [He gestured toward the tree again. I still couldn't tell which one he meant!]
>
> *Massimo*: The cuttings are these three here.
>
> *Andrew*: These three here?
>
> *Massimo*: Sure. Sure, these ones, do you see how beautiful? This one and this one are also beautiful. This one, is already more. . . . Do you see?
>
> *Giuseppe*: In any case, [with] cuttings, there is one thing. When the buds have gotten bigger, the bigger you [graft] them the better it is.[9]

Alessandra ended up tying a pink ribbon to the "good scion" that I had so much trouble seeing. It is certainly hard for the camera to see, but it is hanging like a loop from the upper right branches in figure 4. Deciding which scion to take is tricky. Not just any branch will do. It has to be the right size, somewhat smaller than the rootstock, so that the cambium layers align with each other. More importantly, you have to look closely at the branches and pick out the right one. It has to be the right shape, nice and oblong with full buds, growing vertically and not horizontally. My eye did much better after this conversation, although I would have had to watch a real master like Giuseppe take many cuttings before I could trust myself.

Figure 4. Making cuts / distinguishing the good scion/*marza*, Pozzuolo, Lucca, 2014. The loop of ribbon in the upper right area marks the scion/*marza* that Giuseppe and Massimo thought was a good one. (Author photograph)

From learning to perceive differences in the shape of a branch, the direction it was growing in, and the color of a good bud, I also learned to describe some shoots as "good" and "bad" for the purposes of cutting scions. Massimo, Alessandra, and Giuseppe had succeeded in rewiring my senses. Following Karen Barad, we can see this noticing as a kind of agential cut that momentarily determined what the tree was, at that moment. My interest in grafting enacted branches as possible scions. Other branches could have been "good" for other purposes, such as weaving a basket or cutting a walking stick, but they remained indeterminate, for now. Donna Haraway's thinking on partial and situated knowledges helps me understand how each way of knowing the chestnut tree does not fully define either what I can know or how the chestnut tree might respond to me. If you look closely at this picture, there is much more to know and to notice about branches and buds, but this excess does not matter, for now. There is an indeterminate field of shape, texture, and color for which specific terms are not necessary or available. The plant morphologies that we notice can be quite unstable as particular features of a plant change how we reassess its overall architecture.[10] When I learned to notice a graft scar, I came to see some trees as the meeting of two distinct individuals. I reassessed what I was seeing once again when I learned to notice the presence of plant disease.

The chestnut trees in Pozzuolo were involved in relationships that far exceeded the intentions of farmers or biologists. As we walked across the terraces, Giuseppe gestured angrily at his trees, telling me of the repeated failures of new grafts, as the orange blossom of chestnut canker *Cryphonectria parasitica* spread across the bark around the graft.[11] This fungus often kills trees. If you learn to recognize the tiny orange spores that grow across the bark, you might see a branch or an entire tree as doomed or dying. A particular detail can change your perception of the morphology of a whole tree, as you notice areas of dying or flourishing stems. Alternatively, however, I could learn to see signs of cankers that had calloused and healed over. Another being, *Cryphonectria hypovirus* 1 (CHV-1), could infect the fungus and halt the disease. A dry callus on a formerly cankered trunk would reassure me that a tree was provisionally immune to the disease. From noticing a detail I might learn to see the morphology and destiny of the whole tree differently. This relationship between detail and overall morphology can cause sudden shifts in perception not only across a single tree, but across an entire landscape. Walking across the landscape, the lessons that I learned in Pozzuolo changed how I saw larger patches of forest. Some areas seemed likely to die; in other areas, calloused trees told of a more stable relationship between tree, fungus, and virus. Figure 5 shows a heavily infected tree that will likely die. Figure 6 shows a tree where the hypovirus has slowed down the disease and the tree has formed a callus; this tree will live.

Figure 5. Chestnut canker / *Cryphonectria parasitica* infected stem, Pozzuolo, Lucca, 2014. (Author photograph)

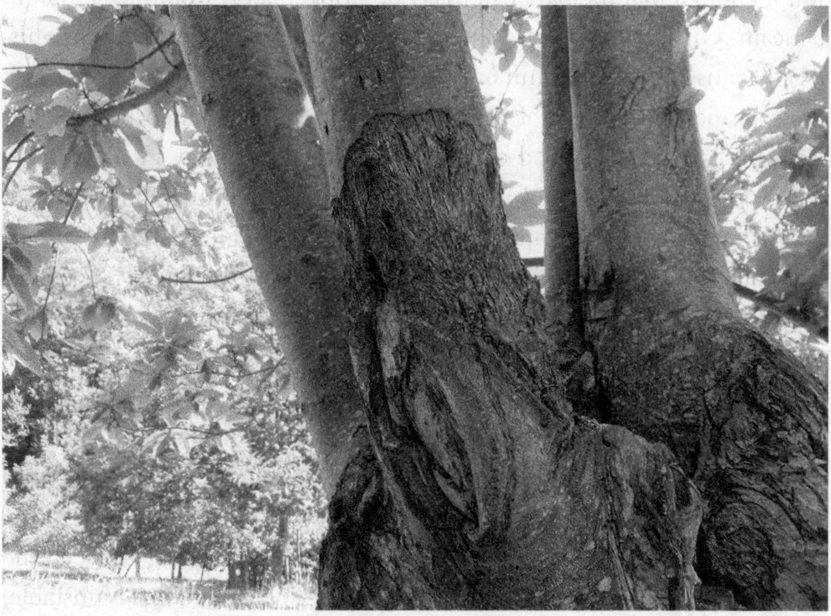

Figure 6. Chestnut tree infected by *Cryphonectria* that is itself infected with *Cryphonectria hypovirus* 1, Orecchiella, Lucca, 2015. (Author photograph)

Grafting as an Encounter with Strangeness

Giuseppe went on to tell me of the skill required for different grafting techniques, but also something of the pleasure: "It was an entertainment to do these things, it was an entertainment," he said. Some kinds of grafts were harder, and there was always the doubt as to whether the graft would take. The key skill lay in aligning the cambium layer of the scion (the grafted variety) with the cambium layer of the rootstock. Giuseppe called the cambium the "skin" (*pelle*) of the tree. Lining up the cambium of scion and rootstock involves the grafter imagining and sensing the cambium layer, the zone of active cell division that lies beneath the bark of the tree like an invisible glove. Grafters try to align the cambium layers of scion and rootstock so that the two can fuse into one organism with different genomes. It takes skills of visual perception and of touch to cut the bark to just the right thickness, to line up the ring of cambium layers so that they take. Timing is important: the weather has to be cold enough that the sap has not yet started rising, yet warm enough that the bark can easily be stripped away from the cambium beneath. Giuseppe tried to show me the technique called *a zufolo* (whistle), because it was both fun and difficult. The bark had to be slipped off the rootstock; a cylinder of bark with cambium would then be removed from the scion and slipped over the rootstock.[12] That day in Pozzuolo, I learned yet another way of appreciating the liveliness and strangeness of trees. Plants enact mundane but very strange ontologies. Even as farmers work pragmatically with them, they respect the uncertainty of how plants may flourish, die, or change shape. New pathogens have only accentuated the indeterminacy of what might come from grafting.

Grafting depends upon a tactile sense of the minutest details of texture. In figure 7 we see skilled hands aligning a plum bud (*gemma*) beneath a triangular incision in the bark of the rootstock. This grower grafts trees both for fun and to produce fruit.

Grafting is a moment of encounter, a partial coordination between the human grafter and two different plant varieties. The grafted tree is unstable, always open to collapse if the wild rootstock sends out shoots that humans fail to cut, or if a pathogen arrives and kills the tree. The tiny details of plant/human grafting encounters can have very long-term consequences, as ex-

Figure 7. Grafting a plum bud, Cappannori, Lucca, 2014. (Author photograph)

pressed across the life spans of chestnut, olive, or other trees, which can live for decades or centuries. The life or death of a grafted tree is always somewhat in doubt. A graft may take or it may die. In the long term, trees may live or die, or appear to die and then sprout from roots. Grafting encounters also produce aesthetic judgments. Neighbors comment on each other's plant care and pruning practices and about the forms of trees and grapevines.

It would be easy to think of grafting as a form of violent control of plants by humans. Recent work on domestication suggests that it is more helpful to see grafting as arising from long-term processes of different species coming into relationship with each other, with morphological and evolutionary consequences for both. There is certainly violence. Reproduction is affected, and diseases can spread more easily, but there is also a kind of symbiosis, as plants elicit ecological relationships with people, animals, and soils. Out of grafting relationships have come the chestnut forests that cover almost 8 percent of the Italian forest landscape. Out of grafting came the terracing systems that supported many chestnut groves, olive trees, and other fruit trees.

From the point of view of classic evolutionary biology, we might think of grafting as a kind of deception, where humans persuade the rootstock of the plant to send its nutrients into the genetically unrelated scion. A less competition-centered view of ecological relationships emerges from the observation that trees can graft roots with their neighbors, both of the same and of different species, and that they can share nutrients with their neighbors through networks of mycorrhizal fungi. In any case, grafting relationships are not unambiguously competitive and, like theories of symbiosis, they cause problems for competition-centered evolutionary biology. The relationship between people and plants that emerges through grafting is one in which different species sense each other and come into a closer relationship, without fully understanding or controlling each other. These encounters are brought into being by the capacities of humans to sense differences in plants, and of plants to respond to what people do to them.[13] Out of a more or less successful graft can come a healthy chestnut tree that can flourish for centuries if it is pruned and cared for. The relationships between grafter and plant are partial relationships: they do not fully define either the human or the plant. For humans, the capacity of the chestnut to graft is helpful if they want to shape chestnut groves, but of no interest if they wish to produce firewood. Human grafters have multiple other identities that emerge from their other social relations, as peasant, landowner, parent. In an analogous way, a chestnut tree takes different forms in relations to its encounters with other organisms, soils, fire, or weather. New ontologies emerge from relationships between beings.

Grafting Diagrams

Walking around their farms with chestnut growers gradually gave me a way of noticing the impact of human care upon tree morphology. This kind of diagrammatic noticing highlighted coordinations between beings.[14] In a chestnut grove in Borgo a Mozzano, the farmer Stefano Fazzi pointed out the bark texture below and above a graft and named the parts of the tree for me. Let yourself look closely at the picture (figure 8), then look at the diagram (figure 9). Now go back and forth a bit and notice how your percep-

Figure 8. Graft scar on ancient chestnut tree near Borgo a Mozzano, Lucca, 2014. (Author photograph)

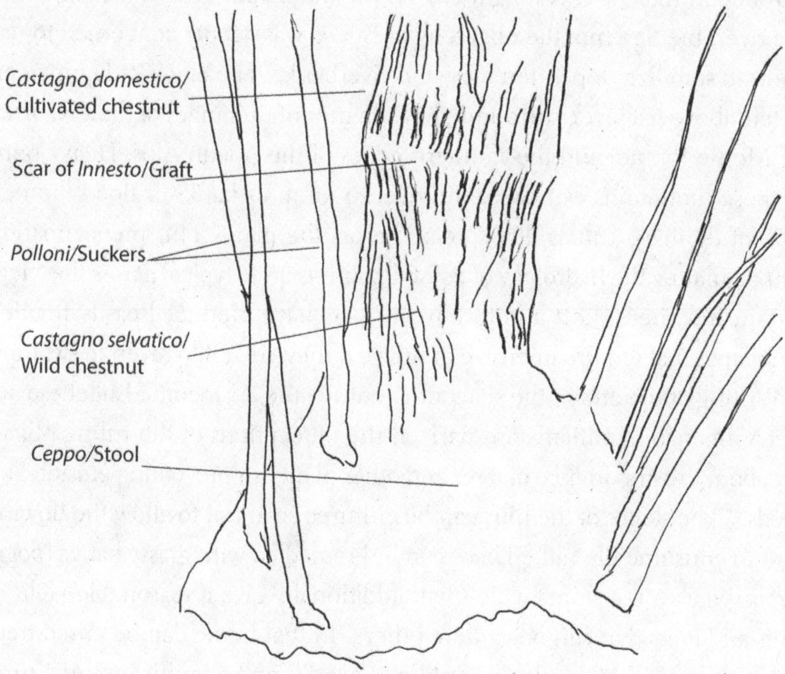

Figure 9. Drawing of a cultivated chestnut tree with named parts, 2015. (Drawing by author)

tions change. Some aspects of the tree are more noticeable, others less so. This is noticing that is both phenomenological and diagrammatic. You can notice much about the tree that is not relevant to this diagram. If you had been there on that day, as I was, you could have touched the mossy bark, you could have noticed the diamond-shaped braiding of bark patterns, the scars left from pruning branches.

From Peasant Plant Care to State Landscape Stabilization

My encounters with chestnut farmers and the plant/soil/water terracing systems they managed helped me make sense of the efforts of early modern Italian states to manage forests and stabilize landscapes. Across central Italy, including in what are now the provinces of Firenze, Pisa, and Lucca, chestnut cultivation was protected and sponsored by early modern states that wished to sustain food supplies.[15] The city-state of Lucca, which remained independent from the Middle Ages until 1805, was particularly concerned with flood protection. Ruling a city on the floodplain of an active and mobile river, the Serchio, the oligarchy of Lucca was deeply concerned to use plants to stabilize slopes, terraces, and riverbanks. The city is only nineteen meters above sea level, surrounded by the mountain ranges of the Pizzorna, the Monte Pisano, and the southern edges of the Apuan Alps. Heavy rains on these mountains can cause the river to jump its banks or flood the network of drainage canals that spreads across the plain. This preoccupation with regulating the hydrology of coastal plains is quite typical across the Mediterranean, where short and torrential rivers have produced easily flooded landscapes that require intensive drainage if they are not to revert to swamps.

Writing at the end of the sixteenth century, the aristocratic Lucchese author Vincenzo Saminiati summarized the perceptions of the ruling oligarchy about the importance of trees and other plants for preventing erosion and floods. "The slopes of the hills can be cultured so as not to allow the flowing rains to consume the soil. [These can be] remedied with grassy banks [*poggi herbosi*] across the slope, which will additionally give a reasonable yield of fruits and grass that can be gathered there. In that home can be raised trees and grapevines that the slope would make it difficult to cultivate." At a time when terraces were almost unknown to literati (although no doubt well known to peasants), Saminiati drew attention to the role of trees in stabilizing grassy banks (*poggi herbosi*, which might now be known as *zolle* or *ciglioni*). He repeatedly called for attention to the role of trees as hedges and as a support for grapevines (*vite maritata*), but also to the role of banked terraces in sustaining olive trees, and of earthen banks (*poggi*) for encouraging chestnut trees in poor or dry soils. Saminiati gives us a glimpse, however filtered, of peasant understandings of plant/soil/water relations. He describes plant/soil/water choreographies of trees, terraces, and drainage ditches as essential to sustaining cultivation and stabilizing the landscape. Saminiati discussed how to recognize good and poor soils by color and texture and which soils were best suited to particular crops, and he saw soil quality as something that could be modified or transformed by careful cultivation, terracing, drainage, and fertilization: "The perfect agriculturalist knows how to give a healthy remedy to bring into cultivation any kind of soil even if it is wholly or partially defective."[16]

This understanding of soil as being improvable through human care was widespread before the arrival of modern soil science, agronomy, and industrial fertilizers. Italy was a relatively poor country with little access to the imperial trade networks that supplied guano fertilizer to Britain and the United States in the nineteenth century. Italian agronomists continued to emphasize the use of plant and animal fertilizers as soil amendments until the arrival of chemical fertilizers after World War II. It was only in the 1950s that plant and animal fertilizers, and related practices of soil improvement, were displaced by modern soil science's conception of soil as a relatively passive reservoir for inorganic nutrients.[17]

Elite concerns over landscape stabilization and food production had caused the Republic of Lucca to establish the Offizio Sopra le Selve (Office of Chestnut Groves) in 1487. In parallel with the Offizio del Serchio (Office of the [River] Serchio), this commission was responsible for protecting food production from chestnut trees and for stabilizing slopes and protecting the flow of the river. This alignment of peasant knowledge of grafting and landscape care with the interests of the Lucchese state in landscape stability and food production has produced a bureaucratic record of land use that I will explore in more depth in the following chapter.

Final Thoughts

We can learn how plants inspire a practical geomorphological politics by being willing to expand our curiosity to notice how plant morphology emerges from encounters between people, plants, soils, and diseases. The long lives of some plants mean that biographies of encounter can have enduring consequences. The capacity of many kinds of grafted trees to flourish in particular soils has caused farmers to build terracing and drainage systems across the Mediterranean over the past two millennia. The capacity of plants to sense soil quality is part of what teaches humans to classify soils and to build and fertilize terraces. The historical record demonstrates how people can come to notice invisible processes through the sensory capacities of the beings they care about. Soil formation and changing tree shape are much too slow for our senses to perceive. Long-lived trees and old terracing systems are proxies: they direct us to consider processes that are too slow for us to notice easily. This capacity of humans to communicate with nonhumans (as with grafting) or to sense them indirectly (as with soil quality) appears to be a ubiquitous part of the anthropological and historical record. Classic studies of Indigenous or peasant ecological knowledge provide clues for how humans might respond to the invisibility of climate, a mathematical construct that we cannot experience directly. Humans care intensely about the cattle, rice, or chestnut trees that they depend upon to make a living.[18] By attending to these beings, we can experience invisible processes such as climate change.

By tacking back and forth between present-day grafting practices and former state policies of regulating and protecting chestnut trees, I have shown how the sensory texture of human/plant encounters can give rise to distinctions, words, bureaucratic classifications, taxation regimes, and projects of reshaping landscapes. Because of the historical accident of the importance of sweet chestnut to the Lucchese state, I focused upon chestnut cultivation, but very similar processes of grafting, soil care, and terrace building took place in response to olive, fruit trees, and grapevines. The horticultural terraced landscapes of Central Italy, and of the Mediterranean more broadly, emerged from the unstable unions between biological individuals that are produced by grafting. Terracing systems and grafted trees are linked with each other.

At the beginning of this chapter, I asked the question, "How do plants come to be political?" Part of an answer is that it is through relations with plants that people come to form ideas of care for plants, soils, and landscapes. The shape-shifting capacities of trees and other plants persuaded people to reshape landscapes. As we shall see, questions of proper plant and landscape care have come to affect contemporary environmental politics in Italy.

In mundane practices of grafting and care through pruning, chestnut trees are long-lived alien beings that can only provisionally be described. Precisely because description is always provisional, new words are always potentially coming into being and going away. It is never clear whether a graft will take, whether a tree will live or die, whether a new plant variety is present or not, and our descriptions of shape-shifting plants are also provisional. A new disease might cause a plant to die, but the apparently fatal disease could be halted by a new pathogen. In Deborah Bird Rose's terms, these trees "shimmer," always at the edge of transformation, of life or death.[19] We can describe such beings even while we remain aware that our descriptions are fallible, limited, both focusing our attention and failing to completely persuade us.

Plants can inspire human cultivation and landscape transformation, and humans can notice plant sensing by paying attention to plant morphology. Plants can change their morphologies in response to people, fires, and disease. Morphology is a different kind of evidence from the interviews or archives that anthropologists are familiar with. Thinking morphologically requires us to use drawings and photographs as primary evidence rather than as illustration. It also requires us to trust our senses and to be alert to the analytic and conceptual relations that emerge with particular perceptions. Morphologies are potentially unstable in relationship to the details that they contain: noticing traces of disease on a tree trunk leads me to reconsider how I see the whole tree or a broader landscape. Morphologies have other properties: they are particularly good ways of looking for evidence of past events, from forest fires, to disease, to human care. Rapid disasters, such as forest fires, or the slow disasters of disease or toxicity, leave morphological traces upon human or plant bodies that can make us attend to other temporalities. Morphologies are empirical evidence of ontologies that emerge through relations between beings. A tree can be a source of firewood, of food, a host of disease, or a survivor of fire. Morphology is a kind of evidence that anthropologists, with our commitment to ethnographic detail, are uniquely well suited to notice. We are, or should be, open to noticing "critters and processes, qualities and quantities," what anthropologist Eduardo Viveiros de Castro calls the "ontological anarchism" of the world. This requires us to be willing to add to our traditional interest in what people say and do, by using our senses to notice the effects that nonhumans have upon each other. We can draw examples from this ontological anarchism, but examples are not enough if they remain unique conjunctures. We risk remaining like Jorge Luis Borges's character Funes the Memorious, who is alert to the uniqueness of the world but is unable to make sense of it.[20] We need to be bold enough to move from our sensory experiences of plants, animals, soils, and people to larger scales in time and space.

My walks across chestnut groves with farmers drew me into thinking about the broader landscapes of the Monte Pisano and the Pizzorna, minor mountain ranges near Lucca. Attunement to the morphologies of individual trees drew my attention to larger-scale landscape structures. Patterns such as areas of burned and unburned landscape are landscape structures, "form coming into being."[21] In my walks across the landscape, I engaged in a practice of speculative noticing, where I tried to imagine the histories that had left traces in plant morphologies and landscape structures. Cultivated chestnut forests have given way to fire-blasted and disease-haunted postindustrial forests. As we shall see, a historical ecology of landscapes allows me to bring slow processes of soil formation and tree growth in conversation with rapid processes of capitalism, forest fires, and plant disease. I invite you first to change pace and spend some time learning to notice the relationships between plant morphologies and the biogeomorphologies of terracing and drainage systems.[22]

INTERLUDE I

Plant Morphology Leads to Geomorphology

Sensing the desires of plants pulls humans into relationships with material processes that we can only dimly perceive. By noticing the forms of plants, the shapes of branches and roots, peasant farmers came to notice and classify soils and build terracing and drainage systems. This was a collective project of remaking the landscape as an infrastructure. Depending upon the perceptual apparatus of plants in order to notice phenomena that are beyond human senses has ancient antecedents. As far back as the classical period, agronomical writers recommended classifying soils through taste, texture, and color, but also by noticing which plants flourished there. Peasant noticing of plant/soil/water relationships had material consequences that cascaded across Mediterranean landscapes. The shape-shifting capacities of plants, and especially tree crops that grew well on terraces, persuaded humans to reshape landscapes across the Mediterranean. Terraces and the less visible drainage systems that these are linked to have attracted the eyes of travelers since the philosopher Michel de Montaigne was struck by the "steps" on hillsides around Bagni di Lucca in 1580. Elite and literary interest is, however, quite recent and rather late in the history of terrace building. Terracing systems were certainly present in classical times but passed almost unrecorded by elites until a flowering of agronomical treatises in the sixteenth century. From the late eighteenth century onward, enlightened agronomists discussed various kinds of terracing systems. By the late nineteenth century, elaborate systems of terracing and drainage were described by agronomists such as Girolamo Caruso.[1] Some of these might have been built by aristocratic owners of model farms, but the vast majority of terracing and drainage systems were inevitably the work of peasant farmers.

Just as philosophers and elites have allowed themselves to imagine that plants were asleep because they did not notice the plant sensing that was recorded in morphology, literati have usually failed to pay attention to peasant practices of shaping landscape morphology.[2] Across the Mediterranean, and elsewhere around the world, farmers have interpreted the morphologies of plants as responses to largely invisible processes of water availability and soil fertility. In Italy, the responses of olive trees, chestnuts, fruit trees, and grapevines to soil and water availability caused farmers to build drainage and terracing systems. Plant morphology can bring humans into caring for soil and landscape form. This is true not only of terraced landscapes, but of cultivated fields everywhere, from Italy to Iowa. These biogeomorphologies are unstable plant/soil/water choreographies that require constant care and maintenance.

Names

Just as trees have many names for varieties and for morphologies that have emerged from plant biographies, terraces also have many names. "Terracing" (*terrazzamento*) is a relatively recent word that contains many older and more precise terms. Driving around the Monte Pisano with Fabio Casella, a planning official who has dedicated his career to fighting fires and preserving terracing and drainage systems, I learned to see differently. Fabio showed me the drainage systems that are the invisible counterpart of visible terracing systems. Older terms for terraces are *ripiani*, *gradinate* (steps, true stone-walled terraces), *scaglioni*, *poggi*, *zolle*, *ciglioni* (vegetated banks), *campi in pendio* (sloping fields). Older Latin terms found in medieval charters include *maceries*, *scala*, *pastinum*, *porca*, *semita*. Drains and ditches of various kinds are called *scoline di guardia*, *zanelle*, *collettori*, *aquidocci*. Terracing systems can extend as banks around chestnut trees in some areas: *lunette (riestrole)*, *ciglioni*. Like trees, terraces do not stay still; soil moves slowly downslope, walls must be rebuilt, soil carried back uphill, and drainage systems maintained. Terraces also imply the production of anthropogenic soils, produced by physical mixing during terrace building and maintenance and further modified by cultivation and fertilization practices.[3] As with grafting and pruning, sensory experiences of the nonhuman world give rise to classifications and names for soil types. The need to manage the movements of soil and water gives rise to projects of caring for landscape form. As we shall see, climate change in Italy is largely apprehended through the danger that improperly maintained landscape form might cause landslides and floods.

Allow your eye to shift from photographs to the drawings by artist Hannah Caisse, and notice how your sensory attention changes as you begin to notice plant/soil/water choreographies. Other textures and relations are still present, but less important now. Something is lost, as well as gained, by this shifting attention. Perhaps this assemblage of photographs and drawings will inspire you to look anew at your own surroundings.

Poplar/Grapevine/Soil/Water Choreographies

This system, in which trees were pruned to support festoons of grapevines, was formerly ubiquitous across the *alberata* and *piantata* landscapes of central Italy, and was typically glossed by officials as mixed (*promiscuo*) cultivation.[4] Fragments of this *vite maritata* are present in the suburban sprawl that surrounds Lucca. In figure 10, you can see poplar (*Populus nigra*), cut at head height as a pollard (*capitozza*), giving rise to multiple branches. Trailing from one tree to the next, if you look closely, you can see a curve like a telephone line. These are grape vines that are held up by the poplars. Formerly, horizontal tree branches would have supported festoons of vines. Now look at the drawing (figure 11), which shows what the eye cannot see but which the feet can feel. The intervals between tree/vine rows have been shaped into gentle banks. Arrows show how water runs into the drainage system and then moves off to the right. You can learn to feel the shape of the land by walking across it, sensing topographies that are too subtle for the eye to see.

Figure 10. *Vite maritata* outside Lucca, 2019. (Author photograph)

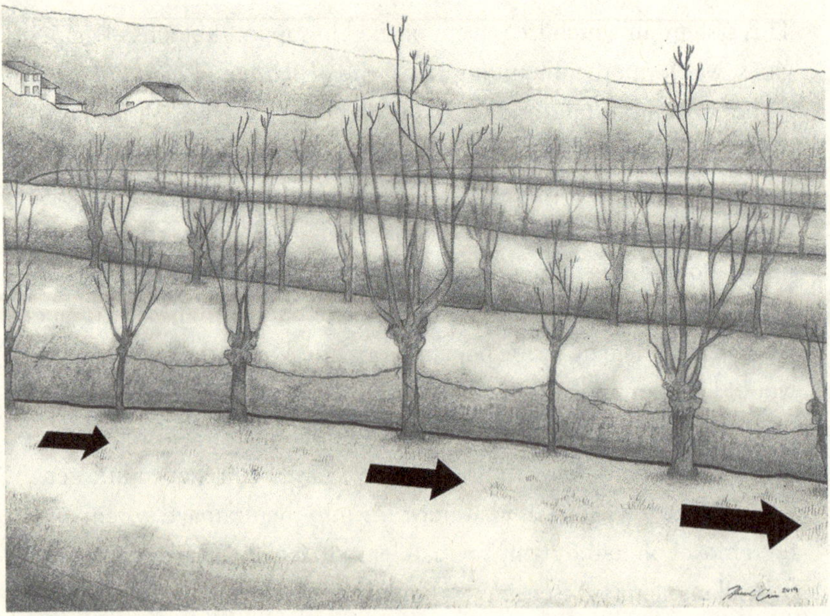

Figure 11. Drawing of *vite maritata* with landform and drainage pattern, 2019. Arrows show direction of water flow. (© Hannah Caisse)

Olive/Soil/Water Choreographies

These dry stone walls (*muretti a secco*, figure 12) are what most of us imagine when we think of terraces. Such walls are sophisticated hydraulic systems. At the base of each wall a ditch carries water *across* the landscape. Multiple terraces join a vertical drain, which moves water downhill without washing away soil. This kind of plant/soil/water choreography requires careful maintenance. As soil moves slowly through terracing systems, so too do drainage channels. After heavy rainfall, farmers would check their terraces to make sure that drainage channels were functioning properly. The invisible drainage channels that haunt this picture are highlighted by an arrow that shows water flow after rain. In figure 13, arrows show a similar pattern of water flow across less formal vegetated banks on shallower slopes.

Figure 12. Olive trees with stone terrace walls, Calci, Lucca, 2018. (Photograph used by permission of Fabio Malfatti)

Figure 13. Olive trees on vegetated banks, *ciglioni*, Palaia, Pisa, 2019. (Author photograph)

Banks and Hanging Fields

These banks (figure 14) might be called *ciglioni* or *zolle*, the fields *campi in pendio* (hanging fields). If you walk across such terraces you can feel the slope that funnels water into ditches, which in turn drain water across the landscape in a herringbone drainage pattern. Fragments of grapevines line the edges of these fields, which might once have sustained barley or potatoes. In figure 15, arrows show the movement of water across the landscape after rain.

Chestnut Trees and Terraces

Forest fires in the Monte Pisano in September 2018 burned off decades of accumulated leaf litter, revealing stone walls in long-forgotten places (figure 16). Look closely at the diagram (figure 17), then look back at the photo. Perhaps you will see the gnarled chestnut shoots on the left

Figure 14. Earthen terraces with grapevines, Garfagnana, Lucca, 2016. (Author photograph)

Figure 15. Drawing of terraces with grapevines and drainage channels, 2019. Arrows show direction of water flow. (© Hannah Caisse)

Figure 16. *Pino marittimo* (*Pinus pinaster*) growing on old chestnut terraces, Calci, Lucca, 2018. (Author photograph)

Figure 17. Drawing of stone terraces with pine trees and chestnut saplings, 2019. Arrows show direction of water flow. (© Hannah Caisse)

of the middle terrace. These walls retain soil, which traps moisture around tree roots and allows water to move through rather than along walls. These permeable walls were built for chestnut trees. The cadastral map, which records ownership and taxable value, confirms that this was a chestnut grove in 1835.

TWO

From Plant Morphologies to Landscape Structures

> The hills have the appearance of so many gardens laid out on steps, rising on small horizontal fields and earthen banks. On each bank vines are planted in rows, supported by peeled posts of acacia or chestnut, which are linked to each other with canes. In the middle of each field, where exposure and soil permit, stand olive trees. . . . Chestnut trees are also planted on banks but less regularly than the vines. Coppice forests cover the mountains from the side of the aforementioned valley to the summit. In this way, the whole presents a green so varied and full of life that it arouses, in whoever contemplates it for the first time, a sense of pleasure, rare and difficult to explain.
>
> —Antonio Mazzarosa, *Le pratiche della campagna lucchese*, 1846, author translation

The pine and chestnut forests of the Monte Pisano (figure 18), only five kilometers south of Lucca, in Central Italy (figure 19), feel very far from the tourist sights of the city center and from the industrial sprawl of paper, furniture, and shoe factories that spreads across the plain. As in many Mediterranean places, mountains and valleys are near each other, but they seem like different worlds. This distance is a relatively new phenomenon. Over the past century, and especially since World War II, the economic and social connections that formerly linked mountains to lowlands have caused the progressive abandonment of many parts of the Apennines.[1] These are certainly not the landscapes that most people think of when I tell them I am working

Figure 18. Monte Pisano with the city of Lucca in the background, 2013. (Author photograph)

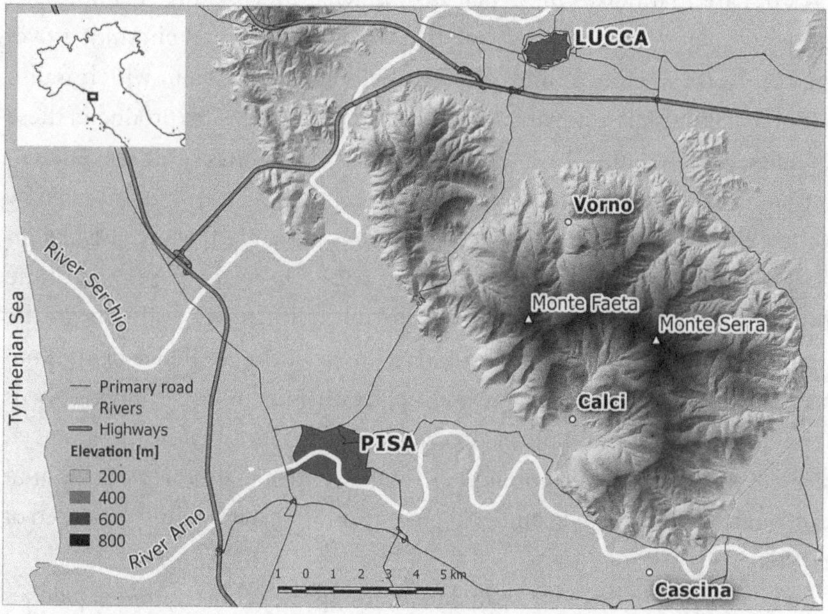

Figure 19. Location map of Lucca and Pisa. Monte Serra and Monte Faeta mark the crest of the Monte Pisano. (Map used by permission of Fabio Malfatti)

in northern Tuscany, nor do many people come here. The few human visitors are mushroom pickers, hunters, and the occasional mountain biker. Although these forests are often empty of people, they are empty in a particular way; evidence of former human use is omnipresent. This is a place where people, trees, and other nonhumans have been entangled for a very long time. Traces of these past relationships are visible in the forms of trees, of areas of forest, of drystone terrace walls, and of drainage systems. By walking, looking, and wondering, I have learned to notice the ghostly forms that have emerged from past encounters between people, plants, animals, and soils. From such practices of wondering, I have learned to notice landscape structures and to tell histories of social and ecological change. Telling such histories is a way of engaging with the politics of global environmental change, a topic I begin to explore in the following chapter.

I find walking through these abandoned chestnut (*Castanea sativa*) and maritime pine (*Pinus pinaster*) forests a little sad. It is the feeling of lack of care that makes these places somewhat melancholy. The forms of remaining large chestnut trees are fragments of cultivated chestnut groves (*selve*). Large ancient stumps known as stools (*ceppi*), from which multiple stems grow, tell a story of peasant firewood cutters who produced these coppices, or perhaps of more recent industrial biomass cutting. Ancient terracing and drainage systems are covered in a thick scrub dominated by yellow-flowered *Ulex europaea* or the yellowish white flowers of *Erica arborea*, both of which regrow after forest fires. On lower slopes, maritime pines loom over the sprouts of ancient chestnut trees, testifying to the abandonment of chestnut groves and to the stubborn resilience of chestnut trees in the face of neglect. In other places, ruined chestnut drying sheds (*metati*) recount the complex agrosilvopastoral systems that formerly linked peasant chestnut growers, premodern Italian states that protected chestnut cultivation, upland sheep and goat grazing, and lowland farmers in need of fertilizer.[2]

The morphologies of individual trees, the species composition of patches of forest, and the physical structures of terraces and buildings are evidence of *longue durée* encounters between humans, plants, animals, fungi, bacteria, and soils. This is a story of the relations between capitalism, state formation, and plant colonization, of the capacity of nonhumans to escape human imaginations, and of the ways that different forms of human politics have emerged from encounters with nonhumans. Over the past 1,500 years, peasant agriculturalists across Italian mountains worked to shape chestnut, oak, and pine trees into the forms that produced nuts, timber, fodder, and fuelwood, while also providing sufficient pasture for sheep and goats. Peasant and animal labor linked mountain wood pastures with terraced and lowland agriculture, through the fertilizing dung provided by mobile sheep and goats, and through the leaf litter that peasants formerly raked from the forest floor. Over the past 150 years, industrialization, rural outmigration, the arrival of alternative forms of fertilizer, and successive plant pathogen epidemics have undermined chestnut cultivation, grazing, and litter raking, leaving a haunted and ruined landscape. Through my practices of walking, looking, and wondering, I have traced the ghostly forms that have emerged from past encounters between people, plants, animals, and soils. Rather than recounting a single history that produced a unified landscape, I describe overlapping and interwoven landscape structures, patterns that are linked to histories of human and nonhuman interaction.[3]

Industrialization caused a rapid transformation of smallholder peasant farmers and sharecroppers into industrial and service workers after World War II, and the wholesale abandonment of grazing and farming in these hills. This abandoned landscape is increasingly swept by large forest fires. Fire-prone pines colonize burned areas, making the landscape more flammable still. Another history, however, can be recovered by combining direct observation of the landscape with visits to the archive. The Monte Pisano is one of the places that has been most heavily affected by pathogens that were brought by the global trade in live plants. Ink disease, *Phytophthora cambivora* (*male del inchiostro*), arrived in Italy in the 1840s, devastating low-elevation chestnut groves that had been cared for by peasant farmers. Chestnut canker, *Cryphonectria parasitica*, arrived here in the 1940s, further damaging chestnut cultivation. The presence and absence of chestnut is largely the result of these diseases, linking chestnut more to the history of the global trade in live plants than to industrialization.

Morphologies, Landscape Structures, and Histories

The word "landscape" has a rich and ambiguous history. Art historians have looked at landscape as an ideological construct, a canonical standard of elite taste that might support capitalism or state control. More recently, geographer Kenneth Olwig has reclaimed a substantive understanding of landscape as "a place of human habitation and environmental interaction" with particular legal, cultural, and economic histories. As Anna Tsing points out in *The Mushroom at the End of the World*, landscapes emerge through encounters between people and other beings, including soils, mushrooms, and disease organisms. I follow the kinds of landscapes and histories that have emerged from encounters between people, trees, pathogens, and soils in formerly cultivated landscapes in central Italy. This kind of landscape description pushes us to think about how particular forms emerge through histories of encounter. The changing shape of a tree tells me how it has been changed through encounters with wildfire, human cutting, grazing goats, and fungal diseases. This transformation is a change in what kind of a thing the tree is. The anthropologist Marianne Lien and the sociologist John Law use the term "empirical ontologies" to describe realities that are enacted in practices between people and salmon. I extend their insight to observe the realities that are produced through the effects that nonhumans have upon each other. Trees bear the scars of fire and disease, and terraces bear traces of building and abandonment. These are practical ontologies that emerge through partial relations between beings, where the difference between life and death is not necessarily relevant. Plants, soil, rocks, fire, and water affect each other.[4]

Encounters with individual organisms and with landscapes have inspired me to explore research methods of drawing, natural history, and historical ecology.[5] These methods prove well suited to the open-ended and partial nature of what I can notice, and to tracing the forms that result from encounters between people and nonhumans (people, sheep, trees) and between nonhumans and other nonhumans (trees, soils, disease, fire). Such an ethnography of the landscape requires attention to the temporal rhythms of processes as disparate as rapidly moving fires and slow-growing trees, soil formation, daily cycles of weather, and the structural violence of political economic transformation and state formation.

In emphasizing landscape as the product of collective human and nonhuman action, I find echoes with studies of landscape as a material infrastructure, as in the road and river networks described by Ashley Carse for the Panama Canal watershed, or the irrigation and drainage systems described by Jessica Barnes for Egypt. Landscapes, however, contain indeterminacy, texture, and a possibility of scale change and transformation that are rather different from most studies of infrastructure. What we know about landscapes always contains indeterminacy and fields of unresolved texture, smaller details that can become significant and change our understanding of what we take to be larger scales (or vice versa). This is not just a feature of the landscapes that we ordinarily think of. Come close to a tree and you will see entire landscapes of relations at every scale, from the pattern of bark that tells you of an ancient tree to the tiny orange fungi that show a tree to be infested by chestnut canker. Farmers like Giuseppe del Chiaro notice these spores with fear. You might see the dry, crackled callus that shows that the canker has itself been infested by a virus that prevents it from killing the tree. Chestnut farmers wait breathlessly for such signs of disease stabilization. Come close to look at such details and your understanding of whether an area of forest landscape is doomed or healthy can change drastically. The relations between details and large-scale patterns are always provisional. In my study of the Monte Pisano, I learned to know the landscape both analytically and phenomenologically, through a practice of moving back and forth between intimate encounters with details of tree morphology and landscape pattern, between interviews with farmers and visits to archives. As I moved back and forth, I gradually came to foreground two histories in accounting for some of the morphological details and landscape patterns that had come to be significant for me. My practices of noticing more-than-human relations of people, plants, and soils pull me beyond the more usual anthropological practices of interview, archive, and observation.[6]

In a classic article, the feminist geographer Diane Rocheleau drew on Donna Haraway's concept of situated knowledges to argue for the use of multiple methods in political ecology. We can expand on this insight to think of our current task as one of linking coexisting processes, histories, and ontological transformations that emerge through relations among beings in landscapes. This is a phenomenological historical ecology that is open to wonder and surprise. Drawing on multiple lines of evidence and attending to details of plant and terrace form has allowed me to notice landscape patterns that are linked to different histories of human and more-than-human encounters. These patterns are heterogeneous assemblages containing plants, soils, and animals that are continuously transforming each other's morphologies. I have learned to see the "form coming into being" of these large-scale patterns as *landscape structures*. Landscape structures are intensely real. I apprehend them with my senses, but they are also analytics, coordinations between different kinds of beings that I can also show through conceptual diagrams.[7] I have learned to notice these landscape structures by linking sensory curiosity to archive and map, by linking drawings and photographs with field notes from walks and conversations with farmers, biologists, and others. Out of this mass of evidence, I have come to be attuned to two landscape structures as being the most important ones. The landscape structures that matter in the Monte Pisano are the fire-blasted landscapes of twentieth-century agricultural abandonment, and the remnant chestnut forests that record the effects of pathogen epidemics in the nineteenth and twentieth centuries.

Through my movement between forest, field, and archive, formerly unnoticed landscape patterns have come into ever-sharper relief as structures that are linked to histories of political, economic, and ecological change. Such structures allow me to project my imagination from my phenomenological experience of the world into larger-scale stories of political economic change and environmental destruction. In this practice of landscape ethnography, every perception is at once speculative, partial, and resolutely empirical. Noticing landscape features, trees, or soils takes a double form of wondering (*What is this thing that I am in relation with?*) and wonder at the mysteriousness and indeterminacy of the world, where our descriptions are always provisional and partial. Tim Ingold has long argued that material forms emerge from ecological relations in a world of process.[8] I link this world of process to larger-scale patterns, which are simultaneously provisional, analytic, and intensely phenomenologically real. Just as the descriptions of a particular organism are partial and tentative, so too, landscape descriptions are partial and tentative, inhabited by many details not relevant at that level of perception. It is through a principled tacking back and forth between details and patterns that I become attuned to new patterns and histories. The ghosts of peasant landscape making, pathogen epidemics, and industrialization gradually become apparent.

Reading Ghostly Presences in Forests

Walking through the forests of the Monte Pisano with my botanist assistant Francesco Roma-Marzio, I note what tree, shrub, and understory plant species we see and what forms they have, jotting these down as sketches in my notebook, making notes of impressions and speculations. As a botanist, Francesco names understory plants for me, and the two of us provoke each other with stories of human use of landscapes. Drawing on my training as a forester, I tell him how the shapes of trees and shrubs tell me stories of tree cutting and regrowth, of fire and grazing. Echoes of conflicts over property and landscape are present in tree form. Remnant ancient cultivated *castagneti* (chestnut groves) tell us of centuries-long relationships with peasant agriculturalists who formerly sculpted chestnut, oak, and pine trees into the particular forms that produced food, timber, fodder, and fuel, while also providing pasture for sheep and goats, and leaf litter to fertilize their fields. Notebooks, interviews, photographs, and sketches contain something of my phenomenological experience of encounters with shape-changing ancient trees and terrace systems. Perhaps a stump is truly dead, but it may also resprout and come alive. Figure 20A shows a sample from my field notes, recording our first encounter with a really large chestnut tree. Figure 20B shows this ancient chestnut tree. Note the *polloni* (shoots known as suckers) sprouting from the base of the tree (see also figures 8 and 9). We guessed that the size of the *polloni* told us that they had been cut back five to eight years earlier, but based on later experience, I would now guess more like two or three years. This tree was at least two hundred years old and perhaps several centuries more, a sign of a human/plant collaboration that had lasted for a very long time.[9]

(A)

(B)

Figure 20. Field notes (A) and ancient grafted chestnut tree (B) in Vorno, Lucca, 2014. (Author photographs)

Drawing is the method through which I do justice to the shape-shifting capacities and the mundane ontological indeterminacy of plants. The form of a cultivated chestnut tree tells me a story of its responses to encounters with peasants, diseases, fires, and soil movement processes. This morphology is somewhat indeterminate. I draw it in different ways, depending on whether I notice the details of disease cankers and imagine that this tree is doomed, or whether I notice the scarring produced by disease containment and guess that it is on its way to a new symbiosis. From these encounters I learn to produce a drawing that summarizes my perception of human/plant and plant/nonhuman interaction as they manifest in tree form. Sometimes I accompany a drawing with the linguistic terms that sharpen my capacity to notice some differences and not others. My sensory apparatus is transformed by my own curiosity and by my journeys with farmers and foresters. They teach me words that change my sense of landscape patterns and my capacity to notice tree form. My capacity to notice is not fully contained or tamed by the words I learn from farmers, foresters, or scientists. Their words are provisional; they capture some aspect of the indeterminacy and shimmer of plant ontologies. My perceptions might shift again. I might need to tell other stories with other words or drawings.

Walking and paying attention to color, shape, and form press me to be alert both to textures (the background, which remains indeterminate) and to the emergent forms that come to matter (the foreground), which I highlight through sketches and drawings. A few pencil strokes can summarize the patterns that I notice when I take a picture, as in figure 20A. These line drawings can be the shapes of trees whose ontology is indeterminate, but they can also be larger-scale landscape patterns whose boundaries could be drawn otherwise, perhaps in relation to encounters with details that come to have a larger significance. In many cases plant form gestures toward processes that I cannot see. A line drawing makes visible my relationship with a particular tree or terrace, my effort to show that this was a partial relation that failed to grasp other aspects of a chestnut stump that might live or die or change shape over time. A strong tradition of line drawings exists in archaeology, natural history, and field biology, as well as, formerly, in cultural anthropology. Because of the nature of their material, archaeologists have never abandoned drawing changing animal anatomy or seed morphology as an important way of tracing histories of domestication that tell of human/nonhuman relationality. Biologists continue to use drawings to highlight the key features that they track in telling stories about evolution and adaptation. Cultural anthropologists might find line drawings or diagrams suitable for recording morphologies that emerge from relationships across ontological and temporal difference, not only in forests but in cities, agricultural fields, or irrigation systems.[10] Drawings are well suited to reflexively showing our involvement with the beings that we care about, and they are uniquely well suited to capturing interactions between processes that proceed at very different rates. Fast and slow disasters such as disease, forest fires, and climate change are best followed through the morphologies that emerge from these processes. The slow violences of toxicity and global environmental change call for attention to form and diagram.

Encountering a Strange Being

A few weeks after that walk in Vorno, Francesco and I encountered a strange being. This image (figure 21) may not be very imposing. Perhaps it looks like a slightly blurry field of shades of gray and black (in the image you are looking at), certainly nothing to remark upon if you happen by something similar on your next walk in the countryside. For me, primed as I was by talking to chestnut farmers, by my training as a forester, and by many walks across similar landscapes, this particular stump told a fascinating story. It reminded me of something I greatly admire about plants—their capacity to change shape. One of the great pleasures of fairy tales is the shape-changing magical beings. The plants that we often fail to notice can also do this trick. Let me tell you a bit more about what you are looking at. Perhaps my brief account may help you notice the weird shape-shifting capacities of plants the next time you go for a walk.

This picture is an ancient chestnut stool. It tells me a story of centuries of careful grafting, pruning, and cultivation, of an ancient tree that was over three meters in circumference and was probably at least two hundred years old when it was cut. The shape of this stump is an echo of disaster, of the moment in the 1950s when rural abandonment and the arrival of the fungal

Figure 21. Ancient chestnut stump, Pizzorna, Lucca, 2014. (Author photograph)

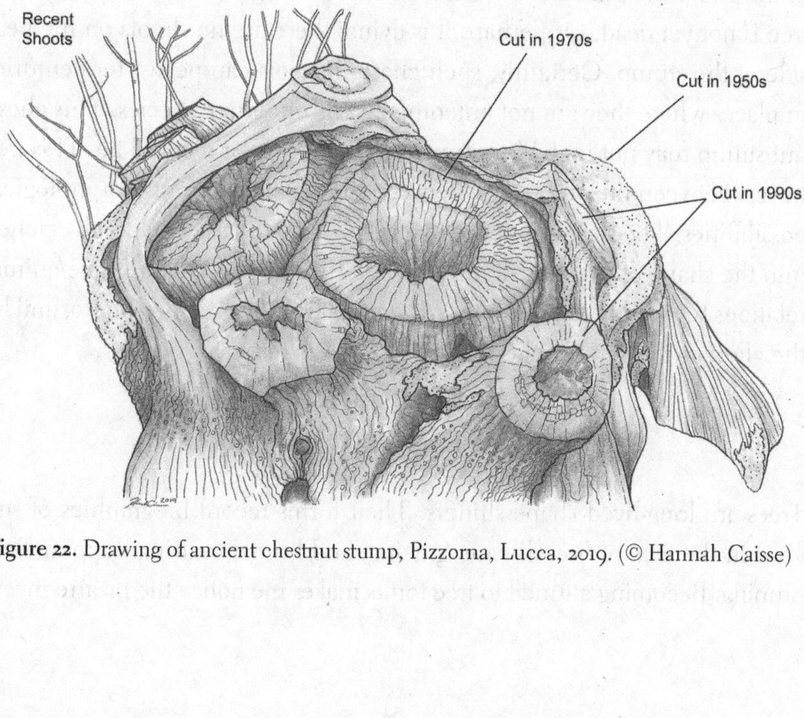

Figure 22. Drawing of ancient chestnut stump, Pizzorna, Lucca, 2019. (© Hannah Caisse)

chestnut canker *Cryphonectria parasitica* made cutting this tree seem like the only sensible thing to do.[11] Faced with the imminent death of all chestnut trees, or perhaps because growing chestnuts for food made little sense compared to taking paid employment in factories, the peasants who cared for this tree decided to cut it down and sell the massive trunk to the tannin factory at Bagni di Lucca, about fifteen kilometers away. Cutting the tree did not kill it. On the contrary, cutting caused a sudden wild flourishing of dormant buds that had lurked as potential growing shoots in the cambium layer beneath the bark. Cutting the main trunk removed hormonal signals from the dominant dormant buds in the upper crown and shed a flood of sunlight on the bark, triggering the emergence and rapid growth of shoots near the stump.[12] Gradually, the number of shoots diminished, due to competition that left perhaps half a dozen stems of about ten to fifteen centimeters in diameter, allowing the tree to change form to become a coppice. Look at the diagram in figure 22, and see if you can see the circular patterns of two ages of pole-sized stems, evidence of the tree's response to cuts that took place twenty years apart. The diagram might help you see the photograph differently, as it emphasizes the differences in texture between different cuts. Older cuts leave rougher, more eroded circles. If you look closely, on the top left of the photo in figure 21, you will see a new round of shoots emerging. This tree is not yet dead. Or perhaps it is dying; there are no shoots on the near side of the stump. Certainly, such chestnut stools can persist for centuries in places where they are not outcompeted by other tree species. This chestnut stump may not look like a tree to you, but it is, or it could be. This tree hovers between life and death, between drastically different morphological possibilities. The slow disasters of capitalism and disease are literally etched into the shape of this tree, as are the older histories of peasant/tree/animal relations that produced this formerly grafted tree. Look at this photo, and let the ghost of this former chestnut grove emerge for you.

Shape Shifters in the Forest

Trees are long-lived shape shifters. Their forms record biographies of survival in the face of fire, disease, grazing, and human cutting, lopping, and pruning. Becoming attuned to tree forms makes me notice the bizarre inven-

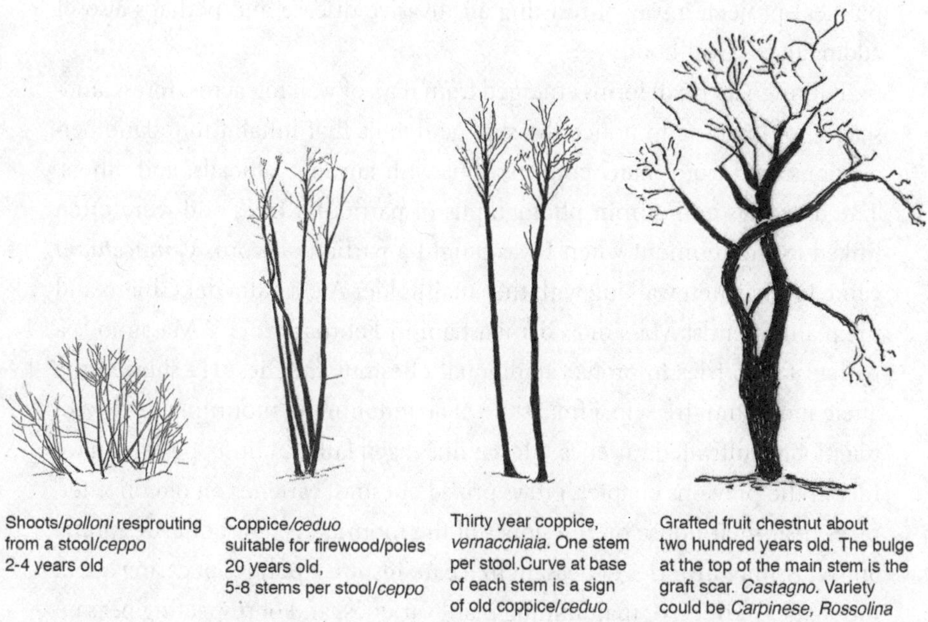

Figure 23. A menagerie of chestnut forms, a family of names. (Drawings by author)

tiveness of plants that change shape and move across the landscape too slowly for me to notice easily. The drawings in figure 23 make visible some of the different forms that chestnut trees can take. Names for these forms emerged from the daily work of peasant farmers who worked with plant/soil/animal assemblages, and from conversations between peasant cultivators and the officials and literati who occasionally talked to them. In Italy, a host of traditional technical terms for chestnut trees, terraces, and forests are now falling into disuse, known mainly to old people as well as historians, foresters, and anthropologists like me. Old words tell of old relationships, but new words and plant varieties are also always potentially emerging from acts of noticing and care. In the winter of 2014, the farmer Stefano Fazzi, who lived in the nearby Garfagnana area, told me that he had noticed that a chestnut variety on his land appeared immune to the invasive gall wasp *Dryocosmus kuriphilus*, which was then devastating chestnut production.[13] Stefano hoped to have his variety recognized and named and to build collaborations with the academic establishment and the state. This was a speculative Anthropocene political project, a way of resisting an invasive disease and perhaps also of adding to his livelihood.

This menagerie of forms emerged from days of walking across forest landscapes, of learning to notice the strange details that inhabit mundane perceptions, and from many conversations with farmers, officials, and others. The drawings come from photographs of particular trees and were often linked to the moment when I was taught a particular word. *Vernacchiaia* came to me when walking with the smallholder Alessandra del Chiaro and the plant scientist Massimo Giambastiani in February 2014.[14] Massimo is a biologist who tries to protect traditional chestnut varieties. He showed me ancient chestnut trees in a final state of abandonment, mourning the loss of traditional cultivated varieties. Alessandra's aged father, Giuseppe, whom we met in the previous chapter, grows prized chestnut varieties on old olive terraces near their house on the slopes of the mountains. For both Alessandra and Massimo, histories of peasant tree care inspire a politics of caring about the shapes of trees, of maintaining plant varieties, and of respecting peasant knowledge. The drawing of a coppiced tree came to me on a field trip with government foresters, who told me how this multistemmed plant might become a tall single-stemmed tree (released coppice, *ceduo affrancato*). Italian foresters love the idea of tall straight trees (ideally conifers), and historically they have tried to avoid the gnarled fruit trees or the multistemmed firewood forests desired by peasant farmers. Farmers and peasants told me that to allow trees to grow too large was to risk having them classified as high forest (*alto fusto*), which might become bureaucratically impossible to cut and which might destabilize hillsides and terraces. These drawings are as much concepts as representations. They contain politically contested futures; they include my guess at how I can best communicate what I see (as a forester and anthropologist with a lifelong practice of walking landscapes) or have been taught to see by others. These drawings come from highly atypical photographs in which I have removed a tree from its context with other trees; no photograph can communicate what the skilled eye learns to see. Photographs are too realistic, almost the worst means to communicate stories about form. My seeing emerges from walking, talking, touching, and wondering; each drawing is a diagram, a story, a description.

Plant Form and State Power

Plant morphologies record social histories, the tense and intimate relations between peasants and landlords, between the government officials who tried to control grazing and prevent fires, and the farmers and pastoralists who needed somewhere to feed their animals. Areas of multistemmed trees, known as coppices, tell me of peasant firewood cutting and of the capacity of trees to resprout from a stump (see figure 23). In English people coppice trees by cutting, while a plant that resprouts after cutting is also said to coppice. Trees and people coppice in relation to each other. This is a rare trace of mutual plant/human responses in our vocabulary. Remaining fruit chestnut trees tell me of the Lucca oligarchy, which wished to maintain food supplies and stabilize landscapes. Conifer plantations at the top of the mountain tell me of twentieth-century struggles between the Italian state and pastoralists.

The advance and retreat of state presence in forests has reshaped relations between people, trees, and landscape over the past two hundred years. From the late Middle Ages until the early nineteenth century, Lucca was a republic ruled by a small and conservative aristocratic oligarchy. In this ancien régime, most peasant households in the mountains had access to at least some land, usually a mixture of pasture, chestnut grove, woodland, and arable land. This integrated agrosilvopastoral system, together with rural industry and migrant labor, allowed smallholders to put together a reasonable living. In most mountainous areas, a critical element of rural livelihoods was common land (*usi civici*) for grazing and fuelwood. In the Monte Pisano, so close to the cities of Lucca and Pisa, community forests had been largely privatized in the sixteenth century, but common grazing areas remained on the crest of the mountains. Transhumance, the practice of moving grazing animals from one grazing ground to another on a seasonal cycle, brought shepherds from summer pastures in the northern Apennines to the Monte Pisano, on their way to coastal winter pastures to the south. Forest owners usually had to allow local people customary access for grazing and firewood collection. Land and trees were tightly confined to local uses, and setting up new industries could be a difficult process. The historian Renzo Sabbatini describes how iron founders in eighteenth-century Lucca were repeatedly prevented from drawing on chestnut groves for charcoal by the Offizio Sopra le Selve. Property owners often did not own the trees that grew on their own land, and often they could not prevent grazing in their woods. A typical example was the iron industry in the nearby province of Pistoia, which owned the fuelwood in its surrounding territory, a source of tension with landowners and pastoralists. On the southern side of the Monte Pisano, the medieval republic of Pisa and its successor, the Grand Duchy of Tuscany (1569–1801), claimed ownership of all pine trees for shipbuilding, while the land belonged to someone else. On the northern side of the mountains, the Republic of Lucca protected chestnut groves as a source of food. In all these cases, what grew on the land was destined for a specific, usually local, user, and the property rights of landowners were hedged in by customary uses and legal restrictions.[15] Forest regulations were administered (or ignored) by local notables, sometimes assisted by local forest guards, but the state apparatus was minuscule.

The end of this world came suddenly. In Tuscany the regime of Archduke Peter Leopold (1765–1790) dissolved legal restrictions over property rights and privatized most commons in a series of decrees between 1769 and 1783. In 1800, invading Napoleonic armies overthrew the Republic of Lucca. Whether driven by liberal absolutism or by Napoleonic conquest, the result was much the same for the forests and inhabitants of the Monte Pisano. Chestnut groves and pine trees could be cut at will, church lands were sold off, remaining commons were privatized, and smallholders were forced into increasing dependence on wage labor. With the unification of Italy in 1861, the Kingdom of Italy sold off public and church lands to real estate speculators, who in many cases logged the forest to pay off their debts. In the southern Apennines, this resulted in widespread deforestation, followed by soil erosion, landslides, and floods. In the Monte Pisano things played out differently. With most communal lands long privatized, there was little land to sell off, although the removal of remaining forest protections did allow private landowners to liquidate forests. On the southern side of the mountains in particular, the booming olive oil market led residents in the communities of Calci, Vicopisano, and Buti to clear forests, build terraces, and plant olive groves, a process that was already well underway in the eighteenth century.[16]

By 1866, national debates over the environmental consequences of eliminating forest protections found an echo in Pisa, where the provincial government commissioned a report that called for reforestation to repair the effects of excessive logging. The national forest law that was passed in 1877 was the result of over a decade of debate about the impacts of deforestation. This law gave the national forest service the authority to restrict access to forests "up to the limit of the chestnut" as well as in areas vulnerable to erosion and landscape instability. In the Monte Pisano, the recently installed Royal Forest Service interpreted this limit as applying to areas "between 500 and 800 meters" and to steep and erodible areas, effectively restricting access to the entire crest of the mountains. Much of this area was pasture critical to the livelihoods of shepherds and farmers on both sides of the mountains. Although pastures were recorded as private property on tax maps, in 2019 elderly shepherds told me that they were grazed as a commons, while property boundaries were recognized for firewood and leaf-litter gathering. Sheep manure and leaf litter were a critical source of fertilizer for booming olive cultivation, and Tuscan landowners who were used to having access to pastures and woodlands fiercely resisted access restrictions. By 1915, the forest service accepted defeat and withdrew the regulation from this area.[17]

Although there had been limited efforts to reforest denuded mountains after the unification of Tuscany into the new Kingdom of Italy in 1861, the national forest service had modest budgets to plant trees and little manpower to enforce forestry regulations. The first large-scale afforestation began after World War I, and especially during the Fascist regime of Benito Mussolini (1922–1943), which launched a new forest law in 1923. Afforestation campaigns concentrated on planting conifers on the crests and slopes of denuded mountains, the very places that shepherds depended upon to feed their sheep. Under the confident and authoritarian Fascist regime, forestry regulations became stricter and more detailed and were much more seriously enforced than previously. From 1927, goats and sheep were excluded from protected mountain forests and from young tree plantings on mountain pastures across Italy. The 1929 agricultural census records over eight thousand sheep on the Pisa side of the mountains alone, while the Lucca side of the mountains supported slightly lower numbers. Thanks to the successful resistance campaign before World War I, shepherds in the Monte Pisano seem to have been less of a target for forestry officials than in other parts of the Apennines. In 2019, for example, an old shepherd told me of his pleasure in seeing young tree plantations damaged by fire, but he did not recall grazing exclusions by the forest service as having been a serious problem. The approximately four hundred hectares of forest laboriously planted on the Monte Pisano during the 1930s were heavily damaged by fires in 1944–1946, as were plantations on the nearby Pizzorna mountain range. These fires may have been caused by the war, but it seems likely that some were set by local people who hoped to halt the takeover of mountain pastures. In the Monte Pisano, as on other nearby mountains, damaged Fascist era plantations were replanted in the late 1940s and early 1950s as a kind of Cold War–era rural employment program.[18] The last gasp of these reforestation efforts were plantings at the top of the Monte Pisano in the late 1970s. By then rural abandonment had taken hold. Sheep numbers were plummeting as elderly shepherds retired, abandoned pastures were colonized by fire-prone scrub, and forest fires were becoming larger and fiercer. From the 1860s to the present, most foresters have seen tall and straight conifer trees as valuable and scientifically manageable. Planting conifers was a way of providing rural employment, of producing timber, and of halting environmental degradation. By the 1970s, conifer plantations were seen as a solution to the abandonment caused by industrialization and urbanization. Rural people have remained skeptical of these plantings. For Alessandra del Chiaro, the daughter of the peasant smallholder Giuseppe, the Douglas fir (*Pseudotsuga menziesii*) plantations near her farm lower down the mountain were a tax boondoggle for rich landowners and an ecological mistake.

This history of natural-resource extraction and state making in the forest has left traces on tree forms, on landscape structures, and in popular understandings of the state. Even as we notice the details of plant morphology, my companions and I often discuss history, politics, state making, and global environmental change. My assistant Francesco can recognize the multitude of understory plants (I cannot do this). He names native species and notices more recent alien arrivals, leading us to wonder about international trade and the mule trains that might have given a lift to the seeds of the non-native plants that he sees by the side of the trail. The path from Calci to Vorno formerly linked different states, a good route for trade and smuggling! These trails also supported the transhumance that brought sheep and goats from the high Apennines every year. This trail may be almost abandoned now, but it was a busy place in the past, and herb species tell us of histories of human and animal mobility. When we encounter old pastures covered with conifer plantations, Francesco notices the meadow species *Crocus biflorus* hanging on beneath the conifers loved by the forest service. The persistence of these pasture flowers is a trace of the centuries of grazing by sheep and goats on mountain pastures. Stories of sheep, grazing, and pastures launch us into conversations about the displacement of pastoralists by the forest service. He tells me of the contented outdoor life of his shepherd grandfather in Puglia, who lived into his nineties.

Historical Ecology: Linking Natural History and Drawing with Cadastral Maps

Attunement to landscape patterns does not only take place in the forest. Sometimes it is a conversation with an official or a visit to the archive that makes me rethink what I see in the landscape. The plant morphologies, landscape patterns, and histories that emerged from my interviews and landscape walks encountered bureaucratic landscape classifications in the tax maps of the former Republic of Lucca, which was so interested in protecting and supporting chestnut cultivation. This archive allowed me to build a large-scale systematic account of the landscape of the Monte Pisano in the early nineteenth century, at the very end of the ancien régime. In 2014 I walked from the village of Vorno, at the base of the Monte Pisano, to the top of the mountain, at Campo di Croce. Overlaying my landscape observations, field notes, and drawings from 2014, and comparing these with geographically referenced tax maps from 1835–1846, I was able to build a diagram that showed dramatic landscape transformations. By comparing historic tax maps with botanical surveys carried out in 2000, I could contrast a systematic account of former land use with a systematic survey of plant communities across the entire mountain range.[19] These comparisons allow me to extrapolate large-scale stories about the landscape, but they also force me to accept the freezing of ontologies and relationships in tax officials' landscape classifications and in the vegetation classifications of the botanical survey. We can think of tax maps as a kind of systems account of the world, similar to the infrastructure of data collection used by climate change modelers that reduces the complexity of weather to a few key variables. The tax register's simplified version of the world is alert to land-use types, to who owned land, and to what it was worth, but it tells me nothing about ontological transformations that take place when a tree changes shape, when a fire transforms a chestnut grove into a pine forest, or when a farmer becomes a worker in a nearby paper factory. Systems accounts allow a certain kind of spatial and temporal projection, while silencing the kind of storytelling and noticing that I can build from landscape ethnography. Nevertheless, it was through the deliberately simplifying systems thinking of the tax register that I came to appreciate the full scale of the disaster wrought by the arrival of *Phytophthora cambivora* in this region in the 1840s.

Telling Stories to the Tax Inspector

Old maps can tell stories if you can link them with other kinds of landscape evidence. I combined georeferenced historical tax maps from 1846 with my own observations of present-day landscapes in the Monte Pisano. Working backward, I consulted the *Giornale di Campo* (*Field Journal*) which recorded what people told the tax assessor on that long ago day. The cadastral map divided the land into tax parcels linked to a tax register called the *Giornale della Misura e Stima* (*Register of Measure and Estimate*). The *Giornale* recorded who owned each piece of property, what was growing there or what a building was used for, and what tax was owed. Such tax records are a simplified description of industrial labor and of choreographies of human care for plants and animals. Like all utopian projects, tax assessments faced frictions with reality, as landowners, farmers, and tax inspectors negotiated what land use would be recorded. The *Catasto Nuovo Lucchese* of 1846 applied a cadastral logic according to which each piece of land had one use, to the complex tree/animal polycultures that covered not only Lucca, but much of the landscape of Central Italy. The archive registers traces of politically fraught encounters between landowners and the peasants who cultivated land on their behalf. We can hear something of the words they shared to talk about cultivation systems, and the kinds of industrial work that took place in water-powered paper, grain, and olive mills. This record allows me to understand the species and forms of the trees that people cared about and to guess at the plants, animals, and terracing systems that were present but unrecorded.[20] Reading a multispecies assemblage off a tax record is only possible if we read the archive imaginatively and combine this reading with art history and natural-history field notes. In figure 24 you can see something of the minute level of detail of the register, where the taxable value of every building and piece of land is recorded around the aristocratic Villa Minutoli-Tegrimi.

Beginning on the valley floor, near the Villa Minutoli-Tegrimi, the *Giornale* registers an echo of elegant villas, of their walled gardens (*chiuse*) cultivated with mixtures of trellised vines (*vigne a pergola*), and of vines trained upon trees, usually poplar or mulberry. We read of *prato con un pergolato a frutti*, "meadow with a pergola on fruit trees." Perhaps this was some kind of mixture of grapevines growing on wooden stakes and along the branches of fruit trees? What was the meadow like? Maintaining it would have required a skilled choreography on the part of animal herders, who could bring sheep or cattle through and keep them moving before they got hungry enough to eat grapevines and nibble fruit trees. These kinds of fruit tree/vine/pasture/grain mixtures dominated the level lands at the bottom of the valley of Vorno and were largely attached to elegant villas. In reading the archive, one gets the impression of the landowner and the farmer trying hard to come up with a description that approximated a complex multispecies choreography. The variety of descriptions hints at the complexity that they struggled to describe. Many descriptions are unique and seem to have been invented on the spot. Consider, for example, *pometo con pochi gelsi e pochi pergolati*, "apple orchard with a few mulberries and a few vine pergolas"; or *seminativo in parte e in parte prativo con pergolati frutti, gelsi, e pioppi con vite unita*, "partly grain and partly meadow with fruit trees trained as a trellis, mulberries, and poplars trained with grapevines."[21] This was a world of vegetative complexity

Figure 24. Section of the map of the *Catasto Nuovo Lucchese*, Vorno, Lucca. The map shows property boundaries and buildings around the Villa Minutoli-Tegrimi. Each numbered parcel was linked to a land use and a taxable value. (From "Mappa Catasto Nuovo Lucchese, Sezione di Vorno, Foglio I, N2." 1846. By permission of the Ministero della Cultura—Archivio di Stato di Lucca. Reproduction by any means is forbidden.)

that demanded extraordinary skill to maintain and that almost defied description.

These detailed descriptions emerged from a meeting between the local landowner who had been delegated the authority to assess taxes and the person responsible for working the land.[22] This could be an estate manager (*fattore*), a sharecropping peasant (*mezzadro*), or an independent smallholder. Such conversations must have been fraught. Landowners who were also tax assessors had an interest in minimizing the taxable value of their own property and increasing that of others. Landowners could lay a heavy finger upon the scales of these estimates. On the other hand, the city of Lucca was only an hour or two away on foot, and complaints would have been easy to lodge, so landowners could not push too hard. Peasants and landowner tax assessors had a relatively intimate (if potentially oppressive) relationship. Out of these awkward intimacies came the description that ended up being passed to the authorities in Lucca and entered in the tax register that recorded what was grown on each parcel of land.

The variety of land use descriptions makes it hard to tell exactly what a particular agrosilvopastoral mixture looked like. We do have a good general sense of what these complex polycultures might have looked like, drawn from across the history of Italian landscape painting by the great landscape historian Emilio Sereni. This was the *alberata*, a landscape that combined trees, animals, and grain crops, separated by hedges of trees carefully pruned to sustain vines. Trees pruned to sustain grapevines were known as the *vite maritata*, but many other plant/soil/water choreographies existed. The *alberata* of Central Italy and the similar *piantata* of Northern Italy were sustained by careful soil and water management, through terracing, banks, and drainage systems, dominating much of Italy over at least the past five hundred years and in some form as far back as the classical period.[23] The state archive of Lucca contains an enchanting drawing of this cultivation system from the valley of Vorno itself (figure 25). This is a plant/soil/water coordination, where poplar trees support the soil of canal banks, grapevines grow along carefully pruned branches, and water moves constantly. Maintaining this choreography would have required peasants to do the constant work of pruning and cutting vines and trees, as well as the less frequent work of maintaining the canal banks.

The *alberata* landscape was shaped by the work of peasants who coordinated plants, animals, soils, and water, as well as by relationships between peasants and landlords. The social injustices, the histories of subordination, but also the skillful evasions by farmers who avoided tax and labor demands from elites, are inscribed in the morphologies of trees, terracing, and drainage systems. A few words are required here to explain what I mean by the slippery term "peasant," so often and so vaguely used.

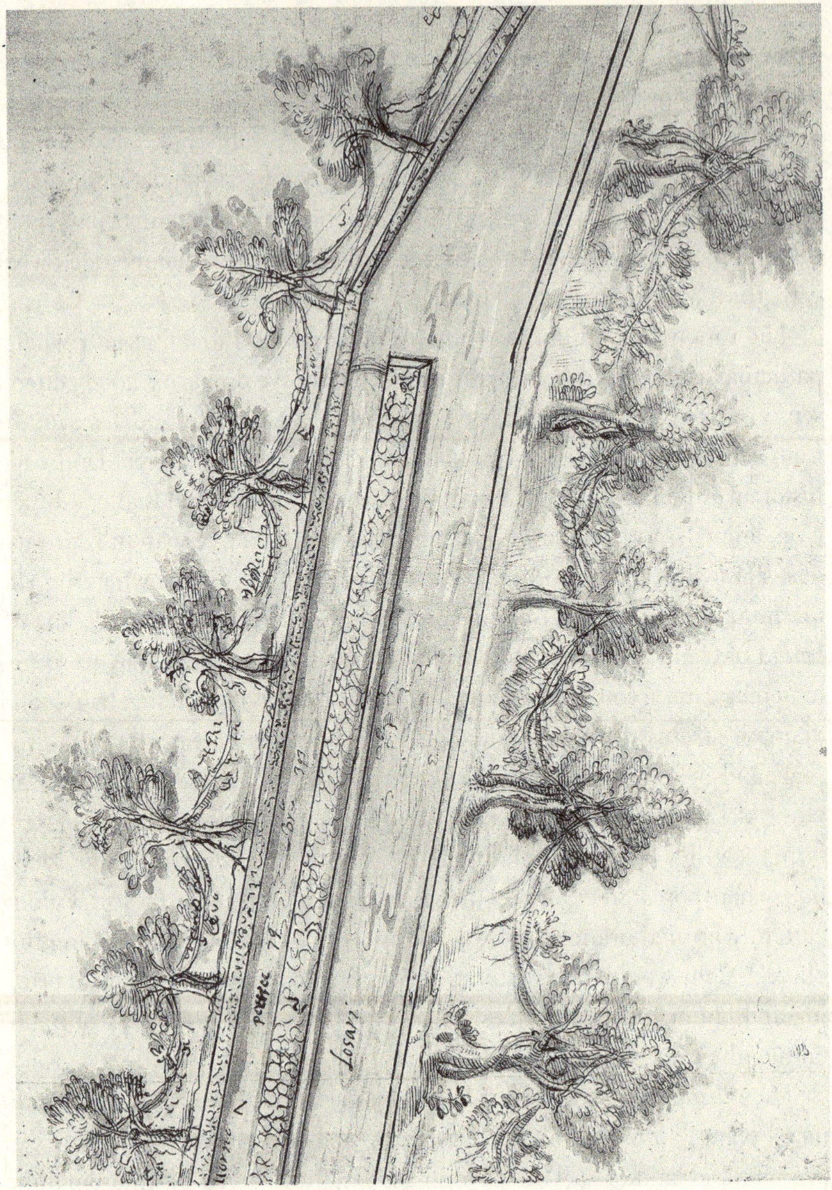

Figure 25. *Vite Maritata.* Grapevines trained across poplar branches (*pioppi con vite unite*) along the junction of the River Vorno with the River Ozzeri, Lucca. (Section from ink drawing on paper circa 1820. Archivio di Stato di Lucca, Direzione poi Commissariato delle Acque e Strade, filza 728, n. 2; N. 29. "Disegno dello sbocco del rio di Vorno in Ozzeri." By permission of the Ministero della Cultura—Archivio di Stato di Lucca. Reproduction by any means is forbidden.)

Peasants and Landlords

In Italy, as in most of Europe, landscapes have been shaped by millennia of peasant agriculture and pastoralism. Across this lengthy period of time the meaning of the term "peasant" and the social conditions that it describes have shifted continuously. Added to this difficulty, the term itself is overlaid with dense layers of academic and scholarly debate. In Italy, the word *contadino*, which I translate as "peasant," historically referred to rural cultivators who were politically and economically subordinated to the *contado*, the territory subordinated to a town. Some of the older people I talked to would describe themselves as *contadini*; younger farmers describe themselves as direct cultivators (*coltivatori diretti*). The social categories that have historically mattered in this part of Italy were the small number of larger landowners who leased land to sharecroppers (*mezzadri*) under the direction of an agent (*fattore*). A larger number of independent smallholders could make a living from their own land, while a much larger number of day laborers who owned only tiny scraps of land worked for sharecroppers or larger landowners. In the Apennine mountains and in the hills, independent smallholders managed to retain control of much of the land, including chestnut cultivation. From the sixteenth century onward, fertile land in the valley of Lucca had been an attractive investment for urban elites, and this concentration of ownership extended up into the hills. By the 1830s, many chestnut groves near Vorno, as in other villages near Lucca, had fallen into the hands of urban or local elites. Large landowners controlled most of the fertile valley bottomland, and more than half of residents were landless and worked in olive mills or paper factories. Women in towns at the base of the mountains often worked as clothes washers for the cities of Lucca and Pisa. Higher up the hill and in the mountains, smallholdings were more common, but on the Monte Pisano wealthy families owned large chestnut groves that were worked by sharecroppers. During the Fascist era (1922–1943) the *mezzadria* (sharecropping) system was heavily weighted on the side of landlords. After World War II Socialists and Communists led efforts to renegotiate or dissolve the system entirely, giving rise to social conflict and the dissolution of sharecropping in the 1960s. In hilly areas that were unsuited to industrial agriculture, former sharecroppers like Giuseppe del Chiaro often managed to buy their land. In the plains or in areas with high-value agricultural production, landlords were able to invest in tractors and enter the world of industrial monoculture.[24] In many places in the hills, smallholder polycultures were plowed up and converted into wine or grain monocultures. Higher up the mountain, pastures and chestnut groves were often abandoned.

Already during the nineteenth and early twentieth centuries, many people had migrated to North and South America. After World War II people also moved to work in factories in Italian cities, from Milan to nearby Pontedera. Woodlots, chestnut groves, and mountain pastures alike were abandoned to regrowth and, ultimately, to large forest fires. Due to inheritance laws, this abandoned land is now fractionally owned by descendants who are scattered across the globe. Fire-blasted pine scrub on the lower slopes of the mountains, and abandoned chestnut groves higher up, are kinds of land that lack the social-ecological relations that sustain property. People/plant/soil relations sustain the property forms and agrarian politics that we so often take for granted. In walking across the Monte Pisano with Francesco in 2014, I moved from the world of wealthy villa owners and industrial service workers in the valley to largely abandoned mountain landscapes, haunted by pastoral abandonment and state-sponsored conifer plantations.[25]

Walking a Transect from Vorno to Campo di Croce

This transect drawing (figure 26) is an empirical diagram resulting from sensory noticing during a walk from the village of Vorno to Campo di Croce, a pass across the crest of the Monte Pisano. The diagram combines what I saw and sensed on a spring day in 2014, with the land uses recorded in historical tax maps.[26] It is also a result of many other walks and conversations with Francesco, of my interviews with foresters, farmers, and officials, and of my visits to the Archivio di Stato in Lucca. This drawing records histories of ruination, disastrous pathogen outbreaks, and the slow disaster of capitalism.

In 1846 the landscape was dominated by chestnut groves, with some pine forest (*pineta*), a smaller area of coppice managed for firewood, and a communal pasture at the top of the mountain. In 2014 the chestnut groves are almost entirely gone, maritime pine (*Pinus pinaster*) occupies many areas, and chestnut coppice covers most of the rest. At the top of the mountain exotic conifer plantations (*Pinus nigra*, *Cedrus libani*) have replaced the for-

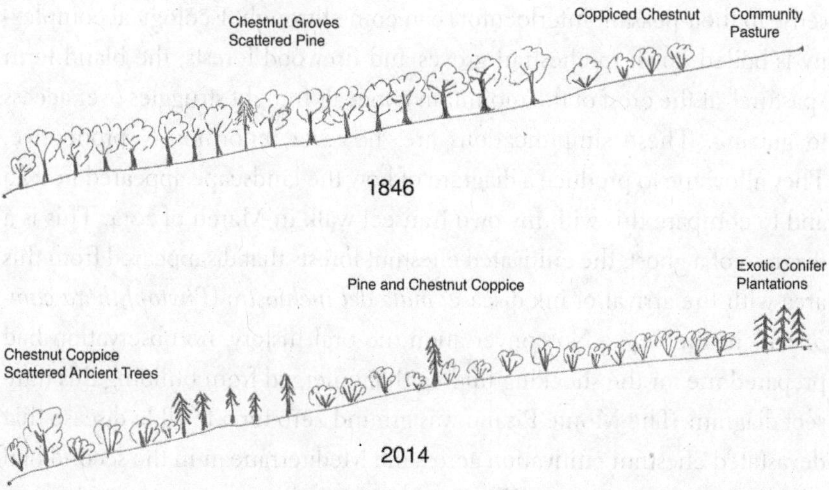

Figure 26. Transect from Cima di Vorno to Campo di Croce, at the top of the Monte Pisano, comparing dominant tree forms in 1846 and 2014. (Drawing by author)

mer common pasture. In many areas, maritime pine has completely taken over, with scrubby stumps of ancient chestnuts lingering in an understory dominated by bracken (*Pteridium aquilinum*), with occasional manna ash (*Fraxinus ornia*), arbutus (*Arbutus unedo*), and, on drier and higher areas, drought-adapted and fire-prone scrub species such as heath (*Erica scoparia*) and gorse (*Ulex europaeus*). Often Francesco and I would see ruined *metati* (chestnut drying sheds) and abandoned terraces in areas now covered by pine forest. Dense conifer plantations at the top of the mountain are the last echo of Cold War workfare programs that sought to prevent peasants from becoming Communists. Some of the coppice is still cut for domestic firewood, but much is destined to become wood chips for biomass energy production, an effort to stave off the slow disaster of climate change.

This drawing projects my capacity to notice many ontologies and relationships through direct observation of trees and plants into a much simpler story about landscape change. This is a kind of systems diagram that combines the bureaucratic simplification of the tax map with my own much more open-ended curiosity. Out of the many kinds of trees and plants that Francesco and I could notice, almost nothing is represented. Only the categories of land use that mattered to Lucchese elites and made some sense to their peasant interlocutors can come through. Ecological complexity is boiled down to chestnut groves and firewood forests; the bland term "pasture" at the crest of the mountain conceals fraught struggles over access to grazing. These simplifications are, however, enormously productive. They allow me to produce a diagram of how the landscape appeared in 1846 and to compare this with my own transect walk in March of 2014. This is a diagram of a ghost, the cultivated chestnut forests that disappeared from this area with the arrival of ink disease, *male del inchiostro* (*Phytophthora cambivora*) in the 1840s. No conversation, no oral history, no observation had prepared me for the shocking finding that emerged from building this transect diagram. The Monte Pisano was ground zero for a terrible disease that devastated chestnut cultivation across the Mediterranean in the second half of the nineteenth century. The impact of ink disease was reported across France, Corsica, and Italy, but it has left little trace in the historical record or in popular memory. Nation-states in the second half of the nineteenth century were interested in agricultural reclamation and grain cultivation, sustained by powerful ideologies of modernization. The fate of "backward crops" was of little interest to officials and literati. It was only through diagram, archive, and landscape walks that I was able to notice the impact of this slow disaster in the Monte Pisano. Historical ecology methods detected an epidemic that archival evidence and oral history alone would struggle to notice.

These transect diagrams are a kind of speculative projection from my capacity to notice details of morphology and to link this noticing to archival evidence of land use. Such diagrams move from plant morphology to landscape structures; they link the details of particular trees with my experience of larger-scale landscape patterns and histories. I become confident that these diagrams have a partial grasp upon the world through a gradual process of sensory attunement, as I move back and forth between archive and field, between map and interview.[27]

From Plant Morphologies to Landscape Structures

My close encounters with pines and chestnuts and my conversations with farmers and biologists have changed how I see the world. From these encounters, I am pressed to see two different, provisionally stable landscape

Figure 27. Detail from photograph of the crest of the Monte Pisano as seen from the walls of Lucca; pine (dark gray) and chestnut (light gray), 2014. (Author photograph)

structures that lie through each other and do not foreclose each other. This kind of noticing is at once sensory, analytic, and diagrammatic. By coming near and close and becoming involved with particular trees, I learned to see color and texture, so that a few days later, when I looked back at the Monte Pisano, my eyes were attuned to the particular reddish color of chestnut buds (light gray) and the gray-blue of maritime pine (dark gray) in figure 27. As you can see, light and dark gray are mixed, but two landscape patterns are clearly visible. Even as these patterns literally mix and lie through each other, a diagram sharpens the distinction between pine and chestnut in figure 28. The landscape structure of remnant chestnut forest dominated by ancient trees and living stumps is linked to histories of international trade, peasant tree care, plant disease, and emerging symbioses between pathogens, plants, and viruses. The landscape structure of pine forest is linked to the absence of sheep and peasants who formerly raked leaf litter, as well as to the recent forest fires that help young pines expand across the landscape. There is a continuous cross talk between my close encounters with particular trees or ruins and my experiences of landscape structures.

In this chapter I have described what we might call realist diagrams, projections that emerge from sensory attunements that lead me from the

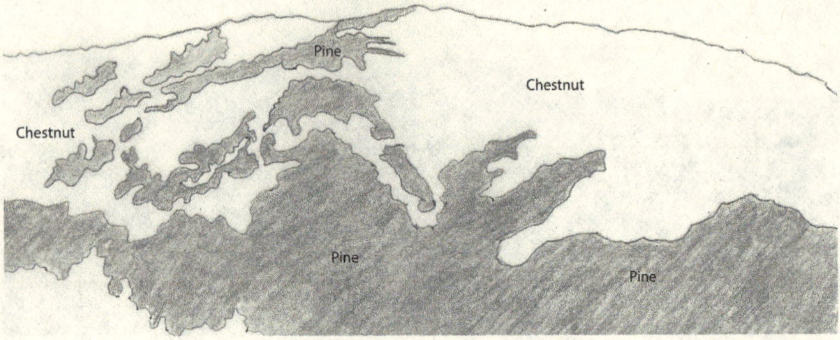

Figure 28. Chestnut and pine landscape structures on the Monte Pisano, as seen from the walls of Lucca. (Drawing by author)

morphologies of trees to landscape structures. Transect diagrams provoked me to wonder how large the impact of plant disease and land-use change had been, making me turn to less realistic forms of diagram. Other diagrams move from what I can apprehend through my senses to nonrealist representations that link past and present, the sensed and the invisible. In the following chapter we will see the maps and photographs with which I have tried to capture the ongoing echoes of disease in the forest fires that increasingly ravage the Monte Pisano.

THREE

Fast and Slow Disasters

Plant Disease, Forest Fires, and Climate Change

The social and ecological histories of the Monte Pisano inform contemporary environmental politics, but they do so selectively. Some histories remain largely unknown, even as they haunt the contemporary landscape. This is the case with the slow disaster of plant diseases that devastated low-elevation chestnut groves on the Monte Pisano between 1860 and 1880. Former chestnut groves have become fire-prone pine forests, which are an increasing danger to life and property. In contrast to the slow and sly progress of disease, forest fires are spectacular and memorable. People now see forest fires as the result of lack of care and abandonment. The urban professionals and ecotourism operators who have restored abandoned peasant houses have gradually learned that this is a landscape that has been made dangerous by lack of care.[1]

Beginning in the late 1970s, volunteer firefighters took up the task of fire prevention. The flammability of the landscape was not only due to the presence of pine forest, but to the abandonment of a way of making a living. The pastoralists who grazed sheep and goats in these mountains, and the farmers who raked leaf litter from forest floors to produce fertilizer for their olive trees, made forests much less flammable. Elderly people told me how litter raking was a daily task for the whole family, including women and young children, who carried heavy baskets of pine needles and leaves down from the mountains. Every home had a long pile of leaf litter outside, ready for use as bedding in sheep stalls. Stable litter, mixed with urine and dung, provided critical fertilizer for olive trees. The abandonment of litter raking in the 1960s caused a buildup of dry vegetation in forests, which burn fiercely when fires come. After fires, the introduced maritime pine (*Pinus pinaster*) reproduces prolifically and colonizes burned sites. If fires return too often, even the pine has little chance to grow, and fire-prone scrub grows. The consequences of the ecological transformation caused by the abandonment of grazing and litter raking came as a nasty surprise to the urban professionals and hobby farmers who have moved to the area since the 1980s. The significance of litter raking and firewood gathering is now known mainly to old people, to a few fire managers, and to people who remember the last days of peasant agriculture.[2]

In the fall of 2018, the latest and largest fire swept across the mountains, revealing the flammability that had been produced by decades of agricultural abandonment. Most people thought the fire was caused by human incompetence or criminality. The immediate collective response to this disaster was for volunteers to rebuild terracing and drainage systems so as to prevent landslides and mudflows. With time, people have begun to discuss ways of managing overgrown forests and olive terraces, including by bringing back sheep grazing. Restoration practices of managing vegetation and repairing terraces and drainage systems draw upon historic (even if poorly understood) traditions that linked trees, soils, and waters. A younger generation of concerned citizens has learned from retired peasants about older traditions of landscape care. These responses to forest fires reveal a remembering and a recognition of ancient traditions that connected forests, soils, and waters to landscape stability. This is a mundane Anthropocene environmental politics of landscape care, which has very little to say to the climate change of policymakers and scientists. Caring for landscape stability is a political and practical project that connects plants and soils to weather.

Historic pathogen epidemics, long-term land-use change, and recent weather events have come together to produce these disastrous fires. Two disasters have had compounding effects upon each other. The first, slow disaster was the chestnut disease *male del inchiostro* (*Phytophthora cambivora*). Almost unknown in contemporary memory, this disease has left the landscape structure of remaining chestnut forests on the heights of the Monte Pisano, and of chestnut stumps scattered in pine forest on the lower hills.

This landscape pattern is linked to the history of international trade and botanical exploration that brought live plants from Southeast Asia and East Asia to Europe in the nineteenth century. It is likely that chestnut plants brought from Japan or China to Europe in the 1830s brought the fungus-like oomycete water molds *Phytophthora cambivora* and *Phytophthora cinnamomi* with them. The second, much faster disaster of expanding forest fires is linked to industrialization and to the abandonment of grazing, burning, and litter raking by peasant farmers. As farmers left the land for industrial work in factories around Lucca and Pisa after World War II, litter raking and grazing were increasingly abandoned. The landscape structure of fire-prone pine forest is also linked to industrial agriculture on the plains. Forest leaf litter and animal manure were replaced by chemical fertilizers. As peasants became industrial workers and forests and pastures were abandoned, accumulating dry vegetation and leaf litter provided an opportunity for fire. Maritime pine (*Pinus pinaster*), which seeds prolifically and grows well in the ashes of forest fires, sensed an opportunity and expanded across the landscape.[3] Other fire-adapted species such as the yellow-flowered spiny gorse (*Ulex europaeus*) flourished on burned areas. The landscape was ravaged by fire, choked with dry vegetation that fueled ever fiercer fires, allowing fire-adapted trees and shrubs to expand at the expense of oaks, chestnut trees, and human beings.

Climate change is increasingly bringing strange new forms of fire to this landscape. The climate of meteorologists and modelers is an abstract category, the long-term average of weather conditions in a particular region. This expert version of climate has little connection with vernacular understandings of weather patterns, which are another version of climate, nor upon the imaginations and experiences of people who live with droughts, strange winds, and the forest fires that these can spread. Climate modelers tell us, through their averaging of long-term measurements, that average temperatures have begun to increase significantly in the Monte Pisano, as in other mountains across the Mediterranean.[4] What matters for forests, though, is the long-term drying of soils and leaf litter caused by the interaction of weather and changing land use. Rare and powerful events such as heavy rainstorms, intense droughts, or late-season windstorms are not easily predicted by climate models that deal with long-term averages, but these are the events that matter for producing the dramatic ecological transformations that people and plants care about. The term "climate" fails to capture the intersecting effects of wind, drought, leaf litter accumulation, and agricultural abandonment. "Climate," a term laden with assumptions of long-term averaging and stability, has little traction upon ecologies or on human experiences of what kind of weather it is reasonable to expect. People rarely link forest fires to climate change. Incompetence, criminality, and landscape abandonment by peasants and by the state are explanations that make more sense. A detailed landscape history shows that legacies of plant disease epidemics are also responsible for current fires, but these are events with little traction on the present.

Ink Disease and Chestnut Landscapes

Sometime in the 1840s the disease known as *male del inchiostro* (ink disease), began to kill chestnut trees in several parts of Italy. The first sign of the blight was of yellowing leaves that would wilt and drop off affected trees. Some would last a year or two, others would die within a few weeks or months. Dying trees produced a foul-smelling black liquid from their roots and trunks, giving rise to the name. Ink disease is caused by the oomycete water molds *Phytophthora cambivora* and *Phytophthora cinnamomi* and was first reported in Portugal in 1838. The disease likely traveled from China, Japan, or Southeast Asia in soil attached to the roots of live plants of Chinese chestnut (*Castanea mollissima*) or Japanese chestnut (*Castanea crenata*) that were being shipped to botanical gardens and plant nurseries in Europe. Global trade and the movement of live plants were the likely triggers for landscape transformations in chestnut-growing regions across the Mediterranean, from Portugal, to Spain, Corsica, France, and Italy. The first reports of ink disease in Italy were near major ports or transportation routes, including the Monte Pisano, and Biella, near an alpine pass to France. The disease spread rapidly, attacking low-elevation chestnut groves across Italy. Accounts of the effects of the disease on the Monte Pisano are devastating. Writing in 1884, an anonymous author described how "in the hills and mountains which surround the plain of Lucca on the south and west the destruction was almost complete. Chestnut groves that were destroyed became woodland and pine forest. Lower down, in places suited to chestnut groves, olive trees followed, but in the hills . . . they became scrub with scattered pines, a few oaks, and other forest trees."[5]

Writing about the valley of Calci in 1874, the eminent agronomist Girolamo Caruso gives a detailed account of the progress of the disease:

> It manifests itself with the yellowing of the [tree] crown, and the gradual death of the highest branches of the plants. It attacks both old and young trees, but it prefers ancient trees that have had heavy cutting of branches. Sometimes the disease runs through several periods: in the first year, yellowing leaves are noticed. In the second, the decline is more noticeable, and also affects fruits, which are smaller than usual. In the third year, the plants die, almost struck by a rapid drying up, and death can happen at any time of the year. There are trees that instead of dying within two or three years of the first manifestation on the upper leaves, die after one, two, or three months, as if they had been struck by a *sun stroke* or *boiling*, in the words of our peasants.[6]

Peasants on the Monte Pisano told Caruso that they had been noticing the disease since the 1840s. By the 1880s, the lower slopes of the Monte Pisano had been transformed: "Certain mountains previously completely covered in chestnut are now completely naked, as at . . . Buti and Vorno," and chestnut cultivation had almost disappeared below five hundred meters. Attention to the epidemic was somewhat diverted by the expansion of olive agriculture. In some areas, olives replaced chestnut trees, but in most places, fire-prone pine forest or mixed woodland took over. The initial spread of the ink disease struck particularly hard at lower elevations. By the 1930s ink disease was relatively quiescent, although sporadic outbreaks continue to the present.[7]

When a pathogen eliminates a species from a whole landscape, there can be surprisingly little memory. When I talked to old people in the Monte Pisano in 2019, no one recalled ink disease, even in areas that had been struck particularly hard in the nineteenth century. Thirty kilometers north, in the Garfagnana, where the disease arrived in the 1930s, a few people still remembered the disease. The smallholder Stefano Fazzi told me, "Ink disease has been here. There were beautiful chestnut groves, down below town. . . . Where it is all acacia now there were chestnuts [before]. My father says they were spectacular three hundred year old trees."[8]

Just when the impact of ink disease had begun to wane in the 1930s, a new disease was brought to Italy. This was *cancro del castagno* (chestnut canker, *Cryphonectria parasitica*), first reported in Italy in 1938. In 2013 in the village of Pozzuolo, the elderly chestnut farmer Giuseppe del Chiaro told me how hard it was to graft new trees on his land. Where formerly most chestnut grafts "took," many were now struck by disease. An orange bloom of fungus would grow across a new graft or a young stem, often killing the plant. Walking across his chestnut terraces with a pruning knife in hand, Giuseppe pointed to one stem that he had grafted four or five times. He hadn't given up, but he pointed to trees whose trunks were covered with orange-flecked lesions. In other places chestnut farmers told me how chestnut canker would often fail to kill a tree. The plant would form a dry callus, leaving the tree scarred but living (see figures 5 and 6 in chapter 1). This callus forms when the *Cryphonectria* fungus is itself attacked by the virus CHV-1, which attenuates its virulence.[9]

Diagramming Ghost Forests

Oral history and contemporary accounts can give only a very approximate sense of the magnitude of the effect of disease upon chestnut forests. An alertness to material traces on the landscape can combine with interviews and archives to give a sense of the pattern of destruction caused by disease, which is difficult to pick up through history alone. Walking through pine forests and ruined chestnut groves on the Monte Pisano, Francesco and I often saw the ruins of small stone buildings. These were traces of the world of subsistence agriculture, where perishable fresh chestnuts were dried on their way to becoming the chestnut flour that was a staple part of rural diets. Noticing ruined drying sheds (*metati*) led me to talk to chestnut growers in mountains

Confronting One Disease and Introducing Another: The Role of Plant Nurseries and Researchers

It is likely that chestnut canker, *Cryphonectria parasitica*, traveled to the United States with Chinese and Japanese chestnut species, which were widely disseminated by plant nurseries from the 1870s onward. The disease spread rapidly, causing the near-total destruction of the American chestnut (*Castanea dentata*) within a generation of the first reports of the disease in 1904. Tragically, even as the American chestnut was being destroyed by *Cryphonectria*, scientists in Europe were diligently seeking to overcome ink disease by cultivating Chinese and Japanese chestnut species. The first European efforts to cultivate Chinese (*Castanea mollissima*) and Japanese chestnut (*Castanea crenata*) took place in Spain and southern France around 1899. Italian researchers followed these experiments with interest and brought *Castanea crenata* seedlings to Italy, although they were also well aware of the role of Japanese and Chinese chestnuts in introducing *Cryphonectria* to the United States. The leading Italian researcher concerned with ink disease, Lionello Petri, organized nursery plantings of Japanese chestnut in the 1920s. It is likely that, as in the United States, *Cryphonectria* was introduced to Italy by plant nurseries, whether experimental or private, and further spread by government forest nurseries that disseminated seedlings to farmers. In Lucca the disease was first reported in forest nurseries that provided Japanese chestnut trees to farmers in 1947. First reported in 1938 near Genoa, chestnut canker spread rapidly across Italy. At first it rapidly killed many trees, and it seemed that Italian chestnut groves were facing the total destruction that had happened in North America. Faced with this looming disaster, and knowing of the fate of American chestnut, Italian foresters believed that there was no option but to cut down chestnut groves and replace them with conifer plantations. In the 1950s and 1960s many ancient chestnut groves were cut down and processed by tannin factories. This destruction only slowed down when people began to notice that not all trees struck by *Cryphonectria* were dying. The arrival of the CHV-1 virus made the disease no longer virulent: callused trees are a sign of this emerging relationship. Chestnut growers watch their trees carefully and hope to see these signs of the stabilization of the disease.

north of Lucca, where drying and milling chestnuts into flour is still a part of daily life.

Metati are small two-story stone structures divided into an upper and a lower level. On the lower level, during the harvest season in October and November, smoldering chunks of chestnut wood are kept slowly burning beneath layers of chestnut husks (*pula*). Over about a month, with constant tending of the fire, chestnuts are dried. The dried chestnuts are peeled and then ground into a long-lasting flour that can be used in chestnut breads, soups, and other recipes. If you walk through chestnut groves during the drying season, the smell of chestnut smoke is pervasive. An essential practical reason for locating drying sheds in chestnut groves is that they are fueled with chestnut prunings and husks. Drying sheds in tax maps from the early nineteenth century are a strong argument that there are nearby chestnut groves. The sensory curiosity of landscape walk and interview can be combined with the bureaucratic simplification of the tax map to produce a diagram of ghost forests, the low-elevation chestnut groves that formerly surrounded the Monte Pisano. In figure 29, you can see an active chestnut drying shed. Note the low door on the left, which provides access to the fire. The small door on the right provides access to the upper level, where chestnuts are laid out on a cane grating.

Chestnut gathering and processing required specialized tools, as well as buildings, including drying sheds and flour mills. This was an entire rural industry, something that is hard to imagine now. A diagram of a former world emerges in figure 30. Thanks to the work of Massimiliano Grava, we have a complete record of land use and rural industries for the valley of Calci in 1825. Through a collaborative analysis with anthropologist Fabio Malfatti, I learned to link past to present. The black cones of *metati* are almost all located in the light gray of chestnut groves, and the dark gray of pine is restricted to lower slopes.[10] Look at the pictures of ruins and working *metati*, and allow yourself to imagine this former landscape. Much is lost by the cartographic simplification provided by this map, but when paired with sensory curiosity and interview, a ghostly diagram emerges. This was the world before ink disease, when chestnut was cultivated almost down to sea level. Ecologists and natural scientists do not know this world. It is only through

Figure 29. Active *metato,* a chestnut drying shed, Fosciandora, Lucca, 2013. (Author photograph)

natural history, landscape walking, and ethnographic interviews, archives, and tax maps that these diagrams of disaster have acquired their significance.

Now I ask you to combine past and present in another diagrammatic comparison.[11] In figure 31, drying sheds gesture to absent chestnut groves. The dark cones of *metati* are now located deep in the dark gray of pine forest. The light gray of chestnut has moved higher up the mountains. This is the fire-threatened landscape of the present, haunted by the ghosts of disease epidemics and by the world of peasant chestnut cultivation and grazing.

A panoramic view of the Monte Pisano (figure 32) makes the comparison of past and present still more stark. In this view, drying sheds come from the slightly later cadastral survey of Lucca, completed in 1846. The lower slopes of the mountains are dominated by the dark gray of pine forest; the black cones of *metati* are located primarily deep in an entirely new landscape of pine forest.

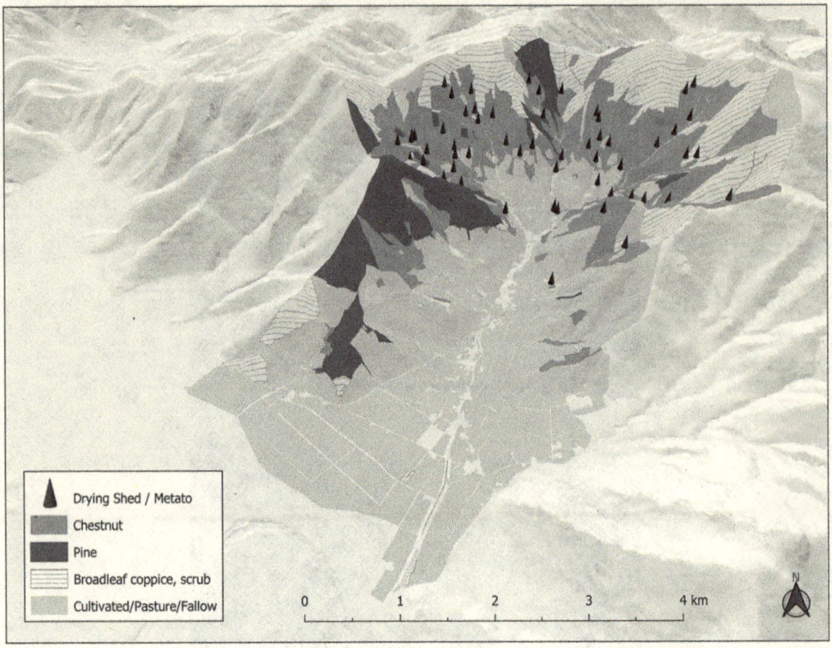

Figure 30. Chestnut drying sheds and land use in the valley of Calci, Monte Pisano, 1825. (Map used by permission of Fabio Malfatti)

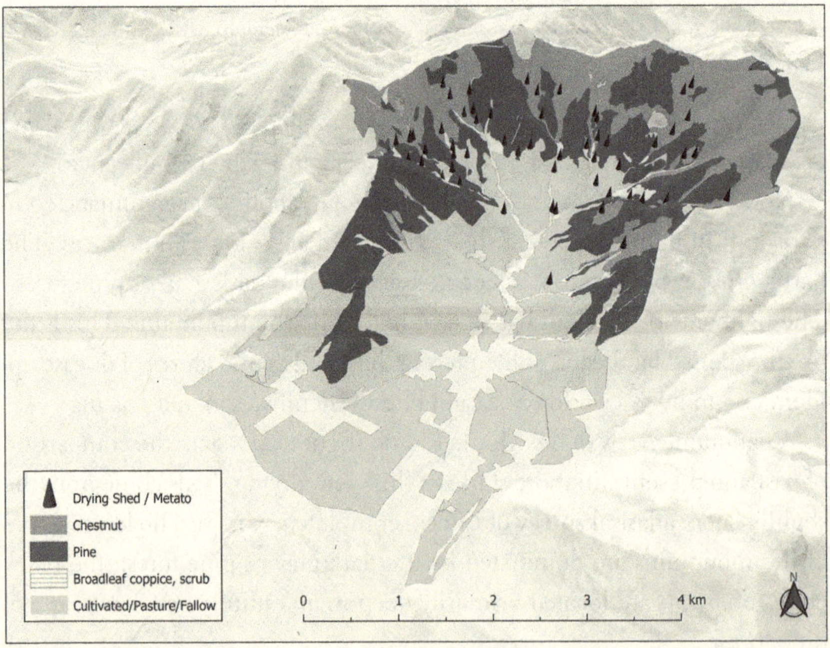

Figure 31. Chestnut drying sheds in 1825 and contemporary vegetation in the valley of Calci, Monte Pisano. (Map used by permission of Fabio Malfatti)

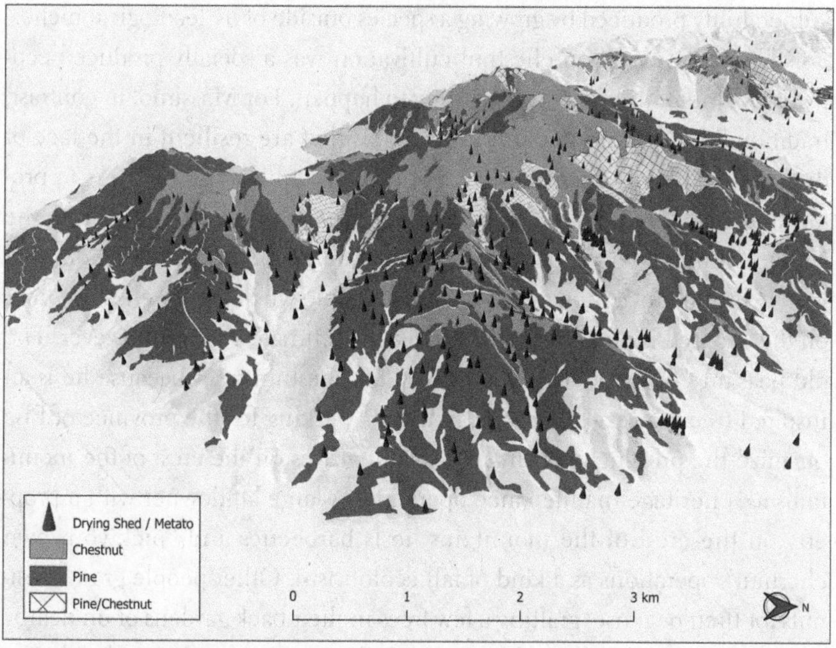

Figure 32. Historic drying sheds and contemporary vegetation in the Monte Pisano. (Map used by permission of Fabio Malfatti)

Landscape Politics

Oral history and landscape diagrams showed a world of loss and destruction that came as a surprise to me and that has left little contemporary resonance. The landscape structure of remaining chestnut forests, together with memories of the history of their loss do, however, inform a politics of landscape care. I first learned of the history of chestnut diseases from the biologist Massimo Giambastiani. It was he who pointed me to the obscure nineteenth-century agricultural journals where the impact and progress of the disease were reported. He is one of the people who documents and seeks to maintain the diversity of traditional chestnut varieties in this area.[12] For him, the chestnut forests of the Monte Pisano are a ruin, but also a source of resistance to the damage that climate change might bring. For many biologists, the loss of low-elevation chestnut groves across Italy is a clear example of a vulnerability produced by growing a species outside of its "ecological niche." For them, low-elevation chestnut cultivation was a socially produced ecological vulnerability, a disaster waiting to happen. For Massimo, in contrast, traditional low-elevation chestnut varieties that are resilient in the face of drought are a sign of the brilliance of peasant cultivators. He seeks to protect and maintain traditional chestnut varieties. Chestnut varieties from the Monte Pisano might be better suited to the dryer and hotter conditions that will be brought by climate change. Most people who care for chestnut trees on the Monte Pisano do not talk much about climate change, however. The old peasant Giuseppe del Chiaro cares for chestnut trees because he is an inspired tree grower. Landscape architects working for the province of Pisa organize the pruning of remnant chestnut groves on the crest of the mountains as a heritage maintenance operation. A large landowner with a property on the crest of the mountains hosts barbecues and "pick your own chestnut" operations as a kind of fall ecotourism. Other people grow chestnuts for their own use, grafting a few trees in their back gardens or on nearby terraces. The vast majority of these people, however, are concerned with care for trees and do not connect them to climate change at all.

Fast Disasters: Forest Fires

Pathogen epidemics like ink disease are slow disasters. Forest fires, in contrast, are rare but fast events that restructure social-ecological coordinations. Fires are difficult research subjects, episodic, fugitive, dangerous to approach, and surrounded by prohibitions. In the Mediterranean, fire has always been a feature of pastoralism, agriculture, and plant care, but it has almost always been forbidden, stigmatized, and misunderstood by states.[13] The abandonment of agriculture and pastoralism, and of traditional fire management practices, have caused a buildup of dead and dry vegetation, resulting in ever larger and fiercer forest fires. In the Monte Pisano, as in many other parts of Italy and elsewhere across the Mediterranean, large forest fires are relatively new, a result of agricultural abandonment since the 1960s. In the Monte Pisano, fire use is so controversial that present and former shepherds deny ever having used fire on pastures. As with pathogen outbreaks, however, the *effects* of fires can be read by the material traces that they leave upon plant forms, upon soils, and upon the species compositions of forests. Walking through forests and talking to people about fires are ways to learn about the impacts of fire. After fires, maritime pine and rapidly growing Mediterranean scrub (*macchia*) replace chestnut, oak, and holm oak (*Quercus ilex*), leaving charred stumps and dense scrub. Fire-scarred chestnut stumps that are a legacy of cultivation are overshadowed by a scrub of gorse (*Ulex europaeus*) and heather (*Erica* species), which are legacies of the most recent fire. Stories told about fire, about the effects of land abandonment, of the withdrawal and indifference of the state, and about lazy neighbors who allow dry vegetation to accumulate on their land are some of the ways that fires leave echoes in daily conversations.

In the Monte Pisano, increasing forest fires are the result of intersecting processes of ecological and social change. The low-elevation pine forest produced by ink disease between 1840 and 1880 was kept more or less stable by peasant practices of firewood gathering, grazing, and leaf-litter raking. Much of this work was likely done by women.[14] Old shepherds and farmers told me how they used to burn dry grass on olive terraces in preparation for the olive harvest. Chestnut growers would burn piles of dry leaves in preparation for their harvest season. All of this was illegal, but it was tolerated by the forest service. Litter raking, firewood gathering, and agricultural burning combined to produce a fire-resistant landscape. The numerous farmers, shepherds, and firewood gatherers who moved through this landscape knew how to put out fires quickly with pine branches. In the 1950s, agricultural abandonment disrupted vegetation and fire management practices. Industrial agriculture, with its complex of tractors and chemical fertilizers, had no use for the nutrients in leaf litter and took place not in the hills but in the lowlands. This transformation also changed gender relations. In interviews in 2019, elderly women who had worked as peasants and shepherds talked of the forest as a busy and social space and remembered how they had moved freely across the landscape. Women and children were out on the land gathering firewood, herding sheep, raking leaf litter, making this a safe and inhabited place. One old shepherdess from the Pisa side of the mountains told me how she used to meet friends from the Lucca side of the mountains. As rural work receded, forests have become lonelier, less busy, and less welcoming to women. Mountain communities had always been linked politically and economically to their respective provincial capitals. With industrialization, contacts with neighboring mountain communities became more attenuated, as people turned their eyes from mountain pastures to cities. In communities at the base of the mountains where there was abundant water, as at Vorno and Calci, women had traditionally washed clothes for the cities of Lucca and Pisa.[15] With industrialization and the arrival of washing machines, this work too disappeared. During the postwar economic boom, young people could find work at the Piaggio scooter factory in Pontedera or at the other factories that have spread across the plains of Lucca and Pisa. Work in factories drew young people away from the land. Changing energy systems meant that firewood was less important for heating and cooking. In combination, these changes meant that forests ceased to be a valued resource, kept "clean" by firewood cutting, leaf-litter raking, and grazing. Newly emptied of people, forests became fire prone, and maritime pine and spiny *Ulex* advanced.

Old people remembered how the landscape literally looked different. The red of soil was visible from across a valley; pastures were trimmed short by sheep and goats; fallen tree branches were picked up instantly. Forests were kept *puliti* (clean) by daily labor: "One cleaned, one went in the broadleaf woods[;] in the pine woods, you gathered up everything beneath to make a bed for the sheep."[16] Children, women, and some men carried huge baskets of leaf litter from forests to sheep sheds. After a few days, the mixture of sheep dung, urine, and leaf litter would be piled up to make compost and eventually dug into the ground beneath olive trees as fertilizer (*sugo*). "Everyone did it," Maria Lenzarini said. The forest was an entirely different place, almost a garden, where every scrap of land was divided by nearly invisible lines of small stones that demarcated woodlots and pastures. This was an open landscape where "you could walk almost everywhere, whether there was a path or not" and "whether because of litter raking, or . . . if a tree fell someone immediately made it into firewood." I remember the last echoes of this horticultural landscape, in the tidy gardens and terraces that I saw as a child, where every blade of grass was trimmed and every tree was pruned. Maria went on:

"When heating came in, everything, everything was abandoned[; now] a tree falls and stays in the woods[;] you can't pass anymore, and it is harder to put fires out." At first the abandonment of sheep grazing was gradual, but with many shepherds retiring or dying in the 1980s, sheep have now almost disappeared from the landscape. Where formerly most farm households had twenty or thirty sheep, and professional shepherds had a flock of several hundred, there are now only one or two shepherds still grazing their sheep on the plains. This landscape is haunted by the absence of people and animals.

Litter raking was likely ubiquitous in hill farming across Italy, in hills and mountains across Central Europe, as it was until quite recently in places as far afield as Switzerland, Nepal, and India. In many of these places litter raking is relatively unnoticed women's work. As one of a myriad mundane peasant practices, often carried out by women and children, litter raking has attracted little attention from governments, and Italy is no exception. Forest codes listed leaf-litter raking as a minor "usage" (*usanza*), but regulations focused mainly on firewood and timber.[17] Government foresters must have seen women, children, and men carrying heavy baskets of leaf litter down from forests, but they seldom found this worthy of mentioning. The abandonment of this little-noticed and now almost-forgotten practice has triggered the devastating forest fires that are now of such concern to officials and ordinary people. Few people imagine that the vulnerability of forests to climate change is linked to histories of gendered labor and to the nutrient cycles of peasant and industrial agriculture. This is likely true not only in Italy, but across the Mediterranean and in many other parts of the world where peasant landscape care has receded. In figure 33 you can see chestnut leaves being gathered for stable litter or for burning. In the Monte Pisano, people carried leaf litter on their backs in tall baskets, but such a mundane task has not attracted photographers.

The accumulation of now useless leaf litter makes abandoned forests in dry places vulnerable to forest fires. Touch the forest floor almost anywhere in the Monte Pisano and you will feel a layer of pine needles, fifteen or twenty centimeters thick. It is bouncy and pleasant to walk on, fragrant with the smell of resin, but also ideal kindling for fires. This is the smell and the feeling of danger. These material legacies of agricultural abandonment

Figure 33. Anonymous farmer gathering leaf litter, Garfagnana, circa 1960. (Photograph by Pasqualino Remedi, reproduced by permission of the Museo del Castagno, Colognora, Italy.)

encounter the effects of climate change. In the Monte Pisano, as in many Mediterranean mountains, temperature and precipitation have increased rapidly since the 1980s, further drying untended forests.[18] Mundane practices of landscape care by peasants and indigenous people affect how forests around the world respond to climate change, but as in Italy, they are often little understood by officials and scientists. It is only through the slow work of oral history and interview that we can learn to understand how people care for plants, soils, and fires. Anthropologists who are willing to talk to old shepherdesses or to collaborate with fire users, and who are also willing to walk around the landscape and trust their senses, may notice other such social-ecological surprises. Mundane landscape processes can have large-scale and long-term consequences.

It took me a while to understand the impact of litter raking. It was Fabio Casella, a planning official in Calci who grew up in a peasant household in the 1960s, who really opened my eyes. In the summer of 2016, driving around

Figure 34. Fabio Casella recounts the effects of fire, Monte Serra, Lucca, 2016. Vegetation in the foreground is spiny *Ulex* that has grown up after a fire. (Photograph used by permission of Fabio Malfatti)

the Monte Pisano, he drew my attention to the dense layers of leaf litter that covered the forest floor. In figure 34 we see Fabio pointing to the expanding areas of pine forest and postfire scrub. He told me of the threat that burned areas posed to landscape stability. After fires, he warned, rainstorms could cause mudflows and floods. The terracing system that formerly kept this landscape safe was falling into ruin. Forest fires were a threat not only to people who lived near forests, but to the stability of the landscape itself.[19] A landscape pattern of pine forest and dense dry vegetation on forest floors, as well as recurring intense forest fires, were linked to the histories of abandonment of litter raking and grazing, of crumbling walls, and of clogged drainage systems.

Casella and volunteer firefighters in Lucca and Pisa remember that it was only in the 1970s, a decade or two after litter raking was abandoned, that large forest fires became an increasingly severe problem. These new, increasingly dangerous fires are "post–litter raking" and "postgrazing" fires. These

Figure 35. Old pasture reemerges after fire on the crest of the Monte Pisano, 2016. (Author photograph)

fires have called into being an increasingly professionalized corps of highly trained volunteer firefighters. A firefighting school near Siena exposes these volunteers to the latest methods and thinking in international fire management. Professional fire managers, learning from experience in Australia and the United States, have begun to experiment with prescribed burning, seeking to restore fire to a landscape where its absence has come to be seen as dangerous. In the summer of 2016 Fabio Casella took me to the crest of the Monte Pisano and showed me the effects of prescribed burning (figure 35). After controlled burns, dense brush had disappeared and wildflowers and grasses had come back, a ghostly return of the pastures that had formerly covered these slopes.

These experimental fire management practices responded to the landscape structures of accumulated dry vegetation, to the morphologies of maritime pine and spiny *Ulex* expanding on burned areas, and to the histories of loss and abandonment of peasant agriculture. This landscape history and structure informed a practical politics of bringing fire back into the landscape, not to restore the world of peasant agriculture, but to address some of the loss caused by its disappearance. Prescribed burning did some of the work that grazing and litter raking had formerly done. This political project of fire restoration inspired fire managers and well-informed planning officials like Fabio Casella, who grew up in a peasant household. For most people the idea of controlled fire was alien and strange. Media coverage of fire is relentlessly hostile, and fire is depicted as monstrous and destructive. Over the past century, traditional fire management practices have been so relentlessly stigmatized by the state that the possibility of restoring prescribed burning is almost unimaginable. Old people told me of burning on agricultural terraces or in chestnut groves, but in interviews I carried out after forest fires in 2018, no one mentioned prescribed burning in pastures.[20] Although the details of traditional landscape care were little known, people agreed that it was abandonment and lack of care that made landscapes flammable and dangerous. Strikingly, fire was seen as a threat to the stability and morphology of the landscape itself. Traditions of building terraces and drainage systems to sustain trees had traveled into a contemporary politics of landscape morphology.

Fire Returns to the Monte Pisano

On the night of September 24, 2018, a major forest fire struck. Growing rapidly from an ignition point above Calci, raging winds drove the fire across a vast sweep of forests and olive groves. A column of fire and smoke was visible from the cities of Pisa and Lucca, attracting national television coverage. Canadair fire planes dumped water on the fires; work crews of volunteer firefighters arrived from across Italy; and hundreds of people were evacuated. At one point the fire threatened the Certosa di Calci, a former monastery of international artistic and cultural significance. By the time the fire was out a week later, hundreds of people had been evacuated from their homes, seven houses had been destroyed or severely damaged, and almost fourteen hundred hectares of forests, olive groves, and vineyards were in ashes (figure 36).[21] In the wake of the fire, a wave of volunteerism and civic action emerged and

Figure 36. The valley of Calci after the 2018 fires. (Photograph used by permission of Fabio Malfatti)

an intense political debate took place. The predominantly urban people who have settled in this area over the past generation and who make a living from ecotourism or professional work in nearby cities, joined postfire restoration work and attended public meetings. Municipal officials, forest service representatives, and regional planning officials tried to figure out how to restore the landscape and how to make it more resistant to fires.

At first people hoped that the Italian state would provide funds to rebuild roads and drainage systems and replant trees, but these hopes were soon dashed. Volunteers, including members of the Pisa soccer fan club, swarmed the hills, clearing out drainage channels, building check dams (figure 37), and rebuilding terrace walls under the guidance of retired masons and local mayors.[22] People feared that winter rainstorms would wash over bare soil in burned areas and cause floods and mudflows in the towns below. Landscapes that had formerly been stabilized by peasants who built drainage systems were in need of a new politics of landscape care.

Figure 37. A check dam (*briglia*) built by volunteers after the 2018 Calci fire. Compare with check dams in figure 50. (Photograph used by permission of Fabio Malfatti)

Most people blamed the fire upon individual criminality, arguing that it was out of season and that a nighttime ignition was inherently suspicious. Tragically, these suspicions seemed to be confirmed when a volunteer firefighter was arrested and put on trial for starting the fire. While there was a general consensus that the major cause of the fire had been landscape abandonment, the larger political blame was placed upon an indifferent and parsimonious Italian state. In conversations with local mayors in the spring of 2019, I heard that anything that brought people back *into* the landscape would reduce fire risk and improve the local economy. This was a landscape that had lost its people and had become overgrown, fragile, and unstable. Overgrown forests required people to cut trees and remove brush; crumbling walls required someone to rebuild them; drainage systems needed to be cleared. Discussions now focus on finding ways to pay for the costs of rebuilding walls and flood-control works, of encouraging neighbors to thin their forests, and of reclaiming abandoned woodland.[23]

While the details of former peasant practices are not widely known, people agree that plants and landscapes are linked and that this is a landscape that has been made dangerous by overgrown vegetation and lack of care. The terracing and drainage systems that were built by peasants who tended tree crops have left a residual echo in present-day fears that the abandonment of forests and drainage systems may cause landscape instability. After the fire, people pointed out how well-mowed olive groves had resisted fires and how houses near overgrown pine forests had gone up in flames. These details informed a larger-scale account of landscape structure that was linked, if rather generally, to histories of peasant cultivation and abandonment. At public meetings in 2016 I heard forest fire technicians warn of the risk of floods and landslides and of the need for building banks, check dams, and drainage systems in the wake of fires. In the spring of 2019, planning officials, municipal leaders, environmentalists, and ordinary people all told me that trees and terracing and drainage systems were linked to flammability and landscape stability. That fall, a newspaper article harked back to the sudden violence of the fire, describing how twenty minutes of torrential rain had filled streams and threatened the town of Calci with mud and ash flows: "A water bomb, also sudden, unleashed fear among the inhabitants of the slopes of Monte Serra."[24] Such media coverage supports a geomorphological politics of maintaining landscape stability. This linkage of forest fires with landslides is found in many places around the world, including California, where I live.

On February 25 of 2019 fire returned yet again. Sudden winds seized upon a fire that had been set by a smallholder trying to burn back overgrown scrub.

A controlled fire became something different, a conflagration that spread rapidly, burning over two hundred hectares of woodland. Fortunately this fire was contained within a few hours and a second disaster was averted. The smallholder argued that a sudden, unexpected, and unnatural winter wind had invalidated his careful efforts to burn scrub that was two years overdue for burning. "This morning, I swear, there was no wind. . . . At 9:15 I got to work putting fire to the brambles[;] I had marked off the area carefully. Here, if you don't continually keep your farm [*podere*] clean, you can't stay."[25] The causes and blame attributed to this fire say a great deal about how people understand personal and community responsibility for environmental change. In a series of interviews only a month later, not a single person accepted climate change or unnatural weather as a contributor to this unnatural fire. People blamed the smallholder as incompetent and ignorant; they mentioned that he was an outsider lacking local ecological knowledge, and they praised volunteer firefighting crews. Climate change provided no purchase for the practical question of how to manage vegetation nor for the political questions of personal and collective responsibility for protecting landscapes.

On the Monte Pisano, political projects of landscape restoration recognize different landscape structures, different morphologies within landscape patterns, and different histories. Municipal officials, fire managers, and citizens discuss thinning and cutting back vegetation in abandoned pine forests. These proposals build upon the landscape structures of fire-blasted *Ulex* scrub and upon the morphologies of dense young pine forests, thick leaf-litter layers, and abandoned terracing systems. A history of agricultural abandonment and lack of human care that stretches back to the 1960s era of agricultural abandonment is linked to this landscape structure. A different landscape structure, that of the abandoned chestnut groves that survived disease on the upper slopes of the Monte Pisano, is taken up by those who care for chestnut trees. The morphologies of remnant grafted trees, of chestnut coppices and remnant chestnut shoots in low-elevation pine forests, are linked to the history of successive pathogen epidemics. This history of chestnut decline is linked not to the political economy that caused agricultural abandonment in the 1950s, but to the older history of biological globalization that brought ink disease to this area in the 1840s and chestnut canker in the 1930s.

For the biologist Massimo Giambastiani, planting and maintaining traditional chestnut varieties is a way to confront climate change. Pruning old trees and grafting new ones are his way of building a more productive and climate-change-resistant landscape.

The history of pathogen epidemics that destroyed the chestnut groves of the Monte Pisano is almost completely forgotten. It was only through archival research, oral history, and interview—and, most importantly, by trusting my own senses—that I learned to recognize the traces of destruction in the landscape. My sensory curiosity traveled from the details of ruined walls and plant morphology to a gradual perception of landscape patterns and a dawning awareness that these landscape structures were linked to a history of disease. A strange and beautiful past emerged, where fire-resistant and heavily tended chestnut groves were formerly cultivated down almost to sea level in places that are now dominated by fire-scarred pine forests. A tragedy emerged also, of the death and disappearance of beautiful plant/animal/soil coordinations, with a new and more unstable relationship between people, plants, fire, soils, and pathogens emerging. My capacities of observation and description allowed me to travel from the ontological indeterminacy of beings that were transformed through relations with other beings, to the "form coming into being" of landscape structures, to historical and political storytelling.[26] This kind of structural storytelling depends upon speculation, doubt, and wonder.

Anthropologists and historians usually focus on the domain of human behavior, of actions, words, and texts. By adding to this curiosity a concern with people/plant/soil/pathogen relations, I can make a strong argument about social and ecological possibility. The case of the Monte Pisano shows us that plant disease can transform landscapes, even as people often forget these transformations. The international trade in live plants and the cultivation of plants in nurseries are, I argue, of comparable seriousness to climate change. There is an exponential growth in invasive pests and pathogens happening around us, a process that is accelerated by international trade and by climate change that expands the range of pathogens. We need to restrict the most dangerous and destructive ways of moving plants around the world—live plants with soil attached to their roots.[27] Pathogen invasions can have long-term consequences that make forests less able to resist climate change generations later, as in the fire-prone pine forests of the Monte Pisano. Ecologists are not well equipped to notice such legacy effects. This is partly because of the short timescale of their research, but also because their commitment to systems analysis and quantification can make it difficult for them to notice the transformations that emerge from historic encounters between such beings as fires, diseases, and people. Ecologists need the open-ended historical and structural curiosity of anthropologists and historical ecologists. The history of the Monte Pisano suggests that human care and labor might alleviate some of the worst effects of climate change. People are able to work with plants and soils in very different ways than are contemplated by most scientists and policymakers, who are unaware of the kinds of dramatic social and ecological changes that I have described. If Italian peasants were formerly able to cultivate chestnut trees down to sea level, this suggests that alternative cultivation practices, plant varieties, and forms of social organization could be ways to respond to climate change, not only in Italy, but around the world. This is a place-based and relatively humble practice of socionatural experimentation rather than the bold solutions so often imagined by policymakers.

So far I have said very little about climate change. This might seem strange at first. Climate change is clearly interacting with land-use change and pathogen epidemics to make the forests of the Monte Pisano more vulnerable to forest fires, floods, and mudslides. The recent decades of gradually increasing average temperatures have certainly made the accumulated leaf litter in forests likelier to burn. When I talk to people about the reasons for forest fires and the threat of floods, however, climate change is routinely accepted as real, and just as routinely brushed aside, as they turn to discuss how to care for the landscapes they live in. As a systems account of long-term environmental change, climate change has little traction on the practical question of how to live and work in an abandoned landscape, where the state is in retreat, pine forests grow relentlessly, and fires return too often. As mathematical constructs that average long-term temperature and rainfall patterns, official ideas about climate change do not engage with people's experiences of plants, abandoned terraces, and crumbling drainage systems, nor with the larger-scale landscape structures of expanding pine forests and fire-prone scrub. Climate change has little to say to remembered histories of subsistence agriculture, of the regretted and criticized world of subordinated and often exploited peasant sharecroppers. Through their capacity to notice their mundane daily surroundings and to link their noticing to landscape structures and simplified histories, ordinary people engage in political ecologies that build walls, call municipal officials to account, and demand government action. From their perceptions of the details of the plants, soils, and terracing systems that surround them, people build an account of landscape structures that are vulnerable to fire and in need of care. A simplified history of how these landscape structures came into being inspires a politics of landscape restoration that draws in volunteers, municipalities, and citizens. This is a contentious politics of landscape morphology that links processes as rapid as fires and as slow as agricultural abandonment. People's understandings of the state affect how they experience landscape change and who they feel is responsible for restoring the landscape. Climate change coexists with, but does not dominate, these concerns.

Even while they largely accept climate change as a reality, people around the Monte Pisano craft a politics of climate change mitigation that fails to mention climate change. As we shall see, people do have a sense of changing weather patterns, of storms and floods, that are different from the past. This is a vernacular climate knowledge that builds upon experiences of weather and notes the effect of weather upon the landscape features that people care about. The most coherent accounts of weather and the environment, however, link weather, forests, landscape stability, mudflows, and landslides. I long hesitated as to whether to call this "vernacular climate knowledge." Certainly, people do link weather to landscape and disaster, but it seems to me that the connections made between the subterranean, the cultivated, and the atmospheric are different from what we usually mean when we say "climate change." A plant/soil/water/weather knowledge animated practical projects of landscape maintenance at a political scale that made sense to ordinary people. I find it unhelpful to call this "climate" because no one I talked to did so. This is a helpful finding if we consider the struggles of climate change policymakers and scientists who seek to persuade people that climate change is "real." Such expert framings of climate change assume that ordinary people are ignorant, in need of education and persuasion, and it ignores the things that they already know and care about. A better approach starts by asking how people know and experience their surroundings, including, but not only, climate. As I have shown in this chapter, climate change is for most people not called into doubt, but also, for most, climate is an abstract process that is not linked to the nonhumans, to the landscape structures, or to the political scales of action to which they are committed. The case of the Monte Pisano suggests that we should study climate change politics by focusing on people's relationships with the nonhumans they care about, the landscape structures they live in, and the histories that they recount.[28] In the following chapters we will begin to move out from the Monte Pisano to the politics of landscape care in Italy more broadly. As we shall see, the politics of weather/plant/soil connections have permeated environmental politics and climate change science in Italy.

Even when, as will increasingly happen in the future, people begin to talk more about climate change, we should notice the political contexts in which they use these words and how they link them with the landscapes in which they live and work. Ranchers in the American West, who worry about the decline of pastures and the health of their cattle in the face of drought, and who resent government oversight, should not be asked how or if they "believe in climate change." The political scales that they attach to their experiences of environmental change may not connect with the scale of global climate change, nor does caring for one's surroundings always produce positive environmental outcomes. Hill farmers in Italy who do not "believe" in climate change, as well as those who do, may find more detailed and dramatic ways of noticing and talking about environmental change, through their capacity to notice droughts, forest fires, terracing systems, and pest epidemics. When and if people do blame fires or floods upon climate change, as is increasingly happening in Italy and around the world, the term "climate" will be given concreteness and political traction through people's sensory experiences of the environments they live in. This could include cities and suburbs, as well as the rural places that I describe. These kinds of noticing are not tied to a "local" scale. Structural accounts of landscape, linked to dramatic histories of environmental change, can transform climate science and policy. As we shall see, through shared understandings of Italian landscapes as abandoned and unstable, through agreement that mudslides and floods can be averted by managing the morphologies of terracing and drainage systems, ordinary people have reworked climate change policy in Italy. Through stories about landscape form, people find ways of linking the temporality of environmental change with the demands of present-day politics.

INTERLUDE II

Pine Cultivation and Pine as an Agent of Landscape Transformation

Stone Pines

Stone pines have been cultivated for their production of pine nuts from Spain to Afghanistan for several thousand years. In the coastal park of San Rossore, the morphologies of pine trees tell of care by *pignaroli*, the pine nut gatherers who trimmed the leading shoots of young trees eighty or a hundred years ago. Forked trees allowed gatherers to climb trees and pick pine cones more easily. Look from the photograph (figure 38) to the diagram (figure 39) and notice how you see this forked tree more clearly. Care for pine trees has persuaded humans to reshape this landscape.

Stone Pine Plantations and Sand Dunes

Coastal dunes in the park of San Rossore have formed as the sediment-laden River Arno and River Serchio flow into the Tyrrhenian Sea, depositing their burdens of sand and silt. Beginning in the eighteenth century, this coastal strip was stabilized with salt-tolerant maritime pine, *Pinus pinaster.* Further inland, old sand dunes are planted with stone pine, *Pinus pinea.* Walking across this landscape, your feet feel the undulations of old dunes. In the hollows between dunes, water puddles after the rain and forms swamps. Glance from photo (figure 40) to diagram (figure 41) and perhaps you will see dunes and water more clearly. These trees have been shaped with one goal in

Figure 38. Cultivated stone pine (*Pinus pinea*) in the park of San Rossore, near Pisa, 2014. (Author photograph)

Figure 39. Drawing of cultivated stone pine (*Pinus pinea*) in the park of San Rossore, near Pisa, 2019. (© Hannah Caisse)

Figure 40. Cultivated stone pines on ancient sand dunes, park of San Rossore, 2014. (Author photograph)

mind, pine nut production. The machinery that picks nuts from these trees no longer requires the trees to be fork-shaped, which had formerly been required by pine nut gatherers who climbed trees. These unforked trees are the result of more industrial forms of pine cultivation.

Pine/Fire/Chestnut Interactions

Maritime pine, *Pinus pinaster*, expands aggressively after forest fires. Fire-killed chestnut trees in the foreground (figure 42) stand bare above young pine trees. This photograph shows a landscape patch that was devastated by fire about five years previously. Look from

Figure 41. Drawing of cultivated stone pines on ancient sand dunes, park of San Rossore, 2019. (© Hannah Caisse)

Figure 42. Fire, pine, and chestnut interactions, Sant'Andrea di Compito, Monte Pisano, 2013. (Author photograph)

photo to diagram (figure 43) and imagine the expanding presence of pine across the landscape. Plants are in motion if you can learn to notice.

Fire/Pine/Oak Interactions

Plants and fire are in an uneasy dance. Where forest fires remain absent for long enough, less flammable species can slowly spread across the landscape. In these pictures (figures 44 and 45), the overstory of maritime pine (*Pinus pinaster*) looms over a dense understory of holm oak (*Quercus ilex*). This is an uneasy dance: if the forest remains unburned for another generation, the short-lived pines will give way to a dark and dense forest of holm oak. This would be a less fire-prone

Figure 43. Drawing of fire-killed chestnut with pine, 2019. (© Hannah Caisse)

Figure 44. Maritime pine growing over holm oak, San Lorenzo a Vaccoli, Monte Pisano, 2016. (Author photograph)

Figure 45. Drawing of maritime pine growing over holm oak, 2019. (© Hannah Caisse)

landscape, closer to the forests that preceded human presence in this area. If another fire arrives, young pine trees and *Ulex* scrub will dominate a newly fire-blasted landscape. Climate change makes such fires more likely. The destination is indeterminate, a drama unfolding under your eyes if you can learn to notice the landscape pattern that tells this story. Pines, people, and holm oaks are negotiating the future together.

FOUR

Plant Morphology, Geomorphology, and Weather

As with many mountainous areas in Italy, the valleys near Castelnuovo di Garfagnana are narrow and steep (see figure 1 in the introduction for a regional map). In many places, slopes are covered with a dense green canopy of young multistemmed coppice forest, the result of centuries or millennia of firewood cutting. In other places, earthen banks or stone terrace walls sustain remnants of cultivation. Higher up the mountains, areas of open pasture show signs of encroachment from expanding woodlands. For the farmers, loggers, and city people who live here, these are landscapes that perpetually threaten to move, a geomorphology that might be transformed by sudden landslides and that is kept in place only by continuing care. Through practices of careful logging and clearing waterways of fallen trees, farmers and firewood cutters seek to keep the entire landscape stable. This is a world where extreme weather events are mitigated by managing the relationships between plants and soils, and where the stability of the landscape is seen as a fragile achievement. People who live here constantly note the effects of recent weather on the condition of slopes, roads, and trees. Through detailed observations of landscape features, many kinds of people think about a politics of landscape stability.

Slopes Need Haircuts

Gazing at a steep wooded hillside in the Garfagnana in the winter of 2014, the biomass energy entrepreneur Giuseppe Mela told me that these trees had to be cut regularly in order to prevent landslides. He recounted a concise history of the shift from peasant firewood management to abandoned and unstable landscapes, of how formerly each peasant head of household managed their small woodlot "because he couldn't ever lack firewood." Government supervision was unnecessary because the myriad peasant landowners knew what they were doing. "There was no need for the *forestale* [forest service] to say, 'cut this one or that one,' there was no need for a management plan, but there was a management plan drawn on the method of the good father of a family."[1] Things changed with the disappearance of peasant logging practices: "The problems came later, when there was an abandonment of the woods, and this has created a big problem for the defense of the ground [*terreno*]. Because [it produces] landslides, landslides [*frane*]. All the watercourses are full of plants, because no one goes to gather [wood] anymore." Drawing on the details of the morphologies of trees on particular hillsides, Giuseppe argued for care for landscape form. He linked the dangerous landscape-scale consequences of overgrown trees to the political and economic changes that had caused land abandonment.

According to Giuseppe, it was a cardinal mistake to think that tree roots alone would stabilize slopes. Even well-rooted trees would become unstable if they became too large: "Now we don't have respect for the land. Now every time it rains there is a landslide, because no one cuts the woods anymore, because it's not worthwhile." Dramatic weather events could combine with lack of care for trees and waterways to produce floods and landslides. I gradually realized that for many of the people I talked to, trees mediated relationships between soil and weather, potentially stabilizing or destabilizing landform. Firewood cutters and foresters told me how, in order to stabilize slopes and keep soil in place, trees had to be kept to the right size, not too large and not too small. The pressure of the wind on the crown of an overly tall tree might overwhelm the grip of its roots on the soil. The tree would then tip over, falling, and its roots would loosen a mass of soil. In the worst case, a single tree fall could knock over other trees, launching an expanding landslide across an entire hillside. Weather, soil, and trees were an unstable choreography that had to be maintained by human attention to the morphology of trees. In linking weather events to tree morphology and landscape form, foresters and loggers were linking a vernacular model of climate to the nonhumans and landscape features that they cared about.

People everywhere around the world have a strong sense of what kind of weather is reasonable and expectable and what kind is exceptional or bizarre. These expectations are what we might call a vernacular model of climate. People in Italy were happy to talk to me about hot summers, recent droughts, or dramatic weather events. Thinking about weather did not, however, inspire their most urgent environmental concerns. It was through talking about and noticing the interactions between weather, trees, and landform that they crafted a mundane biogeomorphological politics that addressed the intense weather events that are a characteristic feature of Mediterranean climates. Even as people's expectations of long-term weather patterns provided them with a sense of what was ordinary and seasonally appropriate, they also had strong recollections of the kinds of rare and intense downpours that might cause floods or mudflows. Their vernacular model of climate contained expectations of possible disastrous weather events, which they sought to manage by attending to the morphologies of trees and to the form of the landscape. Cleared riverbeds or overgrown slopes were landscape forms that mattered. Landscape structures of overgrown or cared-for forest inspired a profoundly Anthropocene environmental politics, in which excluding people from ecosystems was neither possible nor desirable. The relationships between soil formation, tree growth, human labor, and weather were managed by attending to the forms that emerged from the interactions between these diverse temporal rhythms. Climate was experienced through its effects on the nonhumans that people cared about—the coppiced trees, the slopes, terracing, and drainage systems, and riverbeds through which landscape stability was maintained.[2] Morphological thinking of this kind was historical because it was alert to contingent encounters between beings that had different temporal rhythms. Brief and intense weather events left mudflows; firewood cutting changed the morphologies of long-lived trees. Morphological thinking led people to notice the causal forces and histories that had produced the landscape structures of abandoned forests and debris-filled riverbeds. These histories inspired arguments about the responsibility of the state.

As geographer Mike Hulme points out, people have always linked climate to their experiences of place and to such features as trees and buildings that are affected by weather.[3] In thinking about the influence of weather upon soil, trees, and waters, people in Italy think about processes and relationships that are not fully captured by the term "climate," however. Their primary concern is not climate but the relationship between the morphologies of the nonhumans and the landscape forms that they care about. From attention to the morphologies of trees, slopes, riverbeds, and from perceptions of landscape structure, they build arguments about landscape morphology and human care. These are arguments that notice the decay and abandonment of the landscape and that seek to hold the state to account.

For Giuseppe, as for almost everyone I talked to in the countryside, the landscape would only remain stable if trees were cut regularly. I learned to think of this as something like getting regular haircuts in order to look respectable. There was a strong aesthetic component to people's distrust of an "overgrown" landscape where riverbeds were "dirty" (*sporchi*) with fallen trees. There was something quietly dramatic about seeing the landscape as always potentially in motion. Young coppices, perhaps of chestnut, oak, or acacia, held together steep slopes on unstable sedimentary soils. Should these trees get too tall, they could switch from being a reassuring and stabilizing presence and become, instead, a source of danger and instability. A small landslide (*smottamento*) could become a larger one (*frana*). Fallen trees and underbrush could block gullies and ravines, trapping water and mud that might erupt into dangerous mudflows and floods. Landslides could undermine roads or carry them away entirely. It is no wonder that government officials, loggers, and many citizens saw a dense green layer of coppice canopy, not too tall, as a reassuring sign. From the details of trees, groups of trees, and broader landscape structures, people could build politically consequential narratives of care and abandonment.

It is not at all unusual that people in Italy think of forests as stabilizing hill and mountain landscapes. Around the world, foresters and citizens often agree that well-established forests protect watersheds and prevent landslides. What is strikingly different about Italy is the understanding that forests fulfill their stabilizing role *only* if plant/soil/weather relations are constantly nudged and cared for. Trees must not be too large and riverbeds must be kept clean if slopes are to be kept stable in the face of extreme weather events. This is a vernacular plant/soil/weather politics that attends to maintaining the morphology of trees and landscape. In thinking this way, people in Italy combine their understandings of climate with their interest in trees and landforms. In insisting on the role of humans in landscape care, they engage in a kind of Anthropocene conservation that attends to history, land-use change, and state abandonment and which does not make climate the most important consideration. People generally agreed that a gardened and tended landscape was more stable than an abandoned one and that the absence of human care was a source of danger. This might seem strange for many people in North America, where many people see danger as emerging from human interference *into* nature, rather than from the absence of human care. Indigenous people, who practiced diverse forms of land care, as well as their descendants who have been violently prevented from caring for the landscapes they live in, see things differently.[4] Italy provides a valuable example for those concerned with conservation in the Anthropocene, where landscapes need care, and political and aesthetic choices respond to long-term histories of human/nonhuman relations.

The Practical Politics of Plant Form

Firewood cutters and foresters have good reasons for worrying about the forms of trees, slopes, and streams. They often disagree, however, about what shapes of trees might best protect the land. This became clear to me when walking or driving across hillsides and looking at trees with firewood cutters and foresters, who had a rather different sense of what they were seeing. Foresters usually prefer tall trees that can supply construction timber for the building projects desired by the state or elites. In my former training as a forester I learned to look at tall and straight trees with pleasure and to look past multistemmed trees. Foresters sometimes describe a forest landscape as degraded or lacking in timber, when what they mean is that it lacks large trees.[5] Firewood cutters might see a landscape rich with multistemmed coppices.

The firewood cutters I talked to cared about whether an area of forest had enough stems, of the species and size that could find local markets.[6] They thought about the practicalities of getting logs out of the woods, whether by dragging with a cable or by towing in a small tractor trailer. In the Apennines, many areas of forest are too remote to bring logs down to a road. Other areas are too steep to log with machinery. Slopes matter a lot to tree cutters for these practical reasons, but they also think about the possibility that cutting or failing to cut might cause landslides. On my trips through the mountains, I was continually impressed by the extraordinary skill with which apparently precipitous slopes had been logged. Neat piles of cut and stacked wood were a record of the skilled work of loggers, many of whom are now immigrants from the Balkans.

Firewood cutters and foresters agreed that invasive acacias were particularly prone to growing too tall, being toppled by the wind, and dragging hillsides with them. Uniquely, forestry regulations allowed firewood cutters to clear-cut acacia, in the hope that this might kill the trees once and for all (although this never seemed to work). More generally, a coppice of any species could become a source of instability if it grew too tall. One winter day, the firewood cutter Michele Gozzi drove me around the forests on the Pizzorna mountain range north of Lucca, telling me stories about trees and landscape stability. Gesturing to the shapes of trees, he criticized the judgment of foresters and officials. Foresters, he told me, loved to protect *alto fusto* (high forest). This is what many of us might consider to be true forest, unlike the shorter and humbler coppiced forests that cover much of the Mediterranean landscape. For a firewood cutter like him, letting trees get too big might mean losing control of trees to the distrusted *forestale.* Tree cutters and rural people firmly told me that the forest service would ban logging of tall trees; foresters just as firmly denied it. It is certainly the case that foresters have historically tried to persuade firewood cutters to leave a certain number of stems, known as *matricine* (standards), after each cut. Gazing at an area of forest that had been thinned out so as to become high forest, Michele pointed out to me how some of the remaining stems had fallen and taken out a section of road: "Look at that dead one there, that one should be cut. If there is one that is maturing [that is one]. Now you can see here from below, that it has fallen. There is one that has carried away the road too. Look, there, look, do you see? That one down there. Practically, that one fell, it fell because it was dead, it started . . . from the roots."[7] The trees that Michele was pointing to resembled the coppice in figure 46. Like other firewood cutters, Michele saw well-established stools with their attached roots as capable of maintaining landscape stability, but only with timely cutting. Failing care and attention, stems could become too tall and be snapped or toppled by the winds. He thought of stems as "maturing," of becoming ready to be cut, but also of threatening to become "overmature," when they might loosen their grip on a slope and fall across a road or a stream. Maturity could be discerned by a skilled eye that noticed the size of tree trunks.

Allow your eye to move from the photograph to the drawing (figure 47). These are chestnut stools in action, sending up new shoots. The height and thickness of the stems in each cluster of shoots gives a sense of time since the last cut. The remaining tree trunks are standards that could become high forest. Foresters who like big trees tend to focus on the promise of these stems, which could grow back to become "released coppice." These could become the kinds of tall trees that foresters love and which are familiar to most of us from picture books and suburban streets. A firewood cutter might focus on the young shoots emerging from the stumps, a promise that they are doing their job of holding together the hillside, and of producing a healthy crop of firewood in a dozen years or so. He might also wonder if the standards are healthy, mature, or overmature and in danger of snapping or of falling and bringing a section of hillside with them. He would think about the role of tree roots in holding the slope together, and he would consider the threat that overtall trees might snap or uproot and cause a landslide. Look at the road cut on the bottom left of figures 46 and 47 and you will see some of the tree roots that hold this slope in place. Roots interact with the mobility of soil.

A profound rift in assessments of tree and landform emerged in the divergent views of firewood cutters and foresters. Smallholders and firewood cutters unanimously saw high forest (*alto fusto*) as a risk to their livelihoods and a threat to slope stability. Anything that looked like high forest could become bureaucratically impossible to log, and tall trees could snap or fall over and cause landslides. Foresters insisted that *alto fusto* could be legally converted to coppice as long as the right permits had been applied for. Smallholders and loggers just as insistently told me that this wasn't true, that foresters loved *alto fusto* and were known to use its presence as a pretext to prevent logging.

Figure 46. Chestnut *matricine* (standards) and *ceppi* (stools) on a three-to-four-year-old cut on the Monte Pisano, 2014. (Author photograph)

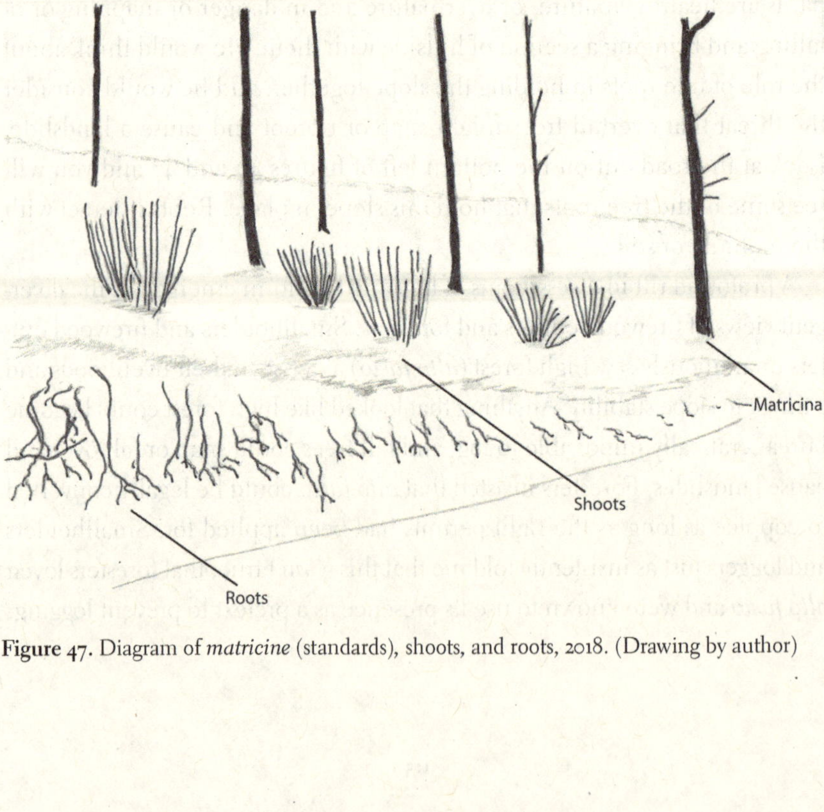

Figure 47. Diagram of *matricine* (standards), shoots, and roots, 2018. (Drawing by author)

In this scenario we see how different kinds of time emerge from attention to the morphologies of trees and slopes. The time of coppice emerges from attention to the size of wood that is suitable for firewood or poles and from the stability of stems and their rooted bases. Firewood cutters link the morphologies of coppiced trees to firewood production and to the stability of slopes. The forms of stem, stump, and hillside are connected to each other. Attending to tree form is the way that firewood cutters *do* a particular kind of time. A tree is ready to cut when it is large enough, not when a certain number of years have passed. Although logging regulations regulate coppice through the time since the last cut, firewood cutters and foresters know how to recognize when trees have the right shape (thickness of stems, height) and are ready to cut. Some foresters hope for a different tree form, and a different kind of time, for tall trees with thick trunks, which might live to be eighty or a hundred years old. The differences between foresters' and tree cutters' interpretations of plant form are mundane differences in practical ontologies.[8] Foresters and firewood cutters understand each other's readings reasonably well, but they have different ideas as to which is best. Firewood cutters want to keep on producing firewood. Foresters dream of producing the kinds of tall trees that their textbooks teach them are "real forest." In Italy, most of the time, foresters have had to acknowledge that steep slopes and postpeasant firewood cutters get to decide what kinds of forests will grow there. For both foresters and firewood cutters the morphologies of trees and slopes help them imagine the slow rhythms of tree growth and the possibility of slope failure, landslides, mudslides, and flooding.

Cleaning Out Streams and Caring for Riverbeds

The specialized knowledge of loggers, foresters, and farmers is shared in less specific ways by ordinary people, who also think about abandoned and unstable postpeasant landscapes and of the need to keep the landscape "clean" so that water can move safely across it. In the winter and spring of 2014, heavy winter rains generated a ripple of reports of roads closed and villages cut off in the mountains north of Lucca. In the steep valleys of the Apennines and the Apuan Alps, a landslide across a narrow road can cut off a town or a village for days or weeks. That winter many people mentioned the need to keep streams and drainage channels clear in order to prevent landslides. With the abandonment of practices of tree care, they talked of the drainage systems and riverbeds as being "dirty" with overgrown vegetation. When heavy rains came, such blockages could cause small landslides (*smottamenti*) near roads, or perhaps larger landslides (*frane*) that could affect entire hillsides.

Across Italy, a history of flooding and mudslides, of state-sponsored land reclamation and drainage, has produced a collective understanding that rivers and hillsides are unstable and must be cared for. Ordinary people complain when riverbeds are full of vegetation and fallen wood, noticing these details as they travel to work or pick up the children from school. Local newspapers in Tuscany insistently link floods, landslides, and mudflows with lack of care for forests, slopes, riverbanks, and riverbeds. The details of particular floods and landslides are linked to a coherent discourse of an unstable landscape in need of human care. This argument departs from the kinds of details that anyone can see, to make arguments about landscape form and political responsibility. In the winter of 2014 my local paper, *Il Tirreno*, was full of stories about *dissesto idrogeologico*, "hydrogeological imbalance." There were stories about floods and landslides, descriptions of the engineering work required to repair damage, and of its likely cost. In a typical story from Pistoia, a town councillor argued, "Without the presence of human intervention, of the terraces and the daily care of drains and small ditches, from the cleaning of riverbanks [*argini*] and check dams [*briglie*] . . . our mountains and hills crumble." What was needed, he went on to say, was a return to caring for nature. The term he used, *governare*, referenced governing as a political practice, but it also echoed the dialect term for animal care. A town councillor from Barga claimed that a recent landslide, like a string of others, was due to the "abandonment of forests or the 'cementification' [overdevelopment] of the territory—a phenomenon evident precisely in the Candia area with alterations of watercourses, slopes, of the shapes of hillsides by construction and poorly planned and often illegal interventions." Such newspaper stories show a picture of a particular landslide or damaged road, a detail that launches a discussion of the need for landscape care and of increased support from the state. This is an argument that builds upon readers' knowledge of a familiar road or bridge before making a political argument about the need to care for landscape morphology. Popular knowledge of the condition of roads, bridges, and hillsides is a widely shared expert knowledge of details, what Science and Technology Studies (STS) scholar Sheila Jasanoff calls a "view from somewhere." This is knowledge that escapes the slot of "local knowledge" so often allocated to the kinds of evidence advanced by environmental justice movements.[9] This is a sensed and experienced knowledge of daily surroundings that is articulated with vernacular knowledge of climate, even as it seldom mentions climate at all.

Preventing a catastrophic reshaping of the landscape and maintaining road systems is largely seen as the responsibility of the government, which must pick up the burden formerly carried by peasants who cut trees and cleared out streams. The second theme that emerges here, and that emerges still more strongly in national discussions of hydrogeological instability, *dissesto idrogeologico*, is the role of the government in allowing or colluding in real estate development. In mountainous regions paved roads were major achievements by the Italian state. Many Apennine villages were only connected to surfaced roads in the 1970s or 1980s. The crumbling of this road system is read as a sign of the crumbling of the state.[10] Discussions of landscape instability seek to hold the state accountable to maintain roads, drainage infrastructure, and the shape of the landscape itself. In demanding that the state maintain landscape stability, ordinary people think about which environmental histories and landscape structures will inform politics. People talk of the history of landscape abandonment caused by industrial agriculture and industrialization after World War II, which has produced overgrown forests, clogged riverbeds, damaged roads, and mudslides. This is an Anthropocene environmental politics, in which climate is a less important category than land-use change, social change, and state abandonment.

It was not only the loggers and foresters whom I talked to on my travels through the countryside who were worried about keeping riverbeds and drainage channels free of fallen trees. In Italy, rural places are often quite well connected to urban places. Mountains are visible from almost every Italian city, and floods and landslides are not a solely rural concern. Giuseppe Mela, the rural biomass energy entrepreneur who wanted to care for the landscape by cutting overgrown forest, was united with the electrician who came to my apartment in town to do a minor repair. Massimo, who lived on the outskirts of Lucca, told me that in the past people used to gather fallen wood from streams and riverbeds, something now forbidden by the *forestale*. As a result, riverbeds were now clogged with debris and flooded easily. Other people told me how riverbeds used to be kept "clean" by firewood gatherers, who would mark desirable logs as their own and take them home. This recollection of former care for riverbeds was shared by almost everyone I talked to. All in all, the disappearance of peasants who cut trees, and the ban on gathering fallen wood, had left a landscape that was "dirty" (*sporco*), laden with an accumulation of brush and fallen trees that blocked streams and clogged riverbeds. These blockages could become dangerous if heavy rains caused mudslides or landslides. Catastrophic landscape instability could be produced by lack of care for the land and the furrows (*solchi*) that channeled water safely across the landscape. As I drove around the hills and mountains, I began to see steep slopes as potentially in motion. I began to sense unstable soils and slippery landscapes and to share the sense of soil permeability and plant/soil/water relationality that I learned from my interlocutors. It was not that everyone agreed about the precise connections between trees, soil, water, and roots. On the contrary, foresters, loggers, and others had divergent views. What they did agree on was that there was an unstable connection between biological, meteorological, and geomorphological processes.

The traditional firewood cutting systems of coppicing woodlands, developed over the past millennia by peasant cultivators across the Mediterranean, are as much about cultivating root/soil assemblages as the arboreal parts of trees that interest foresters. For peasant farmers, tree roots can matter as much as trunks, and tree roots are trusted to hold together hillsides, not only in coppices, but in other forms of cultivation, from chestnut trees to olives. Like olive and chestnut cultivation on terraces, traditional management of coppice woodland requires an attentiveness to plant form that gestures toward invisible soil and water processes. The long lives of trees and the capacities of their roots link human life spans with processes of soil formation and land movement. Although people in the countryside are deeply aware of the con-

Figure 48. A roadside in the Garfagnana, with coppice forest in the background, 2016. (Author photograph)

nections between trees, slopes, and weather, they almost never mention the words "climate change" when talking about these processes. Vernacular ideas about climate are linked to human care and management of plant/soil/water relationships. With the disappearance of peasants, the responsibility for maintaining these relationships increasingly falls upon the state.

Notice the sharp edge of the cut on the hillside above the highway in figure 48. For many people this cut is reassuring because it promises that the hillside is being cared for and that there is less danger of a landslide that might slip down onto the highway. Every year across these mountains heavy rains bring landslides that block roads and highways. This clear-cut is a sign that acacia (black locust, *Robinia pseudoacacia*) is an invasive alien that is not loved. Rather than leaving standards, loggers have clear-cut this patch of acacia, hoping to discourage its further reproduction. The vigor of the regrowth suggests that they have not succeeded. If you look closely you might notice the stacks of firewood at the side of the road to the right.

Thinking about landscape as the product of human care and plant/soil/weather interactions was widely shared, albeit in different levels of detail and with different emphases. Farmers, loggers, and city people shared a broad understanding that these were landscapes that perpetually threatened to move. This was a geomorphology that might give way to sudden landslides and that was kept in place only by continuing care. Loggers and foresters focused much more on the details: they said that by keeping trees the right size and shape, the form of the landscape as a whole could be stabilized. Professionals and people who lived in cities were more likely to mention a general abandonment and lack of care. Concern for landscape stability gave rise to a more general concern for *form*. The shape of the entire landscape had to be stabilized in order to prevent the rapid effects of rainstorms and mudflows.

Morphological politics works by linking an attention to the details of plant/soil relations, from the shape of trees to the state of riverbeds and terracing systems, to accounts of the structure of the entire landscape. These perceptions of landscape structure inform a lively biogeomorphological politics, through which ordinary people evaluate and seek to hold to account both their reckless neighbors and an often distant and indifferent state. Concern with trees and geomorphology becomes part of a broader politics of maintaining long-term landscape stability, not only in the countryside, but in cities. In Italy, citizens judge the state on the basis of its ability to maintain, in some measure, a well-cared-for landscape. The morphologies of trees and the related forms of hillsides, as well as flood and landslide events, make landscape form deeply political. Thinking about landscape as a fragile infrastructure, in need of human care for forests, canal banks, riverbeds, and slopes links landform and tree form to multiple temporalities. The slowness of river system formation and the forms of riverbanks and riverbeds are linked to the rapid effects of floods and landslides. The slow rhythms of tree growth give rise to the shapes of trees that persuade humans to build terraces, maintain riverbanks, and clean riverbeds. The shapes of trees, terraces, and riverbanks are morphologies that emerge through the encounters between processes that have very disparate temporal rhythms. The temporal rhythms of long-lived trees help people to link the slow processes of geomorphology with rapid processes such as floods, downpours, and landslides.

Abandonment

Italian landscapes are haunted by millennia of peasant land management. Unlike in the United States or Britain, where most people's memories of an agrarian past are something that comes out of books, or perhaps from highly inaccurate period dramas where actors sheepishly wave rakes or scythes, many people in Italy have personal memories of peasant landscapes. Italy was a profoundly agrarian country as recently as the 1960s. Scratch an accountant or an engineer in Milan or Rome, a bureaucrat in Firenze, and as often as not, you will find that their grandparents who were peasant farmers. Peasant pasts are often romanticized and no more accurately remembered than anyone else's knowledge of their grandparents' lives. Nevertheless, a key feature of environmental politics in Italy is that *everyone,* from firewood cutters, to officials, to ordinary citizens, respectfully invokes the knowledge and care with which peasant farmers shaped the landscape. For readers who are familiar with the industrially farmed landscapes that dominate Northern Europe and the United States, or with the intensely gardened suburban landscapes that many of us live in, this is an unfamiliar world. Like most of the people around my age whom I talked to, I remember the 1980s as the last years of a smallholder agriculture that focused on keeping polycultural landscapes in order. Weeding, cutting, pruning, and hoeing were needed to keep assemblages of fruit, olive trees, and vines in place.[11] After every downpour, people would come out to clear the drainage ditches that kept water moving across the landscape without washing out roads and terraces. As I grew older the peasants got older, too, and they are now largely gone. The drains and ditches that they used to care for either clog up or take care of themselves, but many people, as I do, notice the absence of care. Many people talk about the landscapes they live in as being abandoned, ruined, and in decay. These are ruined peasant landscapes that have also been abandoned by the state.

This sense of abandonment and neglect might at first look familiar to American or Northern European audiences. After all, rural people from Vermont in the United States to Dorset in England also complain, with justice, about the indifference of the state. In Italy an additional sense of ruin emerges from collective memories of peasant worlds. This sense of ruin and abandonment adds an additional layer to people's daily experiences of the Italian state. Memories of peasant grandparents and daily experiences of slow and capricious bureaucracies give rise to people's experiences of landscapes as being abandoned, ruined, and uncared for by the state.[12] People combine their experiences of political and economic change, with their sense of abandonment (by peasants who left the land) and their sense of abandonment by the state (which has drastically cut back on infrastructure investment). These experiences inspire an Anthropocene environmental politics that sees the landscape as a kind of abandoned and ruined infrastructure.

The countryside of Lucca and Pisa is haunted by the withdrawal of the state and the disappearance of peasants. Many mountain villages and towns are occupied by aging populations of retired smallholders who are sustained by state pensions. Smaller and more remote villages have been abandoned entirely, and the state struggles to maintain roads. Abandoned pastures are colonized by expanding forests, but you would have to walk far from roads to see this. Firewood cutting continues near the highways that most visitors see. The children and grandchildren of peasants live in other ways, looking for the few available factory jobs, government employment, or in tourism. The mother of a childhood friend was born in a now-abandoned village in the high Apennines. Of her three sons, one is a policeman and two are nurses. The relatively few young people whom I meet during my travels in the hills have little hope either of state employment or of a steady job in industry or agriculture. In the summer of 2016, near the village of San Pellegrino in Alpe, I was returning from a long walk to look at ancient chestnut trees. The day was hot and we were thirsty, so we stopped to ask for water at a hamlet by the side of the road. The old people who lived there were proud of their water; it tasted good, and it was good to be up in the cool mountain air. We talked some more. They had grown up in this house, but all the siblings had moved to Firenze. Now that they were retired they could come here in the summers with their Sri Lankan caregiver. Their pensions allowed them to pay their caregiver and spend part of every summer in the mountains, but none could live here year-round. Scattered across the mountains around us were abandoned villages and houses. The humans who used to be out on the landscape, clearing ditches after rains and cutting trees for firewood, are mostly gone. These landscapes are empty of people and of the cattle, sheep, and goats they used to accompany to and from pastures. This emptiness is in part the echo of industrial agriculture, and of the processes of enclosure and intensification that confine animals into barns in the lowlands. This emptying out of the landscape is particularly common in countries with declining populations, such as Italy and Japan, but it is increasingly a feature of rural places around the world. When landscapes are abandoned, property registers fail to record ownership and inheritance, and land often becomes unowned and unknown as well as uncared for. The social form that we call property is revealed to be a fragile achievement, perhaps a brief moment in longer histories of human/nonhuman relations.

Even as practices of tree cutting, animal care, and clearing drains and ditches gradually disappear, the tradition of linking plant form, weather, and landscape stability continues to inform contemporary environmental politics. The sense of living in a landscape that is permeable to weather, wherein caring for plant morphology and landform is a way of maintaining stability, has come to inspire a powerful environmental politics. Ordinary people display a vernacular knowledge of climate, trees, and soils. Their knowledge of climate includes expectations of occasional intense rain events. They seek to manage these deluges by caring for the morphologies of plants and the forms of drainage systems and riverbeds. Drawing on their observations of the details of particular trees, banks, and riverbeds, people build arguments about the stability of the landscape and the role of the state. Through attention to the forms of the nonhumans they care about, people try to manage predictably unpredictable weather and its unstable relations with trees, soil, and water. Official theories of climate change that focus on present-day atmospheres and weather encounter older ways of linking climate to people, plants, and landscapes and to the effects that these beings have upon each other.[13]

FIVE

Biogeomorphological Politics

Walking on the Monte Pisano was often hard work. In many places, slopes were steep and the ground was broken by gullies and ravines. I had to clamber over fallen trees and push through dense brush. In November of 2013, I was walking through abandoned chestnut groves with Francesco, measuring and counting trees, looking for the traces of human/plant encounters in tree form. It was not a good day for fieldwork. Struggling across the ruins of fallen trees, scrambling through deep ravines, I dropped a precious notebook. We went back to look for it, but then the rain began to fall. Slowly the ground beneath our feet became still more slippery, still more treacherous, as dry clay soils turned into a slippery soup. We abandoned our search for the notebook and I gave up forest work for the winter. Rain, soil, and landscape form had colluded to make our work impossible.

Many Italian landscapes share the instability and capacity for transformation in response to weather that I experienced on the Monte Pisano.[1] The tectonic processes that lifted up the Apennine mountain range have produced deeply unstable landscapes, where former marine sediments are exposed to weather. Touch the ground beneath your feet on a winter day and the slippery feeling of clay soil will remind you of a seafloor a few million years ago, where fine sediment particles sank slowly into the depths. In many places, these former marine sediments have become slippery landscapes, mutable, crumbling, and in motion. Most landscape transformation takes place through relatively slow processes of erosion, but sometimes landslides or

Figure 49. Folded sandstone, Manarola, Liguria, 2014. (Author photograph)

earthquakes can shift mountainsides. The tectonic processes that lifted the Apennine mountains from ancient seabeds are visible in the folds of rock strata by the side of the road almost anywhere in the mountains. The inhuman slowness of plate tectonics is visible in the morphology of folded sandstone in figure 49.

The inhuman temporalities of geology and soil formation are linked to human lives through practices of caring for plant and landscape morphology and through experiences of disaster and transformation, when landscapes change form due to earthquakes or landslides. Soil, without being alive, is a mutable mixture of living and nonliving, permeable to the effects of weather, and responsive to human care. Plants produce soil in collaboration with bacteria, fungi, and weather. Once established, plant roots hold soil in place. The slow rhythms of plate tectonics, soil formation, and plant growth are linked to human lives through practices of caring for trees and building and maintaining terracing and drainage systems across vast parts of this unstable landscape. This is a biogeomorphological politics, where the shape of the landscape is seen as bearing traces of human/plant/soil encounters that demand care.[2] Much of the time this work passes unnoticed as part of the background of daily life. It is only after disasters that biogeomorphology becomes obviously political.

Disaster

People in Lucca were haunted by memories of a day when rain, soil, and bedrock had come together to change the shape of the landscape with disastrous consequences for humans. During a walk on the Monte Pisano with the biologist Massimo Giambastiani and the smallholder Alessandra del Chiaro, we paused to look north across the valley of the River Serchio toward the steep limestone ridges of the Apuan Alps. We shared the pleasure of noticing what one part of the landscape looked like when seen from another, of how a familiar hill changed shape from a new point of view. They took turns pointing out mountaintops, a former seminary, locations that I was just beginning to recognize. Soon the conversation took a darker turn, as they began to recount a disaster, a moment when the shape of the land had changed. On that day on June 19, 1996, over five hundred millimeters of rain poured down on the mountains north of Lucca in the space of twelve hours.[3] Massimo remembered seeing the rain clouds over the mountains that summer afternoon and feeling that something unusual was happening. Later that day, he and others learned to their horror that in addition to floods and hundreds of small landslides, flows of mud and debris had poured down from the mountains, burying the villages of Cardoso and Fornovolasco and killing fourteen people.

This disaster has had a lasting impact in the region. To this day people remain alert to the possibility of floods and mudflows when heavy rains fall. Again and again people told me of the need to clean out riverbeds (*alvei*) and to restore the banks of rivers (*argini*). Riverbeds that were clogged by fallen trees and scrub could become temporary dams. When such dams finally broke, the eruption of mud and debris that followed could produce disaster downstream. When I visited the office of the regional head of the forest service, the Corpo Forestale dello Stato, in the fall of 2013, he showed me the monitoring system that kept him up to date on rainfall and the level of water in dams on the Serchio watershed.[4] A network of instruments now seeks to allow officials to give early warning of possible floods and mudflows.

Contemporary newspaper accounts give some idea of how people understood this disaster. As we might expect, the immediate coverage in local and national press focused on the human impacts of the disaster, on the physical presence of mudflows that buried houses, on the desperate search for survivors, and on the predicament of people forced into inadequate temporary housing. Newspaper accounts described roads and railway lines blocked and villages cut off in the floodplain of the River Vezza, which runs through Seravezza (see figure 1 in the introduction). Initially there was little mention of the role of humans in causing the disaster, and the relatively few criticisms focused on the speed and efficiency of disaster relief. A typical story in the national newspaper *la Repubblica*, only two days after the disaster described a brutal transformation: "The Town Is No Longer There: Look for It Under the Mud" and recalled the time of the disaster (13:40 in the afternoon), after only twenty minutes of rain.[5] This was an account of apocalypse, of ordinary life interrupted, of abandoned kitchens, escaped pet rabbits, and the search for survivors.

Quite soon an intense discussion emerged as to the biogeomorphological causes of the disaster and of the steps that should be taken to avoid such events in the future. Writing only a few weeks later, on August 12, the same journalist expressed the complaints of the town's inhabitants.[6] The government had moved quickly after the initial flood event, already allocating 450 billion lire (about €225 million) to cleanup operations. Returning townspeople had been shocked by a new downpour and flood and complained that restoration work was moving too slowly. What they were most concerned about, however, was that "until now no one has taken the trouble to clear the riverbed [*alveo*] of wreckage, nor to raise temporary river banks [*argini*]. In these conditions it is logical that as soon as it rains the river rises and floods." Attention focused on the desirable morphology of the riverbed (clear of debris) and of the riverbanks (properly raised). Townspeople demanded a visit from the minister and pointed out that in the two preceding years there had been too many floods, that there had been no "real project of restoration [*bonifica*] of the river and of the mountain." Although it was riverbanks and riverbeds that were the immediate issue, people were also concerned about the repair of mountain slopes above the town. This story conveys ordinary people's distrust and skepticism about the capacity of the Italian state to disburse funds quickly, fairly, and efficiently. Complaints about the slowness and inefficiency of state disaster response are a common feature of natural disasters in Italy, as in many other parts of the world. Emergency services, often provided by volunteers, are widely admired and trusted. It is in the long aftermath of disaster, when rebuilding is taking place, that people become cynical. Budget cycles are long, money arrives slowly or not at all, and there are often stories about murky bidding processes in which well-connected people profit from disaster.

Disastrous floods and mudflows are not particularly rare events either in Italy or around the Mediterranean. We might almost call them normal disasters. Mediterranean climates are characterized by great interannual variability in precipitation, as well as by occasional intense weather events, when enormous amounts of rain that fall over a few hours or days can transform landscapes. Geomorphologists using archival data to reconstruct past floods and mudflows on the Versilia plain found 159 events between 1328 and 2000, or an average of one every 4.2 years.[7] Over these centuries there have been many attempts to divert and reshape the riverbed so as to move water safely across the coastal floodplain between the Apuan Alps and the Tyrrhenian Sea. People's demand to reshape the morphologies of riverbeds and hillsides is inspired by a vernacular model of climate that recalls the predictable recurrence of deluges.

For geomorphologists, landslides are the result of interactions between processes with different temporal rhythms. In their writings about the Cardoso events, the geomorphologists D'Amato Avanzi, Giannecchini, and Puccinelli noted that a predisposition to shallow landslides was influenced by land-use change (abandoned fields and terraces), by soil thickness, and by the presence of impermeable metamorphic bedrock. In a few sentences they considered how changing landscape morphology (landslides) emerged from encounters between intense rain events, historic processes of land cultivation and abandonment, slow processes of soil formation and movement, and still slower processes of rock formation. As well as thinking about weather, they discussed the roles of changed settlement patterns, river canalization, and water management in affecting floods. Amid the multiple temporalities that geomorphologists and hydrologists had to consider, climate and climate change (which are concerned with long-term averages) mattered less than rare but powerful downpours that encountered human-shaped landscapes. Scientists, however, only partially agreed with the widely held popular opinion that keeping riverbeds "clean" would prevent floods and debris flows by moving water downstream. As one engineer told me, the problem was not so much to move water downstream quickly as to dissipate energy across the landscape safely. Clearing a watershed of undergrowth or a river of debris only risked magnifying floods downstream.[8]

Most climate scientists think that climate change will make the Mediterranean hotter, dryer, and more prone to the kinds of extreme precipitation events that caused the Cardoso and Fornovolasco disasters.[9] It is striking, therefore, that popular interpretations of these disasters focused not upon climate change, but upon human responsibility for caring for the landscape by managing vegetation, cleaning riverbeds, and maintaining riverbanks. This was a biogeomorphological politics that drew upon people's experiences of landscape and weather. By caring for the morphology of the landscape they lived in, people could imagine managing processes of such different temporalities as weather, soil, and plant growth. Climate, with its insistence on atmosphere and water, was less important than biogeomorphology.

A Brief History of Biogeomorphological Politics in Italy

The Italian peninsula is dominated by the Apennine and Alpine mountain ranges. Few places are far enough from mountains that they are not always present, perhaps somewhere on the horizon, only visible on clear days, perhaps an immediate presence that cuts across the sky. Most rivers are quite short, with high peak flows after heavy rain events, when water and mud rush down from the mountains. Near the coasts many areas are swampy and require constant drainage if they are not to return to their former condition.

Collective action to pay for and maintain drainage systems and banks has been a constant feature of Italian history, from Roman efforts to drain swamps and maintain river systems, to the forestry laws of early modern Italian states, to modern interests in erosion, deforestation, and land reclamation. As we have seen, forestry legislation was concerned with connections between soil, water, and trees as far back as the late Middle Ages, as recorded in the forest regulations of Lucca and Firenze. The possibility of draining and moving rivers and of reshaping entire landscapes has been a recurrent feature of Italian politics and economy, from the fifteenth-century river diversions that prevented the siltation of the lagoon of Venice, to twentieth-century land reclamation efforts that drained the Pontine marshes south of Rome. Although the state might organize collective action, it was typically the neighbors of streams and rivers who were expected to pay for the costs of dredging the riverbed and removing debris, of repairing riverbanks, of straightening the course of the river, and of building overflow basins. Across Italy, landowners have historically banded together to pay for the costs of draining swamps, of maintaining riverbanks, and of diverting rivers. Although these associations have operated under a variety of names, they are collectively known as *consorzi di bonifica* (improvement consortia). In Tuscany the *maestri delle aque* (water masters) were responsible for maintaining the Arno from the sixteenth century; in Lucca the Offizio del Serchio played a similar role for the Serchio. In Vorno, at the base of the Monte Pisano, landowners were organized into *circondari* (administrative districts) responsible for paying for flood protection works from 1743 onward.[10]

The erodibility and mobility of the Italian landscape became of increasing interest to literati in the sixteenth century, as agronomical writers began to notice the existence of the terracing and drainage systems, which had been an immemorial feature of the Italian landscape. State involvement in land reclamation increased in the eighteenth century, with major efforts to drain coastal swamps in the Maremma of southern Tuscany, and in the Pontine Marshes south of Rome. A fascinating form of land production, the *colmata*, flooded swampy areas with sediment-laden waters from the mountains, and gradually transformed the internal swamp of the Val di Chiana into cultivable land from the late eighteenth century onward. After the unification of

Figure 50. Check dams (*briglie*) for reducing stream erosion in the mountains in Veneto. On the right-hand side is the same site after five years. Compare with the present-day check dam in figure 37. (From Giuseppe Di Tella, *Il bosco contro il torrente. La redenzione delle terre povere*, Touring Club Italiano, Commissione di propaganda per il bosco e per il pascolo, Vol. Pubblicazione 191, Anno XVIII [Milan: Capriolo & Massimino, 1912]. Image used by permission of the Touring Club Italiano.)

Italy, elites became increasingly worried about soil erosion and accelerating deforestation, inspiring proposals to protect forests, stabilize slopes, and manage riverbeds (figure 50), although, as we have seen, major efforts toward reforestation did not take place until after World War I. Fears about soil erosion and deforestation inspired projects of state making in the mountains in the twentieth century, but a longer historical perspective reveals this to be but one stage in long-running debates about how to manage an unstable landscape. The peasants and pastoralists who reshaped the landscape were largely silent in these conversations, but they carried on their work. The most visible impact of state landscape modification was on the coastal floodplains, where long-standing efforts to drain swamps were given additional impetus by Italian scientists' identification of the connection between *Anopheles*

Figure 51. Mussolini inspecting drainage works in the Agro Pontino, 1931. (Footage supplied by Istituto Luce Cinecittà Historical Archive)

mosquitoes and malaria in the late nineteenth century.[11] During the Fascist period (1923–1943), malaria control and agricultural development inspired the newly confident state to invest large sums of money in reshaping the landscape, from building concrete check dams in the mountains, to building canals and pumps to drain coastal swamps. For the Mussolini regime, the integrated reclamation (*bonifica integrale*) of malarial swamps and the resettlement of populations onto this "new land" was a major triumph, much celebrated in propaganda (figure 51).

Agricultural land along the Serchio (figure 52), as along many river systems in Italy, is protected by embankments. In many areas former swampland is kept drained by pumping stations known as *idrovore*. In English, this word sounds like a creature that devours water. I like to imagine these pumping stations as water-eating beasts!

Many people in Italy are familiar with the broad outlines of the history of state-sponsored landscape transformation that maintains landscape stability,

Figure 52. Agricultural fields from the embankment of the River Serchio, Vecchiano, Lucca, 2019. (Author photograph)

and almost everyone can remember particular floods or landslides. Across the country, improvement consortia maintain embankments, canals, and pumps, moving water safely across the landscape and preventing swamps from returning. The morphology of riverbeds and riverbanks is the result of work by the state, landowners, and peasants, but also a result of the work that rivers do to reshape riverbeds and mobilize sediments. Just as the morphology of trees is a record of encounters between fires, diseases, and peasant farmers, the morphology of drainage systems is the visible trace of histories of encounters between people, soil, vegetation, and moving waters. Across the *longue durée*, a biogeomorphological politics has produced a constant renegotiation of the relationships between citizens, landowners, and the state in collective projects of shaping the land. In the hills, biogeomorphological politics is concerned with terracing systems, drainage systems, forest cover, and hydrogeological instability. In the coastal plains people worry about floods and mudflows and about maintaining the drainage systems that keep swamps at bay. Near Pisa and Lucca, for example, elaborate embankments, canals, and drainage systems prevent the Rivers Arno and Serchio from escaping their banks and reshaping the floodplains. On spring mornings, I would look down from the Monte Pisano and see puddles of water settling across the plain of Lucca, a ghost of the Lake of Bientina that was drained during the nineteenth century.[12] Older people called this the Lake of Sesto. This was a well-remembered ghost that threatened to return as reality.

Weather and Landscape Stability

In recent years long-standing concern over erosion and landslides has been reformulated as "hydrogeological instability" (*dissesto idrogeologico*). This term, initially used by hydrologists and geomorphologists in the 1950s, has traveled into the worlds of policymakers and citizens and draws attention to the way that landscapes are vulnerable to weather. Not all parts of Italy are equally vulnerable, but wherever steep mountains abut narrow coastal floodplains, and wherever river basins have been channeled between cement banks, floods and mudflows are a possibility. A 2013 report by the national environmental organization Legambiente summarizes major urban mudflow and flood events over the past fifty years: Valtellina, 1987, 53 dead; Cuneo, 1944, 70 dead; Firenze, 1966, 34 dead; Sarno, 1998, 160 dead; Salerno, 1954, 318 dead.[13] In this report, pictures of familiar streets, bridges, embankments, culverts, and riverbeds are juxtaposed with stories of disaster and linked to a demand to stabilize the landscape. The details of people's environments are linked to an argument that landscape morphology requires human care. This is an urban biogeomorphological politics that seeks to maintain infrastructures that are vulnerable to weather.

On October 25, 2011, only a few kilometers from the sites of the 1996 Cardoso/Fornovolasco disaster, 540 millimeters of rain fell in six hours. Landslides, mudflows, and floods in the famous Cinque Terre heritage landscape and across the region of Liguria killed nineteen people. In media accounts, floods and mudflows were blamed upon the failure to dredge river systems and on the rural abandonment that had left forests and riverbeds choked with dying trees. In spite of the increased coverage of climate change since the

1996 disaster, climate change was almost never mentioned in accounts of this new disaster. People blamed officials for the lack of warning and for failing to dredge riverbeds and cut excess trees, and they demanded the resignation of mayors and park managers.[14] The vulnerability of the landscape to weather demanded human care for the morphology of drainage systems and for the condition of abandoned forests. The land was responsive to weather, but this vulnerability could and should be managed by attention to landscape morphology.

Media coverage of a more recent weather event illustrates the disconnection between climate change science and popular understandings of the landscape/weather/politics nexus. On September 10 of 2017, a heavy downpour caused catastrophic flooding and mudflows in the coastal town of Livorno, south of Pisa, killing nine people. A few days after the disaster, the finger of blame turned to municipal authorities who had allowed real estate development in flood-prone areas. Corruption, incompetence, and collusion were suspected, all the more because elaborate and expensive flood expansion basins had not worked. The court system ground into action and a criminal investigation was launched. Although climate change was mentioned, geomorphological politics remained a more satisfactory way of making sense of these events. This was not a "natural disaster" but a "tsunami of lack of care" for the landscape. When the meteorologist Giampiero Maracchi explained that these floods had been a predictable effect of climate change, the newspaper article went on to give extensive coverage of an engineer who blamed "too many laws and the lack of cleaning of riverbeds."[15] In the wake of these urban environmental disasters, many people see blaming climate change as a way of deflecting attention from the real estate/government nexus that puts people in houses on floodplains. Government investments in flood management infrastructure do not inoculate officials from blame. Such investments can easily be framed as an opportunity for corruption or financial wrongdoing.

In regional and national media, climate change, *cambiamento climatico*, is typically framed as a question of national and international political responsibility and is seldom linked to the details of the landscapes that people live in. This stands in striking contrast to media coverage of landslides and floods, which focuses upon local responsibility for forests, rivers, riverbanks, and drainage systems, while making little mention of climate. Articles about climate change discuss global impacts and policies, from species extinctions to problems with agriculture, from global warming to the need to reduce fossil fuel burning. This is a framing that is linked to national or international institutions and publics, rather than to the municipalities or regions that might respond to the demands of citizens who seek practical actions. Global climate change is a concept that proceeds at another scale and highlights other phenomena than widely shared understandings of connections between trees, land, water, weather, riverbeds, drainage systems, and humans. Climate change is not connected to the vernacular models of climate through which people make sense of weather, nor to their interest in the biogeomorphology of the landscapes they live in. This disconnect is all the more striking when we consider that Mediterranean mountains are experiencing particularly rapid climate change. Newspaper articles about floods and mudslides refer to specific locations, dates, and times; they link disasters to the details and landscape structures that readers can recognize, and these details are in turn linked to larger-scale questions about landscape morphology and political responsibility. Climate change, an abstract and long-term secular change in average rainfall or temperature, has not yet been effectively linked to popular understandings of the slow temporality of landscape, to the rhythms of care for drainage ditches and rivers, and the rapid uncertainties of rainstorms that link weather to landform. There is a mismatch between the scale of global climate change and vernacular understandings of political responsibility, the feeling among ordinary people that they have been abandoned by the state. The condition of a slope or of a riverbank is the responsibility of a landowner or of a government institution.[16] Buildings next to streams might be the responsibility of real estate speculators and planners. Who can you blame for changing climate, beyond that nebulous collective "everyone"?

After a major rainstorm, newspaper stories recount a litany of towns cut off, of the number of small and large landslides (*smottamenti*, *frane*); they estimate the costs of repairs and lament the lack of funds to do this work. When they can, officials respond to this geomorphological political pressure by announcing the allocation of money to repairs. A typical headline announces the amount to be spent, the location, and the source of funding. In the wake of the 1996 Cardoso events, the Tuscany region allocated a large part of the restoration budget to the forestry cooperative, Terra Uomini e Ambiente (TUA). This cooperative, based in the small town of Castelnuovo di Garfagnana, north of Lucca, grew from seventy to two hundred employees in three years. TUA became a pioneer in "natural engineering" techniques (*ingegneria naturalistica*), also known as *bioingegneria* (bioengineering). Ingegneria naturalistica forgoes the use of the heavy cement structures that are associated with real estate speculation and corruption. Instead, landslide and riverbank repairs use boxes of chestnut logs and plantings of willow stakes to retain soil and stabilize slopes. These methods draw upon older traditions of Sistemazioni Idraulico-Forestali developed in the Alps in the nineteenth century. An engineer who developed these techniques while working for TUA recounted this Alpine influence and a rediscovery of traditional local techniques that are still visible in the landscape.[17] As a low-cost method that used locally available materials and employed a large labor force, bioingegneria was politically and economically attractive to the regional government. This was a charismatic infrastructure that avoided the whiff of corruption that attached to concrete.

In figure 53 we see how a January 2014 landslide is being restored with a palisade of chestnut logs. Since the mudflows of 1996, the cooperative Terra Uomini e Ambiente has been the main organization responsible for *ingegneria naturalistica* across the Tuscany region, but provincial and local governments also undertake these repairs. Such engineering works always have a sign explaining who is responsible for the work and how much it costs, a message of fiscal responsibility and governmental care.

As one might expect, national newspaper coverage in the wake of weather events focuses on urban riverbeds and hillsides. Stories talk of the need to keep riverbeds clear of debris, of the role of real estate development and the government in building on steep slopes that can collapse in mudslides, or of channelizing rivers between concrete walls that turn mudflows and floods into disasters. Weather reports focus on the increase in intense rainstorms, described as *bombe d'acqua* (water bombs), and on the sudden and unpredictable changes

Figure 53. Bioengineering in Seravezza, Lucca, 2014. (Author photograph)

in weather that are produced by climate change. It is only in the past three or four years that some articles have begun to link climate change to the increase in downpours, tornadoes, floods, landslides, infrastructure damage, and heat waves. This emerging language of climate change focuses on the effects of intense storm events upon familiar infrastructures. In these stories, weather combines with "cementification of territory," a wonderful term for excessive real estate development and urban sprawl, to cause floods and landslides.[18] Cities such as Genoa or Naples, which are built on steep hillsides with channelized watercourses that flow directly through town, are particularly vulnerable to mudflows and floods. After disasters, criticism focuses on the relationships between officials and real estate developers that allowed construction in dangerous places.

With recent increases in floods and landslides, popular, governmental, and scientific interest has led to the creation of national maps of landslides and landslide risk. Because landslides can be reactivated after decades or centuries, ancient "stabilized" landslides are always potentially in motion, morphologies that are also events that could be made more likely by extreme weather. A national landslide inventory in 2015 recorded over five hundred thousand landslides, or over 7.3 percent of national territory, with 7.9 percent of the country at high or very high landslide risk. This inventory was a map of geomorphological potential. Just as in the United States you can find out whether you are living in a flood zone, in Italy you can find out if you live on an old landslide.[19] I began to imagine the apparently stable landscape of fields, forests, and buildings as lying over treacherous morphologies that could be reactivated by a heavy rain or by an earthquake. An apparently stable landscape was in a motion that was both too slow and too fast to observe—too slow because it had happened decades or centuries in the past, and too rapid because if a landslide did occur, it would be almost impossible to witness. I should have known better. When I was a child, a landslide swept away several abandoned terraces near my grandmother's house. Decades later, this slide is a steep slope covered by woodland, but I remember the bare soil and the sense of excitement. A bend in the path is the place where we used to climb over the landslide. This is a provisionally stable morphology, perhaps waiting to change form if it encounters the right rainstorm.

Climate Change Talk

Unlike the dense field of geomorphological observation and political conversation, conversations about climate change are rarely connected with people's experiences of their contemporary landscape, nor with the histories of landscape care and abandonment that older people can tell. Although people in the countryside were deeply aware of the connections between trees, slopes, and weather, they almost never mentioned the words "climate change." Even as they talked about the world having changed, and agreed that there had been an increase in "water bomb" rainstorms, they linked these monstrous events not to "climate change" but to vernacular models of climate and weather and to the relationship between plant morphology, biogeomorphology, and official responsibility. Toward the end of my interviews I would always ask people what they knew about climate change, whether it was happening, and what effects they saw. Most would agree, somewhat hesitantly, that climate change was indeed happening, but they usually had little more to say beyond a limited range of platitudes. For loggers and farmers, for retired peasants and shopkeepers alike, the words *cambiamento climatico* (climate change) were a showstopper, a halt to conversation. Often they would say something like, "I don't know much about that." Climate was a language for engineers or scientists, but not for them. A few people advanced conspiracy theories about the causes of climate change. My favorite was that climate change was due not to greenhouse gas emissions, but to the Apollo moon landings, which had changed Earth's orbit.[20] Most people, however, agreed that climate change was real and that it was caused by atmospheric pollution, before changing the subject.

Old people in particular were more hesitant about climate change. They always shifted the conversation to talk about changing seasons, recent weather, and their life experiences of environmental change. Simone Polli, a retired peasant farmer in the village of Vorno, told me that the weather had changed from that of his childhood, but the changes he noticed were not at all what I was expecting. He thought that the temperatures used to be more extreme: people used to go about barefoot in March, while winters were colder, with long icicles forming on waterfalls. It was not only older people who remembered the hot summers of their childhood. Middle-aged people also talked of hot summers and recalled the colder winters of their childhoods, but these simple comparisons were bland generalizations. On rereading my notes from one interview, I had to laugh. When I asked Simone about climate change, he replied with an account of the social and economic changes that he had lived through. "It's changed a bit, it's a whole different business, it's changed that there is more money now."[21] I couldn't help but agree with him. While older people like Simone were vague or doubtful about climate change, they had a great deal to say about how the landscape had changed. They would talk about changing work and the changing economy, of the abandonment of grazing and increased forest fires, and they could cite the material traces of these events in the landscape.

It was quite easy to get people to say that the seasons had changed: "Le stagioni sono cambiate." Most would say that there used to be a proper winter with ice and snow, and a pleasant spring before the hot summer. Now there were only two seasons—a mild wet winter, and a hot summer. Farmers in particular commented on unusually mild winters or dry summers, but they would quickly change the subject to iniquitous agricultural regulations or fuel prices. Some people were less sure that seasons had changed. I remember discussing a particularly oppressive heat wave with a friend who ran a grocery store. I asked her if she thought the climate had changed and how she was handling the heat. She pretended to whisper (to avoid offending imaginary customers complaining about the heat). "Don't tell anyone. I don't really mind the heat. It was hot like this when I was a child."[22] Even as people agreed that the seasons had changed, it was striking how little they talked about climate change when discussing strange weather, including floods and landslides. The time of biogeomorphological politics and landscape care did not align well with the urgency of global climate change.

In the winter of 2015, a series of windstorms devastated the Pizzorna mountains and the town of Bagni di Lucca, north of Lucca, as well as the Versilia region of the coast. Thousands of trees were blown down and many roofs were damaged. When I went back in the summer, people were still talking about these dramatic events. They told me of the sudden hurricane-force wind, of the plummeting temperature that preceded the storm, and of the terrifying sound of trees snapping. This was a monster, a strange and unnatural event, but much to my surprise they did not mention climate change, discussing instead the responsibility of the state to pay for the cleanup and repair costs. It was only municipal officials in Bagni di Lucca, who showed me pictures of fallen trees and damaged roofs, who connected this storm to climate change. They quickly shifted the conversation to talk about the millions of euros in repair costs, which they hoped would come from the regional and national government or the European Union (EU). Climate change, as a global problem caused by a global collective "we" was not doubted by many people, but it did not provide political traction upon the environments in which they lived. Their vernacular model of climate saw abnormally intense weather events that interacted with the landscape as a predictable feature of the world. Local authorities were responsible for caring for forests and drainage systems and for repairing the damage caused by extreme weather.

In the summer of 2016, Ornella Rossi, one of the managers of an estate at the base of the Monte Pisano, eloquently summarized this way of thinking. It was no good talking about sudden downpours as unnatural "water bombs" (*bombe d'acqua*) she said. These were events that happened almost every year now. The only solution, she believed, was to restore the drainage systems that had formerly kept the landscape in equilibrium, that maintained the shape of the landscape.

> The ditches are open, cleaning them out has restored us. With a ditch we restored the balance [*sesto*] of a piece of the slope. We gave shape to a piece of the territory. Not giant walls, but opening ditches. Given the shape of this territory, modified by man, it has to be kept in equilibrium, keeping in mind that man has already modified it. Therefore this is not a territory that goes ahead by itself. . . . It is a territory that needs the work of the humans who transformed it, and therefore, humans need to take responsibility for what they have done, to carry on the care, to carry on taking care, to keep it in the best [possible condition].[23]

She reiterated the importance of caring for landscape morphology (shape, slope, territory) as a way of preparing for extreme weather. Humans maintained landscape stability by keeping water moving across the landscape. A young and educated person like Ornella was quite happy to attribute increasingly intense downpours to climate change, but even for her, it was more interesting to talk about how to care for an unstable landscape.

This sense of living in an unstable landscape that is permeable to weather is found in regional and national media, in oral history, and in *longue durée* histories. Aldo Ferri, who grew up on a farm on the Monte Pisano, told me that according to legend, rains and floods had caused the abandonment of the previous village of Vorno high up on the mountain near Selvavecchia, leaving nothing but chestnut drying sheds (*metati*) scattered through the forest. The local historian Giovanni Massoni records a fourteenth-century disaster, which may be the source of this story.[24] The distant past is present in living memory, animated by contemporary experiences and media accounts of storms, floods, and landslides.

It was only in the spring of 2019, with the rise of the Extinction Rebellion movement, and with intense media coverage of climate change activist Greta Thunberg, that climate change became a more interesting topic. This framing of climate demanded that governments take action to reduce greenhouse gas emissions and that individuals choose to consume less energy or eat less meat. The understanding of climate change that inspired protests in the streets had little connection to the vernacular models of climate that people used to make sense of changing weather, nor was it linked to the scales of practical political action and weather/landscape connections that they understood best. Climate change talk in newspapers was not linked to the potentially unstable landscapes that people lived in, nor to the practical projects that they might engage in.

Living in a Permeable Land

Had I focused on climate alone, I would have had a very poor understanding of people's understandings of environmental change. They saw the landscape very differently than I had expected, mutable and permeable to weather, sensitive to human care for terraces, trees, and drainage systems. This sense of landscape gave rise to visions of infrastructure care and to a biogeomorphological politics that proceeded at a very different tempo to climate change policy. This is a politics that is almost invisible if we focus too closely on "climate" as the question that matters. The Italian landscape is haunted by the absence of the peasants who sculpted terraces, drainage systems, riverbeds, and riverbanks. Fascist projects of coastal land reclamation are well remembered, as is the possibility that swamps might return should state-sponsored drainage retreat. Whatever solutions are proposed to particular environmental disasters, such as floods and landslides, there is a collective understanding that it is the loss of care that has made the landscape particularly vulnerable to disastrous changes in morphology. In Italy, people typically interpret natural disasters as demonstrating a need for *more* human intervention, for more care.[25]

Geomorphological politics moves from details to landscape structures in ways that call upon people's capacity to notice their daily surroundings, from the hillside outside their houses to the bridges they cross on the way to work. Specific features of the landscape have to be cared for, and these details appear in media descriptions of disasters. By comparing the details of particular riverbanks, mudslides, and floods with a recitation of other such events in the past, people build arguments about the need for the state to maintain the morphology of the landscape. This is a kind of popular expertise that makes claims upon the state. Drainage systems must be kept clear of trees and debris, especially in the hills. Rivers must be regularly dredged and banked in the lowlands and in cities. Both in the countryside and in cities, demands for the maintenance of landscape form drive popular criticism and official response. This biogeomorphological politics contrasts the slow mobility of a geologically unstable landscape with the fast rhythms of floods and downpours that penetrate a permeable and mutable land. Wherever floods and landslides threaten human desires, the details of riverbeds, riverbanks, and flood control measures are woven into media accounts, popular commentary, and court cases. This is a contentious politics marked as much by failure as by success. Many houses were built on floodplains and unstable slopes in the postwar boom, and corrupt real estate development is a phenomenon in many regions. If after disasters it is easy to say "never again," it is often the case that after the next one people say "once again."

The temporal and spatial scales of official climate change, which focus on long-term averages of temperature and precipitation and on national and global political scales of action, have little resonance with the model of a climate/landscape interaction through which people notice ordinary and extraordinary weather. In Mediterranean mountains, climate change is likely causing more rapid impacts than in other parts of Europe. Paradoxically, in Italy, the floods and landslides that are some of the likely effects of climate change are not recognized as such by most people. It is not that climate change talk is not a constant and increasing feature of contemporary media and conversation, but rather that this talk proceeds unconnected from people's concerns about the environments they live in. This is not a problem of climate change skepticism. There are relatively few skeptics in Italy compared with in the United States, although right-wing skeptics do seem to be increasing. It is simply that popular understandings of climate/landscape relations inspire a biogeomorphological politics that focuses on landscape as an infrastructure that should be cared for by citizens and by local and regional governments. By contrast, official climate change language and policy is linked to energy systems and carbon emissions, to atmospheric pollution, and to international treaties. This is not only a problem of scale nor of phenomenological immediacy, but a problem of ontological difference. The weather/landform/tree assemblage that sustains rural understandings of landscape stability, and even the weather/landform assemblage that is more prevalent in cities is more than climate, and it is not helpful to reduce caring for this assemblage to "climate change mitigation." When rural people advocate for repairing abandoned terracing and drainage systems, they are thinking more of abandoned peasant landscapes than of climate change futures. So too, when people advocate reformed real estate development policies and changing riverbeds in cities, they are thinking more of state irresponsibility than about climate change. Once we recognize the difference between official climate change policy that is linked to international climate change science, and a biogeomorphological politics that is linked to vernacular models of climate/landscape relations, it becomes possible to imagine productive alliances between these different projects. Climate can become "more than one but less than many," not only in relation to multiple concepts of climate, but in relation to Anthropocene histories of peasant landscape care and postindustrial abandonment.[26]

In recent years many social scientists have warned of the dangers of defining climate change as a single future and a single problem, or as an impersonal and apolitical knowledge distant from people's experiences of the world. Recent scholarship finds that people make sense of climate change through their experiences of the impacts of weather on the environments they live in.[27] People will experience climate change very differently as a result of the environmental and political histories of the places they live in. I would add to this, however, that climate and weather should be nested within a broader field of social and environmental change, where climate is one among many processes that people care about. In Italy people care about abandoned postpeasant landscapes, drainage systems, or channelized urban rivers. These are the morphologies through which they think about the presence of the past in the present. In other parts of the world, people will have other vernacular models of weather and they will link weather to other environmental processes and histories. They will have other political scales of action and other ways of thinking about the state. There too they might not find official "climate change" the most important thing to think about, or they might even deny official models of "climate change" while working to care for the plants, animals, and landscapes that matter to them. Farmers addressing the problems of drought-stricken pastures in the American West or of flooded fields in England will have their own vernacular models of climate/landscape connections. They will draw upon other understandings of environmental processes and histories and of the duties of citizens and governments. Ordinary people, from commuters in Manhattan to cattle ranchers in California, might engage in activities that accelerate climate change, for reasons that make environmental and political sense to them. This is not always a comfortable prospect for those of us who, as I do, instinctively sympathize with ordinary people.

The insight that people notice environmental change by paying attention to the nonhumans that they care about is relevant to many other places and times. Attention to morphology is a way of stepping outside the present and of attending to the slow violence of toxicity and disaster, as in Rob Nixon's account of the environmental picaresque, or historian Kate Brown's detection of impacts of radioactivity upon the morphologies of plants and human bodies in post-Chernobyl landscapes. Attention to landscape morphologies reduces climate change to its proper dimension, as one among many processes that people reckon with as they go about their daily lives in a profoundly human-transformed world. By attending to morphologies, people can reckon with the histories that have produced vulnerability, toxicity, and environmental injustice. Climate justice movements around the world have criticized technocratic climate change policies and pointed to the histories of colonialism and natural resource extraction that have produced present-day environmental degradation.[28] The example of geomorphology and landscape politics in Italy shows how climate change policy can be situated within a broader field of environmental politics, where the ongoing environmental consequences of colonialism and capitalism may be more urgent than climate change.

In Italy, the sense of living in a profoundly human-modified landscape is pervasive and long-standing. Even as scholars have discovered the Anthropocene, as an era when human beings have affected ecological processes around the world, people in profoundly anthropogenic landscapes, as in Italy, have been living in the Anthropocene all along. The Italian tradition of seeing landscape as a morphology that demands care will find increasing resonance with other efforts to engage with the Anthropocene. Climate change might be easier to imagine if it is nested within other Anthropocene processes of global environmental change. In Italy, a sense of living in unstable and mobile landscapes is sedimented in ordinary people's consciousness, a resource that they bring to bear upon climate change politics. This sense of landscape is one of permeability, where atmosphere, soil, landform, and people transform each other, where the subterranean and the atmospheric are in communication. As I move across the landscape at home in California, I now think about the slow mobilities of bedrock and of soil, and of how these are linked to climate through people's interest in preventing landslides and fires. The capacity to think across multiple temporal rhythms by attending to landscape morphology, which I have learned in Italy, is a hopeful possibility for confronting global environmental change. The architect Manuele Manigrasso, writing in a national report on floods and landslides, called for a "rediscovery of a more natural dialogue between land, atmosphere, water, and rain."[29] The strange fact of unstable Italian landscapes is already in motion, already transforming and reworking climate change science and environmental policy. As we shall see, scientists, activists, and ordinary people bring their knowledge of the strange and unstable Italian landscape into such places as biomass energy politics and climate change science.

SIX

From Landscape Histories to Climate Models

One early summer morning I was high up above the treetops, looking out over coastal pine forest in the park of San Rossore, near Pisa, Italy. It was an idyllic moment. The white peaks of the Apuan Alps were clear in the distance; the day was sunny but not yet too hot.[1] Most of the time when I look at trees, I have to look up at them from below. It was a rare pleasure to see the canopy up close, to be able to lean out and touch vivid green pine needles, to look across the crowns of trees gently moving in the breeze. I could imagine the work of photosynthesis through which these pine needles were absorbing red/far-red sunlight (hence the bright green color), converting carbon dioxide and water into sugar and oxygen. I was high up in a tower that had been built to measure the flux of carbon dioxide above the forest canopy, part of an international network of towers that measured the capacity of forests to absorb carbon and slow global climate change. The breath of these forests on that spring day could be used to detect the global scale of human impacts upon the environment.

Climate change is a phenomenon that was detected by global scale networks of weather stations, data infrastructures of meteorological reports, and by models run by supercomputers. This is the biggest of big science, a network of thousands of people and instruments that historian Paul Edwards aptly calls a "vast machine." This machine has made it possible to describe global climate change.[2] The models that simulate the impacts of increasing greenhouse gas concentrations on the world's climate simplify the world down to a relatively small number of state variables, such as wind, temperature, precipitation, humidity, cloudiness, air pressure, and air quality. Once values for these variables are known, a computer calculates their transformations over time. Such systems models of global climate, with their necessary simplifications, are in tension with the focused attention to time and place that are the stock in trade of anthropology and history. This is perhaps one reason that anthropological and historical discussions of climate change have often focused upon how people respond to climate change as a global force that, as it were, comes from above. Predictions of global climate change are very different from the vernacular models of climate, the landscape histories, and the plant morphologies and landscape structures that I have described so far. How might practical and phenomenological experience be relevant to global climate change? In this chapter I bring historical accounts of political economic change, plant disease, and forest fires into conversation with data infrastructures and ecological modeling practices that seek to detect the impacts of global climate change. Scientists who simplify and abstract the myriad interactions of ecological processes in order to model the response of forests to climate change have to decide when landscape history matters and when it can be allowed to subside into the background. Even impressive data infrastructures are connected to landscape histories through the practical skills of scientists and modelers. There is an unlikely echo, an assonance, between the practices of ecological modelers and my own practice of landscape ethnography. Both of us, in rather different ways, project our phenomenological experiences of forests, soils, and trees into accounts of landscape change.

Measuring the Breath of Forests

From the point of view of the Anthropocene and of climate change, the capacity of forests and soils to absorb or emit carbon dioxide is supremely important. About 25 percent of greenhouse gas emissions currently arise from agriculture and land-use change. Adding to their importance, the growth of trees and plants is as yet the only practical means of removing carbon dioxide from the atmosphere. Expanding forest cover has been proposed as a way to reduce atmospheric carbon dioxide levels by up to 25 percent, a project that would require the displacement of other human activities on a vast scale. Forests and forest soils seem to confer a kind of environmental absolution, a relatively painless delay to the drastic changes in the global energy system that will be required in order to reduce carbon emissions. In the tropics, policies known as REDD+ (Reducing Emissions from Deforestation and Forest Degradation) seek to encourage carbon retention in forests. In industrialized countries, studies that estimate the net absorption of carbon into European forests of 109 million tons of carbon per year, or that forest growth can provide 17 percent of California's emissions reductions goals, make the lives of politicians a little bit easier. Caring for forests can allow us to carry on burning fossil fuels for a just a little longer.[3]

How much, where, and when carbon dioxide is absorbed or emitted by forests is critical information for nation-states that are negotiating emissions reductions in international treaties. In many industrialized countries forests are recovering from histories of logging for firewood and timber. In Italy, abandoned mountain pastures are being colonized by firs and pines, and abandoned firewood forests are becoming high forest in more remote areas. In the United States, forests in New England have increased since the abandonment of agriculture in the mid-nineteenth century, and loblolly pine plantations grow on abandoned farmland across the South. Forest regrowth is a valuable way to reduce the burden of changing energy systems in industrialized countries.

Due to forests' importance for climate change policy, national and global carbon-emissions budgets are affected by how forests respond to increased temperatures, droughts, and rainstorms. Some studies show increased forest growth due to the fertilization by increased carbon dioxide, good news for policymakers. Other studies warn that higher temperatures might cause increased respiration or that droughts might slow down growth, eliminating the absolution that forests seemed to offer. In an effort to reduce this critical uncertainty, scientists around the world try to measure respiration and photosynthesis from forests, using instruments that monitor airflows, energy flows, and fluctuations in carbon dioxide and water vapor above tree canopies. San Rossore was one of five towers in Italy that were part of the global FLUXNET network.[4] Data from eddy covariance sites such as this one (figure 54) is shared through websites, allowing researchers to simulate carbon absorption by forests.

The instruments at the top of this impressive tower were quite modest but they could sustain big stories. The ecologist Eugenio Moretti explained to me how an ultrasound gas anemometer, which measures air movement, and a carbon dioxide detector (figure 55) could support calculations of the absorption and emission of carbon dioxide from the forest. This monitoring system, along with many simplifying assumptions, allowed the calculation of the overall flux of carbon in or out of an ecosystem, a number known to ecologists as Net Ecosystem Exchange (NEE). As Eugenio told me, "That is what the politician is interested in, to know, also in relation to quotas, if the ecosystem is absorbing or emitting [carbon dioxide]."[5] Quotas were the quantities of carbon-emissions reductions allocated to nation-states in international negotiations. The continued burning of fossil fuels in power plants was potentially linked to measurements at the top of this tower.

The day-to-day running of the tower required Eugenio to respond to alarms about malfunctions and power outages and to measure the leaf-litter fall that contributed to decomposition and respiration. The complex relations between plants, soils, bacteria, and atmosphere in an entire ecosystem could be monitored by an anemometer that measured air speeds twenty times a second and by an infrared detector that measured carbon dioxide levels every half hour. This data was continuously transmitted from a hut at the base of the tower. Computer models "cleaned" the data, rejecting anomalous high and low measurements and interpolating missing values. From these measurements the breathing of forests and soils could be inferred, the absorption of carbon during daytime photosynthesis partially canceled by the respiration of plants (autotrophic respiration) and by the animals, fungi, and bacteria that broke down organic material (heterotrophic respiration). Carbon flux measurement required theoretical assumptions that partitioned carbon emission and absorption into conceptual compartments: soil, atmosphere, autotrophs, and heterotrophs. These simplifying assumptions supported models of the movement of air over the forest canopy, making it possible to use the eddy covariance technique to measure the breathing of forests and soils, ultimately allowing the calculation of NEE.[6] Many models, each with their own simplifying assumptions, were needed to sustain this global network of flux monitoring towers. This data and modeling infrastructure

Figure 54. Eddy covariance tower, San Rossore / Migliarino, Pisa, 2014. (Author photograph)

Figure 55. Ultrasound gas anemometer and infrared carbon dioxide detectors, San Rossore / Migliarino, Pisa, 2014. (Author photograph)

required the practical skill of people like Eugenio to make sure that the complexities of ecosystem processes did not undermine the credibility of the data it produced.

The practical limitations and theoretical assumptions that sustained the carbon flux towers dictated the choice of location for the monitoring station. An uneven forest canopy would have produced turbulent air and wildly fluctuating results, invalidating the theoretical model that supported the eddy covariance technique. The tower had to be set up above the kind of even canopied high forest that is extremely unusual in Italy, where millennia of peasant landscape management have produced heterogeneous woodlands with uneven canopies. Still worse, the hilly landscapes of Italy provided relatively few places where flat and even forest canopies could form. Finally, the need for long-term measurements required a forest that was protected from fires and firewood logging, disturbances that are typical of Italian landscapes. There is an intense Anthropocene catch-22 for ecologists who work in Mediterranean landscapes. Because almost the entire landscape has been modified by millennia of peasant firewood cutting, cultivation, burning, or grazing, those who wish to study long-term ecological processes struggle to find undisturbed ecosystems to monitor. Even in the wake of rural depopulation, most Italian forests are divided into a myriad of tiny woodlots that are regularly cut for firewood. Confronted with these kinds of disturbances and canopy unevenness, scientists who build ecological monitoring networks often locate their instruments in parks and protected areas. In Italy many such parks are former aristocratic estates that exclude the histories of human/nonhuman encounter that are typical of postpeasant Mediterranean landscapes.[7] By careful interpolation San Rossore could be made to stand for an Italian landscape with a very different history.

Landscape History in San Rossore

Walking through the forest with Eugenio, the morphology of trees told me stories of human/plant encounters (for photographs and drawings, see figures 38–45 in interlude II). When I visited the park, the forester Francesca Logli showed me how stone pine (*pino domestico*, *Pinus pinea*) was cultivated for pine nut production. Pine nut gatherers told me how disease had transformed their livelihoods. Until the arrival of the western conifer-seed bug, *Leptoglossus occidentalis*, in the early 2000s, San Rossore had been one of the major pine nut producers in Italy.[8] The tall well-spaced trees I saw with Eugenio had been planted and tended. Regular thinning had shaped trees with few lower branches and large crowns in order to maximize pine nut production. The forest understory was kept clear of competing vegetation so as to make pine cone gathering easier. Formerly even the lower branches of pine trees were pruned. The tower was located among hundred-year-old pine trees whose morphologies testified to encounters with humans. As we walked toward the tower Eugenio pointed to the remains of a cooking fire, perhaps set by pine nut gatherers, and explained that gathering pine cones or burning deadwood could invalidate the tower's measurements. Human presence was ubiquitous, but it had to be carefully managed if the tower was to do its work successfully.

The park at San Rossore is the result of a history of aristocratic hunting and state protection. Aristocratic expropriation of peasant wood pasture in the sixteenth and seventeenth centuries, including by the Medici grand dukes of Tuscany, combined grazing, hunting, and pine nut production, a system that became more formalized with pine nut plantations in the nineteenth century.[9] After the fall of the Savoy monarchy in 1945, the park became a presidential retreat that hosted visiting heads of state, and it was only in 1979 that it became a regional park. This history of exclusion remains a feature of the park to this day. Visits are carefully regulated, and large areas are closed to the public, to some frustration from municipal leaders in the nearby city of Pisa.

The presence of stone pine in the park is the result of care by humans who like to eat pine nuts. Beginning in the nineteenth century, salt-tolerant maritime pine (*Pinus pinaster*) was planted to stabilize dunes and protect areas farther inland from salt spray. The stone pine trees that surrounded the tower stood on ancient sand dunes, geomorphologies that had emerged from encounters between wind, water, and sediments brought down from the mountains by the Rivers Arno and Serchio. The land has expanded by about seven kilometers out to sea since Roman times, with successive dunes forming parallel to the coast. More recently the combination of afforestation

Figure 56. Plant disease and landscape transformation, San Rossore / Migliarino, Pisa, 2014. (Author photograph)

and sediment trapping dams on the upper watershed has starved rivers of sediment, and the sea now advances by as much as twenty meters a year. Geomorphology emerges at the intersection of coastal wave patterns, human cultivation practices inside the park, and dam building and afforestation many kilometers away.[10]

The park forester Francesca Logli worried about losing the salt-tolerant coastal strip of maritime pine due to disease. Growing on a sand dune, perched above a fluctuating water table, the pine trees of San Rossore rely upon mycorrhizal associates to extract nutrients from dry and sandy soils. Less than a meter below these dry sands lies the water table and even the shallowest ditch finds water (figure 56). In lower-lying areas between former dunes, strips of swamp forest (*lame*) are dominated by water-tolerant alder and poplar. Park officials worry that the drainage and pumping system might not be properly operated, perhaps making trees vulnerable to disease. Even the most intense human care cannot prevent unexpected disturbances from transforming the landscape. Since the 1980s, an invasive scale insect, *Matsucoccus feytaudi*, has devastated maritime pine populations, moving from southern France to Corsica and Liguria.[11] Affected trees shed heavy sap and become vulnerable to pests and pathogens. Francesca Logli pointed to the reddish-brown color of dying foliage and the white gummy sap on diseased trees. Park foresters and biologists had largely given up on saving maritime pine, seeking only to slow the advance of the *Matsucoccus* with pheromone traps and by cutting areas of diseased trees. Their experiences of the advance of the disease have led foresters like Francesca to plan for the disappearance of maritime pine, replacing it with plantings of native holm oak (*leccio*, *Quercus ilex*). In figure 56 we see holm oak in the foreground with stone pine in the background. Dying maritime pine was cut so as to favor native leccio. Note the sandy soil and the water-filled ditch in the foreground.

How Landscape Thinking and Systems Thinking Interact

The morphologies of trees in San Rossore tell me of histories of peasant expropriation and of emerging insect pests, of ongoing pine nut gathering and of excessive deer browsing. The rolling topography and receding shoreline are the result of encounters between sediment-laden rivers and ocean waves. These morphologies tell of the unique histories of trees in patches of forest; they draw my attention to landscape structures and to the histories that brought these structures into being. The landscape structures that matter most here are the areas of flourishing and tended stone pine, the strips of maritime pine that remain near the coast, and the areas of holm oak planted in their place. I can link morphologies of trees and larger landscape structures to the social and economic transformations that changed a peasant landscape into a state park, the unfettered trade in live plants that brought insect pests and pathogens here, and the dam building that has trapped sediments and shifted coastlines. The scientists operating the flux tower were well aware of the ecological complexities of the site and they had a good idea of the history of this landscape. These histories of socioecological transformation did not fit within the systems models that they used to simulate the breath of forests at a national or global scale. By freezing the entities that they measured (carbon dioxide concentrations, energy flow, wind speed) their models allowed them to tell large-scale stories of regional or even global environmental change. These necessary simplifications prevented their models from attending to the transformations that emerged through encounters between plants, soils, people, and diseases.

Complexity surfaces in different ways for ecologists and ecologically minded anthropologists and historians. Eugenio is a skilled ecologist who notices the details of soil and weather and thinks about bacterial responses to rain and drought. It was he who taught me about the spikes in carbon dioxide production that are the result of increased bacterial respiration when dry spells are broken by a light rain. For ecologists from Northern Europe and the United States, these spikes could have been interpreted as artefacts or errors to be cleaned by algorithms, or they could have completely undermined the credibility of San Rossore data. Italian ecologists had to persuade their northern colleagues that these spikes were due to the sandy soils and Mediterranean climate of San Rossore. Once these concerns had been allayed, droughty soils and hot summers no longer mattered to outsiders. Complexity had been tamed in order to sustain valuable simplification and the production of clean data. Once a data infrastructure, such as the carbon flux network, has been established, it limits the entities that can be measured, and it prevents the transformations of these entities until a new data infrastructure is built.[12] Once the flux tower was set up, disease, drought, or pine cone gathering could have invalidated the simplifying assumptions that sustained calculation of the value of Net Ecosystem Exchange. A global data infrastructure of instruments, algorithms, and data standards was kept going by Italian scientists, who prevented the complexities of bacteria/leaf litter/drought/rain relationships from overwhelming necessary simplification.

The forester Francesca Logli and I share an orientation to complexity and to the morphological transformations that emerge through relationships between entities. We notice the sap flows that show insect infestation, the shape of tree crowns that tells of histories of cultivation, the subtle shifts in topography beneath our feet that tell of ancient sand dunes. For this kind of landscape knowledge, each encounter and moment of noticing is a potential surprise. As I encounter each pine tree, I ask myself if it resembles previous trees or whether it is something new. Is this tree like other trees I have seen so far, healthy and shaped to maximize pine nut production? Or is it sick and on the verge of death because of a new relationship with an invasive pathogen or an insect pest? Each tree I encounter might have a different morphology and history; it might suffer from a new disease or it might demonstrate traces of a different kind of human care. At its best, a perception of landscape structure emerges from an alertness to the morphologies of trees and soils as form coming into being. At its worst, a perception of landscape structure can make me confident and incurious, allowing me to assume that I know what I am looking at. "One more stone pine just like the last," I might mumble under my breath, thinking about getting home in time for dinner. Toward the end of my visit to the park, Francesca directed my attention to certain trees and changed my understanding of landscape structure and of the humans who had cared for trees. Driving along an alley of stone pine, she pointed out a series of Y-shaped forks (figure 57). The shapes of these trees had been produced by pine nut gatherers who trimmed the leading shoot of young trees in order to produce a forked shape that was easier to climb.[13] Tree climbing was abandoned forty years ago when US army surplus vehicles were adapted to vibrate pine cones off trees. The park foresters had retained these trees out of a sense of tradition.

I learned from Francesca to notice a new landscape structure of areas of forked and of straight pine trees. I learned to imagine the social histories of pine nut gatherers who had changed their tending practices and of the trees that had responded to them. This history of commodity production and human/plant interaction reached beyond the moment when Francesca taught me to notice these pine trees as something different. Noticing landscape structures required me to continually imagine the histories that had produced them. Alertness to landscape structure requires an openness to what anthropologist Eduardo Viveiros de Castro calls the "ontological anarchy" of the world, but it also requires us to extend our imagination from particular encounters to large scales.[14] As trees are transformed by relations with new beings (diseases, sand dunes, climate change, pine nut gatherers), new histories are required to account for new landscape structures. This way of thinking is intensely concerned with the phenomenological experience of

Figure 57. An alley of forked *pino domestico* in San Rossore, 2014. These trees are forked because the leading shoot was trimmed when they were saplings. (Author photograph)

encounters with strange ontologies but also willing to tell large-scale stories of changing political economies and ecologies.

Changing land use, invasive insects, and pathogen outbreaks are often greater immediate threats to forests than climate change. International trade is an increasing contributor to pest and pathogen outbreaks that damage forests around the world. International travel and the consumption of wild animals for food may have driven the coronavirus epidemic that is raging as I write these words. Climate change can increase the geographical range and intensity of fires, pests, and pathogen outbreaks, potentially undermining the calculations of carbon absorption by forests that climate change negotiators care about. In San Rossore dying maritime pine and plummeting production of pine nuts by stone pines were both the result of insect pests. On the Monte Pisano, as we have seen, chestnut distribution and cultivation changed drastically as a result of the pathogens *Phytophthora cambivora* and *Cryphonectria parasitica*. There too maritime pine has been struck by the

Matsucoccus feytaudi scale insect, leaving dead and dying trees and a dangerously flammable landscape. The 2019 fires on the Monte Pisano were due to a combination of climate change, disease, and land-use change. For pine nut gatherers in San Rossore, pest and disease outbreaks were the environmental change that mattered, rather than climate change. As the pine nut gatherer Alsio Grassini told me, "For me all of nature is sick. We are nature too."[15] Plant disease was everywhere, involving human bodies and landscapes. Our conversation in the fall of 2013 took place at an apocalyptic moment. In nearby mountains the gall wasp *Torymus sinensis* had caused a 90 percent decline in chestnut production. Pine nut production in San Rossore had declined by a similar fraction. Other diseases had attacked his peaches and pears. It was no wonder that climate change had little traction on his imagination. Francesca Logli was more worried about reducing deer populations and managing dying *pino marittimo*. It was not that either of them doubted that climate change was real, but they had more immediate concerns. The global environmental change that mattered most to them was the landscape of disease that they had to live with.

Ecological Modeling as Empirical Storytelling

Much work is required to translate data from San Rossore into models of forests' response to climate change. This is not merely about data collection and formatting. Italian ecological modelers draw upon their sense of history and their phenomenological experience of landscape as they adapt ecological models built elsewhere to drought-prone postpeasant forests. The results of their work are not straightforward predictions. These are extrapolations from model simplifications, "as if" accounts that partially capture uncertainty and indeterminacy. This is bold and important thinking, a kind of scientific cartooning that communicates some part of the indefinite complexity of ecosystems. These ecological models are modest relatives of the giant global climate change models that are run on supercomputers. They share the same properties of necessary simplification, of freezing entities and relations, and of ignoring historical contingency. By following these ecological models, we can learn how systems models both silence and illuminate environmental change, and we can see how ecologists connect the abstractions of global climate change to the landscapes they work in.[16]

In June of 2014 I visited one of the places where the response of Italian forests to climate change was being modeled, on the CNR (Centro Nazionale di Ricerche) research campus outside Firenze. On the mountains behind, as often in Italy, blocks of conifer plantations testified to Cold War–era reforestation. Blocky red buildings were scattered across a grassy plain that was grazed by a few sheep. When I went inside, I found that peasant landscape practices also haunted the computer models through which scientists simulated the movements of carbon, nitrogen, and water through Italian forests.

The ecologists Fabio Maselli and Marta Chiesi have combined two well-respected models to simulate the response of Italian forests to climate change. The widely used C-Fix model, developed by Belgian scientists, combined satellite images of forests with data about solar radiation and air temperature to estimate net photosynthesis. The second model, BIOME-BGC, built at the University of Montana, simulated the fluxes of carbon, nitrogen, and water through ecosystems, combining daily climate data with information about soil and vegetation. BIOME-BGC had been built to make sense of North American forests, and Fabio and Marta had to adjust it to make it work with dry and hot postpeasant Mediterranean forests. Huddled over a computer screen, they showed me the results of their simulations, colored images of carbon absorption by Tuscan and Italian forests. Between them, Fabio and Marta had modified BIOME-BGC to incorporate their sense of the ecology and history of the Italian landscape, of the water stress produced by long and hot summers, and of the histories of firewood cutting that left forests with incomplete canopy cover. In deciding to use BIOME-BGC, they had to consider the genealogy of this model, the fact that it had been shown to work for a range of forests, and the availability of data required by the combined C-Fix and BIOME-BGC models. They had to decide which data to trust, and they had to estimate or measure required parameters. Their empirical storytelling took place within the limits imposed by their institutional location, by their access to resources, and by their sense of the ecosystems that they lived in.[17]

The forests of the American West are very different from those of the Mediterranean. Crucially, BIOME-BGC assumes that in mature forests, Net Primary Productivity (NPP), respiration, and decay will be in a "quasi-climax" equilibrium with each other.[18] Italian forests have been cut for firewood and charcoal for many centuries and continue to be cut heavily. These forests are very far from attaining any assumed equilibrium. Fabio and Marta, as do I, have a clear sense of the histories of firewood cutting, charcoal burning, and grazing that have reduced the biomass of Italian forests. I remember the patch of woodland above my grandmother's house near Arezzo. Centuries of firewood cutting had left stunted *cerro* (*Quercus cerris*, Turkey oak) growing achingly slowly on shallow and dry soils. In many industrialized countries, firewood cutting decreased with urbanization and industrialization, but in Italy it has continued unabated.

Fabio and Marta had to figure out a way to incorporate their sense of the difference of Italian forest landscapes into an American model. Their solution was pragmatic and imaginative. They made the simplifying assumption that "tree volume, which is directly related to woody biomass, can be taken as an indicator of ecosystem proximity to equilibrium condition," and they decided to exclude shrubs and grasses, as "they only marginally accumulate woody biomass and tend to a climax equilibrium." This decision addressed the reality that data on tree volume could be produced by combining satellite images with the forest inventory of Tuscan forests.[19] As in most of the world, the Tuscany region and the Italian government have historically been concerned with timber and firewood production, and forest inventories have concentrated on the volume of tree trunks. Foresters have paid little attention to shrubs, and forest inventories rarely measure such trees. The history of state forestry gives rise to the kinds of data available to ecologists.

In response to data constraints and landscape history, Fabio and Marta came up with an additional simplifying term to add to the core equation of BIOME-BGC. This added term, "NV_A"—normalized actual volume—compared heavily logged postpeasant Italian forests with the "quasi-climax" forests assumed by American modelers. The histories of Italian forests, and Marta and Fabio's sense of the ecological relations present in these forests, were condensed into a single variable in a relatively simple equation for Net

Primary Productivity, NPP. (See appendix 2 for a discussion of these modifications.) A helpful way of thinking about equations is as stories about relationships between entities. The NPP equation is a story about plants photosynthesizing solar energy and growing in biomass, and about the loss of biomass through maintenance respiration. Net Ecosystem Exchange, NEE, adds the respiration by animals and other organisms. These equations are both causal accounts of relations between entities and means of defining which entities will be measured. The measurements taken by the carbon flux tower at San Rossore rely upon the distinction between plants (autotrophs) that produce their own biomass, and the beings who break this biomass down through respiration (heterotrophs), allowing the compartments of the NEE equation to be filled in.

Heat, Drought, and Parametrization

Summers in Italy, as across the Mediterranean, are fiercely hot with long dry spells. Most rain falls in the winter, and the year-to-year variations in precipitation dwarf the long-term changes in average rainfall caused by climate change. In these challenging conditions plants have evolved morphological adaptations and physiological strategies that help them retain water and function with a limited water supply. Mediterranean oaks, for example, have waxy or hairy leaves; they close their stomates to retain water, and they build deep root systems to drink water from the soil. Pines are still better adapted to drought, with waxy needles and sunken stomates. Like these plants, Fabio and Marta had experienced dry and hot summers in the course of their daily lives and research work. They knew that BIOME-BGC would have to be modified to accommodate these extremes. In earlier work, Marta had measured and remeasured leaf-area index and sap flow in an oak forest near Radicondoli, a particularly hot and dry area in southern Tuscany, seeking to characterize the responses of plants to heat and drought. From such measurements and from skilled estimations, she produced parameters for "maximum stomatal conductance" (which expressed the capacity of leaves to retain water) and "fraction of leaf N in Rubisco" (which expressed the capacity of leaves to photosynthesize). Modifying these parameters to fit

Mediterranean forests gave the equations at the heart of BIOME-BGC ecological realism and purchase on the landscape.[20] A single number contained a story, of how evergreen oaks tolerated drought stress by closing their stomates; another number, of how mountain beech forests struggled to grow during dry summers. Equations contained stories about scientists' experiences of Italian forests responding to weather.

In order to run their models, Fabio and Marta had to evaluate the credibility of available data and think about the limitations of the instruments or surveys that had produced it. For example, they excluded eddy covariance flux data with anomalies that they could not account for. One such anomaly might have been caused by the retirement of the scientist responsible for a particular data series. They were also doubtful of regional and national forest inventories, wondering whether there might have been a systematic failure to measure small trees. Good scientists like Fabio and Marta have to distrust their data and inquire about the histories that brought it into being. When anomalies surface, they do archaeology and ethnography to figure out if the data can be trusted or how it should be adjusted. They ask about the location of a weather station or the biographies of people and institutions in ways that are familiar to anthropologists and historians. Historical climatologists reevaluate weather station data by reconstructing histories of the instruments and measurement practices through which weather data was originally gathered.[21] Such work becomes ever more burdensome as models and data sets become larger, and the moments when history can be thought about are often limited to the moments of model building and parametrization.

Models as Diagrams that Capture Uncertainty

Once key equations have been formed, parameters have been measured, calculated, or guessed, and data has been collected, cleaned, and standardized, a model can be run. Ontologies of key entities have been fixed; the relationships between these entities has been defined; history has been baked into key equations and variables. Only then can speculative projections of these necessary simplifications take place. Fabio and Marta, for example, classified forests into types that were assumed to respond to climate change in the same way. This was a simplifying "as if" story, which allowed a principled extrapolation of the response of Italian forests to climate change. In their conversations with me and in their publications, Fabio and Marta did what modelers are expected to do. They demonstrated how well the model accounted for the available data and they carefully discussed sources of error and uncertainty. Their personal experiences of hot summers, and their knowledge of the shallow dry soils on which many Italian mountain forests grow, led them also to have a strong sense of the ecological processes that mattered for these particular forests. We might say that they were crafting their model as a literary/causal account that emerged from their experiences of particular forest landscapes and that imperfectly captured the uncertainty of the world. This new model was validated by assessing errors and by comparison with more established models.[22]

Ecological models of this kind do not so much represent what the world *is* as produce understandings of aspects of the world that can be explored with carefully chosen simplifications. A model is a projection, a kind of empirical cartoon that emerges from a provisional stabilization of entities and relationships. Forests are breathing, leaves are growing, and carbon and water are moving in and out of forests. Simplifying and simulating these processes helps scientists understand ecosystems better, perhaps ultimately helping make predictions about how forests will respond to climate change. Such empirical cartoons are not judged as representations of the world, but as creative simplifications that contain uncertainty and indeterminacy and increase ecological understanding. The map in figure 58, for example, used the combined and domesticated BIOME-BGC/C-Fix models to show primary productivity of Italian forests, drawing upon many data sets, including carbon flux data from San Rossore. At first glance this may look like a realist representation of the world. Perhaps it looks like a satellite image? It is stranger and more interesting. It is a diagram of how forests *could* grow if the authors' simplifications are ecologically sensible and are not invalidated by new surprises. Through many webs of translation and transformation, Fabio and Marta's sense of hot summers and postpeasant landscapes inhabited this projection.

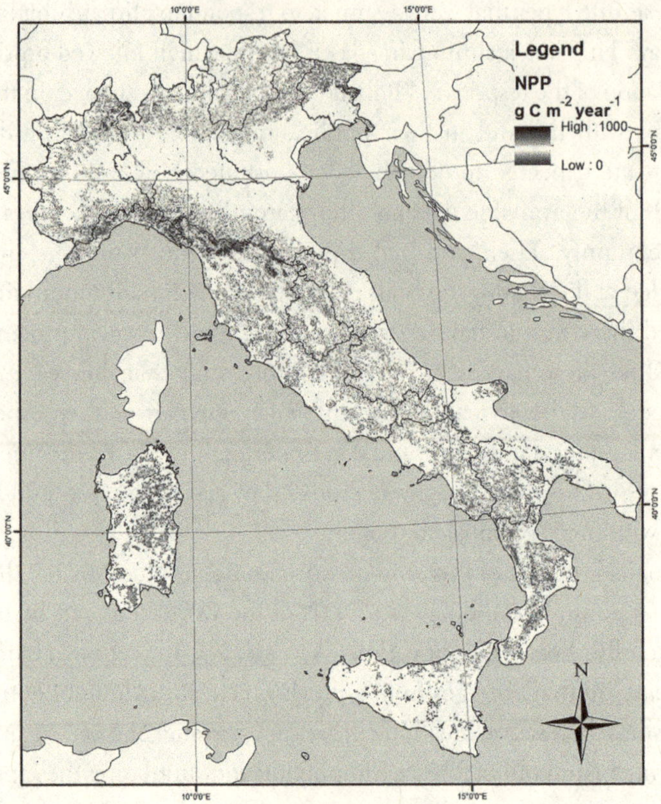

Figure 58. Net Primary Productivity of Italian forests. Darker areas are more productive: Chirici, Gherardo, Marta Chiesi, Piermaria Corona, Nicola Puletti, Matteo Mura, and Fabio Maselli. (Reprinted by permission from Springer Nature, copyright 2015. "Prediction of Forest NPP in Italy by the Combination of Ground and Remote Sensing Data." *European Journal of Forest Research* 134, no. 3 [2015]: 453–67. https://doi.org/10.1007/s10342-015-0864-4)

This image was deeply political, as the scientists who produced it were well aware. It showed how much and where carbon was being absorbed across the Italian landscape. The location of carbon absorption was of interest to European Union policymakers, to the national and regional government, and to biomass energy entrepreneurs who were trying to build a sustainable energy system in Italy. This image implicitly called for regional or national institutions to manage this carbon, what STS scholar Sheila Jasanoff calls the coproduction of knowledge and political authority.[23] As we shall see, efforts to map carbon stored in forests inspire state efforts to support biomass energy plants.

Histories of the Future

Simulation models such as BIOME-BGC necessarily simplify and freeze ontologies and relationships between entities. Modelers call changes in these simplifications violations of the "stationarity assumption" required for their models to work properly. This necessary assumption makes models rigid in the face of surprising events and ontological transformations. Simulation models, including the models built by Fabio and Marta, cannot contemplate the impacts of events such as insect pests, pathogen epidemics, or socioeconomic changes that might radically change the carbon absorption capacities of forests. One way that modelers address these problems of surprise and transformation is to simulate the effects of multiple scenarios of the future. If model thinking requires a freezing of history in order to allow projections of the future, historical thinking reemerges in scenario modeling that takes place *after* model building. Scenarios are story lines about plausible futures whose probability is inherently incalculable. Standard scenarios of plausible climate futures, generated by the United Nations Intergovernmental Panel on Climate Change (IPCC), are known as Representative Concentration Pathways (RCPs). These scenarios incorporate expert ideas about changes in greenhouse gas concentrations, landscapes, economies, and energy systems. RCPs are used by scientists who wish to model the effects of climate change upon ecosystems or societies. The range of futures produced through these scenarios brings some diversity of relations and ontologies back into conversation with simulation models.[24] Most scenarios are produced by consultations between small groups of experts who may have little experience of the kinds of rapid social and ecological changes that I have described for the Monte Pisano. Plant disease epidemics and rapid social change are not easy to imagine. In the end, many scenarios are staid and conservative, lacking in the drama that we often see in the world around us.

Scenarios met the BIOME-BGC/C-Fix model in an article wherein Marta Chiesi and her coauthors explored the effects of different climate futures on Tuscan forests. The future climate they chose was produced by one of the most important climate change models in the world, the HadCM3 global circulation model produced by the Hadley Center in the United Kingdom. This climate future, with a 2°C warmer climate by 2046, was considered a "soft landing" by EU scenario builders who had thought about likely trajectories of economy, energy systems, and carbon emissions. A laboratory such as Marta and Fabio's relied upon information about future climates produced by powerful laboratories and institutions. This particular story of the future found that oaks and pines in the lowlands would suffer from hot summers, and that cooler and moister beech and chestnut forests in the mountains would be less affected. Look closely at such an article and you can imagine sweltering summers and slow-growing or dying trees. You would have to look still more closely to find the socioeconomic and ecological futures imagined by the scenario builders who inspired climate change models. Ecologists are careful to underline that any given simulation or model gives a very partial and speculative kind of knowledge about ecological complexity. Marta and her collaborators warned that the assumptions that underlay their model could easily be invalidated, from changing nitrogen deposition to changed species distributions and land-use decisions: "Consequently, all model applications imply a simplification and generalization of these processes, which are strictly dependent on our degree of knowledge of the observed phenomena." Their results were plausible and credible, but they were also partial and humble.[25]

The data infrastructures and the simplifications used by scientists who simulate environmental processes necessarily limit the ecological relationships that they can incorporate into their models. Scientists' much more expansive theoretical and phenomenological sense of ecosystems and landscapes, of glaciers, or of atmospheres are the preconditions for the simplifications required by systems models. Even the relatively uniform and simple pine forests of San Rossore have to be greatly simplified if they are to be incorporated into measurements of carbon dioxide absorbed and emitted by growing trees. Model simplifications and data infrastructures support Marta and Fabio's accounts of regional and national environmental change.

History enters their models when they build equations and set parameters. The success of their modeling approach is a sign that they have addressed the socioecological history of Italian landscapes. The absence of history from ecological modeling (and from climate change modeling) is caused more by the rhythms of work than by scientists' lack of appreciation for its importance. Ecological modelers may find it impractical to consider the kinds of histories of changing plant, pathogen, and social behaviors that I have described for San Rossore and the Monte Pisano. Nevertheless, their underlying awareness of ecological complexity resonates with the landscape descriptions in previous chapters.

The kind of evidence that anthropologists and historians produce about landscapes is important for broadening our understandings of the kinds of events that can cause regional and global environmental change. Through our keen eyes and our open-ended curiosity we can notice the possibility of changing relations between beings that are registered in the morphologies of plants, in changing landscape structures, and in unanticipated social transformations. The disappearance of a key tree species or forest type due to a pathogen has major consequences for carbon emissions, water, and nitrogen cycling. The transformation of smallholder agriculture to industrial agriculture, as happened in Italy in the 1960s, has large-scale consequences. Like modelers, we think about systems, but we are more interested in political economy than in carbon and water cycles. These different systems accounts can complement each other.

As we link systems to landscapes we should remember that model simplifications can give a false sense of stability or inevitability. The real world is likely much less stable than the models we build to describe it, something that natural scientists increasingly worry about. Earth systems modelers have warned that some of the largest global models do not accommodate the possibility of "biogeophysical feedbacks" and "tipping cascades" that can cause sudden changes in global systems.[26] They list disastrous events ranging from permafrost thawing to the release of methane from ocean methane hydrates, from increased bacterial respiration from oceans to Amazon forest dieback due to drought. Events such as the disappearance of a key plant species due to a pathogen epidemic, or the devastating economic and social consequences of a global flu pandemic are recurring features of history. The kinds of ecological and social surprises that anthropologists and historians notice through accounts of changing morphologies, landscape structures, and social transformations may have large-scale systems-transforming consequences and undermine our expectations of the future.

By walking through the forests of San Rossore I have learned to recognize the impact of the insects *Matsucoccus feytaudi* upon *pino marittimo*, and of *Leptoglossus occidentalis* upon stone pine. I have also learned to recognize the difference between forked trees planted by pine nut gatherers who were willing to climb trees, and trees that have been planted to be picked by machines. Insect pests and pathogen epidemics are surprising new relations between pathogens, insects, and plants. New machines and collecting practices emerged through contact with American machinery after World War II. Such ecological and social surprises are predictably increased by globalization and international trade. As we have seen, ecological and climate modelers cannot easily incorporate these kinds of surprises, while scenario builders are usually unaware of the long history of pathogen outbreaks, and they are often unaware of social diversity and transformation. In the Monte Pisano, sweet chestnut entirely changed its distribution in response to the first wave of *Phytophthora cambivora* in the 1860s. Such an event is entirely beyond the capacities of most people to imagine. It was only by patiently walking and looking at these landscapes, by the work of tacking back and forth between oral histories and contemporary accounts, between tax registers, maps, and descriptions of contemporary landscapes, that I was able to pick up the echo of this devastating event. Through the combination of archival research with my own capacities to notice and to speculate as to the causes of landscape patterns, I produced a historical account of the destruction of low-elevation chestnut forests. This was a horror story, where moving plants around the world caused a punishment out of all proportion to the crime. This horror history could inspire a scenario about the changed behavior of a plant species in response to the combined effects of disease and land-use change. The rapid spread of the *Xyllela* bacteria currently attacking olive trees in Italy demonstrates that this is an all-too-realistic scenario.[27] The social transformations caused by the current

COVID-19 pandemic further underline how narrow our imaginations of social change can be.

A second disease, the chestnut canker *Cryphonectria parasitica,* produced a different story. This story is a story of horror halted and averted but not eliminated. As we saw in chapter 3, *Cryphonectria* fungus was made hypovirulent by a virus.[28] A surprising new relation between the fungus and the disease changed it from a devastating killer to a more mundane annoyance. Whereas in North America *Cryphonectria* almost eliminated the American chestnut between 1900 and 1940, in Italy it largely lost its power to kill. The killer in Italy was not the disease, but the fear that the disease elicited, the intentional cutting of chestnut groves that seemed to be doomed, of little use in a world of industrial agriculture and urbanization. Climate change mitigation policies that boldly assume the disappearance of a species or an economic system can benefit from such stories of surprising survival and of official mistakes. Plants and animals change forms and behaviors, and people change their imaginations of how they wish to live in the world. These transformations are not captured by stories of modernization or decline. Climate change mitigation policies that seek to convert forests to biomass energy might be worse than climate change impacts.

Final Thoughts

In this chapter I have set up an awkward comparison between the kind of knowledge that a historically minded anthropologist with a curiosity about trees and landscape can produce, and the kinds of simulations and projections that ecologists can produce. I have suggested that there is a surprising echo between our different forms of curiosity. Each places a call upon the other. We might think of this as a kind of assonance, a partial rhyming between ways of knowing that does not insist upon too much similarity. First of all, let us consider the similarities.

Both for model thinking and my practice of ethnographic historical ecology, descriptions are partial, conditional, and humble. A description is a kind of sketch that explains some of the uncertainty in the world but remains anchored against uncertainty and indeterminacy. The line drawings I used to describe chestnut trees and landscape structures in the Monte Pisano are cousins to the algorithms and simulations produced by Fabio and Marta. Both are deliberate simplifications, partial descriptions that contain uncertainty and indeterminacy. For all of us, the relationships that we notice in particular landscapes inspire storytelling at larger temporal and spatial scales.

An important difference between anthropological and ecological thinking lies in the *way* that we extend our empirical imagination from our phenomenological experiences of landscapes. Anthropological and historical storytelling is to some extent open-ended and departs from the mundane ontological indeterminacy of trees, soils, and people. By comparing morphological details across landscape patches we can notice landscape structures, and we can come up with the histories that produced them. When I notice that pine forests in San Rossore and chestnut forests in the Monte Pisano are both dying due to exotic pathogens and pests, I can come up with an account of the history that has produced these disasters. Global trade is increasing the spread of pests and pathogens. Plant nurseries and the trade in live plants accelerate these processes. Ecological modelers, in contrast, have to choose a relatively small number of state variables and causal relations to track through the lifetime of their model run. In exchange for this simplification they can describe regional or global environmental change, but they have little chance of thinking about global trade, plant disease, or social change. Anthropological and historical ecology methods can support regional accounts of social and ecological change that provide a critical counterpoint to the simplifying effects of national or global ecological models, including climate change models.

Ecological modelers have a gift for anthropologists and historians who often assume that ecological models, including climate models, are realist representations of the world. This is an understandable mistake, especially when scientists produce images that look so much like satellite images. The heat maps of global climate change familiar to many of us are similar. These are not representations of climate or of forests absorbing carbon, however. These are diagrams that communicate modelers' understandings of climate systems or forests. Simulation models are formal accounts that give some sense of processes and events in the world. In model thinking, description is partial and sits with uncertainty and indeterminacy. Ecological models, including climate models, are the diagrammatic forms of reasoning that build from modelers' practical experiences and theoretical understandings. Ecological modelers can help anthropologists think about how their empirical practices of noticing might be extended to other scales in time and space in order to accompany our long-standing interest in such topics as capitalism or the state. Thinking with modelers suggests that we can be bolder in coming up with diagrams that represent the ontologies and relations that matter. We can escape Cartesian space, as in Bruno Latour's recent collaboration with critical-zone scientists, or we can diagram coordinations between people and plants.[29] Such diagrammatic forms of reasoning are a kind of imaginative extension of encounters with the morphologies of trees, terracing and drainage systems, and with landscape structures. Extending our noticing to think about larger scales in time and space by attending to morphology and pattern helps us notice the histories and material rhythms that inhabit the world.

Ecological modelers, anthropologists, and historians agree on other things. Historians and anthropologists do not usually tell one history. We are comfortable with what anthropologist Anna Tsing calls a "rush of stories." So too, scientists understand that their models are formally independent from one another and that no one model is the best description of the world. Climate change modelers understand that every model works better for some processes, for some geographical and temporal scales than for others.[30] The ecologists I talk to think hard about which models work best for which processes and at which scales. The landscape structures of pine and chestnut forests on the Monte Pisano visibly overlap each other while being linked to different histories of land use and disease. Multiple histories are like multiple models. They partially capture the uncertainty and indeterminacy of the world, and they can operate at different time scales. Scientists' tolerance for multiple models should inspire us to provide accounts of socioenvironmental change that contain multiple temporal rhythms.

Historical ecology, anthropology, and history can broaden our imaginations of social and ecological change, but these methods also raise political and ethical dilemmas. I have compared ordinary people's understandings of climate, landscape, and history with the impersonal frame of climate change science. This distance between official and vernacular conceptions of climate is one reason for the failure of climate change policies. We might feel comfortable with supporting ordinary people against impersonal science. This is too easy. The evidence of pathogen epidemics that I have recovered through historical ecological methods and oral history with elderly people is, like climate change, unknown to most people. I find myself disagreeing with some of the people I talk to about environmental change in the Monte Pisano, even when I am in sympathy with them. If we are producing evidence of intertwined social and ecological changes, we are no longer commentators on or (very occasionally) participants in social action—the more usual roles for social scientists. We are no longer delegating to natural scientists the task of describing the environment while we take up our allotted task of describing the social. We are implicated and accountable both to social and ecological processes. We have to trust our senses as well as what people tell us. We can produce accounts of socioecological transformation that are not known to others. Part of an answer to this uncomfortable dilemma is that we have to be willing to hold in tension the kinds of knowledge that climate scientists, ordinary people, historical ecology, and our own senses can produce. Each has something to say and they will not always agree. The tension between these different accounts can be productive. The rhythms of pathogen epidemics, twentieth-century landscape abandonment, and twenty-first-century climate change can coexist.

As we have seen, global climate change and landscape history are brought into conversation through the work of ecological modelers who study forests. Even for natural scientists, it takes work to link the climate of global circulation models to the landscapes they live in. Climate is one thing for climate change modelers, a slightly different thing for ecological modelers, and still another for ordinary people. Keeping these distinctions clear makes visible the work of translation that takes place as ideas about climate change are moved around the world by officials, scientists, and ordinary people. The climate change of policymakers is not the climate of scientists. The kind of model thinking that I learned by traveling from San Rossore to Sesto Fiorentino is not the kind of carbon modeling that drives sustainable energy policy in Italy or elsewhere around the world. Ecological modelers like Fabio and Marta wish to learn about complex processes; they care about nitrogen, water, and species distributions as well as about carbon. They carefully link their understandings of ecological processes and histories to climate change models, but they are deeply aware of the limits of models and carefully humble in their conclusions. The models they build are "models of," which increase understanding, rather than "models for," which support state policies.[31] Not far from the campus where they worked, a much simpler and more deterministic model of connections between forests and climate was built by policymakers who used national forest inventories that showed forests as a "carbon sink," which absorbed carbon dioxide from the atmosphere. The location and quantity of carbon absorbed in Tuscan forests supported a political project to slow down climate change by building biomass energy plants across the region.

SEVEN

From Climate Change to Biomass Energy

On a cold January morning I was stamping my feet, trying to keep warm, and waiting for the speeches to start.[1] About fifty or sixty people had gathered to celebrate the inauguration of a biomass energy plant on the outskirts of the small town of Montevarchi (figure 59). Tucked in next to a highway overpass, across the road from a tangle of untended grapevines, was the two-story green steel structure of the biomass energy plant. The power plant would provide enough electricity to supply about 250 average American homes. By burning wood chips to produce heat and electricity, this power plant, with a peak production of one megawatt of electricity, took a small step toward replacing the fossil fuel combustion that is causing climate change.

On this cold winter morning the mayor of Montevarchi and regional politicians explained how this modest structure had been financed and how it would heat homes and provide electricity and jobs. At this moment European Union climate change policies and the commitments of the Italian state were translated into concrete actions. Entrepreneurial officials, scientists, and politicians in the regional capital of Firenze had seen a way to attract government subsidies that would help translate Tuscany's forest wealth into jobs for local people. Their goal was to build a supply chain that would link forests to a web of biomass energy plants across the region. As a forest-rich region with a long tradition of scientific forestry and a cadre of well-trained scientists, Tuscany could take the lead in converting forests into a supply of sustainable energy that would boost rural employment and care for the landscape.[2] Subsidies for sustainable energy could be captured by towns and companies that had the necessary connections and bureaucratic skills to put projects together.

As is customary at ribbon opening ceremonies around the world, political and administrative supporters were warmly acknowledged. The representative of the mountain communities, Oreste Giurlani, told us how this project had been made possible by his close collaboration with regional officials. "Two years ago the regional premier and I got to work, saying that a short supply chain [*filiera corta*] from wood to energy could be an opportunity for the territory, for employment, and above all, for doing something fundamental for cultivating the forest, which is at risk that no one [is cultivating it] anymore, and then seeing the disastrous effects of the hydrogeological instability that results."[3] Tuscany was rich in trees, indeed, too full of trees! In some parts of the world, he told us, people planted trees when babies were born. In his town in the mountains, when a baby was born they had to cut a hectare of forest because otherwise humans would be hemmed in. "If trees voted in the mountains, we would have another weight," he told us.

A councillor from the regional government spoke of the need to link agriculture, environment, and landscape (*paesaggio*) into a unified concept of territory (*territorio*). He warned of the "interests that are behind cultural positions" that saw landscape as a solely aesthetic resource. This remark hinted at the fearsome powers of the Soprintendenza Archeologia Belle Arti e Paesaggio of the Ministry of Culture, which can prevent development in the name of "landscape values" (*beni paesaggistici*), and at the difficulties rural people face in a tourist-dominated economy. He offered an alternative vision of territory as a working landscape cared for by humans: "The forest has to be worked because if we don't work it the forest will be finished." The idea of leaving the forest to itself, was, he told us, "a bucolic imagination that has never existed," a dream that had been made possible because some people thought that oil and natural gas could allow them to do without forests.[4] This power plant was helping people take care of forests and landscape stability while also protecting air quality, verified by the fearsomely independent bureaucracy of the local health authorities. The biomass that went into this plant would be "virgin biomass," not the urban food wastes or industrial residues that might produce contamination. Short supply chains would link forests on nearby hillsides with a local economy of firewood cutters, truck drivers, and plant operators, providing one megawatt of electricity for the national power grid and four megawatts of heating for nearby residences.

Listening to these speeches I began to realize how many kinds of energy there are. Energy is measured in different ways for different uses, from the theoretical energy rating of a power plant, to the kilowatt hours on an electricity bill; from the thermal units used by heating engineers, to the therms in my monthly gas bill. Energy produced in Montevarchi could be expressed as electricity or heat, and the plant could be rated by peak energy production or by average energy production across the year. Energy can support transportation in cars and airplanes or it can be reduced to measures such as kilojoules, tons of oil equivalent, or kilowatts. Energy produced in Montevarchi could be consumed locally as hot water piped into radiators in nearby homes, or it could travel across the national electricity grid, disappearing into networks of power lines in order to reemerge as light in my apartment in Lucca.

The Montevarchi power plant, with its piles of wood chips, was small enough for me to grasp. With a little additional effort and a few back-of-the-envelope calculations scrawled in my notebook, I began to imagine connections between forests and energy, between visible trees and the invisible energies that powered my daily life. This power plant would burn forty tons of wood chips every day. Call it two large truckfuls a day. I had often seen such trucks of wood chips on the highways. I did another conversion from the tons quoted by engineers to the cubic meters used by firewood cutters and foresters. Something like eighty cubic meters of timber would be cut and chipped by machines every day and converted into energy in this little power plant. This was an imaginable area of forest, something like one hectare of twenty-year-old coppice per day. Approximating greatly, my back-of-the-envelope calculations helped me imagine what this looked like: a square of forest one hundred meters on a side. I knew what that looked like and I could walk across it in a few minutes. Every day another block of forest would disappear into the furnace of this small power plant. I began to wonder about its impact upon the landscape. Could there be enough forest to supply a whole network of such power plants? What would this look like if these were typical industrial-scale power plants of over one gigawatt? That would be a thousand times the size of Montevarchi. I began to worry. Montevarchi would consume fifteen thousand tons a year. That was thirty thousand cubic meters of chipped tree trunks, limbs, and branches. That was something like three hundred hectares of the kind of hardscrabble coppice that I had walked across in the Monte Pisano.

Considering that the key rationale for this plant was the replacement of fossil fuel burning in order to prevent climate change, I was struck that climate change itself was not mentioned. The long-term renewable energy goals of the European Union, Italy's obligation to comply with these goals, and a generic commitment to a sustainable future all made an appearance, but climate change was an echoing absence. The possibility that officials could bring national funds to Montevarchi was strongly canvassed, and jobs, air quality, and landscape stability were promoted. The councillor told us that he had to leave early to go to an important congress where "carbon credits" and "renewable energy" would be discussed. These were exciting conversations that might bring jobs to the area. Once again there was no mention of climate change. Somehow climate was too obvious and too abstract, too long-term and too difficult to narrate. He reminded us that "fossil fuel energy supplies are finishing, and in any case, they generate *environmental dramas, dramas against life*, which have an impact upon all of us."[5] Dramas indeed. These politicians were skilled public speakers who knew how to reach their audiences. Collectively they knew that climate change was not dramatic enough and that it could not be part of a persuasive political performance. Climate change could not easily be narrated as a "drama against life." These politicians knew that global climate change was too abstract a concept at too large a scale to have emotional traction. Politicians shared vernacular understandings of climate/soil/land connections that inspired the biogeomorphological politics of landscape care, and they knew that local jobs and air quality mattered more to their audience than climate. Histories of landscape care and abandonment mattered more than stories of global climate crisis.

Figure 59. Waiting for ribbon cutting at the Montevarchi biomass energy plant, 2014. (Author photograph)

In addition to officials and journalists, biomass energy entrepreneurs and opponents were listening, as I found out when chatting with a former municipal official from a nearby town. He told me of "dark forces" that were trying to convert a former sugar mill in his town into a biomass energy plant. He hinted at nameless commercial entities and investments by southern Italian companies with Mafia connections. Biomass might not be biomass at all. Burning this "pseudobiomass" might transform toxic waste into smoke and recycle illicit profits. This kind of conspiracy theorizing is pervasive in daily life in Italy. Speculation often focuses on "southern" support for prominent companies that might be linked to organized crime, from the American-owned wine company that I harvested grapes for as a student, to the roots of the fortune of Silvio Berlusconi, to a proposed biomass energy plant at Bagni di Lucca. In the case of sustainable energy projects, this doubt is further supported by the slippery nature of the term *biomassa* (biomass). In common usage biomassa can range from municipal organic waste, to lawn clippings, crop residues, or "virgin" wood chips straight from the forest. People fear that other kinds of waste could be concealed as biomassa, and their doubt about materials extends to institutions. The fear that waste disposal companies can be colonized by organized crime is well founded. Near Naples, the fertile Campania countryside has become a dumping ground for toxic wastes, as the Camorra services the heavy industries of Northern Europe.[6] Garbage incineration is big business, and people in other parts of Italy fear that organized crime could turn biomass energy in their town into something darker.

The power plant at Montevarchi was part of a network of biomass energy plants that were being promoted by the regional government. Tuscan policymakers had responded rapidly to European Union sustainable energy policies, declaring that as a forest-rich region Tuscany had over 2.5 million cubic meters of "usable biomass" available every year. This estimate did not come from a close understanding of forest use. It was a number that came, as it were, "from above"—an extrapolation of national forest inventories and of estimates that only 40 percent of Italian forest growth was being cut. Rural abandonment had produced overgrown and unused forests, a resource that could be used to build an entirely new infrastructure of biomass energy.[7] Apparently, excess and unused biomass could support up to 135 megawatts of electricity production. We have already seen what a 1-megawatt power plant looks like in Montevarchi and how much forest needs to be cut to sustain it every year. Imagine, then, 135 such power plants spread across the Tuscany region. Move your imagination from megawatts to territory and landscape, from numbers to hillsides and forests. This would be something like four hundred square kilometers of forest cut every year across the Tuscany region.

Biomass energy leaves traces on the landscape, but in order to see them, you have to be willing to travel to firewood depots on the outskirts of towns and to the hillsides where trees are cut. Wood chips and firewood congregate in unglamorous places: the yards of firewood merchants who gather in suburbs, the wood-pellet suppliers who operate from gas stations and supermarkets, the small power plants on the outskirts of towns like Montevarchi. In figure 56 you can see what the aftermath of cutting for biomass energy looks like in the disease-stricken coastal pine forests of San Rossore. Unlike

Figure 60. Yarding machinery and wood chip piles from logging diseased pine for biomass energy in San Rossore, 2014. (Author photograph)

most of the Italian peninsula, this is flat land where heavy logging and yarding machinery can easily reach trees (figure 60). Low-value wood chips from easily logged coastal pine forests, such as in figures 38 and 40, can travel on heavy trucks to power plants across the region. The scale of manual firewood logging is much smaller and can more easily reach the steep slopes where most trees grow (figure 61). Firewood is found in the yards of firewood merchants, in trailers towed at the backs of tractors and delivered to homes. Even as the most remote forests are too expensive to log, forests near roads are intensively cut for firewood. There is little economically accessible "unused" biomass in Italy.

On the flat ancient sand dunes of San Rossore, heavy machinery can easily cut and chip diseased trees. At thirty to forty euros per ton, accessible low-value pine forests near roads are the most profitable to log. The low-value wood chips in figure 60 were likely part of a two-thousand-ton shipload destined for a coal power plant in Sardinia.

Figure 61. Manual logging of firewood in oak forest near Volterra, 2013. (Author photograph)

The coppice of oak and hornbeam in figure 61 was likely destined for firewood merchants in nearby towns, but it could also travel as far as Naples or Sardinia. The standing trees are standards (*matricine*), retained to ensure continuous tree cover. Firewood sells for over ninety euros per ton, making it profitable to manually log steep slopes that machinery cannot reach. Many of the workers who cut such forests are immigrants from the Balkans.

The regional government's decision to build a biomass energy system was the result of a series of translations and transformations, by means of which ideas about climate moved from charismatic global climate models, through the international climate change policy process, to agreements by the Italian government. The simplifications of climate models and national policy documents and energy accounts bumped up against the geomorphological politics of the Italian landscape and were transformed through this encounter.

Biomass Energy and Climate Change

Burning biomass, just like burning oil or coal, emits carbon dioxide and contributes to increasing atmospheric temperatures. It is only through a complex chain of reasoning that burning biomass comes to be seen as a source of renewable energy that also reduces carbon dioxide emissions and slows down climate change. If we look at the diagram of the biogeochemical cycle of carbon (figure 62), we can think of the current epidemic of fossil fuel burning as a vast acceleration of the movement of carbon from underground oil, gas, and coal deposits into atmospheric carbon dioxide. As a result of fossil fuel–powered capitalism, more carbon is now in the atmosphere as carbon dioxide and less is stored in geological formations. In contrast to burning fossil fuels, biomass burning accelerates the movement of carbon dioxide from vegetation into the atmosphere, only to be drawn back out of the atmosphere when plants grow back again. As long as the average quantity of carbon stored in oceans, forests, forest soils, and agricultural landscapes is steady or increasing over time, the energy produced by burning biomass is said to be "carbon neutral." This is a plausible future history, a scenario of forest growth and landscape care in which carbon absorbed from the atmosphere in the future allows carbon to be emitted by burning vegetation in the present. It is this socioecological scenario that makes it possible to imagine that cutting down forests and burning them is "carbon neutral" or "carbon negative," terms that have come from the international climate change policy process. Although many researchers argue that in fact only certain kinds of biomass energy reduce carbon emissions even over the very long term, and that biomass energy accounting is prone to exaggeration and dou-

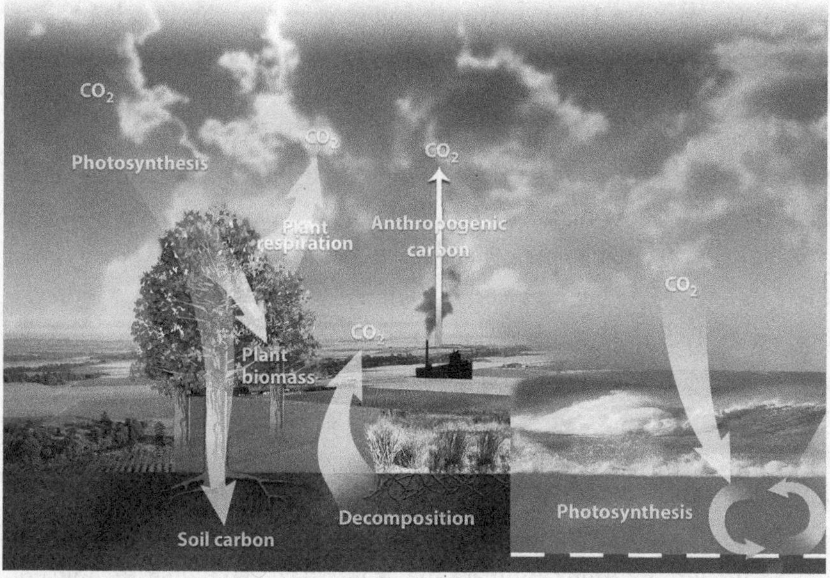

Figure 62. Diagram of the global carbon cycle. (Image from the Office of Biological and Environmental Research of the US Department of Energy Office of Science. science .energy.gov/ber/)

ble counting, global climate policy processes have arrived at the simplification that biomass energy in general is carbon neutral.[8] The political simplification that biomass energy is carbon neutral overrides landscape history, allowing national policymakers to avoid the politically painful task of reducing the fossil fuel burning that still powers our energy system.

The amount of carbon stored in living and dead vegetation is a relatively small part of the complete carbon cycle because most carbon is immobilized in rocks and ocean sediments (see figure 62). The fast carbon cycle, which includes forests, farms, and fossil fuel energy, is another matter, however. In this domain, land-use change and agriculture are major contributors, amounting to about 20 percent of carbon emissions to the atmosphere. Within the field of energy production we might imagine that high-technology solar panels or windmills are more important than burning firewood and charcoal. Even as solar and wind energy are rapidly growing, bioenergy from burning plant material is still the vast majority of the 18 percent of world energy production that is considered renewable. In industrialized countries such as Germany or Denmark, wind and solar energy can be a larger proportion of renewable energy. On a worldwide scale, the most important renewable energy is wood fuel burned by poor people in the global south, as well as biomass burned by a few forest-rich industrialized countries such as Sweden. Faced with the decades that will be required to switch from fossil fuel burning to more high-tech forms of renewable energy, biomass energy provides climate change policymakers with an intermediate stepping stone. Biomass energy can be produced in high-tech energy plants like Montevarchi, but it is almost always a mundane form of energy that is hard to see unless you visit firewood and charcoal depots on the outskirts of towns, or talk to the smallholders and firewood cutters who bring firewood to people's homes. Because of its "carbon neutrality," biomass energy functions as an important placeholder in the UNFCCC (United Nations Framework Convention on Climate Change) treaty process and in national accounts of greenhouse gas emissions. Biomass energy is critical to building credible policy scenarios of a steady shift to a decarbonized energy system that prevents climate change. In spite of treaty commitments by nation-states through the UNFCCC process, fossil fuel emissions have continued to increase steadily. In this context, forests and modern biomass energy have come to take an increasingly important role in the integrated assessment models used by international climate change policymakers. Rather than carbon neutrality alone, "carbon negative" energy systems are increasingly required to balance the books. Biomass energy with carbon capture and storage (BECCS), along with direct air capture of carbon, are the only sources of such negative carbon. These untested and speculative technologies are supposed to safely store carbon dioxide below ground, although for now these are only pilot projects. A recent report from the International Energy Agency, for example, relies largely upon "carbon negative" biomass energy with carbon capture and storage in order to build a scenario of global carbon neutrality by 2050. These "carbon negative" energy systems do not yet exist at any scale. Climate change negotiators find themselves compelled to assume that new and untested technologies will be deployed around the world with unprecedented speed. They also assume that traditional uses of wood for fuel will be entirely replaced by "modern biomass" within a few years.[9] This is a task that generations of rural development projects have struggled with. Smoky fireplaces tended by women in the developing world, and firewood gathering around the world are wrapped into cutting-edge energy policies. Model makers and policymakers know little of the landscapes and lives that their scenarios describe.

International discussions of biomass energy take place in reports and documents that describe national energy accounts. Such reports do not discuss the histories of landscapes or energy systems, nor whether biomass energy is in fact carbon neutral. Industrialized countries such as the United States and the European Union, where forests have grown over the past century, are particularly keen on biomass energy as a preliminary solution to climate change. Rows and columns of figures, of optimistic graphs and pie charts, allow policymakers in conference rooms to imagine that there are large amounts of "unused" biomass available for increased sustainable energy production. This kind of simplification allows modelers and negotiators to engage in what we might call "empty world thinking," which ignores the reality that landscapes around the world are occupied by people who grow food, care for animals, and cut trees for firewood. Such empty world thinking travels through the uncertain channels of policy negotiations and eventually bumps up against full landscapes. Taken to its illogical limit, a total replacement of fossil fuel energy by biomass energy would require a 50 percent increase in the human use of planetary "photosynthetic resources." In a world full of poor farmers and herders, where most agricultural and forest lands are heavily used, this kind of energy shift would be an intolerable impact on ecosystems and societies. Nevertheless, forests seem to promise a kind of "get out of jail free" card, a way of delaying the painful work of reducing or eliminating fossil fuel burning. The importance of forests in climate change imaginaries is demonstrated by the enthusiasm that greeted a study showing that vastly increasing the number of trees around the world could reduce atmospheric carbon dioxide levels by a quarter. Such modeling exercises risk becoming a kind of "empty world" exercise that extrapolates a simplified account of the world to its extreme. Precisely because of its simplicity and attractiveness, planting more trees has become a slogan that unites unlikely allies, from progressives to former president Donald Trump, who committed the United States to the Trillion Tree Campaign at the 2020 World Economic Forum.[10]

One important and almost never fully articulated set of assumptions in efforts to promote biomass energy is the unstated faith that sustainable energy production, including biomass energy, can *replace* fossil fuel energy. It is far from clear how this replacement in fact takes place. In Italy, as in other countries, there are no mechanisms that link the building of a biomass energy plant in one place to the closing of a coal-powered energy plant in another. Faith in energy markets and government subsidies for sustainable energy are the only mechanisms for this transformation. Certainly, cutting down the world's forests is not likely to be a sustainable source of energy if it destroys watersheds, biodiversity, and rural livelihoods. Faced with the disaster of climate change, we might be tempted to forget the other disasters of loss of biodiversity, the displacement of indigenous people and peasants who live in and rely upon much of the world's forests. Critics have rightly focused on the potential damage to forests and livelihoods produced by widespread adoption of biomass energy. This is a demand for climate justice.[11] Nevertheless, around the world, governments have found it easier to propose biomass energy as a "replacement" source of energy, rather than engaging in painful political battles to change their energy systems. Increasing sustainable energy production is not likely to reduce fossil fuel energy production without reductions in energy consumption and without actively changing the energy infrastructure to reduce fossil fuel burning. Concentrating on forests can be a convenient distraction from acting to reduce the burning of coal, oil, and gas.

From Climate Change Treaties to National Energy Policies

Over the past decades, simulation models that demonstrate the existence of global climate change have led to negotiations within the UNFCCC process, where nation-states commit to changing their energy systems and reducing carbon emissions.[12] A series of translations takes place between such international treaties and national government offices, regional planners, and the opening of the biomass energy plant in Montevarchi. Let us follow part of this journey, to see how biogeomorphological politics gradually transformed and silenced "climate" from climate change policies in Italy.

In 2008 the European Union sustainable energy directive established binding goals for renewable energy production by member states. This was known as the 20/20/20 policy because it asked nation-states to reduce greenhouse gas emissions by 20 percent, to increase energy efficiency by 20 percent, and to produce 20 percent of energy from renewable sources by 2020. These goals had teeth. Member states were pressed to take concrete steps toward renewable energy goals through the possibility of fines or other sanctions. Once national baselines of energy production and carbon emissions were agreed upon in negotiation with the European Union, national renewable energy policies were assessed by comparison with a 1990 baseline. For the Italian government, as for most industrialized countries, afforestation caused by rural abandonment meant that biomass energy was a promising component of a national renewable energy strategy. The concept of the "baseline" linked all future energy planning to the past moment against which progress was measured. This baseline was a counterfactual description of what would have happened without renewable energy policies. The lower the proportion of sustainable energy in the baseline year the better subsequent increases would make the country look. It was politically and economically convenient, therefore, for national energy policy to define the baseline renewable energy production very low (5.2 percent in 2010), with a bold national target of 17.5 percent by 2020. For Italy, biomass was to supply the major part of proposed increases in renewable energy because other obvious avenues were closed. As an early-twentieth-century pioneer in hydroelectric power, Italy has already dammed almost all suitable rivers and there would be intense opposition to new dams.[13] The steadily increasing area of forest and the problem of overgrown and unused forests seemed like an easy and politically acceptable source of renewable energy. Drawing upon national forest inventories and firewood production statistics, the government argued that Italian forests were greatly underused and that only 47 percent of annual growth was being cut. These dry statistics summarized a melancholy vision of rural abandonment and overgrown forests, and of the failure to use forest resources that could provide energy and employment. These numbers somehow hovered in the air. Lacking a link to any particular landscape, they allowed officials to find an abundant trove of "unused" biomass. Biomass and biofuels would relatively painlessly supply 44 percent of the country's expanded renewable energy production by 2020. The vision of abandoned and unused forests that drove this plan was based upon official ignorance. Although it is true that the most remote and inaccessible forests are overgrown and uncared for, forests near roads and towns are in fact assiduously logged by a largely invisible network of firewood cutters who help people heat their homes.

According to one estimate, fuelwood consumption in Italy is almost four times the official figures. Far from being an unused resource, a great deal of wood is cut and burned in stoves and small heating plants. Italy had likely already achieved its 2020 sustainable energy goals in 2008 if only one counted the unofficial consumption of firewood for home heating! Many rural firewood users cut their own wood or obtain it from neighbors and friends. In rural Italy it is easy to see firewood advertised through a phone number in a bar. On the outskirts of cities like Lucca people visit firewood merchants to load baskets of logs into the back of cars, or they have someone deliver a load to their home. Many of these transactions are undocumented, passing beneath the legal threshold for a tax declaration, or they are perhaps simply on the margins of the law. Rural producers can avoid the requirement to provide tax documentation if they move firewood with their tractors. Firewood consumption and production are therefore often completely or partially unrecorded by the state. In the wake of the economic crisis of 2008 firewood production increased. In the winter of 2014 farmers and firewood cutters told me that this was the only part of the rural economy that was making any money and that retired people were earning extra money by cutting wood for their friends. Distrust in the state and the need to avoid burdensome documentation meant that rural people avoided declaring firewood production. Distrust and the lack of connection between state and rural people produced the official fantasy of "unused wood" that could be used to produce heat and electricity. Climate change policy was driven by official illusions about rural life and urban firewood use, even as smoke hovered in the air above cities all over Italy. This phenomenon of official ignorance about fuelwood use is not confined to Italy. Around the world climate change policy requires an intense intervention by states into such activities as firewood cutting, livestock grazing, and what is known as "swidden" cultivation in the tropics, whereby farmers cut and burn forest, grow crops for a few years, and then allow forest to return. In many countries, the state has great difficulty eliciting the kind of trust and credibility that would produce reasonably accurate information about what happens in the countryside.[14] Global environmental change has increased the stakes in knowing more about rural landscapes, but the social relations that subordinate rural places to cities produce official ignorance about the countryside.

In Italy firewood burning is one of those public secrets that everyone knows if they stop and think about it. In the winter, columns of woodsmoke rise above small towns and suburban and rural homes. On winter days, a yellow haze of woodsmoke hovers over cities across Italy, as temperature inversions trap smoke and car exhaust for days. Smoke makes visible the morphology of air currents in the basins that surround most cities. As in California, the Italian government tries to control wood burning in order to reduce urban air pollution. In Italy high energy costs and distrust in the state mean that people are determined to continue burning wood. As one young woman on the outskirts of Lucca laughingly told me, "My father burned even more when he heard that it was forbidden!"

A particularly pervasive factoid, which traveled from national energy accounts into official reports and documents, was the statement that only 40 percent of forest increment was being used. This particular number was repeated in the press releases and newspaper accounts that reported the inauguration of the energy plant at Montevarchi.[15] While these rather empty statistics drove the national project of building a renewable energy infrastructure that would mitigate climate change, better informed Tuscan politicians were more interested in using national biomass energy policies and European Union subsidies to stabilize landscapes and secure local jobs. The speechmakers at Montevarchi wove national statistics about lack of tree cutting into local commitments to reduce *rischio idrogeologico* (hydrogeological risk) and build short-distance supply chains that linked forests to furnaces. Popular concern about floods and landslides caused regional politicians to describe an important climate change policy as a project of landscape stabilization and job creation. The biogeomorphological politics linked to histories of peasant labor and land abandonment prevailed over the global climate change that was linked to fossil fuel burning. Concern about landscape stability haunts climate change policy and politics in Tuscany and is the more lively of the two. Even as climate change has become accepted by most people as a reality, it is a concept that has few practical and political connections. Where climate is discussed briefly and in rather abstract terms, care for landscape stability and job creation is something that everyone has an opinion on. People think of the landscape as an infrastructure that is permeable to weather, a morphology that has to be cared for or repaired by state and citizens.

Tuscan Climate Change Science and Biogeomorphology

In contrast to national officials, Tuscan policymakers brought biogeomorphological politics into the heart of climate change and energy policy. The Tuscany region was a leader within Italy in thinking about the impacts of climate change and the potential opportunities that Italian and European Union energy policy might offer. With several major universities and the Accademia Italiana di Scienze Forestali (Italian Academy of Forest Science) near the regional capital of Firenze, Tuscan political and scientific entrepreneurs were well positioned to link forests to climate change policy. By the mid-2000s, the LaMMA research consortium was established in a modern campus on the outskirts of Firenze. The possible climate change impacts they identified ranged from increasing temperatures and declining water supplies that would lead to desertification, soil erosion, effects upon different forest types, the location and quantities of carbon stored in forests, and geomorphological instability. Central to the regional sustainable energy plan were similar concerns over landscape stability. The human modified morphology of the Tuscan landscape combined with climate change to make the region particularly vulnerable to floods and mudslides. The Tuscany region is small enough that environmental officials have a clear idea of the history of the landscape and of its responsiveness to weather. One official, for example, had trained as a geologist and engaged me in a detailed discussion of geomorphology and chestnut cultivation. For her it was intense winter rains, changing seasons, and changing chestnut and hazel flowering that were signs of climate change. She was deeply informed about the details of chestnut cultivation practices in particular Apennine towns, but she also could think about the effect of changing climate. An official who worked on biomass energy had trained as a forester and could talk in detail about the geography of the places where forests were being logged for wood chips or firewood, and about why one power plant was well suited to its location and another, a mistake. This familiarity with landscapes penetrated the regional energy and climate change plan. Postpeasant landscapes and lack of care for landscape morphology haunted a document that declared that investments in flood expansion basins and drainage works were a major climate change policy.[16]

For Tuscan policymakers the possibility of building a biomass energy system was an attractive rural development policy that built on the region's forest wealth and technical expertise, but this project was always firmly connected to geomorphological stability and local markets through an insistence on short supply chains. Biomass power plants were heavily subsidized by the European Union and the Italian government. An additional inducement was the possibility that delinquent regions would have to buy emissions certificates from more virtuous ones. A region such as Tuscany, with the scientific skills to measure the location of carbon stored in its abundant forests, could build a new energy system and increase rural employment. Biomass energy policies were acutely constrained by a commitment to building a short supply chain (*filiera corta*), which would require that wood chips traveled a maximum distance of about seventy kilometers from forest to biomass energy plant. What they did not want, officials firmly told me, was for wood chips to be shipped from abroad and into ports. Short supply chains that linked forests, loggers, truck drivers, and a network of energy power plants would help stabilize overgrown hillsides and provide local jobs.

From Climate Change Models to Energy Landscapes

In this chapter I have sketched the journey from international treaty commitments and national forest statistics to the more confusing reality of building a biomass energy plant in a small town. Climate change models inspired climate change treaty negotiations wherein the simplification that biomass energy was "carbon neutral" took hold. As treaty commitments were translated into national energy policies, aggregated national forestry statistics drove energy policy with only the vaguest connection to landscape history. It was only when energy policy encountered regional and local policymakers that the characteristics of the unstable Tuscan landscape inspired politicians and officials to make biogeomorphological stability a central concern. While climate could be linked to geomorphological stability in regional offices, it became almost unmentionable in the places where climate change policy came to earth, as at the power station outside Montevarchi. The practical politics of building an energy plant that people would trust required that politicians justify the biomass energy plants as a source of jobs and a guarantor of landscape stability. Biogeomorphological politics, which attended to landscape form and to histories of peasant landscape care and abandonment, to the disparate temporalities of floods, landslides, and tree growth, had begun to transform energy plants. The collective popular sense that the landscape was an infrastructure in need of care was more politically compelling than appeals to sustainability or climate change. It was not that climate change did not matter, but rather that the spatial and temporal scale of global climate had few connections to people's sense of the landscape they lived in, nor of the political institutions that they might call to account.

People in Italy find it hard to link climate change to concrete actions in the landscapes they know and care about. This finding is relevant to climate change policy in other parts of the world. In Italy, people use vernacular models of climate/landscape connections to make sense of the riverbeds, hillsides, trees, mudslides, fires, and floods that capture their imagination. These are phenomena that pull humans into fear or love; they demand practical engagement with the biogeomorphological politics of landscape care. In Italy, the Anthropocene rhythm of landscape abandonment is a more immediate disaster than the climate emergency. Even as people talk about summer droughts and warm wet winters as signs of "*cambiamento climatico*," this term has less political traction than their concerns about weather, drought, floods, fires, landscape stability, and employment. In other places around the world, other environmental processes and other political imaginations will produce different responses to climate change. Some people will engage with the term, others will ignore it, and still others will deny it.

Caring for landscape morphology can inspire thinking of landscape as an infrastructure in need of maintenance. In Italy, it was clear to everyone that they lived in a landscape saturated by human care, where history was visible in the shapes of trees and land. One did not have to spend much time thinking about climate change (and most people had little to say about it) in order to act to limit the effects of climate change by maintaining the landscape, whether by cutting trees or maintaining riverbanks. This observation offers a way out of one of the more intractable impasses of climate change policy, the assumption that people need to talk about or "believe in" climate change in order to address it effectively. In Italy people talk in a perfunctory way about climate change before turning to the serious question of how to care for the landscapes they live in. In other places people might not "believe in" or "know about" climate change while acting in order to mitigate its worst impacts. Cattle ranchers in Brazil or farmers in Iowa do not need to use the words "climate change" in order to worry about the conditions of pastures and fields. They are interested in the landscapes that they live and work in. People's experiences of landscape do not always drive the kinds of politics that we might like. In some places people will draw upon their sense of landscape and of politics to support practices that accelerate climate change and damage the environment.

Thinking of landscape as infrastructure makes it possible to imagine the need for investment, maintenance, and repair. The environment becomes a domain that is not an "externality" to pollution, but a kind of green infrastructure that is worthy of investment. Certainly, this is how people I talked to saw this. In recent years, the experience of rural people in Italy, as in much of the industrialized world, has been of abandonment and impoverishment. Industrial agriculture does not need so many workers, and as the older generation retires, young people have few ways of making a living. The biomass energy politics of the Tuscany region responded to this desire for employment through a kind of infrastructural politics. Framing environmental change as a problem of care for landscape as infrastructure does not prevent political conflicts from surfacing. The same questions about the legitimacy of the state, of who should benefit and who be harmed, surface in relation to landscape care and biomass energy, as with any other human project. What is helpful about this way of thinking about politics is that it attends to different temporal rhythms through an attention to landscape morphology. If we see landscape as containing multiple rhythms and histories, we can see how different political projects may call for one or another kind of landscape care. Climate change policy can coexist with political projects that reference Anthropocene histories of landscape change and environmental injustice. As we shall see, climate change policy, and histories of landscape care and of industrial toxicity, were used to support and oppose alternative biomass energy projects near Lucca.

INTERLUDE III

Airscapes

We are used to thinking of the air as a transparent and empty space, somehow not relevant to social life. If we pay attention, however, we notice a sensory "airscape," a domain that can become political. In Italy, where mountains are never far from towns, air becomes visible in the mist, smoke, dust, and plant seeds that it carries and relinquishes to gravity. I suffer from hay fever, and on spring days the air literally feels thick with pollen. I offer these images to pull you into sensing atmospheres that are full, if we only pay attention. In California, forest fires that bring smoke make me notice wind patterns. Try to become attuned to atmospheric morphologies that are revealed by dust, water, and smoke where you live, and the politics of biomass energy in Italy may have a different resonance for you.

Every spring, people prune their olive trees and burn the cuttings, causing pillars of white smoke to rise to the sky (figure 63). Such fires are illegal, but they continue anyway.

Look closely and you can see a haze of smoke across the valley (figure 64). Look still more closely and you can see several pillars of smoke from burning olive cuttings. On winter days the valleys that hold most Italian cities have a brownish/yellowish haze of woodsmoke and smog above them. Atmospheric morphology emerges through smoke and water vapor.

The narrow valley of the Garfagnana, where Bagni di Lucca is located, trapped smoke and vapor on winter days, when I became aware of living at the bottom of an ocean of air. Smoke and steam from a

Figure 63. Olive prunings burning outside Lucca, 2014. (Author photograph)

Figure 64. Smoke and haze across the valley of Lucca, 2014. (Author photograph)

Figure 65. Steam rising from a factory near Bagni di Lucca, in the Garfagnana valley, 2014. (Author photograph)

Figure 66. A hazy summer day near the Larderello geothermal and biomass power plants, Grosseto, 2016. (Author photograph)

factory rise and dissipate (figure 65), making visible the slow movement of air, which feels thicker than on windy days.

A new biomass energy plant is in the foreground; in the background steam emerges from a geothermal power plant (figure 66). On the day I took the picture, the air smelled slightly of sulfur from the geothermal plant.

EIGHT

Landscapes and Energy Politics

If you travel north from the valley of Lucca, the Apennine mountains and the Apuan Alps are an abrupt wall across the horizon. It seems that soon the road will have to start traveling steeply uphill into the mountains. Then, as you come closer, you realize that you will follow the narrow, steep-sided valley of the River Serchio. Beside you, the river powers south, pouring across weirs, passing old mills. Rusting quarry buildings and abandoned factories are interspersed with views of steep cliff faces, of forested slopes and hill towns perched high above. If you are a tourist, you might concentrate on lovely medieval hill towns such as Castelnuovo di Garfagnana and you might prefer not to notice traces of industry. If you consider the morphology of the landscape, however, you will begin to see how mountains and weather have collaborated to make the forty-kilometer valley of the Garfagnana an important location for energy production. On many days the mountains are wreathed with clouds, while sunshine reigns at coastal beach resorts to the west. As clouds encounter these mountains they deposit twenty-five hundred to three thousand millimeters of rain every year, three to four times the precipitation in the valley of Lucca only forty kilometers away. All this rainwater is funneled down steep narrow valleys as streams that run into the River Serchio, which has cut a deep valley through marble and limestone. Wherever the river and its tributaries pass through a gorge or tumble over a rapid, humans have extracted energy from moving water. An infrastructure of water power and hydroelectricity has produced a set of choke points and political opportunities that links the movement of water to human labor and industry.[1] In other places the river spreads across the valley and does work that humans have no use for, depositing sandbars and boulder fields, which are colonized by scrubby poplars and willows. These outwash plains are geomorphological traces of the river's capacity to shift course and to bring sediments down from the mountains. People avoid living in such unstable places. Closer to the coast the river is prevented from spreading by the giant levees that protect the floodplain and city of Lucca.

Tucked into these narrow valleys is a network of dams and old industrial towns that grew up to use first mechanical water power and later hydroelectricity. This was the water-powered industrialization that powered machine works, paper and textile mills in towns such as Barga and Bagni di Lucca in the late nineteenth century. With the rise of fossil fuel–powered industrialization after World War II, many of these towns have declined. Mill buildings have fallen into ruin, and the dams that formerly powered them now produce electricity for the national electricity company, ENEL. There are still paper and pulp factories clustered along the river system. Abundant water makes this a good place to build a factory that needs water for industrial processes or to dissipate heat. Many factories have shut down or need fewer workers than previously. Villages and many small towns are dominated by old people living on their pensions as retired peasants or industrial workers. It can be hard for young people to find a way of making a living here, and well-paid, secure manufacturing jobs are hard to find.[2] As in many rural places, young people who manage to stay often end up working in the tourist economy, whether producing charismatic traditional foods (the cheese, chestnuts, salami, and polenta for which the Garfagnana is known) or working in restaurants and hotels. One such town is Bagni di Lucca, which sits by the River Serchio an hour north of Lucca. This was formerly a spa town favored by travelers who sought out the hot springs. In the sixteenth century the French political thinker Michel de Montaigne visited the hot springs here. By the nineteenth century the town was popular with English travelers and local aristocrats. As travel fashions and ideas of health changed in the twentieth century, the spa entered a long decline. Now it seems like just another quiet country town, with a strip of furniture and shoe stores on the outskirts and a gently fading city center near the river.

When I arrived in the fall of 2013, Bagni di Lucca was the site of a hot controversy. Climate change and the biomass energy policies that it inspired had encountered a tangled politics of postindustrial environmentalism. The Tuscany region's plans for a network of biomass energy plants had been taken up by an alliance of local industrialists and biomass energy entrepreneurs.[3] Their chosen location for a new biomass energy plant was a shuttered paper pulp and tannin factory on the outskirts of town. This would be an enormous installation, producing seventeen megawatts of electricity and forty-eight megawatts of heat and consuming 150,000 tons of wood chips per year. At one fell swoop, over a tenth of regional sustainable energy goals would be taken care of. From the moment it was proposed, the energy plant caused a storm of controversy as local residents argued over its risks and benefits. In 2013 forestry officials told me that after many years of delays, the plant was inevitable. By the fall of 2015, legal proceedings and vociferous local opposition caused investors to withdraw, and the project fell apart. State efforts to build a new biomass energy system encountered rival political factions who drew upon different understandings of landscape and atmosphere to open up the question of what energy was. Local understandings of landscape structure and history and skepticism about the credibility of the state slowed efforts to bring a capitalist supply chain into the countryside. This kind of popular refusal to link forests to electricity has halted or canceled new biomass energy plants across Italy.

A major practical difficulty encountered by biomass energy projects was the problem of accessing tiny parcels of forests scattered on remote mountainsides. This was a landscape laden with "overgrown forests" that were uneconomic to log and administratively difficult to reach. Over 80 percent of forest in Tuscany is privately owned.[4] The vast majority of these properties are less than ten hectares in size, and about 40 percent of Tuscan forests have no officially known owner, a result of the history of land abandonment and migration that has left peasant woodlots overgrown and uncared for. The connections between people and landscape that produced the property form have been broken. Building a new biomass frontier relied upon erasing history and reimagining forests as wood chips, so as to make landscape into property once again. Building a biomass supply chain would bring wood chips to energy plants as a new kind of commodity, but only if logging machinery could reach steep hillsides and if timber buyers could find property owners. Weaving land into property takes ongoing work. This is not a phenomenon unique to Italy. Around the world, wherever population decline and rural abandonment take hold, land can slip quietly beyond ownership, almost without anyone noticing.

Biomass Energy as Landscape Care and Welfare

For supporters of the energy plant, this was an opportunity to reuse abandoned industrial infrastructure to create jobs and stabilize the landscape by cutting overgrown trees.[5] On the outskirts of town the Alce chestnut tannin and paper pulp factory had shut down in 2009. This left over 100 workers in the strange limbo of the *cassa integrazione* (redundancy fund), where the state paid salaries while the company tried to recover.[6] Unlike the vast majority of young and informally employed workers, they could make a kind of welfare claim upon the resources of the state. Founded in 1903, the Alce factory had liquidated the ancient chestnut forests of the region in order to produce tannin, and beginning in the 1950s, it had combined tannin production with cardboard for food packaging. The paper and tannin supply chain had employed 100 workers in the factory, as well as about 350 firewood cutters and drivers. Alce managers argued that a biomass energy plant on the same site would consume little more wood than the former pulp and tannin plant. The new plant would employ some of the former workers and use the existing environmental permits. This was a biogeomorphological politics that promised to provide jobs to laid-off industrial workers and loggers and to remove overgrown trees from abandoned hillsides.

The forested hillsides, the atmospheres of the valley, and the site of the tannin factory were brought into rival histories and projected into different political projects. On the spring day when I visited the site, I saw the rundown buildings around the plant, the rust and soot on the machinery,

Figure 67. Shuttered Alce tannin/pulp factory outside Bagni di Lucca, 2014. (Author photograph)

and the empty parking lot. The hillside behind was feathered with the light green of fresh leaves of invasive acacia that were themselves often laden with ivy. I imagined the industrial workers who had formerly worked here, the trucks that had rumbled through these gates carrying pieces of ancient chestnut trees, the smells and the clouds of steam and dust that had spread across the valley.

This image (figure 67) shows some of what I noticed that day, and I can use it to tell you something about how opponents and supporters of the plant noticed different morphologies and landscape structures. Pay attention not only to the machinery in the foreground, but also to the steep slopes in the background. Opponents and supporters alike noticed the histories of human/nonhuman relationships that had produced the morphologies of overgrown trees, invasive acacias, and destroyed chestnut groves on those slopes. Both opponents and supporters of the energy plant linked the factory to these steep slopes, but they noticed different morphologies, landscape structures, and histories. Both projected their imaginations from the specificity of the social relations of tree cutting that had produced *those* hillsides of acacia and *that* rusty machinery, to larger-scale landscape structures and histories of logging, landscape abandonment, and industrial exploitation. Both could project their sensory experiences from details to large-scale claims as to what the landscape was and how it should be cared for. Everyone could notice tree morphology and claim knowledge of landscape structure, and all could recount history.

The biomass energy entrepreneur whom I call Giuseppe Mela was sure that this plant was a good thing.[7] Crisscrossing much of north and central Tuscany he coordinated purchases of wood chips from landowners and tree-cutting companies. He knew how to talk to woodcutters and officials and how to fill in the forms and reports required to keep this business going. He was deeply versed in the histories of peasant tree cutting and landscape care that had produced this landscape, and he saw the project of biomass energy as offering part of a solution to global climate change. From wood chips that traveled as two-thousand-ton shiploads, to piles of tree limbs at the side of the road, from municipal heating plants in remote Apennine villages to modern biomass energy plants, Giuseppe knew how to stitch together a biomass supply chain.

Giuseppe had an extraordinary depth of knowledge about the history of forests in the region. He told me how people used to cut trees by hand and send firewood to town on the backs of mules, about the technical pros and cons of large and small biomass energy plants. It was he who warned me of the threat of new pathogens, of the danger of oversized biomass energy plants, and of the need for short supply chains. He doubted that in a society where people take hot showers and use computers, energy consumption could be easily reduced. For Giuseppe one of the ways of obtaining clean electricity to feed modern lifestyles was from abandoned forests. Using Italian forests rather than importing wood chips from other countries was also a question of forest health. Local biomass energy could help prevent the arrival of pests and pathogens that were devastating forests in Italy and that had traveled in imported shipping pallets or in wood chips. Giuseppe told me how peasant practices of tree cutting had kept trees from becoming too large and protected hillsides from collapsing into landslides and floods. His argument was based upon observations of tree and landscape morphology. Driving around in his car Giuseppe pointed out to me morphological evidence of forest care and abandonment, of landslide stabilization works, and of ivy climbing on trees, which most people consider a sign of lack of care. The details of particular trees and slopes informed his understanding of a landscape structure of overgrown forests that could be stabilized by skillful logging. Landscape structure was linked to the history of land abandonment in the 1960s, and this history informed the political project of biomass energy.

For biomass energy supporters forested slopes and power plants would be reconnected by renewed cutting. Bringing back loggers to cut trees would stabilize slopes that threatened to slip down onto roads and homes. Logging trucks would once again move through these gates. Industrial workers would once again have the kinds of permanent jobs with benefits that have become so rare in Italy. This was a politics of landscape care that emerged from a skilled reading of tree and landscape morphology and from a sense of landscape structure and history.

Biomass Opponents: Ruined Landscapes and Contaminated Atmospheres

Opponents of the energy plant noticed different details, landscape structures, and histories. They disaggregated forested slopes, as in the background in figure 67, into different kinds of forest. While they too saw steep slopes, they remembered these forests as formerly productive chestnut groves that had been cut by the tannin factory. They noted the invasive acacias that dominated these patches of forest as echoes of industrial destruction, and they mourned the peasant-cultivated chestnut groves that had formerly grown there. While they agreed that this landscape was uncared for, they attributed this ruin as much to the tannin factory as to rural abandonment. Further, they argued, the structure of the landscape was quite different from that imagined by the supporters of biomass energy. Overgrown forest known as *macchiatico negativo* (negative woodland) was unprofitable to log, and this would not change with a biomass energy plant. Far from bringing care to local hillsides, the biomass plant would bring thundering cavalcades of trucks loaded with wood chips from distant forests. The steep slopes of the Garfagnana would remain uncared for.

When I met with members of the anti–power plant Comitato Alce (Alce Committee), they told the story of the landscape differently, but like Giuseppe Mela they were acutely concerned with observable details of their environment. As one committee member told me, it was Alce that was responsible for destabilizing the landscape by destroying forests, making a mockery of their claim to protect the landscape though biomass energy. "Among the ugly things that Alce gave us as a present was exactly that. This area was completely covered with chestnut, and now there are no more chestnut trees. Wherever it was easy to remove [chestnut], they substituted acacia, which is not even a plant of ours. It doesn't hold the soil steady because it is a plant that should be in flat places, because it has shallow roots, so we have inherited land that is too fragile. When it rains landslides happen because there are no longer chestnut roots to keep the land in place."[8]

They found it bitterly ironic that the factory that had liquidated ancient chestnut forests was now claiming to restore the landscape. In focusing on the history of tannin logging, they made no mention of the contribution of plant disease. The ink disease (*Phytophthora cambivora*), which arrived in this area in the 1930s, and the chestnut canker (*Cryphonectria parasitica*), which arrived in the 1950s, had caused foresters and farmers to despair of chestnut cultivation, but this Anthropocene history of pathogen epidemics had less traction than the history of industrial logging and industrial contamination by the tannin factory.

The activists were more worried about air pollution than about landscape stability. They remembered a battle against the horrendous air pollution caused by tannin and paper factories, stretching back to the 1980s. They recalled the indifference of the government to their petitions for redress, how clothing left on clotheslines and farmers working in fields would be blackened by dust. They recounted the long battle to obtain dust filters and reduced odors from the paper factories. Their most urgent environmental concern was the danger of invisible fine particles known as PM10 that are linked to asthma and cancer. They told me the names of local residents who had died of cancer. Biomass energy could produce particles that would penetrate permeable bodies. In addition to the evidence of their senses and their observations of local disease patterns, they had allies in research universities. They had learned to conduct their own air monitoring and to commission epidemiological analyses, finding cancer clusters that they traced to PM10 concentrations.

The retired teacher Cristina Macchetti told me some of the episodes in the long-running legal and political battle, first against the paper factory, and later against the proposed biomass energy plant. Her home looked across the river toward the former tannin factory, and she well remembered the dark dust that accumulated on clothes, the smells and clouds of steam. For her it was atmospheric morphology that mattered. The basin of the mountains trapped smoke and steam, which would visibly linger above the valley on still winter days. Invisible fine particles followed visible air currents. Cutting trees, as for most people in the countryside, was not a concern for her at all. As with many homes in the Garfagnana, firewood was stacked outside her door, and she employed a tree cutter to take care of the small parcels of woodland that she owned. It was not biomass energy as such that she opposed (her house was heated by burning biomass!), but the scale of the proposed plant. Cristina knew about the risk that overgrown trees might cause landslides, but she pointed out that economically accessible woodland (*macchiatico positivo*) was already being cut. The vast majority of woodlands farther from roads (*macchiatico negativo*) was too expensive to cut, and a new biomass energy plant would not bring care to these forests. "Shamefully they have dared to say that [the biomass plant] would be a way to fight against hydrogeological instability, to clean the mountains that are now sliding down. . . . Where we see that the hillsides crumble and come down . . . where they are not cared for it is because it costs too much to go and gather [the wood]."[9] Rather than provide local employment and stabilize hillsides, the Alce plant would draw wood supplies from far away, driving a noisy and polluting cavalcade of heavy trucks along narrow mountain roads. Her argument was based upon a deep knowledge of the morphology of the valley and of the air currents that moved through it. She described a landscape structure of untended forests far from roads and of logged forests near roads, and linked it to the history of landscape abandonment. From the sensory details of daily life, she and her colleagues built an account of landscape structure that had large-scale consequences.

Opponents of the Alce plant were deeply informed about local history, landscape structure, and the movements of the local atmosphere. They also gathered academic articles, published reports, and an extensive gray literature about biomass energy that they deployed in legal arguments and press releases. These kinds of documents are widely shared by activists across Italy. Often these are informational documents with no author, but with a formidable mastery of technical details. While the Bagni di Lucca activists had built alliances with epidemiologists and engineers who could demonstrate disease clusters and question design decisions, the activists' own expertise drew upon experiences of air pollution, memories of forest destruction, and awareness of expanding acacias and devastated chestnut groves. They could speak not only of landscape, but of an airscape, a visible aerial terrain of smoke, vapor, and dust deposition that they traced to the paper factories in the valley. Their affidavits and conversations were relentlessly specific, as to particular locations and experiences. Through their capacity to compare the socionatural histories of different patches of the landscape and atmosphere, and through their attention to morphological details and landscape structure, they had found a way of calling the state and polluting industries to account. Activists and their opponents agreed that credible data came from witnessing, a "view from somewhere" that incorporated personal experiences and suffering.[10] Through their account of landscape structure, however, they claimed a larger-scale significance for their personal experiences. From their sensory experiences of the mundane indeterminacy of daily life they had produced accounts of landscape and atmosphere that repelled the advance of a state-sponsored infrastructure and of a wood chip commodity chain. Climate change policy was reworked by landscape stories.

While bitterly opposed and scathing about each other's motivations, opponents and supporters of the plant agreed about surprisingly many things. They shared a profound sense of the absence of the peasants who had formerly maintained landscape stability, and they tried to imagine how the landscape could be made stable and healthy. Experiences of landscape informed their arguments for and against the power plant, as did their experiences and profound distrust of the Italian state. All concerned remarked on the problem of Italian political culture, hinting ominously about concealed "dark interests" that supported their opponents. Supporters of the plant emphasized that burning industrial or urban waste could never work in Italy, because "Italians are special" (lawless and selfish), and because of their legitimate fear of organized crime. Plant opponents made the same argument. An affect of distrust and doubt, a sense that state institutions were easily manipulated and hard to understand, permeated conversations and inspired people's conversations, whether they opposed or supported the plant. This was a "culture of the state" that emerged from daily experiences of indifferent and incomprehensible state bureaucracies, and in a rural place like the Garfagnana, from their experiences of retreat and abandonment by the state. In Italy everyone knows of complex paperwork, of regulations that are implemented but which few understand, and of the interminable procedures of review, appeal, and counterclaim that make the wheels of government grind achingly slowly and incomprehensibly. In the countryside the state appeared very far away. Small villages crumbled and were abandoned, roads were no longer maintained, and schools and government buildings were progressively shut down. The infrastructural presence of the state was visibly thinning, fraying, and falling into ruin. People were fearful and angry about this abandonment. In 2013–2014, at a time of political crisis, almost every interview I conducted led without any effort on my part to angry denunciations of the Italian state. I well remember when a farmer near Volterra erupted with anger: "The state is a swindle. Write that! It has become a usurer. It has become a usurer!"[11]

Biomass Energy as Infrastructural Politics

Faced with global environmental change, it has become increasingly clear that we need to transform the energy infrastructures that have produced climate change in the first place. As many scholars have noted, infrastructures are typically taken for granted as the background of daily life, only becoming a topic of concern and of political contestation at moments of breakdown or transformation. Invisibility can be precisely the point. As Tim Mitchell points out, an oil-based infrastructure was attractive to twentieth-century states because pipelines made oil-based energy invisible and less amenable to democratic control. Efforts to redesign energy systems undo this invisibility, causing debates as to who will control energy production, transmission, and consumption and who will suffer its environmental impacts. From wind energy in Mexico and Spain, to coal energy in Navajo territory in the United States, to renewable energy in Southern Europe, environmental justice movements have opposed sustainable energy plans and argued for different visions of health, energy, and environment. In the United States fossil fuel energy plants are often located in poor neighborhoods and near people of color, burdening the less powerful with the environmental and health effects of energy production.[12] Energy production is always a political and economic question. A new energy system such as the biomass energy network being built in Italy poses a series of questions. How big will energy plants be? What landscapes will they draw their biomass from, and what effects will energy production have upon these landscapes? What kind of energy will be produced, who can use it, and what will it cost? Whose health will be harmed by energy production?

In Italy, as in most of the world (although unlike most industrialized countries), wood remains a source of home heating from fires and stoves. The energy produced by burning wood produces warm bodies and the smell of woodsmoke. Woodsmoke lingers visibly over cities in the winter as a layer of yellow haze. Changing to modern stoves allows new kinds of wood to be used. Chestnut wood produces sparks, making it difficult to use in open fires, but fine for stoves. When used to heat water, energy from stoves emerges in radiators and showers rather than as the kind of heat from open fires that leaves other parts of a room cold. Stoves and fireplaces are connected to local firewood suppliers, to the work of stacking and moving small logs that come from coppices and to the effort required to keep stoves going. Burning firewood produces a lot of air pollution, but this is a risk that comes from a familiar source, and ordinary people feel comfortable with it. Smoke is air pollution that most people don't mind incurring.[13] They are "experts" as to what counts as air pollution, and they have little trust in official analyses which reveal firewood burning to be a more important source of air pollution than, for example, cars or biomass energy plants.

Modern forms of wood energy break trees into smaller and more uniform matter, producing new kinds of social relations and bodily experiences. In Italy you can buy wood pellets in a fifteen-kilogram plastic sack at a supermarket, a hardware store, or even in a gas station. Wood-pellet stoves need less care than woodstoves. Rather than carry dirty and heavy logs into your living room, you can pour the pellets into the hopper of a stove that you run with a thermostat. There is no need to poke the coals, and the house will be warm when you get home from work. Ever higher quality and more uniformly burning small wood chips are being developed. Wood chips and pellets flow more easily through hands and machines than logs do. Wood chips can be fed continuously into large furnaces, and a truck might deliver wood chips to a district heating plant or a power station. Such trucks travel longer distances; they travel with bills of lading and pay taxes, unlike those in the informal local circuits through which much firewood moves. Many wood pellets in Italy come from Austria, Romania, or farther afield, giving rise to fears that they might come from the pillaging of forests. The familiar mechanisms of consumer labeling and certification come in to play, promising that wood chips come from "virgin" wood that is not recycled from other uses. Consumers are supposed to read the labels on bags of pellets if they are to avoid supporting "timber mafias" in Eastern Europe or producing toxic smoke from contaminated pellets.[14]

Working at a scale that far exceeds local firewood supply chains, biomass electricity production requires large and long-distance supply chains. The Bagni di Lucca plant would have required 150,000 tons of wood chips per year. This almost matched the estimates of available biomass for the province of Lucca, but much of this forest was much too expensive to log for biomass or firewood. The steep slopes, fragmented properties, and environmental constraints of the region meant that much of this biomass would have to travel from farther afield. To place this quantity in perspective and to illustrate the impossibility of substituting the modern energy system with biomass energy, we should compare the Bagni di Lucca plant with the size of the coal, oil, and natural-gas plants that power our fossil fuel economy. Such plants range from producing five hundred to one thousand megawatts at their maximum capacity, but most of us have not seen them. Do you know where the nearest power plant is to you, right now? These energy plants are large, centralized, and far away and often located near the homes of poorer and less powerful people. Should they be converted to burning wood chips, their consumption and pollution would be phenomenal. Consider the giant 3.9-gigawatt coal-fired Drax Power Station in the United Kingdom, which has largely converted to biomass energy. In 2016 this plant burned thirteen million tons of wood pellets, largely imported from the Southeastern United States. Activists, officials, and biomass energy supporters in Tuscany were well aware of this bad example. The biomass entrepreneur Giuseppe Mela argued that importing wood chips from abroad would not prevent climate change nor stabilize local landscapes. Regional officials similarly argued that large biomass energy plants with long-distance supply networks would neither reduce carbon emissions nor provide jobs. In order to avoid what we might call the "Drax B syndrome," they constrained the distance that wood chips could travel to a seventy-kilometer radius, carefully modeling the availability of "unused" biomass in catchment areas, and demanding that new power plants should produce a list of local wood suppliers. In effect, the regional government acknowledged that biomass was not a "proper" commodity that could travel across the world. Rather than the kind of globe-spanning supply chains that we see emerging from industrial agriculture, biomass energy in Tuscany still linked forests, tree cutters, and nearby fireplaces or furnaces. This was a tenuous achievement. In Italy, mountainous landscapes with deeply fragmented or abandoned ownerships have made wood chip production so expensive that it only makes sense near roads or in the lowlands. In other parts of the world, such as the US Southeast, forestry companies have found flat landscapes, accommodating legal systems, and legible property relations, and are able to transport wood chips and wood pellets internationally.[15] In Eastern Europe, timber mafias involved in logging for biomass energy may bypass questions of ownership or co-opt environmental protections. The relative failure of forest biomass production in Italy is due to opposition from anti-biomass groups and steep landscapes. This should be compared with the destructive effects of expanding biomass frontiers, where local people lack the power to block logging and air pollution. Large-scale biomass energy seems to be done best in someone else's landscapes, places that can be sacrificed for the goal of renewable energy.

Political Opposition to Biomass Energy

As biomass energy plants became national and regional policy, a wave of criticism and protest spread across the country. In 2013 there were over a hundred opposition movements to biomass electricity production across the country, with twenty-three active in the Tuscany region alone. "Biomass" was a slippery term that included agricultural waste products, branches and leaves that remained from tree cutting in forests, and waste from urban trees. The possibility that "biomass energy" could conceal the burning of industrial toxic wastes animated vociferous local opposition to energy plants that might cause air pollution by PM10 particles. Across Italy, opponents of biomass energy warned that burning "solid wood" could rapidly turn to burning municipal or even toxic wastes, as expressed in the anonymous document "Everything About the Biomass Lie," which circulated on the Facebook pages of activist groups. Even tiny biomass energy plants could be colonized by toxic-waste incineration. In 2019, a small biomass power plant in northern Tuscany was discovered to be burning toxic waste.[16]

Opposition to biomass energy drew upon fear and distrust of the nation state and a lesser distrust of regional governments, alongside considerable acceptance of the legitimacy of provincial and municipal governments. This fear and distrust was shared by opponents to biomass energy, who lacked connections to national and regional politicians, and by well-connected biomass energy supporters. Although people would often make sweeping accusations of all government officials ("They are all thieves . . ."), they talked about local government as inhabited by lazy bureaucrats rather than by actual criminals. I well remember one firewood cutter commenting on the lack of road maintenance by the provincial government while admitting that his son-in-law worked for the province. A supporter of biomass energy told me that local officials did not prevent him from getting the logging permits he needed, although they kept him waiting around. In daily life and at a local level the state was annoying and infuriatingly slow, but it was only at national and, to a lesser extent, at regional levels that people recounted official decisions as being subverted by dark forces and hidden agendas.

National environmental organizations, while broadly supportive of biomass energy, preferred small district heating plants and short supply chains, echoing activist groups in criticizing larger plants for "wasting heat" while producing electricity. Energy was parsed into heat and electricity and was linked to local landscapes. To ship electricity to the national grid was to send energy far away, with few benefits for local residents. When I started my research in 2013 the Alce energy plant looked inevitable. By 2015 regional officials and local politicians were keen to dissociate themselves from a slow-moving political disaster, emphasizing the importance of respecting local desires for heating from small energy plants. By 2018, a more modest network of district heating plants had spread across the region.[17] Such energy plants accord with rural people's ideas of energy and landscape. Citizens' concerns about the dangers of air pollution and the need for landscape stability, their desire to keep wood production for local consumption, and their sense that wood should be used to produce heat rather than electricity caused the redesign of a small part of the energy system. Popular understandings of energy, landscape, and atmosphere largely constrained state and capitalist efforts to build a new energy system. Government policies and supply chains turned out to be quite fragile processes, liable to change and transformation in the face of citizen opposition.

The movement of wood chips from forests to energy plants required considerable work in the face of steep slopes, fragmented property holdings, and remote trees. It is hard work turning living trees into wood chips of uniform size and dryness. As with other capitalist supply chains, this work takes skill, personal connections, the capacity to format materials into commodities, and then to move these materials across supply chains. Building supply chains calls for considerable attention to the affordances and resistances of the landscapes that wood, minerals, or other commodities come from.[18] I saw some of this work when accompanying Giuseppe Mela on his travels, from roadside conversations when he told woodcutters how and where they could chip and pile a problematic pile of logs, to the docks of Livorno where wood chips arrived in trucks. I watched him tag samples as he organized the transfer of wood chips to a freighter that was destined for a large coal power plant in Sardinia. Mela knew how to look at a stack of logs and talk to loggers; he knew how to measure the humidity of wood chips so as to get the best price; and he knew how to find landowners and forestry companies that would sell him wood. Wood chip quality was a constant struggle. Producing valuable lower humidity wood chips with a higher heat content required careful drying and protection from the weather.

A much more modest supply chain was being built in a village north of Lucca. Over the past six years the community entrepreneur whom I will call Michele has coordinated a consortium of about two dozen small-scale loggers. Rather than facing the kind of contentious geomorphological politics, suspicions about air quality, and memories of industrial pollution that we saw at Bagni di Lucca, Michele's work was of coordination, organization, and persuasion, of budgets, grants, and bank loans. He worked to persuade fiercely independent loggers to buy equipment that they could share so as to reduce labor costs. He looked for grants to build drying yards so as to get the best prices for wood chips, and he tried to develop long-term contracts. The fact that Michele does not have to address the kind of political controversy faced by the Alce plant is a testament to the legitimacy of small-scale logging and local uses of biomass as heat. When I visited in 2014, he showed me a new 770-kilowatt district heating plant that was powered by wood chips. He walked me through the basements and streets of the village, showing me the piping that transported heat from the plant to radiators and living spaces. For a village with only three hundred inhabitants, the dozen or so people employed as woodcutters and the reduced home heating costs were a persuasive project. It was not that people did not have experience with the smells and pollution of the paper industry. On the contrary: in the valley below, ruined paper mills testified to the former importance of paper production. Industrial pollution had been as present here as in Bagni di Lucca. The heating plant was an energy infrastructure that had local allies in people's experiences of heat and in the maintenance of a biomass energy landscape that was linked to the employment of local firewood cutters.

From Landscape Politics to Climate Change

The bitter conflicts over biomass energy in Bagni di Lucca and in other towns across Italy might seem of little importance when weighed against the scale of global climate change. This is a mistake. As I have shown, biomass energy is critical in allowing international policymakers to imagine that they are "balancing the books" of global carbon accounting. The Italian government and other industrialized countries have sustained a fantasy that they could use "excess biomass" to fulfill their climate change treaty obligations without looking too closely at the carbon emissions produced by biomass energy. Although individual biomass energy plants may be small, they are important contributors to what is known as "negative carbon" and "carbon neutral" energy in global climate change policy. These terms need to be connected to the landscapes where people live and plants grow, in order to prevent them from becoming as destructive as other modernist fantasy projects.

The details of landscape politics matter because they can halt or transform biomass energy policies. When climate change policy comes to earth it is rapidly reconfigured as a result of local understandings of landscape that refuse to remain local. In Italy the scale and nature of biomass energy was transformed due to powerful opposition to large electricity plants. In Bagni di Lucca, biomass energy opponents refused to accept official knowledge about the safety of the plant. The activists I talked to were not "anti-science." Rather, they combined scientific literature with their own knowledge of the morphologies of trees and hillsides, of valleys and airflows, of landscape structure and history.[19]

The political coalitions that sought to build or remake biomass energy drew upon people's experiences of landscape and of air pollution and upon their capacities to recount socioenvironmental histories that were not captured by the urgency of climate change policy. People built structural accounts of the landscape by comparing across landscape patches, the steep hillsides, polluted atmospheres, and abandoned forests of the Tuscan Apennines. By noticing the details of trees and hillsides and by linking these to large-scale landscape structures and histories, they came up with visions of alternative futures. These were politically consequential stories that linked people's daily lives to collective projects of landscape care. Caring for landscape was a political project that drew upon experiences of daily life in order to build an account of the world that reached toward larger scales, reworking state projects and political economies.

Popular distrust in the Italian state, and its relative weakness and limited resources, prevented biomass energy from producing the climate change policies that officials had hoped for. It was not at all that people were not concerned about climate change. Most people agreed that seasons had changed, that summers were hotter, droughts more frequent, and that strange weather was a feature of daily life. Climate change was a rather general background condition for life, or perhaps the occasion for the kinds of mass protests inspired by Extinction Rebellion in 2019. These protests were linked to a global and international framing of climate change, and they were not connected to the landscapes that people lived in. This global framing of climate largely failed to justify biomass electricity production to ordinary people. In contrast, biomass energy as heat production and landscape care was connected to histories of rural abandonment and overgrown forests that people cared about. Debates about biomass energy were permeated by an awareness of living in a ruined landscape that had once been cared for. People did not agree on what care would look like. The contest between supporters and opponents of biomass energy produced painful divisions in Bagni di Lucca. What was shared across their differences was a sense that the landscape and forests that surround the town were falling into ruin. This was an Anthropocene politics in which nature was intensely social and wherein removing humans from nature was not a viable solution.[20]

Histories of former peasant landscapes, of industrialization and the destruction of chestnut forests by tannin factories, of rural abandonment and the threat of landslides, and of air pollution from tannin and paper factories displace politics from the urgencies of climate change as the only future to prepare for. The technocratic time of climate change is answered by a politics of attending to histories of landscape transformation, destruction, and care. Humanist critics of climate change policy have rightly criticized its technocratic and monocausal obsessions and noted that people actually experience climate change through personal experiences of weather.[21] The Anthropocene energy politics I describe echoes this insight but links vernacular models of climate to unstable landscapes. People in Italy drew upon personal experiences of the landscape they lived in to recall socioenvironmental transformations that were not to do with climate change at all. The Anthropocene rhythm of postwar rural abandonment was more important than the rhythm of climate change. In many places around the world, as in Italy, caring for landscape will have little apparent connection to climate change but will have major consequences for global environmental change.

Epilogue

Trees Are Shape Shifters

High up in the Italian Apennines, in the summer of 2016, I encountered a being that lives long, changes shape, and remains always partly beyond description. I refer, of course, to a giant ancient chestnut tree (figure 68). In order to see it properly I had to come close, step back, and walk around it, and then step closer once again (figure 69). No image or diagram could do justice to this strange being, which shimmered at the edge of intelligibility. I continue to think about this moment of encounter and wonder. This tree might live or die; it has many names; it has changed shape many times and will change shape again. The shape of this tree gestures to invisible processes and to histories that I can only guess at. This tree has lived from the world of peasant agriculture into the world of climate change. What can such a messenger say to our current predicament?

The morphology of this ancient tree tells a story of human/plant encounters and of the relationships of this tree with soil, weather, and plant disease. The bulging trunk is a sign of the violence of the long-ago moment of grafting. Six hundred years ago a peasant farmer skillfully aligned the cambium layers of scion and rootstock. The echo of this event is the traveling wave front that is the graft scar. The loops and curves of the burls in the second image record histories of cutting for firewood and construction timber. The leaves on the burls record the response of the cambium layer beneath the bark to sunlight and to signals from other parts of the tree. These leaves could each become a shoot, then a branch, and perhaps even a giant trunk. The morphology of this unstable composite being is the result of the care of

Figure 68. The ancient chestnut tree of Pratofosco, Lucca, 2016. (Author photograph)

Figure 69. Detail, the ancient chestnut tree of Pratofosco, Lucca, 2016. (Author photograph)

farmers and volunteers who garden the trunk and cut away branches that could threaten the vigor of the central stem. This unstable graft union has elicited care and inspired imagination for over six hundred years. Through their attention to tree morphology and to the food, firewood, and construction materials that trees can produce, peasant cultivators have cared for this tree for centuries. This shape changer can change the stories we tell about relationships between humans, plants, animals, and soils.

The ancient chestnut tree of Pratofosco is, however, an ambiguous messenger. While it conveys a modest hope that humans can engage in very long-term projects of care, it is also a warning of the disastrous effects of disease and of what can happen when people believe in the inevitability of a particular future. This tree is a refugee from an overwhelming disaster, a remnant of the chestnut groves that once covered these mountains. In the 1960s loggers were cutting all large chestnut trees in the area and shipping them to the tannin factory at Bagni di Lucca twenty kilometers away. Faced with the crisis of the epidemic chestnut canker, everyone assumed that these trees were doomed. When confronting the end of the world, people do things that would make no sense otherwise. Salvage capitalism took hold and ancient trees were converted to tannin, ending up in elegant shoes or handbags in distant cities. The survival of this tree was due to an encounter, a moment, when the inevitability of destruction was called into question. The story goes that a logger, impressed by the beauty and size of the tree, told his supervisor that he would pay its value to avoid cutting it. The forester agreed and the tree was saved. At a moment when industrial agriculture seemed to make chestnut growing irrelevant and when disease seemed to have doomed the species, only a few trees called upon humans so forcefully that crisis capitalism paused in its tracks. Just as the disaster of chestnut blight inspired the rush to tannin logging, our current disaster of climate change might lead us to rush to liquidate forests for biomass energy. This survivor is as much a dire warning as an inspiration.

The shimmering strangeness of plants, slow growing and gifted shape shifters, can pull people into attention to morphology and to longer-term processes that are partially or completely invisible. The shape-shifting capacities of trees persuaded peasant farmers in Italy to build and maintain terraces and drainage systems across an unstable landscape. The shapes of terracing and drainage systems, like the shapes of grafted trees, were morphologies that elicited long-term care. This human capacity to care for biogeomorphological assemblages has been largely overlooked. We have been looking in the wrong places and using the wrong tools. In Italy a mundane biogeomorphological politics took place before the eyes of mostly uninterested scholars and officials. For much of the past two thousand years they failed to notice what they were seeing. Biogeomorphological politics can inspire other projects of reshaping plants and landscapes in other places. These projects of care can be harmful. The sugar plantation complex of the colonial Caribbean used the labor of enslaved Black people to reshape the hydrology of the entire landscape. Fields in Iowa are reshaped to support the needs of industrially grown corn. If we are to notice mundane care for morphology, not only in Italy but elsewhere around the world, we need other tools beyond the archives of historians and the interviews of anthropologists. We need to trust our senses and we need to expand our methods to include diagrams and drawings. This is part of a decolonization of anthropology and history that may help us make better sense of what farmers, peasants, indigenous people, and others have been doing all along. We may find that we need to collaborate with ecologists, landscape architects, and modelers, and we might use diagrams or drawings to analyze our evidence and explain our findings.

The capacity to care for very slow and long-term processes through attention to morphology is not unique to Italy, nor to relations between plants and soils. Long-term care for morphology is a human capacity that is found in other domains and in other parts of the world. We could slow down and notice other morphologies that matter to us, from the built environments that surround us, to the urban water infrastructures and airflows that affect so many of us. As we move through our daily lives, we have allowed ourselves to imagine that the evidence of our senses and the form of our surroundings are of little relevance to such larger questions as climate change or political economy. This is wrong. The mundane beings and processes that we encounter are linked to histories of care, of ruin, and of possibility that are captured neither by stories of economic growth nor of imminent destruction. Anthropologist Joe Masco warns us that "a loss of the collective environment is easier to imagine than a shift in the nature of petrocapitalism."[1] Our surroundings can be a source of that imagination. Attention to morphology can inspire humans to care for slow processes that escape the gaze of the state and the grasp of markets. By noticing the strange behaviors of plants and soils, we can displace our attention from contemporary notions of progress or crisis. By engaging in collective projects of long-term care for our surroundings we might be able to build more-just economies and healthier environments.

The current climate crisis and the multiple crises of the Anthropocene can seem like overwhelming and distant events, too large and slow to grasp, impossible to think your way out of. Historians struggle to link the inhuman scales of geological time to human experience.[2] As we have seen, the climate change of natural scientists is too abstract and at too large a scale for most of us to grasp. The systems models that show us global climate change are not up to the task of showing us how the landscapes we live in might change as a result of intertwined social change, ecological change, and climate change. Morphological analysis, attention to larger-scale landscape structures, and alertness to history and to daily life can help us link long-term processes with lived experience. Our accounts of regional environmental change can give a different kind of purchase on the future, acting as examples and warnings that offer an alternative to the simplifications of climate models. We need both global climate models and regional accounts of social and ecological change. We need both official climate change knowledge and vernacular models of climate.

My own morphological analysis linked plate tectonics, unstable sedimentary soils, intense Mediterranean rainstorms, peasant agriculture, and industrialization with present-day experiences of forest fires, floods, and landslides. In other parts of the world other processes and histories can be made visible by attention to morphology. The history of racial slavery and exploitation that located Black people on flood-prone landscapes in New Orleans was a biogeomorphology that exposed them to the effects of Hurricane Katrina. Histories of Cold War nuclear power and swamp drainage produced the nuclear wastelands of Chernobyl and the toxicity that is visible in the shapes of plants and human bodies.[3] Attention to morphology can help us link the past to the present and to link long-term histories with present disasters. We need multiple histories to help us confront global environmental change.

Historical ecologists often look to the past as a way to plan for the future. Faced with climate change it is not so clear that the past is a guide to the future anymore. Peasant traditions of landscape care might lose their relevance in the face of the droughts, fires, and floods that will come with climate change. Firefighting methods no longer work as they used to in California because forest fires have become too wild to make sense of.[4] Old people in Italy know that the present is unlike the past. Restoring litter raking and pastoral burning or bringing back less flammable chestnut and oak trees might not make the forests of the Monte Pisano sufficiently fire-resistant to survive climate change. The past does not have to tell us solely about tradition, however. It can also be a source of imagination, a reminder of how badly and quickly things can go wrong, that there are alternative ways of being human, and that different kinds of relationships between humans and nonhumans are possible. The radically strange world of peasant agriculture, so different from our postindustrial present, reminds us how quickly human societies can change their relationships with the plants, animals, and soils that we depend upon. The disaster of the destruction of chestnut cultivation by plant pathogens is an exemplary warning, a cautionary tale of regional environmental disaster that supports efforts to control the spread of plant diseases. This example also warns us of what can happen when one version of the future seems inescapable. Cutting forests for biomass energy may make as little sense as liquidating chestnut forests for tannin. While climate change is increasing the range of plant diseases, the most important cause of the increasing frequency of pathogen epidemics is the international trade in live plants. We can alleviate some of the impacts of climate change by questioning the need for instant gardens around mansions, hotels, and houses. Shape-changing trees can inspire stories that travel far beyond forests.

In this book I have approached climate change from an oblique angle. Rather than focusing directly upon climate change, I have situated it within people's other social and environmental concerns and within longer-term histories of social and ecological change. This indirect approach tried to do justice to people's lived experiences and to the reality that climate change is rarely their most important concern. In Italy, official ideas of global climate change encountered a tradition of thinking about plant/soil/climate assemblages, popular concern about landscape stability, and distrust of the state. Even as few people doubted that climate change was a real problem, most were more concerned with practical projects of care for their surroundings than they were with climate change. Where I live in California people are more immediately concerned about forest fires that might threaten their homes than about climate change. Many people around the world will be more concerned with caring for their surroundings than with the distant concept of climate change.[5]

Ecological histories do not leave us unambiguously on the side of local perceptions of environmental problems. In this book, I have traced the effects of pathogen epidemics and social changes that are unknown to most people. Where most people in the Monte Pisano worried about wildfire, landscape instability, and landscape abandonment, I have come to also worry about the impacts of plant diseases. Most people do not know of the histories of burning and litter raking that formerly made the landscape less fire prone. My historical ecology gives me a different perspective and a different account of socioenvironmental change. I try to balance my own history with the accounts of ordinary people and of climate scientists, and to hold these three in tension with each another. Emphasizing the importance of people's understandings of their surroundings for climate change policy does not mean that we should always agree with them. In some places, farmers and cattle ranchers may be deeply knowledgeable about their environments while also engaging in destructive practices. We should study and respect their knowledge, but we should not necessarily agree with them all of the time.

Effective climate change policies will require scientists and policymakers to realize that people link climate to their surroundings and daily lives in different ways and that there are many ways of thinking about climate. They will need to see their task as one of building alliances across different ways of knowing, where agreement on definitions is not necessary for effective collaboration. Policymakers' failure to engage with ordinary people's understandings of their surroundings may doom unpopular climate change policies, just as it did for biomass energy in Italy. Local knowledge can have large-scale consequences. Even when people appear to "believe" in climate change, it is likely that they have their own understanding of climate and that they will be more concerned with the landscapes they live in than with official definitions of climate. Even when people say they do not "believe" in climate change, they are likely to be concerned about the landscapes they live in, and they may link climate to alternative assemblages of plants, soils, and waters or to other processes and beings. The climate of Italian science and policy and the climate of vernacular plant/soil/water assemblages are not the same thing. People's relative lack of interest in climate change policy is not a sign of ignorance but of an alternative politics. People who repair drainage systems in Italy, like farmers who worry about drought-stricken pastures in Iowa, are engaging with landscape structure and history. Their decision to care for some material processes rather than others may seem irrelevant to climate change policymakers, but this is a practical politics of landscape care, a choice of one Anthropocene rhythm over another. People around the world will confront climate change by caring for the landscapes, plants, and animals that matter to them and by calling to account political institutions in ways that make sense to them.[6] They will draw upon their understandings of the landscapes and political institutions that they have inherited. The question to ask then is not "Why don't people act in the name of climate change?" but "How are people already caring for the landscapes they live in and how do they connect these landscapes to climate and to politics?"

Finally, perhaps I have persuaded you to look at your surroundings with new eyes. As you move through the world, you might pause to look at street or garden trees and to wonder what histories gave them their shapes. You might begin to wonder about the shapes of agricultural fields, urban embankments, street drains, and rivers, about the histories of human labor and natural disaster, of exploitation and care that have shaped the world around you. Hillsides are slowly in motion. Forests are breathing. Perhaps you can sense, right now, all around you, the shape shifting of trees.

APPENDIX ONE

Ecology and Climate of the Monte Pisano

The Monte Pisano is a modest-sized mountain range located between the cities of Pisa and Lucca in Central Italy (see figure 19).[1] The mountains are outliers of the main chain of the Apennine mountain range, from which they are separated by the River Serchio and the now-drained bed of the Lake of Bientina to the northeast. The elevation ranges from 15 meters to 917 meters above sea level at the top of Monte Serra. Climate varies with elevation and is in the Köppen Csa class: humid temperate with dry summers, Mediterranean subtype. Average temperatures range from −3°C in the coldest months to over 22°C for the hottest. Precipitation varies from 928 to 950 millimeters per year on the floodplain of the Arno to the south, to 1,203 millimeters at the crest of Monte Serra, which is similar to the plain of Lucca to the north, with most rain falling in the fall and winter. The geology consists of a mixture of sedimentary Oligocene materials of the Tuscan formation, metamorphic Paleozoic and Miocene limestones of the Santa Maria del Giudice unit, and the similar Monte Serra unit of metamorphic Paleozoic and Miocene silicates and limestones.

Several small towns occupy the valleys that are incised into the mountains, including San Giuliano Terme, Asciano, Calci, Buti, Sant'Andrea di Compito, and Vorno. These valleys are dominated by fast-flowing rivers (the Guappero, Vorno, Visona, Calci, and Magno), which were formerly of great importance for powering grain, olive, and other mills.[2] Within the valleys and on the valley floors, agriculture predominates, with olive cultivation particularly widespread on agricultural terraces on the southern side of the mountains. On lower-elevation hills, the forest is predominantly maritime pine (*Pinus pinaster* Aiton), over an understory of xeric species such as *Ulex europaea* L. and *Erica arborea* L. Higher up, mixtures of chestnut and pine predominate, with chestnut prevailing above about five hundred meters, with patches of oak (*Quercus pubescens* Willd.) at lower elevations. Along river galleries more mesic vegetation, including manna ash (*Fraxinus ornus* L.), and hornbeam (*Ostrya carpinifolia* Scop.) dominate. On dryer, south-facing slopes, especially at lower elevations, there are areas of *macchia* scrub, dominated by *E. arborea* L. and *Arbutus unedo* L., with patches of cork oak (*Quercus suber* L.) and holm oak (*Quercus ilex* L.), while on areas of limestone there are areas of true Mediterranean *garrigue* dominated by *Phillyrea angustifolia* L., *Pistacia lentiscus* L., and *Myrtus communis* L. On the crest of the mountains there are areas of exotic conifers (*Pinus nigra* Arnold, *Cedrus libani* A. Richard) established as plantations between the 1950s and the 1980s, while at lower elevations on the northern and eastern slopes there are broad bands of the exotic (and now invasive) *Robinia pseudoacacia* L.

APPENDIX TWO

Equations as Stories

Net Primary Productivity Equation, used in BIOME-BGC Model

$$NPP = GPP - R_{gr} - R_{mn}$$

NPP = Net Primary Productivity
GPP = Gross Primary Productivity
R_{gr} = Simulated Growth Respiration
R_{mn} = Maintenance Respiration

The builders of BIOME-BGC chose to use the Net Primary Productivity equation because it described the fundamental ecosystem processes of increase in biomass due to growth and loss of biomass due to respiration. This equation is a "classic" for ecologists, and many people learn one or another version in high school. Fabio Maselli and Marta Chiesi modified this equation by adding a new term, NV_A, the ratio of actual to maximum tree volume, comparing the "far from climax" condition of disturbed forests in Tuscany with the "near climax" assumed by BIOME-BGC. The term NV_A in turn helped calculate the actual forest cover FC_A, as opposed to FC, the forest cover predicted by BIOME-BGC. Here too the "near climax" assumed by North American modelers was reduced to account for the reality of heavily logged Mediterranean forests. This modified equation is a story about dramatic encounters between entities. The absorption of energy into growing plants is counteracted by the respiration through which these plants maintain themselves and grow in the face of firewood cutting. Centuries of peasant firewood cutting are compressed into the terms NV_A and FC_A.[1]

Modified NPP Equation

$$NPP_A = \frac{GPP \cdot FC_A}{FC} - \frac{R_{gr} \cdot FC_A}{FC} - R_{mn} \cdot NV_A$$

NV_A = normalized actual volume (i.e., volume estimated via remote sensing/ volume predicted by BIOME-BGC)

FC_A = actual forest cover, represents photosynthetic radiation usable by the incomplete tree canopy

FC = forest cover predicted by BIOME-BGC, represents photosynthetic radiation usable by the more complete tree canopy

APPENDIX THREE

Organizations

Alce	Tannin and paper company, operating in Bagni di Lucca from 1903 to 2009
Carabinieri	National gendarmerie, responsible for domestic policing
CNR	Centro Nazionale di Ricerche (National Research Center), a university campus outside Firenze
CFS	Corpo Forestale dello Stato (State Forestry Corps), absorbed by the Carabinieri in 2016
IPCC	Intergovernmental Panel on Climate Change
MiC	Ministero della Cultura (Ministry of Culture)
Offizio Sopra le Selve	Office of Chestnut Groves, the commission charged with protecting chestnut groves in the Republic of Lucca
Offizio del Serchio	Office of the Serchio, which regulated land use on the banks of the River Serchio under the Republic of Lucca, often in joint session with the Offizio Sopra le Selve
Soprintendenza Archeologia, Belle Arti e Paesaggio	Provincial directorates within the Ministry of Culture (MiC), responsible for regulating and protecting landscape aesthetics
UNFCCC	United Nations Framework Convention on Climate Change

GLOSSARY

This glossary contains Italian terms with their English equivalents. Where the English term is technical or not in common use, I have also provided a brief definition.

alberata	Vines trained along tree branches, a historical cultivation system that was characteristic of central Italy at least since the Middle Ages.
alto fusto	High forest, tall single-stemmed trees that are suitable for large buildings and are usually favored by foresters. By comparison, peasants have tended to prefer *ceduo*.
alveo/alvei	Riverbed/riverbeds.
aquidocci	Drainage channels for a terrace.
argini	Riverbanks or embankments.
assessore dell'ambiente	Environment councillor. This can be a municipal-, provincial-, or regional-level position.
beni paesaggistici	Landscape values.
bioingegneria	Bioengineering. Boxes of wooden posts to stabilize slopes and landslides. (See *ingegneria naturalistica.*)
biomassa	Biomass. This could be municipal organic waste, lawn clippings, crop residues, and wood chips from trees.
bombe d'acqua	Water bombs. Unusually intense and damaging downpours.
bonifica	Reclamation, often used to describe drainage or landscape restoration works, as in the *bonifica integrale* (integrated reclamation) of the Pontine swamps under Mussolini.
briglia/briglie	Check dam/dams.

cambiamento climatico	Climate change.
campi in pendio	Sloping fields, a type of earth-banked terrace.
cancro del castagno	Chestnut canker, *Cryphonectria parasitica*.
capitozza	Pollard. Trees that are cut off at shoulder-to-head height, protecting resprouting stems from grazing animals, characteristic of wood pastures that dominated many parts of Europe until the nineteenth century.
cassa integrazione	Redundancy fund.
castagneto	Cultivated chestnut grove or orchard.
catasto	Cadastral tax register.
ceduo	Coppice. Trees that are allowed to resprout from a stump.
ceduo affrancato	Released coppice. Single stems on a coppice stool that have been allowed to grow up to a full-sized tree.
ceppo/ceppi	Stool/stools. Stump(s) from which new shoots grow for coppice (see *ceduo*).
ciglioni	Vegetated banks.
collettori	Drainage channels for a terrace.
colmata	System of land reclamation by flooding swamps with sediment-laden water.
coltivatore diretto	Direct cultivator, a smallholder who would likely have formerly considered himself/herself to be a peasant/ *contadino*.
comune	Municipality.
comunità montana	Mountain community.
consorzio di bonifica	Reclamation consortium.
contadino/contadini	Peasant/peasants.
contado	In the middle ages, the geographical region economically and politically subordinated to a town, hence *contadino*.
dissesto idrogeologico	Hydrogeological instability.
fattore	Agent or estate manager.
filiera corta	Short supply chain.
forestale	"The forest service." Loosely used by rural people to describe the various government institutions responsible for regulating access and use of forests.
frana/frane	Landslide/landslides.
Giornale della misura e stima	Journal of measure and estimate, recorded area, and taxable value of land parcels in the nineteenth-century Lucca *catasto*.

Giornale di campo	Field journal, recorded land use and productive value in the nineteenth-century Lucca *catasto*.
gradinate	Stone-walled terraces.
ingegneria naturalistica	Natural engineering. Boxes of wooden posts used to stabilize slopes and prevent landslides. (See *bioingegneria.*)
innesto	Graft.
leccio	Holm oak, *Quercus ilex*.
macchia	Scrub.
male del inchiostro	Ink disease, *Phytophthora cambivora* or *Phytophthora cinnamomi.*
marza	Scion, a cutting or bud that is grafted onto a rootstock.
matricine	Standards. Residual stems left after an area of forest has been cut for coppice.
metato/metati	Chestnut drying shed/sheds.
mezzadria	Sharecropping system that dominated Central Italy from the late Middle Ages until the mid-twentieth century.
mezzadro	Sharecropper.
paesaggio	Landscape.
pineta	Pine forest.
pino marittimo	Maritime pine, *Pinus pinaster.*
pino domestico	Stone pine, *Pinus pinea*.
poggi	Vegetated banks.
polloni	Shoots/suckers growing from a stump or the base of a plant stem.
portainnesto	Rootstock, usually of a wild plant variety onto which the cultivated variety is grafted.
promiscuo	Polyculture of tree crops, grain, and grapevines.
provincia	Province, analogous to a county.
pula	Chaff, also the chestnut husks that are burned in a *metato*.
regione	Region, analogous to a state; one of twenty regions in Italy.
scaglioni	Vegetated banks.
scolina di guardia	Drainage ditch for a terracing system.
selva/selve	Cultivated chestnut grove/groves.
solchi	Plow or drainage furrows.
smottamenti	Small landslides.
sporco/sporchi	Dirty.
terrazzamento	Terracing, either with earthen banks or stone walls.

terreno	Ground, land.
territorio	Territory.
usi civici	Common lands.
vernacchiaia	In Lucchese dialect, a mature coppice stand where the number of stems on each stool has been reduced due to competition, suitable for construction timber.
vincolo	Legal or customary constraint upon land use.
vite maritata	Festoons of grapevines trained along tree limbs, often of poplar or field maple.
zanelle	Drainage ditches for terracing system.
zolle	Vegetated banks.
zufolo	Whistle.

NOTES

Introduction

1. While it is by now popular knowledge that twentieth-century fire suppression set the stage for more intense forest fires, the 2020 California fires also brought to the fore the role of traditional Native American burning practices in reducing fire risk. See Fimright, "California Native American Tribe Has Been Burning Forests for 10,000 Years: What Can We Learn From Them?"; David, "The Racist Removal of Native Americans." For a discussion of the relative contributions of climate change and settlement density to forest fires, see Syphard et al., "Human Presence Diminishes the Importance of Climate in Driving Fire Activity Across the United States." For the relative roles of fuel load and wind events, see Keeley and Syphard, "Twenty-First Century California, USA, Wildfires."
2. For media accounts of drought, see Gilbert, "US South-West in Grip of Historic 'Megadrought.'" For effects of increased global average temperatures, see IPCC, "Climate Change 2014." For experiences of weather, see Ingold, "Earth, Sky, Wind, and Weather"; and for extreme weather experiences, see Hulme, *Weathered*, 55–67.
3. The Anthropocene concept has inspired a vast literature, with heated debates as to whether it is a useful term and when it started. See Mathews, "Anthropology and the Anthropocene"; Tsing, Mathews, and Bubandt, "Patchy Anthropocene." For earth systems approaches, see Steffen, "Planetary Boundaries." See also Smith and Zeder, "The Onset of the Anthropocene"; Bonneuil and Fressoz, *The Shock of the Anthropocene*; Lewis and Maslin, "Defining the Anthropocene."
4. Grove and Rackham, *The Nature of Mediterranean Europe*; Blondel, "The 'Design' of Mediterranean Landscapes"; Blondel, *The Mediterranean Region*.
5. For a discussion of the relationship between settler colonialism and American ideas of nature, see Cronon, "The Trouble with Wilderness"; and Whyte, "Settler Colonialism,

Ecology, and Environmental Injustice." The description of Mediterranean and Italian landscapes by George Perkins Marsh strongly influenced American environmentalism. See Marsh, *Man and Nature*. See Hall, *Earth Repair*, for influences and differences between Italian and American traditions of environmental restoration. For debates about Anthropocene-inspired conservation in the United States, see Hare, "The Anthropocene Trading Zone."

6. The capacity to resprout from a stump is common among broadleaves but rather rare among conifers. Human cultivation of trees by repeated cutting of main stems or branches is known as "coppicing" or "pollarding" and is found around the world. Lightfoot et al., "European Colonialism and the Anthropocene."
7. For a brief overview of historical ecology, see Crumley, "Historical Ecology and the Study of Landscape." For classic work in North America, see Foster and Aber, *Forests in Time*; in Europe, see Crumley and Marquardt, *Regional Dynamics*. I am particularly influenced by Oliver Rackham's intense focus on direct observation of biophysical evidence and by his skepticism about accounts of landscape change that depend only upon archives or interviews. Oliver Rackham, *Woodlands*; Grove and Rackham, *The Nature of Mediterranean Europe*. Diego Moreno's pioneering research on Ligurian landscapes similarly insists on relating archival and landscape evidence. See Moreno, *Dal Documento Al Terreno*; Cevasco and Moreno, "Historical Ecology in Modern Conservation in Italy." For use of trees as evidence of history in Italy, see Cevasco, "Multiple Use of Tree-Land in the Northern Apennines"; Cevasco, *Memoria Verde*. My use of multiple methods is also inspired by feminist geographer Diane Rocheleau. See Rocheleau, "Maps, Numbers, Text and Context."
8. The patron saint of Lucca, San Frediano, is credited with tracing a new channel for the River Serchio when it changed its course in the sixth century. Squatriti, "Water, Nature, and Culture in Early Medieval Lucca."
9. For a description of the unique capacities of plants, see Francis Hallé, *In Praise of Plants*; Hallé, *Atlas of Poetic Botany*. Suzanne Simard has done pioneering research on nutrient transfer between trees through mycorrhizal associations. See Simard, *Finding the Mother Tree*; Beiler et al., "Architecture of the Wood-Wide Web."
10. Hallé, *Atlas of Poetic Botany*, 8.
11. For drawings of plants and a discussion of terracing systems, see Grove and Rackham, *The Nature of Mediterranean Europe*, 45–71 and 107–17, respectively.
12. Anthropologists moved away from morphological analysis for their own reasons, including the rise of structuralism and the turn toward interpretation of culture, both taking place in the 1950s. Evans-Pritchard's diagrams of cattle coloration and naming in *The Nuer* can be seen as morphological arguments. His comparison of wet- and dry-season cattle grazing is a pioneering analysis of landscape structure. See Evans-Pritchard, *The Nuer*.
13. Tsing, Mathews, and Bubandt, "Patchy Anthropocene"; Mathews, "Landscapes and Throughscapes."

14. This is what Sheila Jasanoff has called a public-ignorance or information-deficit model. See Jasanoff, *Designs on Nature.*

Chapter 1. Sensing the Invisible

1. Chestnut is usually reckoned to grow best between two hundred and eight hundred meters, but thanks to the skill of peasant farmers, it formerly grew from sea level up to one thousand meters in the province of Lucca. I use the term "peasant" to describe those who historically would likely have identified themselves as a *contadino*. This term emerged during the Middle Ages to describe the economically and politically subordinated smallholders who lived and worked in the *contado*, the region surrounding a city. I use the term "farmer" to describe contemporary smallholders.
2. Over the past ten years there has been flowering of research on plants in the humanities. Michael Marder points to the general neglect of plants by the Western philosophical canon and engages with their ontological strangeness. For Patricia Vieira, the inscription of plants in their surroundings inspires literature about plants, *phytographia*. I am concerned with how we can notice the responsiveness of plants by focusing on morphology. As Francis Hallé points out, plants absorb energy through their exteriors and change shape drastically in response to their biographies. As shape-shifting monsters, plants upset our assumptions about the stability of morphologies and pull us into other temporalities: Marder, *Plant-Thinking*; Vieira, "Phytographia: Literature as Plant Writing"; Hallé, *In Praise of Plants*; Hallé, *Atlas of Poetic Botany*.
3. For a discussion of terracing systems across the Mediterranean, see Grove and Rackham, *The Nature of Mediterranean Europe*, 108–18. For archaeology of terracing in Liguria, see Roberto Maggi, "*I monti sun eggi.*" For a review of classical terms for terraces, see Di Bérenger, *Studii di archeologia forestale*, 256. For Renaissance agronomical treatises, see Sereni, *History of the Italian Agricultural Landscape*. For terms for terracing in medieval Lucca and Pisa, see Pedreschi, *I terrazzamenti agrari*. For the political importance of recognizing plants, see Myers, "How to Grow Livable Worlds."
4. As of 2018 the largest chestnut-producing country by far was China, with almost 2 million tons out of the global total of 2.3 million tons. Korea, Italy, Turkey, and Bolivia also each produce 50,000–80,000 tons. Food and Agriculture Organization of the United Nations, "FAOSTAT Statistics Database." Chestnut consumption has been recorded as far back as 1000–500 BCE in China. Hsuan Keng, "Economic Plants of Ancient North China"; Sheng et al., "Some Like It Hot," with archaeological evidence of chestnut consumption in Korea as early as 8000 BCE and of cultivation by 1200 BCE. See Chong Pil Choe and Martin T. Bale, "Current Perspectives on Settlement, Subsistence, and Cultivation in PreHistoric Korea"; Park et al., "Pollen and Sediment Evidence." Cultivation is recorded in Japan as early as 5000 BCE. See Kitagawa and Yasuda, "Development and Distribution of Castanea and Aesculus Culture During the Jomon Period in Japan." Indigenous people in the northeast and southern United States

considered American chestnut an important food source and likely favored it through tending practices. Abrams and Nowacki, "Native Americans as Active and Passive Promoters of Mast and Fruit Trees in the Eastern USA." There is disagreement as to whether chestnut was introduced to Europe from Turkey during the Roman Empire or whether it was also found in glacial refugia in the high Apennine mountains of Liguria and Southern Italy. Mattioni et al., "Microsatellite Markers Reveal a Strong Geographical Structure." Chestnut cultivation for food spread across Italy and the Mediterranean in the early Middle Ages. See Conedera et al., "The Cultivation of *Castanea sativa*"; Squatriti, *Landscape and Change in Early Medieval Italy.* For the history of chestnut blight in the United States, see Freinkel, *American Chestnut.*

5. For burning of leaf litter and chestnut cultivation, see Paolo Ottone, pseudonymous chestnut farmer, notes from interview with the author, Fosciandora, Lucca, November 26, 2013. A monumental survey of the chestnut varieties known in Lucca in the 1950s by Nino Breviglieri found over eighty cultivated varieties with seven or eight in each *comune*. A recent restudy of the same area, by Massimo Giambastiani, added two or three more for each *comune*. Breviglieri, "Indagini e osservazioni sulle cultivar di castagno"; Giambastiani et al., *Le cultivar di castagno della provincia di Lucca.*
6. In the Tuscan Apennines in the late nineteenth century, most households owned or had access to land, with an average of about three hectares per household. This would have been a mixture of woodland, chestnut, pasture, and cultivated land. In the lowlands, dominated by arable farming, most land was owned by larger estates that managed multiple sharecropper households, while many people were landless agricultural laborers: Sarti, *Long Live the Strong*, 101; Lazzarini, *La storia della mezzadria.* For statistics on chestnut cultivation and production, see Ministero delle Politiche Agricole Alimentari e Forestali, *Piano del settore castanicolo 2010–2013*. For a discussion of abandoned chestnut groves in Tuscany, see Bianchi et al., *La Selvicoltura dei castagneti da frutto abbandonati della Toscana*, 4.
7. This section draws upon site visits and conversations with seven chestnut growers across the province of Lucca in 2013–2016.
8. Scholars of multispecies ethnography have focused on affective and sensory attunements through which different species become involved with each other. Donna Haraway, *When Species Meet.* Writing about plant/insect ecologies, anthropologist Natasha Myers describes, "the affective push and pull among bodies, including the affinities, ruptures, enmeshments and repulsions among organisms constantly inventing new ways to live with and alongside each other." Myers, "Involutionary Momentum." These kinds of sensory attunements also take place between grafters and plants.
9. Giuseppe del Chiaro, Massimo Giambastiani, Alessandra del Chiaro, transcription of interview with author, Pozzuolo, Lucca, February 12, 2014.
10. Haraway, "Situated Knowledges." The relationship between determinacy/indeterminacy that we experience when we encounter plant morphologies is produced through the relationship between details and overall form. Sensory interactions with details

and plant morphologies resonate with, but have different properties from, the diffraction experiments investigated by Karen Barad. Barad, *Meeting the Universe Halfway.*

11. Chestnut canker was first reported in Italy in 1938. See Pavari, "Chestnut Blight in Europe." For a recent review of the biology, history, and impacts of chestnut canker, see Rigling and Prospero, "*Cryphonectria parasitica.*"
12. Giuseppe del Chiaro, Massimo Giambastiani, Alessandra del Chiaro, transcription of interview with author, Pozzuolo, Lucca, February 12, 2014. In Italy, grafting is a popular hobby for gardeners and a common practice among farmers and plant nursery growers. Bookstores and gardening centers offer manuals on how to graft fruit trees of many kinds. Experimentally minded cultivators take pleasure in producing cross-species grafts. Grafting techniques have names such as *a spacco, a zufolo, a corona,* and they require particular skills. The cambium layer is the zone of active cell division, which lies between the bark and the heartwood of a tree. On the outer side is the phloem layer; on the inner is xylem, which eventually becomes heartwood. Xylem, heartwood, and bark are dead and dry. In woody plants only a narrow zone of active cell division and nutrient transport a few millimeters beneath the bark is alive. Most Italian farmers think grafting is best done under a waning moon, as this will prevent the plant from "bleeding." Analogies of plant and human body extend to talking about the bark as the "skin" and the rising sap as the circulation of blood. These are productive anthropomorphisms through which people imagine how trees will respond to cutting, grafting, and tending.
13. Zeder, "Core Questions in Domestication Research"; Zeder, "Domestication and Early Agriculture in the Mediterranean Basin." For statistics on chestnut cultivation, see Ministero delle Politiche Agricole Alimentari e Forestali, *Piano del settore castanicolo.* For belowground interactions between plants, see Callaway, "Positive Interactions Among Plants"; Graham, "Transfer of Dye Through Natural Root Graft"; Beiler et al., "Architecture of the Wood Wide Web." The capacity of plants to sense and respond to light, nutrient, and olfactory stimuli is well known. Classic studies had attributed plant sensing to slow signaling through the diffusion of plant hormones within the plant. Over the past two decades the field of plant signaling has found more rapid electrical, hydraulic, and chemical signaling, as well as vesicle-mediated auxin transport. See Brenner et al., "Plant Neurobiology."
14. For drawings of coordinations, see Elaine Gan and Anna Tsing, "How Things Hold." For descriptions of sensing and diagramming, see Mathews, "Landscapes and Throughscapes."
15. For regulations on chestnut in Tuscany, see Gabbrielli, "La legislazione forestale in Toscana." For protection of chestnut in the Republic of Lucca, see Sabbatini, "La rottura degli equilibri di antico regime"; Puccinelli, "All'origine di una monocultura." For state interest in drainage and water control across the Mediterranean, see Braudel, *The Mediterranean and the Mediterranean World,* 60–85. For control of water and drainage in the plain of Lucca, see Squatriti, "Water, Nature, and Culture."

16. Saminiati, "Trattato d'agricoltura," 31. Author translation. Soil classifications likely derived from classical traditions. See Winiwarter, "Prolegomena to a History of Soil Knowledge in Europe." Saminiati was also at pains to emphasize the practical steps required to improve soils. Saminiati, "Trattato d'agricoltura," 27. Author translation.
17. For connections between the networks of the imperial guano trade and "High Victorian" agriculture in Britain and the United States, see Cushman, *Guano and the Opening of the Pacific World.* For an account of the relationship between soil science and farmer knowledge of soil vitality in Colombia, see Lyons, "Soil Science, Development, and the 'Elusive Nature' of Colombia's Amazonian Plains."
18. Conklin, *Hanunoó Agriculture*; Evans-Pritchard, *The Nuer.*
19. Macfarlane, *Landmarks.* Rose, "Dreaming Ecology: Beyond the Between."
20. For fictional accounts of the impacts of toxicity upon human form, see Nixon, "Neoliberalism, Slow Violence, and the Environmental Picaresque." For impacts of radioactivity upon the morphologies of humans and plants, see Brown, "Learning to Read the Great Chernobyl Acceleration." For recent debates on ontologies, see Bessire and Bond, "Ontological Anthropology"; and Blaser, "Ontology and Indigeneity." I follow Marianne Lien and John Law in seeing ontologies as emerging from practices, but I build on their approach to consider the ontologies that emerge through relationships between more than human beings. See Law and Lien, "Slippery." For ontological anarchy, see Viveiros de Castro, "On Models and Examples." Borges, "Funes the Memorious."
21. Tsing, Mathews, and Bubandt, "Patchy Anthropocene."
22. This is not geomorphology but biogeomorphology. Plant/animal/soil/geological beings are in relationship with each other. The distinction between life and nonlife that Elizabeth Povinelli points to as important for secular liberal politics is not relevant when thinking about biogeomorphology. See Povinelli, *Geontologies.*

Interlude I. Plant Morphology Leads to Geomorphology

1. For classical knowledge of soil, see Winiwarter, "Prolegomena to a History of Soil Knowledge in Europe." For Montaigne's visit to Lucca, see Rackham, *The Nature of Mediterranean Europe,* 114. For archaeological evidence of tenth-century-BCE terracing systems in Liguria, see Maggi, "*I monti sun eggi.*" The Lucchese agronomical writer Vincenzo Saminiati recommended the use of grassy horizontal banks to retain soil; see Saminiati, "Trattato d'agricoltura," 31. For nineteenth-century accounts of terraces, see Sismondi, *Tableau de L'Agriculture Toscane*; Mazzarosa, *Le pratiche della campagna lucchese.* For Renaissance and enlightenment agronomical treatises and terracing practices, see the classic work by Sereni, *History of the Italian Agricultural Landscape.* For an illustrated English language survey of terracing and drainage systems and the work of Caruso, see Corti et al., "Italian Soil Management from Antiquity to Nowadays."

2. Grove and Rackham, *The Nature of Mediterranean Europe*, 107–18.
3. Fabio Casella, interview with Andrew Mathews and Fabio Malfatti, Calci, Italy, July 12, 2016. Like irrigation systems, terracing systems are sustained by largely invisible drainage systems. For irrigation systems, see Barnes, *Cultivating the Nile*. For historic and traditional terms for terracing systems in Lucca, see Pedreschi, *I terrazzamente agrari*. For classical terms, see Di Bérenger, *Studii di archeologia forestale*, 256. For terracing and drainage systems on the Monte Pisano, see Rizzo et al., *La gestione delle sistemazioni idraulico-agrarie nel Monte Pisano*. For anthropogenic soils, see Corti et al., "Italian Soil Management."
4. Sereni, *History of the Italian Agricultural Landscape*.

Chapter 2. From Plant Morphologies to Landscape Structures

1. Portions of this chapter have been published as Mathews, "Landscapes and Throughscapes." For a description of the ecology of the Monte Pisano, see appendix 1. This mountain range is known in older sources as the Monti Pisani, but I follow current vernacular usage. Although it is an outlier of the Apennine mountains, the Monte Pisano range has undergone many of the processes experienced by mountain communities across Italy. Far from being a barrier to movement, the Apennines were open to dense transport networks that linked mountain dwellers to the lowlands through seasonal labor, transhumance, and trade. Braudel, *The Mediterranean and the Mediterranean World*, 25–102; Sabbatini, "La rottura degli equilibri di antico regime"; Ciuffetti, *Appennino: Economie, culture e spazi sociali*, 213–43, 139–77. As John McNeill points out, connections to international markets in the second half of the nineteenth century displaced industrial activities from the mountains. McNeill, *The Mountains of the Mediterranean World*, 221–71.
2. Maritime pine (*pino marittimo, Pinus pinaster*) is native to western Spain and Portugal. It was introduced in coastal plantings in this area in the eighteenth century because of its salt tolerance, but it was a source of naval timber on the Monte Pisano as early as the Middle Ages. Flammable and threatened by disease, maritime pine is now considered an undesirable non-native species whose elimination is encouraged by the regional government. The capacity of many broadleaf and a few conifer tree species to resprout from a stump has allowed people around the world to produce a vast variety of products through the practice known as "coppicing." Baskets, barrels, construction timber, fence posts, or vine poles can be produced from coppices; see Rackham, *Woodlands*. Italy was composed of a patchwork of states until reunification between 1859 and 1870. For most of the past thousand years, until 1799, Lucca was a republic ruled by an aristocratic oligarchy. Pisa was first an independent state and then part of Florentine territory from 1406. For cultivation practices in Lucca in the early nineteenth century, see Mazzarosa, *Le pratiche della campagna lucchese*.

3. For the history of chestnut cultivation, see Squatriti, *Landscape and Change in Early Medieval Italy*; Puccinelli, "All'origine di una monocultura"; Giannini and Gabbrielli, "Evolution of Multifunctional Land-Use Systems." The concept of "landscape structures" was developed in conversation with Anna Tsing and Nils Bubandt, in which we define these as "observations of the patterns of human and nonhuman assemblages as these emerge historically." Tsing, Mathews, and Bubandt, "Patchy Anthropocene." See also Mathews, "Landscapes and Throughscapes."
4. For art-historical approaches to landscapes, see Cosgrove, "Prospect, Perspective and the Evolution of the Landscape Idea"; Berger, *Landscapes.* For a response calling for attention to the substance and political history of landscape, see Olwig, "Recovering the Substantive Nature of Landscape." For encounters between beings, see Tsing, *The Mushroom at the End of the World.* For enactment of empirical ontologies, see Law and Lien, "Slippery." My friend Enrico Chiesa could sense invisible lines of energy in the landscape that told him where plants would flourish or struggle. I have not discussed invisible beings and energies in this book, but practical ontologies could emerge in relation to these as well. For a description of ghosts in landscapes, for example, see Tsai, Carbonell, Chevrier, and Tsing, "Golden Snail Opera."
5. The historical ecologist Oliver Rackham insisted on the importance of fieldwork and direct observation over archival evidence alone. See Grove and Rackham, *The Nature of Mediterranean Europe*, 20. My drawings of tree form are inspired by his; ibid., 48–49.
6. For a classic study of infrastructure as an information network, see the work of feminist scholar Susan Leigh Star; Star, "The Ethnography of Infrastructure." For a review of infrastructure studies, see Larkin, "The Politics and Poetics of Infrastructure." For infrastructure as applied to landscape, see Carse, "Nature as Infrastructure" and Barnes, *Cultivating the Nile.* Willingness to trust my senses is an openness to what Eduardo Viveiros de Castro calls the "ontological anarchy" of the world; see Viveiros de Castro, "On Models and Examples." However, I also seek to tell stories about larger landscape structures, and histories of economic and social change.
7. For a multidisciplinary form of political ecology, see Rocheleau, "Maps, Numbers, Text and Context." The interdisciplinary field of historical ecology has long been open to an eclectic use of methods from across the natural sciences, social sciences, and humanities: Crumley, "Historical Ecology and the Study of Landscape." For phenomenological approaches that are inspired by natural history, see the work of the Brown Coal group in Denmark: Bubandt and Tsing, "Feral Dynamics of Post-Industrial Ruin"; Gan, Sullivan, and Tsing, "Using Natural History in the Study of Industrial Ruins"; Højrup and Swanson, "The Making of Unstable Ground." For a discussion of landscape structure, see Tsing, Mathews, and Bubandt, "Patchy Anthropocene." For coordinations, see Gan and Tsing, "How Things Hold."
8. Ingold, "Materials Against Materiality"; Ingold, "Toward an Ecology of Materials."

9. Tree growth is strongly affected by soil fertility and water availability, making size a very unreliable guide to tree age. Borelli and Pettina give an age of 177 years for a tree that was less than half this size, suggesting that this one was at least a couple of centuries old: Borelli and Pettina, "La struttura e la coltivazione dei castagneti."
10. I was inspired to plunge into drawing by a conversation with the biologist Peter Funch. For natural history field notes and drawings, see Canfield, *Field Notes on Science and Nature.* For examples of anthropological diagrams and drawings, see Evans-Pritchard, *The Nuer*; Lévi-Strauss, *Tristes Tropiques.* For imaginative use of diagrams to describe social and environmental change, see Misrach and Orff, *Petrochemical America*; and Tsing et al., *Feral Atlas.*
11. This dating is a principled guess, based upon the size of the two patterns of smaller stems that might have been cut in the 1990s and the 1970s.
12. Older accounts of plant growth emphasize a kind of competitive and hierarchical relationship between "dominant" or "apical" meristems and "suppressed" meristems. Botanists increasingly see growth as emerging through a more collaborative process of signaling between different parts of the plant. See Brenner et al., "Plant Neurobiology."
13. Stefano Fazzi, transcript of recorded interview with author, Borgo a Mozzano, Lucca, February 15, 2014.
14. Massimo Giambastiani and Alessandra del Chiaro, transcript of recorded interview with author, Monte Romagna, Lucca, February 18, 2014.
15. For agro/sylvo/pastoral systems in the Apennines, see Giannini and Gabbrielli, "Evolution of Multifunctional Land-Use Systems." For rural industry and mobility, see Ciuffetti, *Appennino: Economie, culture e spazi sociali.* In Vorno most common lands were sold off to pay taxes in the sixteenth century. Massoni, *La pieve e la comunità di Vorno,* 164–72. Only about forty hectares of publicly owned forest remain, a tiny remainder of the medieval commons. For ancien régime forest laws under the Republic of Lucca, see Sabbatini, "La rottura degli equilibri di antico regime." For the protection of pines on the Pisa side of the mountains, see Martini, *La storia di Calci,* 137–39; Gabbrielli, "Selvicoltura Toscana nel '700: seconda parte," 201–3.
16. For the dissolution of forestry regulations by Peter Leopold of Tuscany, see Gabbrielli, "La Legislazione Forestale in Toscana Dall' Inizio Alla Caduta del Granducato." In Lucca the extremes of liberal reforms (1800–1815) were tempered under restored Bourbon rule between 1815 and 1847, but the tide was strongly in favor of opening access to forests. For the postunification alienation of state lands in Southern Italy, see Armiero, "La ricchezza della montagna"; Biasillo and Armiero, "Seeing the Nation for the Trees"; McNeill, *Mountains of the Mediterranean World,* 260–66. For eighteenth-century economic changes on the Monte Pisano, see Gabbrielli, "Selvicoltura Toscana nel '700: seconda parte," 202–3.
17. For national discussion of hydrogeological instability, see Armiero, *A Rugged Nation,* 21–33. For local views on excessive logging and opposition to the forest regulations

in Calci, see Martini, *La storia di Calci*, 140–41; and for landowner opposition to forestry regulations across Tuscany, see Biagianti, "Boschi e pascoli nella montagna Toscana fra sette e novecento."

18. Forestry regulations were promulgated by provincial administrations, see, for example, Consiglio Provinciale dell'Economia, *Prescrizioni di massima e di Polizia Forestale*. For one shepherd's attitude to afforestation, I spoke with Michele Fazzi, a pseudonymous retired shepherd in Asciano, Pisa, on March 22, 2019. Statistics for grazing animals should be interpreted as very approximate, as shepherds had good reasons to conceal their animals from the state. Statistics are from Istituto Centrale di Statistica del Regno D'Italia, *Catasto Agrario: 1929,VIII Compartimento della Toscana, Provincia di Pisa*; Istituto Centrale di Statistica del Regno D'Italia, *VIII Compartimento della Toscana, Provincia di Lucca*. Most of the 4499 sheep reported for the Capannori region of Lucca would have been from the Monte Pisano. For the Fascist 'war on goats' see Armiero, *A Rugged Nation*, 129–34. For Fascist era reforestation and postwar fires on the Monte Pisano, see Martini, *La storia di Calci*, 141. For pre- and postwar reforestation in Tuscany and Italy, see Ciabatti et al., *I rimboschimenti in Toscana e la loro gestione*.
19. Cadastral tax maps were introduced across Europe during the eighteenth century. Taxation was based upon the productivity of declared land use, with the goal of favoring capital investments and long-term increase in tax revenues. The cadastral tax mapping implemented by the Duchy of Lucca (*Catasto Nuovo Lucchese*) and the Grand Duchy of Tuscany (*Antico Catasto Toscano*, also, *Catasto Leopoldino*) required landowners to report land use for every tax parcel. The cadastral mapping process took from 1819 to 1825 for Pisa, and from 1834 to 1846 for Lucca. For the valley of Vorno, the survey was carried out in 1846. See Grava, "Gli Opifici di Calci all'Impianto del 'Leopoldino.'" Bertacchi, Sani, and Tomei, *La Vegetazione del Monte Pisano*.
20. Systematic comparison of multiple lines of evidence to understand landscape history is a hallmark of historical ecology; see Crumley, "Historical Ecology and the Study of Landscape." For use of maps, historical archives, and direct observation of landscape evidence, see Moreno, *Dal documento al terreno*; Agnoletti, *L'evoluzione del paesaggio nella tenuta di Migliarino*; Cevasco, *Memoria verde*. My interest in plant form as evidence of plant biographies follows approaches pioneered by Oliver Rackham; see Grove and Rackham, *The Nature of Mediterranean Europe*. The maps of the *Antico Catasto Toscano* and the *Catasto Nuovo Lucchese* have been digitized and georeferenced by the Tuscany region, providing evidence of the land-use history of each parcel of land. The *Catasto Vecchio Lucchese* was begun under the principate of Napoleon's sister Elisa Buonaparte Baciocchi in 1807, but it was never completed. The *Catasto Nuovo Lucchese* was incorporated into the *Antico Catasto Toscano* when Lucca was absorbed by the Grand Duchy of Tuscany in 1847, although the Tuscan *catasto* was itself not finally completed until national unification in 1860. The *Catasto*

Nuovo Luccchese: Giornale della misura e stima records area and land use for each tax parcel.

21. All land uses are from the *Catasto Nuovo Lucchese: Giornale della misura e stima.*
22. Massoni, *La pieve e la comunità di Vorno*, 255–56.
23. For classical cultivation practices and descriptions of the medieval *alberata* and *piantata* landscapes, see Sereni, *History of the Italian Agricultural Landscape*, 21–41 and 213–20. Sereni estimates that in Central Italy various forms of *promiscuo* (polycultures) were greater in area than arable farming at the beginning of the twentieth century; Sereni, ibid., 314–20.
24. In modern usage, *contado* means "countryside," but in medieval usage it was closer to our sense of "county." Few topics have attracted as much debate as the *mezzadria* sharecropping system that dominated much of Central and Northern Italy between about 1400 and 1950. It was a flexible and continually changing system that involved a considerable degree of intimacy between landlord and peasant, as well as exploitation and sexual predation by landlords or their representatives. For historical overviews, see Piccinni, "Mezzadria e potere politico"; Biagioli, "La mezzadria poderale." For English-language discussions that build upon Italian-language agrarian histories, see Holmes, *Cultural Disenchantments*; Gaggio, *The Shaping of Tuscany*. Average property sizes in the Apennines and the Garfagnana north of Lucca were only about three hectares in the 1860s. Sarti, *Long Live the Strong*, 101. An investigation of the last days of peasant agriculture near Lucca in the 1950s found that the vast majority of property holdings in the plains and hills were smaller than two hectares. Sharecroppers dominated properties in the two-to-five-hectare range, with a very small number of larger estates accounting for the remainder. For employment in industry as washerwomen in the village of Vorno, see Massoni, *La pieve e la comunità di Vorno*. The numerous parcels of one-tenth of a hectare or less were owned by smallholders who were likely agricultural laborers. See Lazzarini, *La storia della mezzadria*. For an account of social transformations across twentieth-century Tuscany, see Gaggio, *The Shaping of Tuscany*.
25. Abandoned land can become a kind of "outside" to capitalism. Making abandoned and "unowned" land economically productive requires major legal, political, and financial work to bring it into the property form once again. Land abandonment takes place around the world and is especially acute in rural areas in developed countries, where declining and aging populations are causing what we might call "postagrarian" and to some extent "postproperty" landscapes. Japan and Italy are at the forefront of such processes.
26. Use of transect diagrams is a long-recognized analytic method among historical ecologists. See, e.g., Cevasco, *Memoria verde*, 22; Cevasco, "Multiple Use of Tree-Land."
27. These diagrams and my transect walks across the landscape are similar to the "agential cuts" that enact realities, as described by Karen Barad in *Meeting the Universe*

Halfway. Landscape structures are patterns that emerge from the transformations that take place in my perceptions as a result of moving *through* landscapes, of looking from near to far, and of interview and archival research. Landscape structures are less defined and more provisional than agential cuts. Multiple landscape structures can coexist, lie through, or overlap with each other. See Mathews, "Landscapes and Throughscapes."

Chapter 3. Fast and Slow Disasters

1. I use the term "care" to summarize the concerns of rural people with practical activities of plant, animal, and soil care, as well as their aesthetic, ethical, and political commitments to caring for the landscape. They complained of *abbandono* (abandonment), of the need to *badare* (care for) the landscape, and about *mancanza di cura* (lack of care). This practical sense of care, albeit coming from a different direction, resonates with the important feminist literature and theorizations of care; see De la Bellacasa, "Matters of Care in Technoscience."
2. This chapter draws on fifteen interviews with elderly former shepherds and peasants from communities around the Monte Pisano in 2019. For a description of the concerns of contemporary hobby farmers, see Gennai-Schott et al., "Who Remains When Professional Farmers Give Up?" In many areas of the Apennines, charcoal burning would also have reduced flammable vegetation. The Monte Pisano is dominated by pine and chestnut, species that are less suited to charcoal, but some charcoal burning did take place, especially in areas with oak and holm oak, *Quercus ilex*.
3. Japanese chestnut, *Castanea crenata*, and to a lesser extent Chinese chestnut, *Castanea mollissima*, are resistant to ink disease, suggesting that they coevolved with *Phytophthora cambivora* and *Phytophthora cinnamomi*, and that the introduction of Japanese and Chinese chestnut to North America and Europe was also responsible for introducing ink disease. Anagnostakis, "The Effect of Multiple Importations of Pests and Pathogens on a Native Tree"; Heiniger and Rigling, "Biological Control of Chestnut Blight in Europe." With a low seed weight and easily dispersed winged seeds, a thin bark that burns easily, and early reproductive age, *Pinus pinaster* is well adapted to flourish after fires. See Richardson, "Ecology and Biogeography of Pinus"; Keeley and Zedler, "Evolution of Life Histories of Pinus."
4. As the geographer Mike Hulme points out, climate should not be understood solely as a technical term. Cultures around the world have always understood "recognizable and expected patterns of atmospheric behavior and performance": Hulme, "Weather-Worlds of the Anthropocene and the End of Climate." Historical climate modeling for the Monte Pisano found that maximum and minimum mean annual temperature increased by about 1.5°C between 1820 and 1980, and by 0.8°C from 1980 to 2000, while precipitation showed no significant change. See Casazza et al., "Interactions between Land Use, Pathogens, and Climate Change." For historical climate model-

ing in Italy, see Brunetti et al., "Temperature and Precipitation Variability in Italy in the Last Two Centuries."

5. *Phytophthora* water molds are probably the most dangerous invasive plant pathogen globally and are likely spread by the international trade in live plants. Plant nurseries provide conditions of ecological simplification and overwatering and are ideal locations for the proliferation of *Phytophthora*. See Vettraino et al., "Recovery and Pathogenicity of *Phytophthora* Species"; Jung et al., "Widespread *Phytophthora* Infestations in European Nurseries"; Croucher, Mascheretti, and Garbelotto, "Combining Field Epidemiological Information and Genetic Data." Plant nurseries may unintentionally produce the hybridization of native and non-native *Phytophthora* species and cause the rapid evolution of pathogenicity: Brasier, "Rapid Evolution of Introduced Plant Pathogens via Interspecific Hybridization"; Brasier, "Plant Pathology." For descriptions of the initial epidemic in Lucca, see Puccinelli, "Sulla malattia del castagno"; for impacts across Italy, see Selva, *Memorie per servire allo studio della malattia dei castagni*. For descriptions of the ecological effects of the epidemic upon the Monte Pisano, see Anonymous, "Sulla e ginestra," 173–78.
6. Girolamo Caruso, "Intorno alla malattia dei castagni ne' Monti Pisani," 339–40.
7. Girolamo Caruso, "Intorno alla malattia dei castagni ne' Monti Pisani," 339–40. Giuseppe Gibelli, *Nuovi studi sulla malattia del castagno, detta dell'inchiostro*. Pio Fortunato Bonucelli, "Il castagno nella Lucchesia," 2–26; Vettraino et al., "Recovery and Pathogenicity of *Phytophthora* Species."
8. Working in Buti in the early 2000s, Massimo Giambastiani heard of the effects of the 1880s' *male del inchiostro* epidemic: Massimo Giambastiani, transcript of interview with author, Lucca, January 7, 2013. Stefano Fazzi, transcript of interview with author, Borgo a Mozzano, Lucca, February 15, 2014.
9. Giuseppe del Chiaro, Massimo Giambastiani, Alessandra del Chiaro, transcript of interview with author, Pozzuolo, Lucca, February 12, 2014. For the arrival of chestnut canker in Italy, see Pavari, "Chestnut Blight in Europe." The following citations provide information for the inset box. For the role of CHV-1 virus in slowing the disease, see Heiniger and Rigling, "Biological Control of Chestnut Blight in Europe." For the spread of chestnut disease from Asia, see Anagnostakis, "The Effect of Multiple Importations of Pests and Pathogens"; Freinkel, *American Chestnut*, 64–70. For European experiments with Japanese chestnut, see Farneti, Lissone, and Montemartini, "La resistenza del castagno Giapponese alla malattia dell'inchiostro." For the introduction of Japanese chestnut in Italy, see Gabbrielli, "Lionello Petri." For reports of the disease outbreak in Lucca and Italy, see Borelli and Pettina, "Le malattie del castagno." Pavari, "Chestnut Blight in Europe."
10. Land use and industrial buildings are from Grava, "Gli opifici di Calci all'impianto del 'Leopoldino.'" For ease of representation, we have omitted areas of pasture and woodland on the crest of the mountains. For a color version of this map, see Casazza et al., "Interactions Between Land Use, Pathogens, and Climate Change."

11. Figures 30, 31, and 32 were produced by Fabio Malfatti, of the Centro Ricerche Etno-Antropologiche. Present-day vegetation type is from the survey of Bertacchi, Sani, and Tomei, *La Vegetazione del Monte Pisano*. Land use and chestnut drying sheds in the valley of Calci are modified from Grava, "Gli Opifici di Calci All'Impianto del 'Leopoldino.'"
12. Giuseppe del Chiaro, Massimo Giambastiani, Alessandra del Chiaro, transcript of interview with author, Pozzuolo, Lucca, February 12, 2014. Massimo Giambastiani and Alessandra del Chiaro, transcript of recorded interview with author, Monte Romagna, Lucca, February 18, 2014. Giambastiani et al., *Le cultivar di castagno della provincia di Lucca*.
13. For a recent ethnographic study of controlled burning, see Jon Nyquist on prescribed burning in Australia: Nyquist, "Fire and the Creation of Landscape Regimes." For firefighting in the United States, see Petryna," Wildfires at the Edges of Science." For a world history of fire and the opposition of European states to fire, see Pyne, *Vestal Fire*. The intense stigma attached to burning has meant that there has been little empirical work on fire management by peasants or pastoralists anywhere in the Mediterranean. For ethnohistorical descriptions of contemporary fire management in the Pyrenees, see Metailie, "Mountain Landscape, Pastoral Management and Traditional Practices in the Northern Pyrenees (France)"; and in less detail across the Mediterranean, see Grove and Rackham, *The Nature of Mediterranean Europe*, 217–40.
14. Writing in 1890, Pelosini describes women firewood gatherers as carrying three loads of forty-eight kilograms each from the crest to the base of the mountains every day: "Crowds of poor young women are used to a mode of labor that even the strongest of dumb animals could not sustain for long." Pelosini, *Ricordi, tradizioni e legende dei Monti Pisani*, 95.
15. Interviews with twenty-one elderly former farmers and shepherds in communities around the Monte Pisano, carried out in 2016 and 2019, confirmed that leaf-litter raking was a ubiquitous practice. Ten of these interviews were with women, but five of the six people who recounted doing litter raking themselves were women, and it seems likely that more women than men did this work. Women also worked at spinning, as well as washing laundry for the cities of Pisa and Lucca. Washing machines inspired other stories. One of the causes of agricultural abandonment that I used to hear was that young women would refuse to marry peasants who could not provide a washing machine.
16. Maria Lenzarini, pseudonymous elder, transcript of recorded interview with Andrew Mathews, Fabio Malfatti, and Fabio Casella, Calci, Pisa, March 22, 2019. Woodland of oak, chestnut, or other broadleaf species is known as *bosco*, pine forest as *pineta*.
17. For litter raking in Switzerland, see Gimmi et al., "Soil Carbon Pools in Swiss Forests Show Legacy Effects." For Nepal and India, I am indebted to a personal communication from Wendy King in 2019. For a wealth of now-forgotten vegetation management practices in Liguria, see Moreno, "Escaping from 'Landscape.'" Preliminary

analysis of interviews carried out in 2019 suggests that most litter raking in the Monte Pisano was done by women and children. For litter raking regulations, see Consiglio Provinciale dell'Economia, *Prescrizioni di Massima e di Polizia Forestale.*

18. Brunetti et al., "Temperature and Precipitation Variability in Italy in the Last Two Centuries."
19. Fabio Casella, recorded interview with Andrew Mathews and Fabio Malfatti, Calci, Pisa, July 12, 2016.
20. This is strikingly different from media coverage of major forest fires in Australia and the United States, where the need for prescribed burning to cope with excessive fuel loads is routinely discussed. See Nyquist, "Fire and the Creation of Landscape Regimes."
21. Gori, "Dopo il rogo."
22. Research on the postfire response was carried out by my collaborator, Fabio Malfatti. For debates on postfire recovery, see Gori, "Dopo il rogo."
23. In 2019 a group of municipalities, environmental activists, and concerned academics formed a new organization called the Comunità del Bosco (Forest Community) with the goal of caring for and restoring the landscape of the Monte Pisano; see https://www.comunitadelboscomontepisano.it.
24. Masiero, "Maltempo, Calci minacciata da un torrente di cenere."
25. Bianchi, "Il Serra brucia ancora."
26. Tsing, Mathews, and Bubandt, "Patchy Anthropocene."
27. For a discussion of the need for improved regulation in the international live-plant trade, see Roy et al., "Increasing Forest Loss Worldwide from Invasive Pests Requires New Trade Regulations." For impact of trade on plant diseases, see Santini et al., "Tracing the Role of Human Civilization in the Globalization of Plant Pathogens."
28. For the rapid shift from climate change to practical projects, see Orlove et al., "Framing Climate Change in Frontline Communities," which describes how people in Italy, the United States, and Peru found a community frame more helpful in dealing with environmental change, and that "it is possible to take action to address climate change without addressing climate change itself." For a classic study of the "deficit model" of public understanding, see Wynne, "Misunderstood Misunderstandings." For people's interest in nonhumans and their environment, see O'Reilly, "The Substance of Climate."

Chapter 4. Plant Morphology, Geomorphology, and Weather

1. Giuseppe Mela, pseudonymous biomass-energy entrepreneur, transcript of interview with Andrew Mathews, Lucca, January 10, 2014. People in Italy, but especially in the countryside, use the term *la forestale* to vaguely indicate "the forest service." This could mean the Corpo Forestale dello Stato (the national forest service, assimilated into the Carabinieri in 2016), the regional forest service of Tuscany, or even representatives

of local *comuni* (municipalities) or associations of municipalities (in mountainous areas, these are known as Unioni dei Comuni, which are the heirs of former Comunità Montane). The term Giuseppe used, *buon padre di familia,* is embedded in Italian law and derives from the Roman legal term *bonus pater familias*, which indicates the common sense of the average head of household.

2. For different types of climate knowledge, see Hulme, *Weathered*, 28–32. For vernacular expectations of normal and extreme weather, see Hulme, "Weather-Worlds of the Anthropocene and the End of Climate." Anthropocene conservation is marked by an acceptance of human activity in ecosystems. For a discussion of conservation in the Anthropocene, see Jamie Lorimer, *Wildlife in the Anthropocene*; Hare, "The Anthropocene Trading Zone." For ordinary people's experiences of the processes that link earth and sky into a weather world, see Ingold, "Earth, Sky, Wind, and Weather."
3. Hulme, *Weathered*, 58. See also O'Reilly, "The Substance of Climate."
4. Hydrologists and soil scientists think that the relationship between forest cover and floods is more complex. Theories of connections between forests and climate date back to classical Greece and were a prominent feature of colonial forest policies around the world. Recent climate change policies that focus on reforestation and forest protection (known as REDD+) draw upon older ways of connecting forests to climate: Grove and Rackham, *The Nature of Mediterranean Europe*, 141–44; Grove, *Green Imperialism*; Mathews, "Scandals, Audits, and Fictions"; Mathews, "Unlikely Alliances." For a comparison of conservation in Italy and the United States, see Marcus Hall's wonderful *Earth Repair.* Recent approaches to conservation in the United States are beginning to bring human care back in. See Marris, "Rambunctious Garden"; Hare, "The Anthropocened Trading Zone." For Native American land care, see Lightfoot et al., "Anthropogenic Burning on the Central California Coast"; Whyte, "Settler Colonialism, Ecology, and Environmental Injustice."
5. People in medieval Europe paid close attention to the shapes of trees, from smallwood to large timber. See Keyser, "The Transformation of Traditional Woodland Management."
6. Traditional tree management across Europe focused not upon calculating future volumes but upon managing time through attention to the forms of desired timber and firewood assortments. See Moreno, "Querce come olivi"; Keyser, "The Transformation of Traditional Woodland Management"; Di Bérenger, *Studii di archeologia forestale.* In the early nineteenth century the new discipline of forestry represented this traditional way of thinking about tree time as disorganized and illegible. Foresters tried to substitute peasant management of time through form with calculations of volume growth over time. In Italy, as in almost all Mediterranean landscapes, scientific forestry has had relatively little success in controlling peasant-managed forests. Foresters have learned to coexist with peasant management of time through attention to plant form.

7. The acacia (*Robinia pseudoacacia*) was introduced in the nineteenth century and promoted as an erosion-control species from the 1950s onward. It is now considered an aggressive invasive species. The word *matricina* resembles *madre* (mother) to which it may be related. *Matricine* are imagined as a source of seed to produce new trees that will replace coppice stumps that occasionally die after logging. Quotations are from Michele Gozzi, pseudonymous firewood cutter, recorded interview with the author, Lucca, March 26, 2014.
8. Law and Lien, "Slippery."
9. *Il Tirreno* is printed in Livorno with a circulation of about 55,000, with local editions for cities across central and northern Tuscany. A search for the term *dissesto idrogeologico* yielded over 1,000 articles between 1997 and 2018. Even when restricting my search by adding in the term *alveo* (riverbed), I found 59 articles. In comparison, climate change (*cambiamento climatico*) had only 244 articles in the same period, with the vast majority (238) published after 2010. Unlike modern English, colloquial Italian is richly endowed with widely understood terms for drainage and landform. This makes my translations of vernacular language from newspapers seem more technical than they really are. *Il Tirreno*, "Stop all'ubriacatura ecologista." Elmi, "Più manutenzione dei boschi per prevenire gli smottamenti." Jasanoff, "Virtual, Visible, and Actionable."
10. Often, new roads interfere in the hydrology of the landscape, becoming a source of instability of their own, but this is more rarely remarked upon: Agnoletti et al., "Paesaggio e Dissesto Idrogeologico."
11. Faced with the success of mechanized grain monocultures, grain had already largely disappeared from these polycultures.
12. Any conversation in a café can elicit a story of dangerous and oppressive bureaucracies. For an account of encounters with housing bureaucracies in Rome, see Herzfeld, *Evicted from Eternity*.
13. As Mike Hulme points out, "People living in places develop their sense of climate through lifelong experience of how their weather behaves, often mediated through memorialized artefacts in the landscape or through oral histories." This insight also applies to emergent forms, such as trees and riverbeds. Hulme, "Weather-Worlds of the Anthropocene and the End of Climate."

Chapter 5. Biogeomorphological Politics

1. My discussion of Mediterranean landscape instability owes much to the work of Rackham and Grove, *The Nature of Mediterranean Europe*, and to McNeill, *The Mountains of the Mediterranean World*. For a pioneering study of erosion in Lesotho, see Showers, *Imperial Gullies*.
2. Rocks and soil are lively without being alive: indeed, the distinction between *bios* and *geos* outlined by Elizabeth Povinelli is not relevant to the biogeomorphological

politics in chapter 5. See Povinelli, *Geontologies*. Although geomorphologists argue that their discipline is already attentive to the role of biota in shaping landform, some prefer the term "biogeomorphology," defined as "the study of the interaction between geomorphological processes and biota." See Naylor, Viles, and Carter, "Biogeomorphology Revisited." I have avoided the unwieldy term "anthrobiogeomorphology" by including humans within the *bios*. The agronomical literature on the Italian landscape, stretching back to classical times, is in this light a predecessor to the current field of biogeomorphology. For terracing and drainage systems, see Sereni, *History of the Italian Agricultural Landscape*. For an accessible recent review, see Corti et al., "Italian Soil Management from Antiquity to Nowadays."

3. Massimo Giambastiani and Alessandra del Chiaro, transcript of interview with the author, Monte Romagna, Lucca, February 18, 2014. D'Amato Avanzi, Giannecchini, and Puccinelli, "The Influence of the Geological and Geomorphological Settings on Shallow Landslides."
4. The Corpo Forestale dello Stato was absorbed by the Carabinieri in 2016. The Serchio watershed has been heavily dammed to produce hydroelectricity. For purposes of flood control a partially empty dam is ideal, but for electricity production it needs to be kept as full as possible.
5. C.f., "Il paese non c'è più, cercatelo sotto il fango."
6. C.f., "Ma perché non hanno pulito il letto del fiume?"
7. The importance of infrequent intense storm events is also a feature of the "Mediterranean" climates of California, Western Australia, and South Africa. For intense storm events in the Mediterranean, see Grove and Rackham, *The Nature of Mediterranean Europe*, 25–36. D'Amato Avanzi and Giannecchini, "Eventi alluvionali e fenomeni franosi nelle Alpi Apuane (Toscana)."
8. D'Amato Avanzi, Giannecchini, and Puccinelli, "The Influence of the Geological and Geomorphological Settings on Shallow Landslides." Michele Marzi, pseudonymous environmental engineer, recorded interview with Andrew Mathews, Lucca, February 23, 2014.
9. Extreme weather events have increased in parts of the Mediterranean in recent decades: Alpert et al., "The Paradoxical Increase of Mediterranean Extreme Daily Rainfall."
10. See the work of environmental historian Marco Armiero for an account of the critical role of mountains in producing modern Italian identity: Armiero, *A Rugged Nation*; Armiero, "La ricchezza della montagna." For the historic importance of floods and landslides, see Bevilacqua, "The Distinctive Character of Italian Environmental History"; for the importance of earthquakes, see Guidoboni, "Upside-Down Landscapes: Seismicity and Seismic Disasters in Italy." For Fascist era environmental policies and concern with landscape stability, see Armiero and von Hardenberg, "Green Rhetoric in Blackshirts." For river diversions near medieval Lucca, see Squatriti, "Water, Nature, and Culture in Early Medieval Lucca." For forestry regulations, see

Sabbatini, "La rottura degli equilibri di antico regime"; Gabbrielli, "La legislazione forestale in Toscana dall' inizio alla caduta del granducato." For the history of the Venice lagoon, see Tommasini et al., "Changes in the Wind-Wave Field and Related Salt-Marsh Lateral Erosion." For an overview of Italian coastal geomorphology, see Grove and Rackham, *The Nature of Mediterranean Europe*, 328–50. For the drainage of the Pontine marshes by Mussolini, see Snowden, *The Conquest of Malaria*, 142–80. For early modern Tuscan water management, see Maglioni, "Vincenzo Viviani e l'Arno." For water management near Lucca, see Massoni, *La pieve e la comunità di Vorno*, 290–93. Major floods in Vorno are recorded for 1743, 1812, 1813, 1815, and 1826. Maintenance and repair costs for flood prevention structures were the responsibility of the *circondario* (district) that covered the watershed of the river.

11. For the *colmata* system, see Alexander, "The Reclamation of Val-di-Chiana (Tuscany)." For beautiful and deeply ideological images of soil erosion and deforestation, see Serpieri, *Il bosco, il pascolo, il Monte*; Di Tella, *Il bosco contro il torrente*. For the drainage of the Pontine marshes, see Snowden, *The Conquest of Malaria*.
12. In the Tuscany region 48 percent of the land is regimented by *consorzi di bonifica*. See Consorzi di Bonifica della Toscana, *Atlante della bonifica Toscana*, 15. For the history of the Lake of Bientina, see Zagli, *Il lago e la comunità*.
13. For nineteenth- and early-twentieth-century discussions of landscape instability, see Armiero, A *Rugged Nation*, 21–25. For the importance of landscape stability in Italian history, see Bevilacqua, "The Distinctive Character of Italian Environmental History." *Dissesto*, "lack of balance," is a legal term that was first linked to soil/water relations as *dissesto idrogeologico* in the 1950s, to describe the undermining of towns and villages in the erodible badlands of Basilicata in Southern Italy. See Cotecchia, "Sulle cause geologiche che obbligano al trasferimento di taluni abitati dissestati della Lucania." For a summary of historic flood events, see Manigrasso et al., *L'Italia delle alluvioni*.
14. Agnoletti et al., "Paesaggio e dissesto idrogeologico"; Calandri Pignone, "La rabbia di Genova." The poor state of forests was also blamed on the insect pest *Matsucoccus feytaudi*, which has devastated maritime pine over the past thirty years. Calandri Pignone, "Alluvione, migliaia di senzatetto."
15. Lazzotti, "Alluvione a Livorno, la procura nomina cinque ingegneri"; Guarducci, Lazzotti, and Biancolatte, "Alluvione a Livorno, dalla tragica notte all'inchiesta." Zucchelli, "Nubifragio a Livorno." Loreti, "Più forti e frequenti."
16. Between 1997 and 2018 the national newspaper *la Repubblica* published 1,729 articles with the term *dissesto idrogeologico* (hydrogeological instability), and 3,538 with the term *cambiamento climatico* (climate change), but only 54 that mentioned both. In the regional newspaper *Il Tirreno*, *dissesto idrogeologico* was mentioned 945 times, and climate change 230 times, and only 3 mentioned both. I have sampled this array of material for what seemed to me to be typical stories. This mismatch between framings of global climate change and local political responsibility for the causes of floods and landslides is found also in Brazil and may be typical around the world.

See Lahsen, Azevedo Couto, and Lorenzoni, "When Climate Change Is Not Blamed." For accelerated climate change in Mediterranean mountains, see Bravo et al., "Climate Change in Mediterranean Mountains During the 21st Century." Keeping one's land and trees from bothering the neighbors is a principle deeply embedded in Italian law. Roman law gave landowners responsibility for removing soil that had fallen from their land to that of their neighbors: Di Bérenger, *Studii di archeologia forestale*, 257.

17. *Il Tirreno*, "200 Smottamenti e pochi soldi per il risanamento." Evette et al., "History of Bioengineering Techniques for Erosion Control in Rivers in Western Europe"; Preti, "Sistemazioni idraulico-forestali e ingegneria naturalistica per la difesa del territorio." Michele Marzi, pseudonymous environmental engineer, recorded interview with the author, Lucca, February 23, 2014.
18. Riccardi, "Maltempo, Italia sott'acqua"; Cianciullo, "Il clima cambia le città."
19. Trigila et al., *Dissesto idrogeologico in Italia*. Mario Rossi, pseudonym for environmental official, interview with the author, Gallicano, Lucca, June 20, 2015.
20. Studies of climate change communication in Italy do not find many skeptics. See Beltrame, Bucchi, and Loner, "Climate Change Communication in Italy."
21. Simone Polli and Aldo Ferri, pseudonyms, recorded interview with Andrew Mathews and Fabio Malfatti, Vorno, Lucca, June 24, 2016.
22. Many people in Italy refuse to sleep with fans or air-conditioning because they say that drafts cause colds, stiffness, or influenza. The body is felt to be permeable to the air, one of many traces of Hippocratic medical theory in popular culture.
23. Ornella Rossi, pseudonym, recorded interview, Andrew Mathews and Fabio Malfatti, Vorno, Lucca, June 21, 2016.
24. Simone Polli and Aldo Ferri, pseudonyms, recorded interview with Andrew Mathews and Fabio Malfatti, Vorno, Lucca, June 24, 2016; Massoni, *La pieve e la comunità di Vorno*, 63.
25. Hall, *Earth Repair*.
26. David Nogués Bravo et al., "Climate Change in Mediterranean Mountains During the 21st Century." Annemarie Mol, *The Body Multiple*.
27. Hulme, "Cosmopolitan Climates"; Jasanoff, "A New Climate for Society." As Mike Hulme points out, "Climate becomes a rich ensemble of atmospheric processes, material technologies, memories, landscapes, dress codes, social practices, symbolic rituals, and identities": Hulme, *Weathered*, 66. See also Lahsen, Couto, and Lorenzoni, "When Climate Change Is Not Blamed."
28. Nixon, "Neoliberalism, Slow Violence, and the Environmental Picaresque"; Brown, "Learning to Read the Great Chernobyl Acceleration"; Martinez-Alier et al., "Is There a Global Environmental Justice Movement?"
29. For a discussion of anthropology and the Anthropocene, see Mathews, "Anthropology and the Anthropocene"; Tsing, Mathews, and Bubandt, "Patchy Anthropocene." For landscape design and floods, see Manigrasso et al., *L'Italia delle alluvioni*.

Chapter 6. From Landscape Histories to Climate Models

1. The full name of the park is Migliarino San Rossore Massaciuccoli. The marble and limestone peaks of the Alpi Apuane look like miniatures of the actual Alps hundreds of kilometers away.
2. Edwards, *A Vast Machine*.
3. For land use and carbon emissions, see Searchinger et al., "Assessing the Efficiency of Changes in Land Use for Mitigating Climate Change." For tree restoration, see Bastin et al., "The Global Tree Restoration Potential." The origin of REDD+ policy (Reducing Emissions from Deforestation and Forest Degradation) has been told in many ways, but a reasonably solid origin myth traces it back to the Kyoto Protocol of the UNFCCC in 1997; see Hohne et al., "The Rules for Land Use." For estimates of carbon absorbed by European forests, see Luyssaert et al., "The European Carbon Balance." For California forests, see Cameron et al., "Ecosystem Management and Land Conservation."
4. This tower (figure 54) was part of both the European ICOS network and the global FLUXNET network. The United States, China, and Australia manage their own networks of carbon flux towers.
5. Eugenio Moretti, pseudonym, recorded interview with Andrew Mathews, June 3, 2014. In Europe emissions quotas are negotiated through the European Union's commitments to the UNFCCC (United Nations Framework Convention on Climate Change) treaty process, then allocated to individual member states through further negotiations at the EU level.
6. Aubinet, Vesala, and Papale, *Eddy Covariance*.
7. This paradox is found in many landscapes around the world. Perhaps it is only in relatively low-population-density settler colonial societies such as the United States or Australia that it is possible to imagine ecological monitoring networks that exclude human activities. This imagination requires ignoring burning practices by Indigenous people or Aboriginal people, as well as more recent agriculture and invasive plants and pathogens.
8. Francesca Logli, recorded interview with Andrew Mathews, San Rossore, April 3, 2014. Alsio Grassini, notes from interview with Andrew Mathews, San Rossore, October 25, 2013. *Leptoglossus occidentalis* has combined with other pathogens to cause a decline of about 90 percent in pine nut production in San Rossore. Pine nut production has plummeted by a similar proportion across the Mediterranean: Sabbatini Peverieri et al., "Host Egg Age of *Leptoglossus occidentalis*"; Luchi et al., "*Leptoglossus occidentalis* and *Diplodia pinea*"; Bracalini et al., "Cone and Seed Pests of *Pinus pinea*."
9. For a masterful account of the effects of history on the contemporary landscape of Migliarino, see Agnoletti, *L'evoluzione del paesaggio nella tenuta di Migliarino*; see also Panattoni, *San Rossore nella storia*.

10. Stone pine (*Pinus pinea*) has been spread from Spain to Afghanistan by human cultivation. This broad geographical distribution has made it difficult to find the original source region, but recent work points to southwestern Spain as a strong candidate; see Martínez and Montero, "The *Pinus pinea* L. Woodlands Along the Coast of South-Western Spain." For coastal geomorphology in Tuscany, see Pranzini, "Updrift River Mouth Migration on Cuspate Deltas."
11. Since the 1980s the scale insect *Matsucoccus feytaudi* has seriously damaged or eliminated maritime pine from coastal Central and Northern Italy. See Sciarretta et al., "Adaptive Management of Invasive Pests in Natural Protected Areas." Ironically, *Pinus pinaster* is itself a serious invasive in South Africa, Australia, and New Zealand.
12. The spike in respiration after droughts is known as the "Birch effect," discovered by the colonial soil scientist H. F. Birch in East Africa in the 1950s and 1960s. See Birch, "The Effect of Soil Drying on Humus Decomposition and Nitrogen Availability." The "Birch effect" emerges at the interface of plant roots, the rhizosphere occupied by these roots, plant relations with soil bacteria, and changing rainfall patterns. Respiration by soil bacteria is of global significance for affecting the responsiveness of ecosystems to climate change, and bacterial responses to rainfall are affected by the histories of bacterial communities: Jarvis et al., "Drying and Wetting of Mediterranean Soils Stimulates Decomposition and Carbon Dioxide Emission"; Hawkes et al., "Historical Climate Controls Soil Respiration Responses to Current Soil Moisture." Redesigning data infrastructures is tedious and laborious work. The standardization required by data infrastructures prevents them from following historical and biographical change of individual cases: Bowker and Leigh Star, *Sorting Things Out*.
13. Shaping adult trees by bending or trimming young saplings is an ancient tradition of woodcraft across Europe; see Rackham, *Woodlands*; Moreno, "Querce come olivi."
14. Viveiros de Castro, "On Models and Examples."
15. For invasive pathogens, see Santini et al., "Biogeographical Patterns and Determinants of Invasion by Forest Pathogens in Europe"; Seidl et al., "Forest Disturbances Under Climate Change." Alsio Grassini, notes from interview with the author, San Rossore, October 25, 2013.
16. This section draws upon interviews with the botanist Gabriele Casazza in Genoa, July 7, 2015, and with Fabio Maselli and Marta Chiesi in Sesto Fiorentino, Italy, June 26, 2014. For a review of ecological modeling, see Dietze, *Ecological Forecasting*.
17. Veroustraete, Sabbe, and Eerens, "Estimation of Carbon Mass Fluxes over Europe Using the C-Fix Model and Euroflux Data"; Chiesi et al., "Application of BIOME-BGC to Simulate Mediterranean Forest Processes." Fabio Maselli and Marta Chiesi, interview with the author in Sesto Fiorentino, Italy, June 26, 2014.
18. The concept of the ecological climax was developed by the American ecologist Frederic Clements to describe the steady-state community of plants and animals that was best adapted to a local climate and that would dominate the landscape if left undisturbed for long enough. The climax concept was heavily criticized for its organismic

connotations by the British ecologist Arthur Tansley. In contemporary ecology it is considered an outdated but helpful "as if" assumption, as in the term "quasi-climax" used by Fabio, Marta, and the authors of BIOME-BGC. Clements, "Nature and Structure of the Climax"; Tansley, "The Use and Abuse of Vegetational Concepts and Terms."

19. Maselli et al., "Modelling the Forest Carbon Budget of a Mediterranean Region." Maselli and Chiesi, "Evaluation of Statistical Methods to Estimate Forest Volume in a Mediterranean Region."
20. Chiesi et al., "Calibration and Application of FOREST-BGC in a Mediterranean Area." Parameters are constants or equations that help models correspond to actual ecosystems. Parameter values have to stabilize model outputs, and they have to make sense ecologically. "The parameters found for the six ecosystems . . . are generally in accordance with relevant auto-ecological considerations": Maselli et al. "Modelling the Forest Carbon Budget of a Mediterranean Region."
21. Brunetti et al. "Temperature and Precipitation Variability in Italy."
22. This kind of validation by comparison with existing methods is similar to the introduction of new methods for detecting atherosclerosis in clinical settings; see Anne Marie Mol, *The Body Multiple*.
23. Jasanoff, *States of Knowledge*.
24. Scenario building emerged from Cold War military planning but has spread to corporate, environmental, and technical fields over the past forty years. Scenario building can be used to support decision-making under conditions of uncertainty, to explore what future worlds citizens might wish to live in, and to build collaborations between scientific research communities: Van Vuuren et al., "A Proposal for a New Scenario Framework"; Wodak and Neale, "A Critical Review of the Application of Environmental Scenario Exercises"; Westhoek, Van den Berg, and Bakkes, "Scenario Development to Explore the Future of Europe's Rural Areas." Van Vuuren et al., "The Representative Concentration Pathways: An Overview." Scenario builders typically build an even number of scenarios in order to avoid the tendency to see a "middle" scenario as a compromise between two more extreme versions.
25. Chiesi et al., "Simulation of Mediterranean Forest Carbon Pools Under Expected Environmental Scenarios."
26. Steffen et al., "Trajectories of the Earth System in the Anthropocene."
27. Santini et al., "Biogeographical Patterns and Determinants of Invasion by Forest Pathogens in Europe." Schneider et al., "Impact of *Xylella fastidiosa* Subspecies *pauca* in European Olives."
28. Heiniger and Rigling, "Biological Control of Chestnut Blight in Europe."
29. Arènes, Latour, and Gaillardet, "Giving Depth to the Surface"; Tsing and Gan, "How Things Hold."
30. Tsing, *The Mushroom at the End of the World.* Guillemot, "Connections Between Simulations and Observation in Climate Computer Modeling."
31. Viveiros de Castro, "On Models and Examples."

Chapter 7. From Climate Change to Biomass Energy

1. In this and the following chapter I draw upon interviews with firewood cutters (nine interviews), firewood and pellet suppliers (six interviews), biomass energy entrepreneurs and opponents (twenty interviews), and scientists and policymakers (six interviews), as well as upon numerous informal conversations about home heating and energy use. Although I tried to interview firewood cutters *in* the forest while at work, health and safety regulations and the informal or illegal nature of much firewood cutting made this difficult (two interviews).
2. Tuscany has been a historic center of forestry research and training due to its connection with the Austrian Hapsburg-Lorraine dynasty (1765–1860). The first national forestry school was founded in Vallombrosa in 1869, directed by the Bavarian forester Adolfo Di Bérenger, who was trained in Hapsburg Vienna. Gabbrielli, "Adolfo Di Bérenger."
3. Mountain communities in Italy have long been recognized as facing unique economic challenges and have been given additional support by the state. The "Mountain Communities" established in 1971 (Comunità Montane) were transformed into the "Unions of Communities" (Unioni di Comuni) in 2000. Italy is divided into twenty regions, each with its own president, legislature, and quasi-ministerial councillors. The politician at Montevarchi was the regional *assessore dell'ambiente* (environment councillor). In reaction to the centralization under the Fascist regime of Benito Mussolini (1923–1943), and increasingly since the 1970s, regional governments in Italy have acquired ever-greater responsibilities. Inauguration of biomass plant, transcript, Montevarchi, Italy, January 16, 2014.
4. The Ministry of Culture (Ministero della Cultura) is widely resented for its heavy-handed prevention of building in protected landscapes. See also Gaggio, *The Shaping of Tuscany*, 238–80. The councillor echoed writers on the Anthropocene who point out that fossil fuel consumption has made it possible to imagine human societies that are independent of the natural world. Chakrabarty, "The Climate of History."
5. Inauguration of biomass plant, transcript, Montevarchi, Italy, January 16, 2014.
6. The Camorra is the organized crime group that controls the Campania. Armiero and D'Alisa, "Rights of Resistance."
7. For estimates of available biomass, see Regione Toscana, *PAER: Proposta di piano ambientale ed energetico regionale*. According to one estimate, 39 percent of the 3.7 million hectares of *ceduo* in Italy, which was formerly cut every twenty years, has not been cut for over forty years. Fabbio and Cutini, "Il ceduo oggi?"
8. Helmut Haberl argues that only biomass that is additionally available because of human care (such as through forests that grow more rapidly because of thinning and pruning), or that which would otherwise decay rapidly (in organic material destined for landfill, or from agricultural or logging wastes) is in reality carbon neutral or negative. For criticisms of biomass energy accounting, see McKechnie, Colombo, and

MacLean, "Forest Carbon Accounting Methods"; Haberl, "Net Land-Atmosphere Flows of Biogenic Carbon Related to Bioenergy"; Haberl et al., "Correcting a Fundamental Error in Greenhouse Gas Accounting Related to Bioenergy."

9. For the role of land-use change in carbon emissions, see Searchinger et al., "Assessing the Efficiency of Changes in Land Use for Mitigating Climate Change." For sustainable energy figures, see World Energy Council, *World Energy Resources Bioenergy 2016*. For fuelwood burning, see Chatti et al., "Exploring the Mundane." For historical energy transitions, see Smil, "Examining Energy Transitions"; Smil, *Energy*. Mander et al., "The Role of Bio-Energy with Carbon Capture and Storage in Meeting the Climate Mitigation Challenge"; International Energy Agency, *Net Zero by 2050*.
10. Dukes, "Burning Buried Sunshine." Bastin et al., "The Global Tree Restoration Potential"; Lisa Friedman, "A Trillion Trees: How One Idea Triumphed over Trump's Climate Denialism."
11. The climate justice movement draws attention to historic social and environmental injustices and tries to ensure that climate change policies help build a more equitable society. See Ranganathan and Bratman, "From Urban Resilience to Abolitionist Climate Justice in Washington, DC"; Schlosberg and Collins, "From Environmental to Climate Justice." For environmental justice and energy, see Levenda, Behrsin, and Disano, "Renewable Energy for Whom?"
12. The 2018 UNFCCC meeting worked to formulate international standards for reporting greenhouse gas emissions. Climate change policy is, among other things, a giant system of accounting.
13. For renewable energy policy in Italy, see Ministero dello Sviluppo Economico, *Piano di azione nazionale per le energie rinnovabili dell'Italia*. A foundational event for the Italian environmental movement was the Vajont dam collapse of 1963, which marked the last gasp of hydroelectric state making: Armiero, *A Rugged Nation*, 173–94.
14. For EU biomass policy processes, see Giachi, *Quali sono le variabili della governance della biomassa?*; for a discussion of baselines, see Ureta, Lekan, and von Hardenberg, "Baselining Nature." For a description of scenarios and baselines for EU biofuel policies, see Johnson, Pacini, and Smeets, *Transformations in EU Biofuels Markets Under the Renewable Energy Directive*. For wood-fuel consumption in Italy, see Pra and Pettenella, "Consumption of Wood Biomass for Energy in Italy." Around the world, efforts to control land-cover change, forest fires, or firewood use are similarly undermined by poor official statistics and lack of connections between officials, farmers, and firewood users: see Mathews, *Instituting Nature*; Chatti et al., "Exploring the Mundane."
15. Comune di Montevarchi, "A Levane inaugurata la nuova centrale a biomasse"; Crini, "Inaugurata la centrale di cogenerazione a biomasse."
16. Zabini, Magno, and Grasso, *Clima che cambia: gli impatti sul territorio Toscano*; Regione Toscana, *PAER: Proposta di piano ambientale ed energetico regionale*. For carbon absorbed by Tuscan forests, see Genesio et al., "Monitoraggio integrato del

bilancio della CO2 a scala regionale." Interview with Luisa Ferri, pseudonymous official, Tuscany region, June 6, 2014. Interview with Michele Chiesi, pseudonymous official, Tuscany region, July 7, 2015.

Chapter 8. Landscapes and Energy Politics

1. These mountains are of relatively modest elevation, with most peaks near two thousand meters. This chapter draws upon ten recorded interviews between biomass energy opponents and supporters, municipal officials, and representatives of environmental organizations. The river is lively without being alive and does work without being a worker. For a classic account of water and power, see White, *The Organic Machine*.
2. In the early twentieth century Italy was one of the first countries in the world to build a large hydroelectricity network. Until well into the 1950s the vast majority of the country's electricity was produced by large dams in the Alps, with smaller dams in the Apennines. The major hydroelectric dams in the Garfagnana are Pian Rocca, 55 megawatts; Gallicano, 43 megawatts; and Castelnuovo di Garfagnana, 20 megawatts. Such power plants are small when compared with fossil fuel power plants, which typically range from several hundred to 2,000–3,000 megawatts, and even compared with the 1,320 megawatt Luigi Einaudi dam in the maritime Alps. For water power and industrialization in Southern Italy, see Stefania Barca, *Enclosing Water*; Armiero, A *Rugged Nation*, 33–43. As with many mountain areas in Europe, the Apennines have long supplied migrant labor to other parts of the world, from Brazil to San Francisco. See Sarti, *Long Live the Strong*.
3. Regione Toscana, *PAER: Proposta di piano ambientale ed energetico regionale*.
4. Amorini, "Gestione delle foreste toscane pubbliche e private."
5. The plant would have been phenomenally profitable. Subsidized electricity purchases would have covered installation costs after three years, and annual income would have been €15 million per year. See Gabbrielli and Marco, *Valutazione tecnica sul progetto di una centrale termoelettrica cogenerativa a cippato di biomassa*.
6. There is a strong separation between permanent employees with full job security and temporary employees on short-term contracts. Full-time workers are known as *assunti per bene* (properly employed). These positions have a financial and juridical value that allows a job to function as a form of welfare in a society where universal welfare benefits are relatively modest. Possibly the only workers in the United States to have such security are professors or teachers with tenure.
7. Giuseppe Mela, pseudonymous biomass energy entrepreneur, recorded interview with Andrew Mathews, Lucca, January 10, 2014.
8. He used the term *nostra*, referencing nativeness and locality. The rapid-growing acacia (*Robinia pseudoacacia*) was introduced to stabilize slopes and provide firewood in the nineteenth century and was widely promoted by the forest service in the twentieth century. Ironically, it is now seen as an invasive that destabilizes hillsides. Tran-

script of interview with three members of the Comitato Alce, with Andrew Mathews, Bagni di Lucca, Italy, February 25, 2014.

9. Cristina Macchetti, pseudonymous environmental activist, interview with Andrew Mathews, Lucca, July 4, 2015.
10. Supporters of biomass energy claimed that their opponents were inspired by "fake news" and were like anti-vaccination activists. The documents that activists circulated were often a bricolage of academic documents, policy reports, and legal briefs that did not fit any genre. See Grupo di Studio Comitatibiogas Manziana, *Vademecum Per Saperne di Piu Su Biomasse e Biogas*. For "a view from somewhere," see Jasanoff, "Virtual, Visible, and Actionable."
11. The literature on the state is vast, but the most relevant in this context is work by Sheila Jasanoff on the "civic epistemologies" through which people evaluate state efforts to perform authoritative knowledge. People's distrust in the Italian state is due to their conviction that national and regional elites are not responsive to their concerns and due to a well-founded fear of organized crime. See Jasanoff, *Designs on Nature*. For experiences of opaque legal bureaucracies in Italy, see Herzfeld, *Evicted from Eternity*. Antonio Ghezzi, pseudonymous farmer, recorded interview with Andrew Mathews, Volterra, Italy, December 18, 2013.
12. For an introduction to energy systems, see Smil, *Energy and Civilization*. I follow energy infrastructures not as an information network nor as a system of standards, but as a collective project of producing and transmitting energy from forests. For a classic description of information infrastructures, see Bowker and Star, *Sorting Things Out*. For more recent essays that apply the concept to the environment, see Hetherington, *Infrastructure, Environment, and Life in the Anthropocene*. For oil and democracy, see Mitchell, "Carbon Democracy." Dominic Boyer, *Energopolitics*; Howe, *Ecologics*; Franquesa, *Power Struggles*; Powell, *Landscapes of Power*; Frolova, Prados, and Nadaï, *Renewable Energies and European Landscapes*; Bullard et al., *Toxic Wastes and Race at Twenty*.
13. People experience risks differently depending upon their sources, and risk talk often authorizes experts and state institutions. See Jasanoff, "The Songlines of Risk."
14. EU regulations seek to ensure the sustainability of wood pellets, as do various consumer labels. As the largest official importer of firewood in the world, Italy is particularly vulnerable to "eco-mafias," who might relabel pellets from illegal logging. Masiero, Andrighetto, and Pettenella, "Linee-guida per la valutazione sistematica della filiera corta"; Mario A. Rosato, "Sopravvivenza nella giungla europea dei pellet."
15. For regional wood availability and models, see Fagarazzi et al., "Qual e la disponibilità della risorsa biomassa"; Fagarazzi, Nibbi, and Tirinanzi, *Come monitoreare le filiere e gli impianti*. For the Drax power station, see Howe, "No Drax! There's Nothing 'Sustainable' About Big Biomass." The concept of *filiera corta* (short supply chain) arose in the domain of food and agriculture and likely traveled from the food sector to biomass energy in a 2010 ministerial decree. Masiero, Andrighetto, and Pettenella,

"Linee-guida per la valutazione sistematica della filiera corta." For wood chip production in the US Southeast, see Alan Dater, *Burned*; Southern Environmental Law Center, "Biomass Energy in the South."

16. ARPAT, "Nimby forum"; Anonymous, "Tutto sull'imbroglio della combustione delle biomasse"; Nardi, "Sequestrato impianto a biomasse."
17. Legambiente Lucca, "Il contributo sostenibile delle biomasse." Chiesi, pseudonymous regional official, recorded interview with Andrew Mathews, July 5, 2015. Gravano, "Il teleriscaldamento a biomassa in Toscana."
18. See Susan Freidberg's comparison of supply chains for French beans or Anna Tsing's description of the matsutake mushroom supply chain: Tsing, *Mushroom at the End of the World*; Freidberg, *French Beans and Food Scares*. Julie Klinger shows, for example, how the material properties of rare earths and their association with radioactive substances have led to the location of mines in remote places where toxicity can be inflicted upon sacrificial landscapes and people: Klinger, *Rare Earth Frontiers*.
19. Skepticism about mainstream science, including vaccinations, has been promoted by populist politicians from the M5S and Lega Nord parties.
20. For Anthropocene conservation see Lorimer, *Wildlife in the Anthropocene*.
21. Hulme, "Cosmopolitan Climates."

Epilogue

1. Joseph Masco, "The Crisis in Crisis."
2. Chakrabarty, "The Climate of History."
3. Bullard and Wright, "Race, Place, and the Environment in Post-Katrina New Orleans." Brown, "Learning to Read the Great Chernobyl Acceleration."
4. Petryna, "Wildfires at the Edges of Science."
5. This finding is echoed by researchers working in the United States, Peru, and Italy: Orlove et al., "Framing Climate Change in Frontline Communities."
6. Lahsen, Couto, and Lorenzon, "When Climate Change Is Not Blamed." O'Reilly, "The Substance of Climate."

Appendix 1

1. This section is drawn from Bertacchi, Sani, and Tomei, *La vegetazione del Monte Pisano*.
2. Massimiliano Grava et al., "Dalla cartografia storica alla cartografia 2.0 nella Toscana Preunitaria." Massoni, *La pieve e la comunità di Vorno*.

Appendix 2

1. Maselli et al., "Modelling the Forest Carbon Budget of a Mediterranean Region."

REFERENCES

Abrams, Marc D., and Gregory J. Nowacki. "Native Americans as Active and Passive Promoters of Mast and Fruit Trees in the Eastern USA." *The Holocene* 18, no. 7 (2008): 1123–37. https://doi.org/10.1177/0959683608095581.

Agnoletti, Mauro. *L'evoluzione del paesaggio nella tenuta di Migliarino Fra XIX e XX Secolo*. Firenze: Edizioni Regione Toscana, 2005.

Agnoletti, Mauro, Francesca Emanueli, Giacomo Maggiari, and Federico Preti. "Paesaggio e dissesto idrogeologico: il disastro ambientale del 25 ottobre 2011 nelle Cinque Terre." In *Studi e ricerche: biennale internazionale dei beni culturali e ambientali*, 25–46. Firenze: Bandecchi & Vivaldi, 2012.

Alexander, David. "The Reclamation of Val-Di-Chiana (Tuscany)." *Annals of the Association of American Geographers* 74, no. 4 (1984): 527–50. http://www.jstor.org/stable/2562543.

Alpert, P., T. Ben-Gai, A. Baharad, Y. Benjamini, D. Yekutieli, M. Colacino, L. Diodato, et al. "The Paradoxical Increase of Mediterranean Extreme Daily Rainfall in Spite of Decrease in Total Values." *Geophysical Research Letters* 29, no. 11 (2002): 31-1–31-4. https://doi.org/10.1029/2001GL013554.

Amorini, Emilio. "Gestione delle foreste toscane pubbliche e private." In *Rapporto sullo stato delle foreste in Toscana 2005*, 40–51. Firenze: Regione Toscana, ARSIA, 2005.

Anagnostakis, Sandra L. "The Effect of Multiple Importations of Pests and Pathogens on a Native Tree." *Biological Invasions* 3, no. 3 (2001): 245–54. https://doi.org/10.1023/A:1015205005751.

Anonymous. "Sulla E Ginestra." *L'Agricoltore: periodico mensuale del comizio agrario lucchese*. Anno XX (Vol. 20). (1884): 173–78.

———. "Tutto Sull'imbroglio della combustione delle Biomasse." Accessed December 16, 2013. http://truccobiomasse.altervista.org/index.html.

Arènes, Alexandra, Bruno Latour, and Jérôme Gaillardet. "Giving Depth to the Surface: An Exercise in the Gaia-graphy of Critical Zones." *Anthropocene Review* 5, no. 2 (2018): 120–35.

Armiero, Marco. "La ricchezza della montagna. Il bosco dalla sussistenza al superfluo." *Meridiana*, no. 44 (2002): 65–96. http://www.jstor.org/stable/23199876.

———. *A Rugged Nation: Mountains and the Making of Modern Italy: Nineteenth and Twentieth Centuries*. Cambridge, UK: White Horse Press, 2011.

Armiero, Marco, and Giacomo D'Alisa. "Rights of Resistance: The Garbage Struggles for Environmental Justice in Campania, Italy." *Capitalism Nature Socialism* 23, no. 4 (2012): 52–68. https://doi.org/10.1080/10455752.2012.724200.

Armiero, Marco, and Wilko Graf von Hardenberg. "Green Rhetoric in Blackshirts: Italian Fascism and the Environment." *Environment and History* 19 (2013): 283–311.

Armiero, Marco, and Marcus Hall. *Nature and History in Modern Italy*. Athens: Ohio University Press, 2010.

ARPAT. "Il teleriscaldamento a biomassa in Toscana. Intervista ad Elisabetta Gravano—Regione Toscana." Venerdì, 3 Febbraio 2017. Accessed August 26, 2019. http://www.arpat.toscana.it/notizie/arpatnews/2017/024–17/il-teleriscaldamento-a-biomassa-in-toscana.

ARPAT. "Nimby forum. Salgono a 354 le opere contestate in Italia." *ARPATnews* 119 (Venerdì, 7 Giugno 2013).

Aubinet, Marc, Timo Vesala, and Dario Papale, eds. *Eddy Covariance: A Practical Guide to Measurement and Data Analysis*. Springer Atmospheric Sciences. Dordrecht, Netherlands: Springer, 2012.

Barad, Karen. *Meeting the Universe Halfway: Quantum Physics and the Entanglement of Matter and Meaning*. Durham, NC, and London: Duke University Press, 2007.

Barca, Stefania. *Enclosing Water: Nature and Political Economy in a Mediterranean Valley, 1796–1916*. Cambridge, UK: White Horse Press, 2010.

Barnes, Jessica Emily. *Cultivating the Nile: The Everyday Politics of Water in Egypt*. New Ecologies for the Twenty First Century. Durham, NC: Duke University Press, 2014. doi:10.1177/0306312712438772.

Bastin, Jean-Francois, Yelena Finegold, Claude Garcia, Danilo Mollicone, Marcelo Rezende, Devin Routh, Constantin M. Zohner, and Thomas W. Crowther. "The Global Tree Restoration Potential." *Science* 365, no. 6448 (2019): 76. https://doi.org/10.1126/science.aax0848.

Beiler, Kevin J., Daniel M. Durall, Suzanne W. Simard, Sheri A. Maxwell, and Annette M. Kretzer. "Architecture of the Wood-Wide Web: *Rhizopogon* spp. genets Link Multiple Douglas-Fir Cohorts." *New Phytologist* 185, no. 2 (2010): 543–53. https://doi.org/10.1111/j.1469-8137.2009.03069.x.

Beltrame, Lorenzo, Massimiano Bucchi, and Enzo Loner. "Climate Change Communication in Italy." In *Oxford Research Encyclopedia Climate Science*. Oxford University Press online, 2016. doi:10.1093/acrefore/9780190228620.013.462.

Berger, John. *Landscapes: John Berger on Art.* Edited by Tom Overton. London and New York: Verso Books, 2016.

Bertacchi, Andrea, Alessandra Sani, and Paolo Emilio Tomei. *La vegetazione del Monte Pisano.* Pisa: Felici Editori, 2004.

Bessire, Lucas, and David Bond. "Ontological Anthropology and the Deferral of Critique." *American Ethnologist* 41, no. 3 (2014): 440–56. https://doi.org/10.1111/amet.12083.

Bevilacqua, Piero. "The Distinctive Character of Italian Environmental History." In *Nature and History in Modern Italy,* edited by Marco Armiero and Marcus Hall, 15–32. Athens: Ohio University Press, 2010.

Biagianti, Ivo. "Boschi e pascoli nella montagna Toscana fra sette e novecento." In *Economie nel tempo: persistenza e cambiamenti negli Appennini in eta moderna,* edited by Antonio G. Calafatti and Ercole Sori, 153–70. Milan: FrancoAngeli, 2004.

Biagioli, Giuliana. "La mezzadria poderale nell'Italia centro-settentrionale in età moderna e contemporanea (secoli XV–XX)." *Rivista di Storia dell'Agricoltura* 42, no. 2 (Dicembre 2002): 53–100.

Bianchi, Francesca. "Il Serra brucia ancora, l'anziano agricoltore: 'Sono stato io, bruciavo sterpaglie.'" *La Nazione: Pisa.* 26 Febbraio 2019. https://www.lanazione.it/pisa/cronaca/monte-serra-1.4463011.

Bianchi, Livio, Alberto Maltoni, Barbara Mariotti, and Marco Paci. *La selvicoltura dei castagneti da frutto abbandonati della Toscana.* Supporti tecnici alla Legge Regionale Forestale della Toscana. Vol. 4, Firenze: ARSIA, Regione Toscana, 2009.

Biasillo, Roberta, and Marco Armiero. "Seeing the Nation for the Trees: At the Frontier of Italian Nineteenth-Century Modernity." *Environment and History* 24 (2018): 497–518.

Birch, H. F. "The Effect of Soil Drying on Humus Decomposition and Nitrogen Availability." *Plant and Soil* 10, no. 1 (1958): 9–31. https://doi.org/10.1007/BF01343734.

Blaser, Mario. "Ontology and Indigeneity: On the Political Ontology of Heterogeneous Assemblages." *Cultural Geographies* 21, no. 1 (2014): 49–58. doi:10.1177/1474474012462534.

Blondel, Jacques. "The 'Design' of Mediterranean Landscapes: A Millennial Story of Humans and Ecological Systems During the Historic Period." *Human Ecology* 34, no. 5 (2006): 713–29. https://doi.org/10.1007/s10745-006-9030-4.

———. *The Mediterranean Region: Biological Diversity in Space and Time.* 2nd ed. xv. Oxford: Oxford University Press, 2010.

Bonneuil, Christophe, and Jean-Baptiste Fressoz. *The Shock of the Anthropocene: The Earth, History and Us.* Translated by David Fernbach. xiv. London: Verso, 2016.

Bonucelli, Pio Fortunato. "Il castagno nella Lucchesia." *Reale Accademia Lucchese di Scienze, Lettere ed Arti.* Vol. 17 (1939): 2–26.

Borelli, O., and A. Pettina. "La struttura e la coltivazione dei castagneti." In *Studio monografico sul castagno nella provincia di Lucca,* edited by O. Borelli, N. Breviglieri,

C. A. Cecconi, C. Ciampi, R. Morandini, and A. Pettina, 137–56. Firenze: Centro di Studio sul Castagno, 1958.

———. "Le malattie del castagno." In *Studio monografico sul castagno nella provincia di Lucca*, edited by O. Borelli, N. Breviglieri, C. A. Cecconi, C. Ciampi, R. Morandini, and A. Pettina, 169–73. Firenze: Centro di Studio sul Castagno, 1958.

Borges, Jorge Luis. "Funes the Memorious." In *Labyrinths; Selected Stories & Other Writings*, 148–54. New York: New Directions, 1964.

Bowker, Geoffrey C., and Susan Leigh Star. *Sorting Things Out: Classification and Its Consequences*. Inside Technology. Cambridge, MA: MIT Press, 1999.

Boyer, Dominic. *Energopolitics: Wind and Power in the Anthropocene*. Durham, NC: Duke University Press, 2019.

Bracalini, Matteo, Stefano Benedettelli, Francesco Croci, Perla Terreni, Riziero Tiberi, and Tiziana Panzavolta. "Cone and Seed Pests of *Pinus pinea*: Assessment and Characterization of Damage." *Journal of Economic Entomology* 106, no. 1 (2013): 229–34. https://doi.org/10.1603/EC12293.

Brasier, Clive. "Plant Pathology: The Rise of the Hybrid Fungi." *Nature* 405, no. 6783 (2000): 134–35. http://dx.doi.org/10.1038/35012193.

Brasier, Clive M. "Rapid Evolution of Introduced Plant Pathogens via Interspecific Hybridization: Hybridization Is Leading to Rapid Evolution of Dutch Elm Disease and Other Fungal Plant Pathogens." *BioScience* 51, no. 2 (2001): 123–33. https://doi.org/10.1641/0006-3568(2001)051[0123:reoipp]2.0.co;2.

Braudel, Fernand. *The Mediterranean and the Mediterranean World in the Age of Philip II*. Vol. 1. Berkeley and Los Angeles: University of California Press. 1995 [first ed. 1949].

Bravo, David Nogués, Miguel B. Araújo, Teodoro Lasanta, and Juan Ignacio López Moreno. "Climate Change in Mediterranean Mountains During the 21st Century." *Ambio: A Journal of the Human Environment* 37, no. 4 (2008): 280–85. https://doi.org/10.1579/0044-7447(2008)37[280:CCIMMD]2.0.CO;2.

Brenner, Eric D., Rainer Stahlberg, Stefano Mancuso, Jorge Vivanco, František Baluška, and Elizabeth Van Volkenburgh. "Plant Neurobiology: An Integrated View of Plant Signaling." *Trends in Plant Science* 11, no. 8 (2006): 413–19. http://dx.doi.org/10.1016/j.tplants.2006.06.009.

Breviglieri, N. "Indagini e osservazioni sulle cultivar di castagno." In *Studio monografico sul castagno nella provincia di Lucca*, edited by O. Borelli, N. Breviglieri, C. A. Cecconi, C. Ciampi, R. Morandini, and A. Pettina, 65–138. Firenze: Centro di Studio sul Castagno, 1958.

Brown, Kate. "Learning to Read the Great Chernobyl Acceleration: Literacy in the More-Than-Human Landscapes." *Current Anthropology* 60, no. S20 (2019): S198–S208. https://doi.org/10.1086/702901.

Brunetti, Michele, Gianluca Lentini, Maurizio Maugeri, Teresa Nanni, Ingeborg Auer, Reinhard Böhm, and Wolfgang Schöner. "Climate Variability and Change in the Greater Alpine Region over the Last Two Centuries Based on Multi-Variable Analysis." *International Journal of Climatology* 29, no. 15 (2009): 2197–225. https://doi.org/10.1002/joc.1857.

Brunetti, Michele, Maurizio Maugeri, Fabio Monti, and Teresa Nanni. "Temperature and Precipitation Variability in Italy in the Last Two Centuries from Homogenised Instrumental Time Series." *International Journal of Climatology* 26, no. 3 (2006): 345–81. https://doi.org/10.1002/joc.1251.

Bubandt, Nils, and Anna Tsing. "Feral Dynamics of Post-Industrial Ruin: An Introduction." *Journal of Ethnobiology* 38, no. 1 (2018): 1–7. https://doi.org/10.2993/0278-0771-38.1.001.

Bullard, Robert D., Paul Mohai, Robin Saha, and Beverly Wright. *Toxic Wastes and Race at Twenty: 1987–2007. A Report Prepared for the United Church of Christ Justice and Witness Ministries.* Cleveland, OH: United Church of Christ (2007). https://www.nrdc.org/sites/default/files/toxic-wastes-and-race-at-twenty-1987-2007.pdf.

Bullard, Robert D., and Beverly Wright. "Race, Place, and the Environment in Post-Katrina New Orleans." In *Race, Place, and Environmental Justice After Hurricane Katrina: Struggles to Reclaim, Rebuild, and Revitalize New Orleans and the Gulf Coast,* edited by Robert D. Bullard and Beverly Wright, 19–48. Boulder, CO: Routledge, 2009.

Calandri Pignone, Massimo. "Alluvione, migliaia di senzatetto e scattano la prime inchieste è omicidio e disastro colposo." *La Repubblica,* 28 Ottobre 2011.

———. "La rabbia di Genova." *La Repubblica,* 11 Novembre 2011.

Callaway, Ragan M. "Positive Interactions Among Plants." *Botanical Review* 61, no. 4 (1995): 306–49. https://doi.org/10.1007/BF02912621.

Cameron, D. Richard, David C. Marvin, Jonathan M. Remucal, and Michelle C. Passero. "Ecosystem Management and Land Conservation Can Substantially Contribute to California's Climate Mitigation Goals." *Proceedings of the National Academy of Sciences* 114, no. 48 (2017): 12833. https://doi.org/10.1073/pnas.1707811114.

Canfield, Michael R., ed. *Field Notes on Science and Nature.* Cambridge, MA: Harvard University Press, 2011.

Carse, Ashley. "Nature as Infrastructure: Making and Managing the Panama Canal Watershed." *Social Studies of Science* 42, no. 4 (2012): 539–63. https://doi.org/10.1177/0306312712440166.

Caruso, Girolamo. "Intorno alla malattia dei castagni ne' Monti Pisani. Relazione al Comizio Agrario di Pisa, letta nella seduta generale del 1 luglio, 1874." *L'Italia Agricola* 6 (1874): 339–40.

Casazza, Gabriele, Fabio Malfatti, Michele Brunetti, Valentina Simonetti, and Andrew S. Mathews. "Interactions Between Land Use, Pathogens, and Climate Change in the Monte Pisano, Italy, 1850–2000." *Landscape Ecology* 36, no. 2 (2020). https://doi.org/10.1007/s10980-020-01152-z.

Catasto Nuovo Lucchese: Giornale della misura e stima. Comunità di Capannori, Sezione di Vorno. Lucca: Archivio di Stato di Lucca, 1846.

——. "Municipio Di Capannori, sezione N2, foglio 1, detta di Vorno." In *Catasto Nuovo—Faldone 17—Capannori 2–1—n. 426*. Corretta dela Geometra Santi Pinochi. Levata in Pianta dai Geometri Santi Pinochi e Francesco Valentini. Lucca, 1846.

Cevasco, Roberta. *Memoria verde: nuovi spazi per la geografia*. Citta di Castello, Italia: Diabasis, 2007.

——. "Multiple Use of Tree-Land in the Northern Apennines During the Post-Medieval Period." In *Ligurian Landscapes*, edited by Ross Balzaretti, Mark Pearce, and Charles Watkins, 155–78. London: Accordia Specialist Studies on Italy, University of London, 2004.

Cevasco, Roberta, and Diego Moreno. "Historical Ecology in Modern Conservation in Italy." In *Europe's Changing Woods and Forests: From Wildwood to Managed Landscapes*, edited by Tibor Hartel, Keith Kirby, Thomas Ranius, Charles Watkins, Peter Buckley, Peter Savill, Chris Quine, et al., 227–42. Oxford: CAB International, 2016.

C.f. "Il paese non c'è più, cercatelo sotto il fango." *La Repubblica*, 21 Giugno 1996.

——. "Ma perché non hanno pulito il letto del fiume." *La Repubblica*, 12 Agosto 1996.

Chakrabarty, Dipesh. "The Climate of History: Four Theses." *Critical Inquiry* 35, no. 2 (2009): 197–222. https://doi.org/10.1086/596640.

Chatti, Deepti, Matthew Archer, Myles Lennon, and Michael R. Dove. "Exploring the Mundane: Towards an Ethnographic Approach to Bioenergy." *Energy Research & Social Science* 30 (2017): 28–34. https://doi.org/10.1016/j.erss.2017.06.024.

Chiesi, M., F. Maselli, M. Bindi, L. Fibbi, L. Bonora, A. Raschi, R. Tognetti, J. Cermak, and N. Nadezhdina. "Calibration and Application of Forest-BGC in a Mediterranean Area by the Use of Conventional and Remote Sensing Data." *Ecological Modelling* 154, no. 3 (2002): 251–62. http://dx.doi.org/10.1016/S0304-3800(02)00057-1.

Chiesi, M., F. Maselli, M. Moriondo, L. Fibbi, M. Bindi, and S. W. Running. "Application of Biome-BGC to Simulate Mediterranean Forest Processes." *Ecological Modelling* 206, no. 1–2 (2007): 179–90. http://dx.doi.org/10.1016/j.ecolmodel.2007.03.032.

Chiesi, M., M. Moriondo, F. Maselli, L. Gardin, L. Fibbi, M. Bindi, and S. W. Running. "Simulation of Mediterranean Forest Carbon Pools Under Expected Environmental Scenarios." *Canadian Journal of Forest Research* 40, no. 5 (May 2010): 850–60. https://doi.org/10.1139/X10-037.

Chirici, Gherardo, Marta Chiesi, Piermaria Corona, Nicola Puletti, Matteo Mura, and Fabio Maselli. "Prediction of Forest NPP in Italy by the Combination of Ground and Remote Sensing Data." *European Journal of Forest Research* 134, no. 3 (2015): 453–67. https://doi.org/10.1007/s10342-015-0864-4.

Choe, Chong Pil, and Martin T. Bale. "Current Perspectives on Settlement, Subsistence, and Cultivation in Prehistoric Korea." *Arctic Anthropology* 39, no. 1/2 (2002): 95–121. http://www.jstor.org/stable/40316567.

Ciabatti, Giuseppe, Antonio Gabellini, Andrea Perugi, and Claudio Ottaviani. *I rimboschimenti in Toscana e la loro gestione*. Supporti tecnici alla Legge Regionale Forestale della Toscana. Vol. 5, Firenze: ARSIA, Regione Toscana DREAM Italia, 2009.

Cianciullo, Antonio. "Il clima cambia le città. 139 vittime in cinque anni." *La Repubblica,* 13 Aprile 2015.

Ciuffetti, Augusto. *Appennino: Economie, culture e spazi sociali dal medioevo all'età contemporanea.* Roma: Carocci Editori, 2019.

Clements, Frederic E. "Nature and Structure of the Climax." *Journal of Ecology* 24, no. 1 (1936): 252–84. https://doi.org/10.2307/2256278.

Commissione delle Acque e Strade, Archivio di Stato, Lucca. "Disegno dello sbocco del Rio di Vorno in Ozzeri." Mappe, Rio di Vorno (sottofondo 1), filza 728, n. 2; N. 29 1701–1800.

Comune di Montevarchi. "A Levane inaugurata la nuova centrale a biomasse." News release, 16 Gennaio 2014.

Conedera, M., P. Krebs, W. Tinner, M. Pradella, and D. Torriani. "The Cultivation of *Castanea sativa* (Mill.) in Europe, from Its Origin to Its Diffusion on a Continental Scale." *Vegetation History and Archaeobotany* 13, no. 3 (2004): 161–79. https://doi.org/10.2307/23418004.

Conklin, Harold C. *Hanunoó Agriculture: A Report on an Integral System of Shifting Cultivation in the Philippines.* Rome: Food and Agriculture Organization of the United Nations, 1957.

Consiglio Provinciale dell'Economia. *Prescrizioni di massima e di polizia forestale per i boschi e terreni di montagna sottoposti a vincolo nella provincia di Pisa.* Pisa: Tipografia Editrice Pacini-Mariotti, 1931.

Consorzi di Bonifica della Toscana. *Atlante della bonifica Toscana.* Firenze: Edizioni Medicea, 2012.

Corti, Giuseppe, Stefania Cocco, Giorgia Brecciaroli, Alberto Agnelli, and Giovanna Seddaiu. "Italian Soil Management from Antiquity to Nowadays." Chap. 9 in *The Soils of Italy,* edited by Edoardo A. C. Costantini and Carmelo Dazzi. World Soils Book Series, 247–93. Dordrecht, Netherlands: Springer, 2013.

Cosgrove, Denis. "Prospect, Perspective and the Evolution of the Landscape Idea." *Transactions of the Institute of British Geographers* 10, no. 1 (1985): 45–62. https://doi.org/10.2307/622249.

Cotecchia, Vincenzo. "Sulle cause geologiche che obbligano al trasferimento di taluni abitati dissestati della Lucania." *Geotecnica* 1 (1957): 4–15.

Crini, Federica. "Inaugurata la centrale di cogenerazione a biomasse di Levane: Un modello di produzione di energia attraverso la filiera corta." *Valdarno Post,* 1 Gennaio 2014.

Cronon, William. "The Trouble with Wilderness; or, Getting Back to the Wrong Nature." In *Uncommon Ground: Rethinking the Human Place in Nature,* edited by William Cronon, 69–90. New York and London: W. W. Norton, 1996.

Croucher, Peter J. P., Silvia Mascheretti, and Matteo Garbelotto. "Combining Field Epidemiological Information and Genetic Data to Comprehensively Reconstruct the Invasion History and the Microevolution of the Sudden Oak Death Agent

Phytophthora ramorum (Stramenopila: Oomycetes) in California." *Biological Invasions* 15, no. 10 (2013): 2281–97. https://doi.org/10.1007/s10530-013-0453-8.

Crumley, Carole L. "Historical Ecology and the Study of Landscape." *Landscape Research* 42, no. sup1 (2017): S65–S73. https://doi.org/10.1080/01426397.2017.1399994.

Crumley, Carole L., and William H. Marquardt. *Regional Dynamics: Burgundian Landscapes in Historical Perspective.* San Diego: Academic Press, 1987.

Cushman, Gregory T. *Guano and the Opening of the Pacific World: A Global Ecological History.* New York: Cambridge University Press, 2014.

D'Amato Avanzi, Giacomo, and Roberto Giannecchini. "Eventi alluvionali e fenomeni franosi nelle Alpi Apuane (Toscana): Primi risultati di un'indagine retrospettiva nel bacino del Fiume Versilia." *Rivista Geografica Italiana* 110 (2003): 527–59.

D'Amato Avanzi, Giacomo, Roberto Giannecchini, and Alberto Puccinelli. "The Influence of the Geological and Geomorphological Settings on Shallow Landslides. An Example in a Temperate Climate Environment: The June 19, 1996 Event in Northwestern Tuscany (Italy)." *Engineering Geology* 73, no. 3 (2004): 215–28. https://doi.org/10.1016/j.enggeo.2004.01.005.

Dater, Alan. *Burned: Are Trees the New Coal?* Marlboro, VT: Marlboro Films, 2017.

David, Ezra. "The Racist Removal of Native Americans in California Is Often Missing from Wildfire Discussions, Experts Say." 2:04. Sacramento, CA: Capradio, September 16, 2020. Radio story. https://www.capradio.org/articles/2020/09/16/the-racist-removal-of-native-americans-in-california-is-often-missing-from-wildfire-discussions-experts-say/.

De la Bellacasa, Maria Puig. "Matters of Care in Technoscience: Assembling Neglected Things." *Social Studies of Science* 41, no. 1 (2011): 85–106. https://doi.org/10.1177/0306312710380301.

Di Bérenger, Adolfo. *Studii di archeologia forestale.* Firenze: Accademia Italiana di Scienze Forestali, Direzione Nazionale dell'Economia Montana e delle Foreste, 1965 [first ed. 1859].

Dietze, Michael Christopher. *Ecological Forecasting.* Princeton, NJ: Princeton University Press, 2017.

Di Tella, G. *Il bosco contro il torrente. La redenzione delle terre povere.* Touring Club Italiano, Commissione di propaganda per il bosco e per il pascolo. Vol. Pubblicazione 191, Anno XVIII. Milan: Capriolo & Massimino, 1912.

Dukes, Jeffrey S. "Burning Buried Sunshine: Human Consumption of Ancient Solar Energy." *Climatic Change* 61, no. 1 (2003): 31–44. https://doi.org/10.1023/A:1026391317686.

Edwards, Paul N. *A Vast Machine: Computer Models, Climate Data, and the Politics of Global Warming.* Cambridge, MA: MIT Press, 2010.

Elmi, Stefano. "Più manutenzione dei boschi per prevenire gli smottamenti." *Il Tirreno, edizione Lucca,* 7 Gennaio 2011.

Evans-Pritchard, E. E. *The Nuer: A Description of the Modes of Livelihood and Political Institutions of a Nilotic People.* New York and Oxford: Oxford University Press, 1940.

Evette, Andre, Sophie Labonne, Freddy Rey, Frederic Liebault, Oliver Jancke, and Jacky Girel. "History of Bioengineering Techniques for Erosion Control in Rivers in Western Europe." *Environmental Management* 43, no. 6 (2009): 972–84. https://doi.org/10.1007/s00267-009-9275-y.

Fabbio, G., and A. Cutini. "Il ceduo oggi: quale gestione oltre le definizioni?" *Forest—Rivista di Selvicoltura ed Ecologia Forestale* 14, no. 5 (2017): 257–74. https://doi.org/10.3832/efor2562-014.

Fagarazzi, Claudio, Leonardo Nibbi, and Alessandro Tirinanzi. "Come monitoreare le filiere e gli impianti esistenti al fine di massimizzare la resa economica e migliorare l'impatto ambientale." In *Politiche e strumenti per la valorizzazione delle biomasse come fonte energetica rinnovabile. Le biomasse nell'area di cooperazione transfrontaliera: disponibilità di risorsa e proposte di governance*, 53–75. Lucca: Provincia di Lucca, Biomass+ Energia Che Cresce / Energie en Croissance, 2011.

Fagarazzi, Claudio, Alessandro Tirinanzi, Christian Ciampi, and Sandro Sacchelli. "Qual e la disponibilità della risorsa biomassa nell'area di cooperazione?" In *Politiche e strumenti per la valorizzazione delle biomasse come fonte energetica rinnovabile. Le biomasse nell'area di cooperazione transfrontaliera: disponibilità di risorsa e proposte di governance*, 35–52. Lucca: Provincia di Lucca, Biomass+ Energia Che Cresce / Energie en Croissance, 2011.

Farneti, R., E. G. Lissone, and L. Montemartini. "La resistenza del castagno Giapponese alla malattia dell'inchiostro." *Rivista di Patologia Vegetale* 6, no. 1 (1913): 1–7. http://www.jstor.org/stable/42558989.

Fimright, Peter. "California Native American Tribe Has Been Burning Forests for 10,000 Years. What Can We Learn from Them?" *San Francisco Chronicle*, October 14, 2020. https://www.sfchronicle.com/california-wildfires/article/California-tribe-offered-solution-to-wildfire-15638137.php.

Food and Agriculture Organization of the United Nations, "FAOSTAT," statistics database. Accessed March 18, 2021. http://www.fao.org/faostat/en/?#home.

Foster, David R., and John D. Aber. *Forests in Time: The Environmental Consequences of 1,000 Years of Change in New England*. New Haven, CT: Yale University Press, 2004.

Franquesa, Jaume. *Power Struggles: Dignity, Value, and the Renewable Energy Frontier in Spain*. New Anthropologies of Europe. Bloomington: Indiana University Press, 2018.

Freidberg, Susanne Elizabeth. *French Beans and Food Scares: Culture and Commerce in an Anxious Age*. New York: Oxford University Press, 2004.

Freinkel, Susan. *American Chestnut: The Life, Death, and Rebirth of a Perfect Tree*. Berkeley: University of California Press, 2007.

Friedman, Lisa. "A Trillion Trees: How One Idea Triumphed over Trump's Climate Denialism." *New York Times*, February 12, 2020. https://www.nytimes.com/2020/02/12/climate/trump-trees-climate-change.html.

Frolova, Marina, Maria José Prados, and Alain Nadaï, eds. *Renewable Energies and European Landscapes: Lessons from Southern European Cases*. Dordrecht: Springer, 2015.

Gabbrielli, Antonio. "Adolfo Di Bérenger." *L'Italia Forestale e Montana* 59, no. 1 (2004): 75–76.

——. "Lionello Petri (1875–1946)." *L'Italia Forestale e Montana* 59, no. 5 (2004): 131–32.

——. "La legislazione forestale in Toscana dall' inizio alla caduta del granducato." *L'Italia Forestale e Montana* 40, no. 2 (1985): 126–42.

——. "Selvicoltura Toscana nel '700: seconda parte." *Annali Accademia Italiana di Scienze Forestali* 29 (1980): 179–226.

Gabbrielli, Roberto, and Paolo Di Marco. *Valutazione tecnica sul progetto di una centrale termoelettrica cogenerativa a cippato di biomassa da installare presso il territorio comunale di Bagni di Lucca (LU)*. Pisa: Dipartimento di Energetica Lorenzo Poggi, Universita di Pisa, 2010.

Gaggio, Dario. *The Shaping of Tuscany: Landscape and Society Between Tradition and Modernity*. Cambridge: Cambridge University Press, 2016.

Gan, Elaine, Daniel Sullivan, and Anna Tsing. "Using Natural History in the Study of Industrial Ruins." *Journal of Ethnobiology* 38, no. 1 (2018): 39–54. https://doi.org/10.2993/0278-0771-38.1.039.

Gan, Elaine, and Anna Tsing. "How Things Hold: A Diagram of Coordination in a Satoyama Forest." *Social Analysis* 62, no. 4 (Winter 2018): 102–45.

Genesio, L., M. Chiesi, F. P. Vaccari, L. Fibbi, B. Gioli, V. Grasso, R. Magno, et al. "Monitoraggio integrato del bilancio della CO2 a scala regionale: esperienze in Toscana." Atti 14a Conferenza Nazionale ASITA—Brescia, 9–12 Novembre 2010, Brescia, 2010.

Gennai-Schott, Sabine, Tiziana Sabbatini, Davide Rizzo, and Elisa Marraccini. "Who Remains When Professional Farmers Give Up? Some Insights on Hobby Farming in an Olive Groves–Oriented Terraced Mediterranean Area." *Land* 9, no. 5 (2020): 20. https://doi.org/10.3390/land9050168.

Giachi, Anna Maria. *Quali sono le variabili della governance della biomassa?* In *Politiche e strumenti per la valorizzazione delle biomasse come fonte energetica rinnovabile. Le biomasse nell'area di cooperazione transfrontaliera: disponibilità di risorsa e proposte di governance*, 13–34. Lucca: Provincia di Lucca, Biomass+ Energia Che Cresce / Energie en Croissance, 2011.

Giambastiani, Massimo, F. Occhipinti, M. Armanini, F. Bagnoli, F. Camangi, C. Cossu, S. Fineschi, et al. *Le cultivar di castagno della provincia di Lucca—I parte*. Atti dell'Istituto per la Documentazione sul castagno e la Ricerca Forestale. Vol. 2, Lucca: Istituto per la Documentazione sul castagno e la Ricerca Forestale, 2011.

Giannini, Raffaello, and Antonio Gabbrielli. "Evolution of Multifunctional Land-Use Systems in Mountain Areas in Italy." *Italian Journal of Forest and Mountain Environments* 68, no. 5 (2013): 259–68. http://ojs.aisf.it/index.php/ifm/article/view/872/834.

Gibelli, Giuseppe. *Nuovi studi sulla malattia del castagno, detta dell'inchiostro. Memoria.* Bologna: Tipografia Gamberini e Parmeggiani, 1883.

Gilbert, Samuel. "US South-West in Grip of Historic 'Megadrought,' Research Finds." *The Guardian*, May 29, 2020. https://www.theguardian.com/environment/2020/may/29/megadrought-us-south-west-fires-water-research?CMP=Share_iOSApp_Other#maincontent.

Gimmi, Urs, Benjamin Poulter, Annett Wolf, Hanspeter Portner, Pascale Weber, and Matthias Bürgi. "Soil Carbon Pools in Swiss Forests Show Legacy Effects from Historic Forest Litter Raking." *Landscape Ecology* 28, no. 5 (2013): 835–46. https://doi.org/10.1007/s10980-012-9778-4.

Gori, Giulio. "Dopo il rogo: sul Monte Serra, case giù e strage di alberi. Non è un'emergenza?" *Corriere della Sera: Corriere Fiorentino*, 9 Novembre 2018. https://corrierefiorentino.corriere.it/firenze/notizie/cronaca/18_novembre_09/sul-monte-serra-case-giu-strage-alberi-non-emergenza-42eb7e82-e402-11e8-ab4a-0db4f57d3f47.shtml.

Graham, Ben F., Jr. "Transfer of Dye Through Natural Root Grafts of *Pinus Strobus* L." *Ecology* 41, no. 1 (1960): 56–64. https://doi.org/10.2307/1931939.

Grava, Massimiliano. "Gli opifici di Calci all'impianto del 'Leopoldino'": Il Gis applicato all'archeologia industriale." *Storia e Futuro* 30 (Novembre 2012).

Grava, Massimiliano, Michele De Silva, Mariano Gesualdi, Fabio Lucchesi, Alessandra Martinelli, and Cristiana Torti. "Dalla Cartografia Storica Alla Cartografia 2.0 Nella Toscana Preunitaria: Toponomastica Idrografica E Attività Manifatturiere." Atti XIX Conferenza Nazionale ASITA 29–30 Settembre—1 Ottobre 2015, Lecco—Polo di Lecco del Politecnico di Milano. Federazione Italiana delle Associazioni Scientifiche per le Informazioni Territorialie ed Ambientali, 2015: 421–28.

Grove, A. T., and Oliver Rackham. *The Nature of Mediterranean Europe: An Ecological History.* New Haven, CT, and London: Yale University Press, 2001.

Grove, Richard, H. *Green Imperialism.* New York: Cambridge University Press, 1995.

Grupo di studio comitatibiogas Manziana. *Vademecum per saperne di più su biomasse e biogas.* Manziana, Italia: 2013. Accessed October 23, 2021. http://www.cordicom.org/shared/files/3)H7%20-%20Vademecum%20x%20saperne%20di%20piu%20su%20Biomasse.pdf.

Guarducci, Alessandro, Federico Lazzotti, and Tecla Biancolatte. "Alluvione a Livorno, dalla tragica notte all'inchiesta: il dossier." *Il Tirreno*, Settembre 2017.

Guidoboni, Emanuela. "Upside-Down Landscapes: Seismicity and Seismic Disasters in Italy." In *Nature and History in Modern Italy*, edited by Marco Armiero and Marcus Hall, 33–55. Athens: Ohio University Press, 2010.

Guillemot, Hélène. "Connections Between Simulations and Observation in Climate Computer Modeling. Scientist's Practices and 'Bottom-up Epistemology' Lessons." *Studies in History and Philosophy of Science, Part B: Studies in History and Philosophy of Modern Physics* 41, no. 3 (2010): 242–52. http://dx.doi.org/10.1016/j.shpsb.2010.07.003.

Haberl, Helmut. "Net Land-Atmosphere Flows of Biogenic Carbon Related to Bioenergy: Towards an Understanding of Systemic Feedbacks." *GCB-Bioenergy* 5, no. 4 (2013): 351–57. https://doi.org/10.1111/gcbb.12071.

Haberl, Helmut, Detlef Sprinz, Marc Bonazountas, Pierluigi Cocco, Yves Desaubies, Mogens Henze, Ole Hertel, et al. "Correcting a Fundamental Error in Greenhouse Gas Accounting Related to Bioenergy." *Energy Policy* 45 (June 2012): 18–23. http://dx.doi.org/10.1016/j.enpol.2012.02.051.

Hall, Marcus. *Earth Repair: A Transatlantic History of Environmental Restoration.* Charlottesville: University of Virginia Press, 2005.

Hallé, Francis. *Atlas of Poetic Botany.* Cambridge, MA: MIT Press, 2018.

———. *In Praise of Plants.* Portland, OR: Timber Press, 2002.

Haraway, Donna. "Situated Knowledges: The Science Question in Feminism and the Privilege of Partial Perspective." In *Simians, Cyborgs and Women*, 183–201. New York: Routledge, 1991.

———. *When Species Meet.* Minneapolis: University of Minnesotta Press, 2008.

Hare, Lizzy. "The Anthropocene Trading Zone." *Environment and Society* 6, no. 1 (2015): 109–27. https://doi.org/10.3167/ares.2015.060107.

Hawkes, Christine V., Bonnie G. Waring, Jennifer D. Rocca, and Stephanie N. Kivlin. "Historical Climate Controls Soil Respiration Responses to Current Soil Moisture." *Proceedings of the National Academy of Sciences* 114, no. 24 (2017): 6322. https://doi.org/10.1073/pnas.1620811114.

Heiniger, U., and D. Rigling. "Biological Control of Chestnut Blight in Europe." *Annual Review of Phytopathology* 32, no. 1 (September 1, 1994): 581–99. https://doi.org/10.1146/annurev.py.32.090194.003053.

Herzfeld, Michael. *Evicted from Eternity: The Restructuring of Modern Rome.* Chicago and London: Chicago University Press, 2009.

Hetherington, Kregg, ed. *Infrastructure, Environment, and Life in the Anthropocene.* Experimental Futures. Durham, NC: Duke University Press, 2019.

Hohne, Niklas, Sina Wartmann, Anke Herold, and Annette Freibauer. "The Rules for Land Use, Land Use Change and Forestry under the Kyoto Protocol—Lessons Learned for the Future Climate Negotiations." *Environmental Science & Policy* 10, no. 4 (2007): 353–69 https://doi.org/10.1016/j.envsci.2007.02.001.

Højrup, Mathilde, and Heather Anne Swanson. "The Making of Unstable Ground: The Anthropogenic Geologies of Søby, Denmark." *Journal of Ethnobiology* 38, no. 1 (2018): 24–38. https://doi.org/10.2993/0278-0771-38.1.024.

Holmes, Douglas R. *Cultural Disenchantments: Worker Peasantries in Northeast Italy.* Princeton, NJ: Princeton University Press, 1989.

Howe, Cymene. *Ecologics: Wind and Power in the Anthropocene.* Durham, NC: Duke University Press, 2019.

Howe, Francis. "No Drax! There's Nothing 'Sustainable' About Big Biomass." *The Ecologist*, April 10, 2017. https://theecologist.org/2017/apr/10/no-drax-theres-nothing-sustainable-about-big-biomass.

Hulme, Mike. "Cosmopolitan Climates: Hybridity, Foresight and Meaning." *Theory, Culture & Society* 27, no. 2–3 (2010): 267–76. https://doi.org/10.1177/0263276409358730.
———. *Weathered: Cultures of Climate*. London: Sage, 2017.
———. "Weather-Worlds of the Anthropocene and the End of Climate." *Weber: The Contemporary West*, Fall 2018: 64–75. https://doi.org/10.17863/CAM.35055.
IEA. "Climate Change 2014: Summary for Policymakers." In *Climate Change 2014: Impacts, Adaptation, and Vulnerability. Part A: Global and Sectoral Aspects. Contribution of Working Group II to the Fifth Assessment Report of the Intergovernmental Panel on Climate Change*, edited by C. B. Field, V. R. Barros, D. J. Dokken, K. J. Mach, M. D. Mastrandrea, T. E. Bilir, M. Chatterjee, et al., 1–32. Cambridge and New York: Cambridge University Press, 2014.
———. *Net Zero by 2050: A Roadmap for the Global Energy Sector*. Vienna: International Energy Agency, 2021. https://www.iea.org/reports/net-zero-by-2050.
Il Tirreno. "200 smottamenti e pochi soldi per il risanamento." *Edizione Massa-Carrara*, 13 Settembre 2011.
———. "Stop all'ubriacatura ecologista." *Edizione Pistoia*, 2 Febbraio 2014.
Ingold, Tim. "Earth, Sky, Wind, and Weather." *Journal of the Royal Anthropological Institute* 13, no. s1 (2007): S19–S38. https://doi.org/10.1111/j.1467–9655.2007.00401.x.
———. "Materials Against Materiality." In Tim Ingold, *Being Alive*. Oxford and New York: Routledge, 2011.
———. "Toward an Ecology of Materials." *Annual Review of Anthropology* 41, no. 1 (2012). https://doi.org/doi:10.1146/annurev-anthro-081309-145920.
Istituto Centrale di Statistica del Regno D'Italia. *Catasto Agrario: 1929—VIII Compartimento della Toscana, Provincia di Lucca*. Fascicolo 47, 1933.
———. *Catasto Agrario: 1929—VIII Compartimento della Toscana, Provincia di Pisa*. Fascicolo 49, 1933.
Jarvis, Paul, Ana Rey, Charalampos Petsikos, Lisa Wingate, Mark Rayment, João Pereira, João Banza, et al. "Drying and Wetting of Mediterranean Soils Stimulates Decomposition and Carbon Dioxide Emission: The 'Birch Effect.'" *Tree Physiology* 27, no. 7 (2007): 929–40. https://doi.org/10.1093/treephys/27.7.929.
Jasanoff, Sheila. *Designs on Nature*. Princeton: Princeton University Press, 2005.
———. "A New Climate for Society." *Theory Culture Society* 27, no. 2–3: 233–53. https://doi.org/10.1177/0263276409361497.
———. "The Songlines of Risk." *Environmental Values* 8, no. 2 (May 1999): 135–52. https://www.jstor.org/stable/30301700.
———. *States of Knowledge: The Co-Production of Science and the Social Order*. Edited by Sheila Jasanoff. London: Routledge, 2004.
———. "Virtual, Visible, and Actionable: Data Assemblages and the Sightlines of Justice." *Big Data & Society* 4, no. 2 (2017). https://doi.org/10.1177/2053951717724477.
Johnson, F. X., Henrique Pacini, and Edward Smeets. *Transformations in EU Biofuels Markets Under the Renewable Energy Directive and the Implications for Land*

Use, Trade and Forests. Bogor, Indonesia: Center for International Forestry Research: 2012.

Jung, T., L. Orlikowski, B. Henricot, P. Abad-Campos, A. G. Aday, O. Aguín Casal, J. Bakonyi, et al. "Widespread *Phytophthora* Infestations in European Nurseries Put Forest, Semi-Natural and Horticultural Ecosystems at High Risk of Phytophthora Diseases." *Forest Pathology* 46, no. 2 (2015): 134–63. https://doi.org/10.1111/efp.12239.

Keeley, Jon E., and Alexandra D. Syphard. "Twenty-First Century California, USA, Wildfires: Fuel-Dominated vs. Wind-Dominated Fires." *Fire Ecology* 15, no. 1 (2019): 24. https://doi.org/10.1186/s42408-019-0041-0.

Keeley, Jon E., and Paul H. Zedler. "Evolution of Life Histories of Pinus." In *Ecology and Biogeography of Pinus*, edited by D. M. Richardson, 219–50. Cambridge and New York: Cambridge University Press, 1998.

Keng, Hsuan. "Economic Plants of Ancient North China as Mentioned in 'Shih Ching' (Book of Poetry)." *Economic Botany* 28, no. 4 (1974): 391–410. http://www.jstor.org/stable/4253534.

Keyser, Richard. "The Transformation of Traditional Woodland Management: Commercial Sylviculture in Medieval Champagne." *French Historical Studies* 32, no. 3 (2009): 353–84.

Kitagawa, Junko, and Yoshinori Yasuda. "Development and Distribution of Castanea and Aesculus Culture During the Jomon Period in Japan." *Quaternary International* 184, no. 1 (2008): 41–55. https://doi.org/10.1016/j.quaint.2007.09.014.

Klinger, Julie Michelle. *Rare Earth Frontiers: From Terrestrial Subsoils to Lunar Landscapes*. Ithaca, NY: Cornell University Press, 2017.

Lahsen, Myanna, Gabriela de Azevedo Couto, and Irene Lorenzoni. "When Climate Change Is Not Blamed: The Politics of Disaster Attribution in International Perspective." *Climatic Change* 158, no. 2 (2020): 213–33. https://doi.org/10.1007/s10584-019-02642-z.

Larkin, Brian. "The Politics and Poetics of Infrastructure." *Annual Review of Anthropology* 42 (2013).

Law, John, and Marianne Elisabeth Lien. "Slippery: Field Notes in Empirical Ontology." *Social Studies of Science* 43, no. 3: 363–78. https://doi.org/10.1177/0306312712456947.

Lazzarini, Giulio. *La storia della mezzadria nelle colline lucchesi a metà del novecento*. Lucca: Stampa S. Marco Litotipo, 2013.

Lazzotti, Federico. "Alluvione a Livorno, la procura nomina cinque ingegneri per indagare sulle carte edilizie." *Il Tirreno*, 16 Settembre 2017.

Legambiente Lucca. "Il contributo sostenibile delle biomasse nella programmazione energetica per la produzione di energia da fonti rinnovabili." Intervento presso il Consiglio Provinciale di Lucca. 9 Maggio 2013.

Levenda, A. M., I. Behrsin, and F. Disano. "Renewable Energy for Whom? A Global Systematic Review of the Environmental Justice Implications of Renewable Energy

Technologies." *Energy Research & Social Science* 71 (2021). https://doi.org/10.1016/j.erss.2020.101837.

Lévi-Strauss, Claude. *Tristes Tropiques*. New York: Atheneum, 1970.

Lewis, Simon L., and Mark A. Maslin. "Defining the Anthropocene." Perspectives. *Nature* 519, no. 7542 (2015): 171–80. https://doi.org/10.1038/nature14258.

Lightfoot, Kent G., Rob Q. Cuthrell, Cristie M. Boone, Roger Byrne, Andreas S. Chavez, Laurel Collins, Alicia Cowart, et al. "Anthropogenic Burning on the Central California Coast in Late Holocene and Early Historical Times: Findings, Implications, and Future Directions." *California Archaeology* 5, no. 2 (December 1, 2013): 371–90. https://doi.org/10.1179/1947461X13Z.00000000020.

Lightfoot, Kent G., Lee M. Panich, Tsim D. Schneider, and Sara L. Gonzalez. "European Colonialism and the Anthropocene: A View from the Pacific Coast of North America." *Anthropocene* 4, supplement C (2013): 101–15. https://doi.org/10.1016/j.ancene.2013.09.002.

Loreti, Lara. "Più forti e frequenti: alluvioni in aumento." *Il Tirreno, edizione Livorno*, 12 Settembre 2017.

Lorimer, Jamie. *Wildlife in the Anthropocene: Conservation After Nature*. Minneapolis: University of Minnesota Press, 2015.

Luchi, N., V. Mancini, M. Feducci, A. Santini, and P. Capretti. "*Leptoglossus occidentalis* and *Diplodia pinea*: A New Insect-Fungus Association in Mediterranean Forests." *Forest Pathology* 42, no. 3 (2012): 246–51. https://doi.org/10.1111/j.1439-0329.2011.00750.x.

Luyssaert, S., P. Ciais, S. L. Piao, E. D. Schulze, M. Jung, S. Zaehle, M. J. Schelhaas, et al. "The European Carbon Balance. Part 3: Forests." *Global Change Biology* 16, no. 5 (2010): 1429–50. https://doi.org/10.1111/j.1365-2486.2009.02056.x.

Lyons, Kristina Marie. "Soil Science, Development, and the 'Elusive Nature' of Colombia's Amazonian Plains." *Journal of Latin American and Caribbean Anthropology* 19, no. 2 (2014): 212–36. https://doi.org/10.1111/jlca.12097.

Macfarlane, Robert. *Landmarks*. London: Penguin, 2016.

Maggi, Roberto. "*I monti sun eggi*: The Making of the Ligurian Landscape in Prehistory." In *Ligurian Landscapes*, edited by Ross Balzaretti, Mark Pearce, and Charles Watkins, 71–81. London: Accordia Specialist Studies on Italy, University of London, 2004.

Maglioni, Iolanda. "Vincenzo Viviani e l'Arno. Scienza galileiana e problemi di un fiume e del suo bacino nel XVII secolo." *Archivio Storico Italiano* 159, no. 1 (587) (2001): 151–70. http://www.jstor.org/stable/26229538.

Mander, Sarah, Kevin Anderson, Alice Larkin, Clair Gough, and Naomi Vaughan. "The Role of Bio-Energy with Carbon Capture and Storage in Meeting the Climate Mitigation Challenge: A Whole System Perspective." *Energy Procedia* 114, (2017): 6036–43. https://doi.org/10.1016/j.egypro.2017.03.1739.

Manigrasso, Michele, Daniela Chiavarini, Daniela De Rubeis, and Sara Toso. *L'Italia delle alluvioni: gli impatti degli eventi estremi di pioggia nelle città italiane*. Studio

Legambiente, Italia (2013). Accessed October 24, 2021. https://www.legambiente.it/sites/default/files/docs/litalia_delle_alluvioni_studio_ultimo.pdf.

Marder, Michael. *Plant-Thinking: A Philosophy of Vegetal Life.* New York: Columbia University Press, 2013.

Marris, Emma. *Rambunctious Garden: Saving Nature in a Post-Wild World.* New York: Bloomsbury, 2011.

Marsh, George P. *Man and Nature.* Cambridge, MA: Belknap Press of Harvard University Press, 1965 [first ed. 1865].

Martínez, Felipe, and Gregorio Montero. "The *Pinus pinea* L. Woodlands Along the Coast of South-Western Spain: Data for a New Geobotanical Interpretation." *Plant Ecology* 175, no. 1 (2004): 1–18. https://doi.org/10.2307/20146667.

Martinez-Alier, Joan, Leah Temper, Daniela Del Bene, and Arnim Scheidel. "Is There a Global Environmental Justice Movement?" *Journal of Peasant Studies* 43, no. 3 (2016): 731–55. https://doi.org/10.1080/03066150.2016.1141198.

Martini, Mario E. *La storia di Calci: raccolta di notizie, edite e inedite intorno ai luoghi, cose, persone, e fatti della Valle Graziosa.* Pisa: V. Lischi e Figli, 1976.

Masco, Joseph. "The Crisis in Crisis." *Current Anthropology* 58, no. S15 (2016): S65–S76. https://doi.org/10.1086/688695.

Maselli, F., and M. Chiesi. "Evaluation of Statistical Methods to Estimate Forest Volume in a Mediterranean Region." *IEEE Transactions on Geoscience and Remote Sensing* 44, no. 8 (2006): 2239–50. https://doi.org/10.1109/TGRS.2006.872074.

Maselli, F., M. Chiesi, M. Moriondo, L. Fibbi, M. Bindi, and S. W. Running. "Modelling the Forest Carbon Budget of a Mediterranean Region Through the Integration of Ground and Satellite Data." *Ecological Modelling* 220, no. 3 (2009): 330–42. http://dx.doi.org/10.1016/j.ecolmodel.2008.10.002.

Masiero, Gabriele. "Maltempo, Calci minacciata da una torrente di cenere. Il Sindaco Ghimenti: 'Per la nostra zona era stato dato codice verde.'" *La Nazione: Pisa,* 1 Settembre 2019.

Masiero, Mauro, Nicola Andrighetto, and Davide Pettenella. "Linee-guida per la valutazione sistematica della filiera corta delle biomasse legnose a fini energetici." *Agriregionieuropa* 9, no. 33 (Giugno 2013): 74.

Massoni, Giovanni. *La pieve e la comunità di Vorno.* Lucca: Maria Pacini Fazzi Editori, 1999.

Mathews, Andrew S. "Anthropology and the Anthropocene: Criticisms, Experiments, and Collaborations." *Annual Review of Anthropology* 49 (2020): 67–82.

——. *Instituting Nature: Authority, Expertise, and Power in Mexican Forests.* Politics, Science, and the Environment Series. Cambridge, MA: MIT Press, 2011.

——. "Landscapes and Throughscapes in Italian Forest Worlds: Thinking Dramatically About the Anthropocene." *Cultural Anthropology* 33, no. 3 (August 2018): 386–414.

——. "Scandals, Audits, and Fictions: Linking Climate Change to Mexican Forests." *Social Studies of Science* 44, no. 1 (2013): 83–109. https://doi.org/10.1177/0306312713490330.

———. "Unlikely Alliances: Encounters Between State Science, Nature Spirits, and Indigenous Industrial Forestry in Mexico, 1926–2008." *Current Anthropology* 50, no. 1 (2009): 75–101.

Mattioni, Claudia, M. Angela Martin, Paola Pollegioni, Marcello Cherubini, and Fiorella Villani. "Microsatellite Markers Reveal a Strong Geographical Structure in European Populations of *Castanea Sativa* (Fagaceae): Evidence for Multiple Glacial Refugia." *American Journal of Botany* 100, no. 5 (2013): 951–61. https://doi.org/10.1016/j.envsci.2007.02.001.

Mazzarosa, Antonio. *Le pratiche della campagna lucchese*. Lucca: Tipografia di Giuseppe Giusti, 1846.

McKechnie, Jon, Steve Colombo, and Heather L. MacLean. "Forest Carbon Accounting Methods and the Consequences of Forest Bioenergy for National Greenhouse Gas Emissions Inventories." *Environmental Science & Policy* 44 (2014): 164–73. http://dx.doi.org/10.1016/j.envsci.2014.07.006.

McNeill, John Robert. *The Mountains of the Mediterranean World: An Environmental History*. Studies in Environment and History. Cambridge: Cambridge University Press, 1992.

Metailie, J.-P. "Mountain Landscape, Pastoral Management and Traditional Practices in the Northern Pyrenees (France)." In *The Conservation of Cultural Landscapes*, edited by Mauro Agnoletti, 108–24. Wallingford, UK: CABI, 2006.

Ministero delle Politiche Agricole Alimentari e Forestali. *Piano del settore castanicolo 2010–2013, documento di sintesi*. Roma: 2009. Accessed October 24, 2021. https://www.politicheagricole.it/flex/cm/pages/ServeBLOB.php/L/IT/IDPagina/3277.

Ministero dello Sviluppo Economico. *Piano di azione nazionale per le energie rinnovabili dell'Italia*. Ministero dello Sviluppo Economico. Roma: 2010. Accessed October 24, 2021. https://www.gse.it/Dati-e-Scenari_site/monitoraggio-fer_site/area-documentale_site/Documenti%20Piano%20di%20Azione%20Nazionale/PAN%20DETTAGLIO.pdf.

Misrach, Richard, and Kate Orff. *Petrochemical America*. New York: Aperture, 2014.

Mitchell, Timothy. "Carbon Democracy." *Economy and Society* 38, no. 3 (2009): 399–432. https://doi.org/10.1080/03085140903020598.

Mol, Annemarie. *The Body Multiple: Ontology in Medical Practice*. Durham, NC: Duke University Press, 2002.

Moreno, Diego. *Dal documento al terreno: storia e archeologia dei sistemi agro-silvo-pastorali*. Giano Bifronte 1. Edited by Carlo Montanari and Maria Angela Guido. Genova, Italia: Genova University Press, 2018.

———. "Escaping from 'Landscape': the Historical and Environmental Identification of Local Land-Management Practices in the Post-Medieval Ligurian Mountains." In *Ligurian Landscapes*, edited by Ross Balzaretti, Mark Pearce, and Charles Watkins, 130–40. London: Accordia Specialist Studies on Italy, University of London, 2004.

———. "Querce come olivi. Sulla rovericoltura in Liguria tra XVIII e XIX secolo." *Quaderni Storici* 49 (1982): 108–36.

Myers, Natasha. "How to Grow Livable Worlds: Ten Not-So-Easy Steps." In *The World to Come: Art in the Age of the Anthropocene*, edited by Kerry Oliver-Smith, 53–63. Gainesville: Samuel P. Harn Museum of Art, University of Florida, 2018.

———. "Involutionary Momentum: Affective Ecologies and the Sciences of Plant/Insect Encounters." *Difference* 23, no. 5 (2012).

Nardi, Licciana. "Sequestrato impianto a biomasse." *La Nazione: Massa Carrara*, March 28, 2019.

Naylor, L. A., H. A. Viles, and N. E. A. Carter. "Biogeomorphology Revisited: Looking Towards the Future." *Geomorphology* 47, no. 1 (2002): 3–14. https://doi.org/10.1016/S0169-555X(02)00137-X.

Nixon, Rob. "Neoliberalism, Slow Violence, and the Environmental Picaresque." *MFS Modern Fiction Studies* 55, no. 3 (2009).

Nyquist, Jon R. "Fire and the Creation of Landscape Regimes: Wildness and Interconnections in West Australian Forests." PhD diss., University of California Santa Cruz, 2019.

Olwig, Kenneth R. "Recovering the Substantive Nature of Landscape." *Annals of the Association of American Geographers* 86, no. 4 (1996): 630–53. https://doi.org/10.1111/j.1467-8306.1996.tb01770.x.

O'Reilly, Jessica. "The Substance of Climate: Material Approaches to Nature Under Environmental Change." *Wiley Interdisciplinary Reviews: Climate Change* 9, no. 6 (2018): e550. https://doi.org/10.1002/wcc.550.

Orlove, Ben, Kerry Milch, Lisa Zaval, Christoph Ungemach, Julie Brugger, Katherine Dunbar, and Christine Jurt. "Framing Climate Change in Frontline Communities: Anthropological Insights on How Mountain Dwellers in the USA, Peru, and Italy Adapt to Glacier Retreat." *Regional Environmental Change* 19, no. 5 (2019): 1295–309. https://doi.org/10.1007/s10113-019-01482-y.

Panattoni, Rita. *San Rossore nella storia: un paesaggio naturale e costruito*. Firenze: L. S. Olschki, 2010.

Park, Jungjae, Minkoo Kim, Hyoun Soo Lim, and Jinmu Choi. "Pollen and Sediment Evidence for Late-Holocene Human Impact at the Seonam-Dong Archeological Site, Gwangju, Korea." *Review of Palaeobotany and Palynology* 193 (2013): 110–18. https://doi.org/10.1016/j.revpalbo.2013.01.012.

Pavari, Aldo. "Chestnut Blight in Europe." *Unasylva* 3, no. 1 (January–February 1949).

Pedreschi, Luigi. *I terrazzamenti agrari in Val Di Serchio*. Publicazioni dell Istituto di Geografia dell'Universita di Pisa. Pisa: Libreria Goliardica, 1963.

Pelosini, N. F. *Ricordi, tradizioni e legende dei Monti Pisani*. Bologna: Forni Editore, 1970 [first ed. 1890].

Petryna, Adriana. "Wildfires at the Edges of Science: Horizoning Work amid Runaway Change." *Cultural Anthropology* 33, no. 4 (2018): 570–95.

Peverieri, Giuseppino Sabbatini, Paola Furlan, Daniele Benassai, Sarah Caradonna, Ward B. Strong, and Pio Federico Roversi. "Host Egg Age of *Leptoglossus occiden-*

talis (Heteroptera, Coreidae) and Parasitism by *Gryon pennsylvanicum* (Hymenoptera, Platygastridae)." *Journal of Economic Entomology* 106, no. 2 (2013): 633–40. https://doi.org/10.1603/ec12344.

Piccinni, Gabriella. "Mezzadria e potere politico. Suggestioni dell'età moderna e contemporanea e realtà medievale." *Studi Storici* 46, no. 4 (2005): 923–43. http://www.jstor.org/stable/20567326.

Povinelli, Elizabeth A. *Geontologies: A Requiem to Late Liberalism*. Durham, NC: Duke University Press, 2016.

Powell, Dana E. *Landscapes of Power: Politics of Energy in the Navajo Nation*. Durham, NC: Duke University Press, 2017.

Pra, Alex, and Davide Pettenella. "Consumption of Wood Biomass for Energy in Italy: A Strategic Role Based Upon Weak Knowledge." *L'Italia Forestale e Montana* 71, no. 1 (2016): 49–62.

Pranzini, Enzo. "Updrift River Mouth Migration on Cuspate Deltas: Two Examples from the Coast of Tuscany (Italy)." *Geomorphology* 38, no. 1–2 (2001): 125–32. http://dx.doi.org/10.1016/S0169-555X(00)00076-3.

Preti, Federico. "Sistemazioni idraulico-forestali e ingegneria naturalistica per la difesa del territorio." Sintesi dell intervento al Convegno Ingegneria Naturalistica in Ambiente Mediterraneo, Pisa, 22 Aprile 2004.

Puccinelli, C. "Sulla malattia del castagno." *L'Agricoltore* 5 (Gennaio–Dicembre 1869): 289–92.

Puccinelli, Giuliana. "All'origine di una monocultura: l'espansione del castagneto nella Valle del Serchio in età moderna." *Rivista di Storia dell'Agricoltura* 50, no. 1 (2010): 3–65.

Pyne, Stephen J. *Vestal Fire: An Environmental History, Told Through Fire, of Europe and Europe's Encounter with the World*. Cycle of Fire. Seattle: University of Washington Press, 1997.

Rackham, Oliver. *Woodlands*. London: HarperCollins, 2006.

Ranganathan, Malini, and Eve Bratman. "From Urban Resilience to Abolitionist Climate Justice in Washington, DC." *Antipode* 53, no. 1 (2021), 115–37. https://doi.org/10.1111/anti.12555.

Regione Toscana. *PAER: Proposta di piano ambientale ed energetico regionale, libro bianco sui cambiamenti climatici in Toscana*. Firenze: Laboratorio di Monitoraggio e Modellistica Ambientale, 2012.

Riccardi, Katia. "Maltempo, Italia sott'acqua da giovedì: violenti nubifragi in Liguria e nel Lazio. Roma a rischio." *La Repubblica*, 14 Settembre 2016.

Richardson, D. M. *Ecology and Biogeography of* Pinus. Cambridge and New York: Cambridge University Press, 1998.

Rigling, Daniel, and Simone Prospero. "*Cryphonectria parasitica*, the Causal Agent of Chestnut Blight: Invasion History, Population Biology and Disease Control." *Molecular Plant Pathology* 19, no. 1 (2018): 7–20. https://doi.org/10.1111/mpp.12542.

Rizzo, Davide, Fabio Casella, Mariassunta Galli, and Enrico Bonani. *La gestione delle sistemazioni idraulico-agrarie nel Monte Pisano: schede descrittive e operative*. Comune di Calci: Land Lab; Scuola Superiore di Sant'Anna Pisa, 2009.

Rocheleau, Dianne. "Maps, Numbers, Text and Context: Mixing Methods in Feminist Political Ecology." *Professional Geographer* 47, no. 4 (1995): 458–66.

Rosato, Mario A. "Sopravvivenza nella giungla europea dei pellet—II parte." *Agronotizie*, no. 5 (Aprile 2016).

Rose, Deborah Bird. "Dreaming Ecology: Beyond the Between." *Religion & Literature* 40, no. 1 (2008): 109–22. https://www.jstor.org/stable/40059845.

Roy, Bitty A., Helen M. Alexander, Jennifer Davidson, Faith T. Campbell, Jeremy J. Burdon, Richard Sniezko, and Clive Brasier. "Increasing Forest Loss Worldwide from Invasive Pests Requires New Trade Regulations." *Frontiers in Ecology and the Environment* 12, no. 8 (2014): 457–65. https://doi.org/10.1890/130240.

Sabbatini, Renzo. "La rottura degli equilibri di antico regime: alcune considerazioni sull'Appennino Tosco-Emiliano e sul caso lucchese." In *Economie nel tempo. Persistenza e cambiamenti negli Appennini in età moderna*, edited by Antonio G. Calafatti and Ercole Sori, 127–52. Milano: FrangoAngeli, 2004.

Saminiati, Vincenzo. "Trattato d'agricoltura di Giovanni di Messer Vincenzo Saminiati." Archivio di Stato di Lucca. Unpublished manuscript, circa 1598.

Santini, A., L. Ghelardini, C. Pace, M. L. Desprez-Loustau, P. Capretti, A. Chandelier, T. Cech, et al. "Biogeographical Patterns and Determinants of Invasion by Forest Pathogens in Europe." *New Phytologist* 197, no. 1 (2012): 238–50. https://doi.org/10.1111/j.1469-8137.2012.04364.x.

Santini, Alberto, Andrew Liebhold, Duccio Migliorini, and Steve Woodward. "Tracing the Role of Human Civilization in the Globalization of Plant Pathogens." *ISME Journal* 12, no. 3 (2018): 647–52. https://doi.org/10.1038/s41396-017-0013-9.

Sarti, Rolando. *Long Live the Strong: A History of Rural Society in the Apennine Mountains*. Amherst: University of Massachusetts Press, 1985.

Schlosberg, David, and Lisette B. Collins. "From Environmental to Climate Justice: Climate Change and the Discourse of Environmental Justice." *Wiley Interdisciplinary Reviews: Climate Change* 5, no. 3 (2014): 359–74. https://doi.org/10.1002/wcc.275.

Schneider, Kevin, Wopke van der Werf, Martina Cendoya, Monique Mourits, Juan A. Navas-Cortés, Antonio Vicent, and Alfons Oude Lansink. "Impact of *Xylella fastidiosa* subspecies *pauca* in European Olives." *Proceedings of the National Academy of Sciences*, April 28, 2020: 9250–9259. https://doi.org/10.1073/pnas.1912206117.

Sciarretta, A., L. Marziali, M. Squarcini, L. Marianelli, D. Benassai, F. Logli, and P. F. Roversi. "Adaptive Management of Invasive Pests in Natural Protected Areas: The Case of *Matsucoccus feytaudi* in Central Italy." *Bulletin of Entomological Research* 106, no. 1 (2016): 9–18. https://doi.org/10.1017/S0007485315000851.

Searchinger, Timothy D., Stefan Wirsenius, Tim Beringer, and Patrice Dumas. "Assessing the Efficiency of Changes in Land Use for Mitigating Climate Change." *Nature* 564, no. 7735 (2018): 249–53. https://doi.org/10.1038/s41586-018-0757-z.

Seidl, Rupert, Dominik Thom, Markus Kautz, Dario Martin-Benito, Mikko Peltoniemi, Giorgio Vacchiano, Jan Wild, et al. "Forest Disturbances under Climate Change." *Nature Climate Change* 7 (2017): 395–402. https://doi.org/10.1038/nclimate3303.

Selva, Francesco. *Memorie per servire allo studio della malattia dei castagni dominanti nel circondario di Biella.* Biella, Italia: Tipografia Antonio Chiorino, 1872.

Sereni, Emilio. *History of the Italian Agricultural Landscape.* Translated by R. Burr Litchfield. Princeton, NJ: Princeton University Press, 1997.

Serpieri, Arrigo. *Il bosco, il pascolo, il monte.* Vol. 17, no. 165. Milano: Touring Club Italiano, Commissione di Propaganda per il Bosco e per il Pascolo, 1911.

Sheng, Pengfei, Hua Zhou, Jianye Liu, and Hongen Jiang. "Some Like It Hot: Sichuan Pepper (*Zanthoxylum bungeanum*) and Other Spices from a Late Bronze Age Kingdom (Chu State) in Hubei, China." *Archaeological and Anthropological Sciences* 12, no. 10 (2020): 249. https://doi.org/10.1007/s12520-020-01201-3.

Showers, Kate Barger. *Imperial Gullies: Soil Erosion and Conservation in Lesotho.* Athens: Ohio University Press, 2005.

Simard, Suzanne W. *Finding the Mother Tree: Discovering the Wisdom of the Forest.* New York: Alfred Knopf, 2021.

Sismondi, Jean-Charles-Leonard Simonde. *Tableau de L'Agriculture Toscane.* Geneva: J. J. Paschoud, 1801.

Smil, Vaclav. *Energy: A Beginner's Guide.* Oneworld Beginner's Guides. London: Oneworld Publications, 2017.

———. *Energy and Civilization: A History.* Rev., 2nd ed. Cambridge, MA: MIT Press, 2017. http://www.jstor.org/stable/j.ctt1pwt6jj.

———. "Examining Energy Transitions: A Dozen Insights Based on Performance." *Energy Research & Social Science* 22 (December 2016): 194–97. https://doi.org/10.1016/j.erss.2016.08.017.

Smith, Bruce D., and Melinda A. Zeder. "The Onset of the Anthropocene." *Anthropocene* 4 (2013): 8–13. https://doi.org/10.1016/j.ancene.2013.05.001.

Snowden, Frank M. *The Conquest of Malaria: Italy, 1900–1962.* New Haven, CT: Yale University Press, 2006.

Southern Environment Law Center, "Biomass Energy in the South." Accessed April 21, 2021. https://www.southernenvironment.org/cases-and-projects/biomass-energy-in-the-south.

Squatriti, Paolo. *Landscape and Change in Early Medieval Italy: Chestnuts, Economy, and Culture.* Cambridge and New York: Cambridge University Press, 2013.

———. "Water, Nature, and Culture in Early Medieval Lucca." *Early Medieval Europe* 4, no. 1 (1995): 21–40. https://doi.org/10.1111/j.1468-0254.1995.tb00032.x.

Star, Susan Leigh. "The Ethnography of Infrastructure." *American Behavioral Scientist* 43, no. 3 (1999): 377–91. https://doi.org/10.1177%2F00027649921955326.

Steffen, W. "Planetary Boundaries: Guiding Human Development on a Changing Planet." *Science* 347, no. 6223 (2015): 1259855–1-10. https://doi.org/10.1126/science.1259855.

Steffen, Will, Johan Rockström, Katherine Richardson, Timothy M. Lenton, Carl Folke, Diana Liverman, Colin P. Summerhayes, et al. "Trajectories of the Earth System in the Anthropocene." *Proceedings of the National Academy of Sciences* 115, no. 33 (2018): 8252. https://doi.org/10.1073/pnas.1810141115.

Syphard, Alexandra D., Jon E. Keeley, Anne H. Pfaff, and Ken Ferschweiler. "Human Presence Diminishes the Importance of Climate in Driving Fire Activity Across the United States." *Proceedings of the National Academy of Sciences* 114, no. 52 (2017): 13750. https://doi.org/10.1073/pnas.1713885114.

Tansley, A. G. "The Use and Abuse of Vegetational Concepts and Terms." *Ecology* 16, no. 3 (1935): 284–307.

Tommasini, Laura, Luca Carniello, Massimiliano Ghinassi, Marcella Roner, and Andrea D'Alpaos. "Changes in the Wind-Wave Field and Related Salt-Marsh Lateral Erosion: Inferences from the Evolution of the Venice Lagoon in the Last Four Centuries." *Earth Surface Processes and Landforms* 44, no. 8 (June 30, 2019): 1633–46. https://doi.org/10.1002/esp.4599.

Trigila, Alessandro, Carla Iadanza, Martina Bussettini, Barbara Lastoria, Angela Barbano, Michele Munafò. *Dissesto idrogeologico in Italia: pericolosita e indicatori di rischio. rapporto 2015.* Rome: Istituto Superiore per la Protezione e la Ricerca Ambientale, 2015.

Tsai, Yen-Ling, Isabelle Carbonell, Joelle Chevrier, and Anna Tsing. "Golden Snail Opera: The More-Than-Human Performance of Friendly Farming on Taiwan's Lanyang Plain." *Cultural Anthropology* 31, no. 4 (2016): 520–44. https://doi.org/10.14506/ca31.4.04.

Tsing, Anna Lowenhaupt. *The Mushroom at the End of the World: On the Possibility of Life in Capitalist Ruins.* Princeton, NJ: Princeton University Press, 2015.

Tsing, Anna L., Jennifer Deger, Alder Keleman, and Feifei Zhou. *Feral Atlas: The More-Than-Human Anthropocene.* Redwood City, CA: Stanford Digital Projects, Stanford University Press, 2021. Accessed May 15, 2021. https://doi.org/10.21627/2020fa.

Tsing, Anna, and Elaine Gan. "How Things Hold: A Diagram of Coordination in a Satoyama Forest." *Social Analysis* 62, no. 4 (2018): 102–45.

Tsing, Anna Lowenhaupt, Andrew S. Mathews, and Nils Bubandt. "Patchy Anthropocene: Landscape Structure, Multispecies History, and the Retooling of Anthropology: An Introduction to Supplement 20." *Current Anthropology* (2019): S186–97. https://doi.org/10.1086/703391.

Ureta, Sebastián, Thomas Lekan, and W. Graf von Hardenberg. "Baselining Nature: An Introduction." *Environment and Planning E: Nature and Space* 3, no. 1 (2020): 3–19. https://doi.org/10.1177/2514848619898092.

Van Vuuren, Detlef P., Jae Edmonds, Mikiko Kainuma, Keywan Riahi, Allison Thomson, Kathy Hibbard, George C. Hurtt, et al. "The Representative Concentration Pathways: An Overview." *Climatic Change* 109 (2011): 5–31. https://doi.org/10.1007/s10584-011-0148-z.

Van Vuuren, Detlef P., Keywan Riahi, Richard Moss, Jae Edmonds, Allison Thomson, Nebojsa Nakicenovic, Tom Kram, et al. "A Proposal for a New Scenario Framework to Support Research and Assessment in Different Climate Research Communities." *Global Environmental Change* 22, no. 1 (2012): 21–35. https://doi.org/10.1016/j.gloenvcha.2011.08.002.

Veroustraete, Frank, Hendrik Sabbe, and Herman Eerens. "Estimation of Carbon Mass Fluxes over Europe Using the C-Fix Model and Euroflux Data." *Remote Sensing of Environment* 83, no. 3 (2002): 376–99. https://doi.org/10.1016/S0034-4257(02)00043-3.

Vettraino, A. M., G. Natili, N. Anselmi, and A. Vannini. "Recovery and Pathogenicity of *Phytophthora* Species Associated with a Resurgence of Ink Disease in *Castanea sativa* in Italy." *Plant Pathology* 50, no. 1 (2001): 90–96. https://doi.org/10.1046/j.1365-3059.2001.00528.x.

Vieira, Patricia. "Phytographia: Literature as Plant Writing." *Environmental Philosophy* 12, no. 2 (2015): 205–20.

Viveiros de Castro, Eduardo. "On Models and Examples: Engineers and Bricoleurs in the Anthropocene." *Current Anthropology* 60, no. S20 (2019): S296–308. https://doi.org/10.1086/702787.

Westhoek, H. J., M. van den Berg, and J. A. Bakkes. "Scenario Development to Explore the Future of Europe's Rural Areas." *Agriculture, Ecosystems & Environment* 114, no. 1 (2006): 7–20. https://doi.org/10.1016/j.agee.2005.11.005.

White, Richard. *The Organic Machine*. Edited by Eric Foner. New York: Hill and Wang, 1995.

Whyte, Kyle P. "Settler Colonialism, Ecology, and Environmental Injustice." *Environment and Society* 9, no. 1 (2018): 125–44. https://doi.org/10.3167/ares.2018.090109.

Winiwarter, Verena. "Prolegomena to a History of Soil Knowledge in Europe." In *Soils and Societies: Perspectives from Environmental History*, edited by John R. McNeill, 180–217. Cambridge, UK: White Horse Press, 2010.

Wodak, Josh, and Timothy Neale. "A Critical Review of the Application of Environmental Scenario Exercises." *Futures* 73 (2015): 176–86. http://dx.doi.org/10.1016/j.futures.2015.09.002.

World Energy Council. *World Energy Resources Bioenergy 2016*. London: 2016.

Wynne, Brian. "Misunderstood Misunderstandings: Social Identities and Public Uptake of Science." In *Misunderstanding Science? The Public Reconstruction of Science and Technology*, 19–46. Cambridge: Cambridge University Press, 1996.

Zabini, Federica, Ramona Magno, and Valentina Grasso. *Clima che cambia: gli impatti sul territorio Toscano*. Laboratorio di Monitoraggio e Modellistica Ambientale (LaMMA). Firenze: Regione Toscana, LaMMA, Ibimet, 2012.

Zagli, Andrea. *Il lago e la comunità. Storia di Bientina, un "castello" di pescatori nella Toscana moderna*. Nuove Ricerche di Storia. Edited by Ivan Tognarini. Napoli: Edizioni Polistampa, 2001.

Zeder, Melinda A. "Core Questions in Domestication Research." *Proceedings of the National Academy of Sciences* 112, no. 11 (2015): 3191–98. https://doi.org/10.1073/pnas.1501711112.

———. "Domestication and Early Agriculture in the Mediterranean Basin: Origins, Diffusion, and Impact." *Proceedings of the National Academy of Sciences* 105, no. 33 (August 19, 2008): 11597–604. https://doi.org/10.1073/pnas.0801317105.

Zucchelli, Mauro. "Nubifragio a Livorno, ecco le cause. È lo tsunami dell'incuria." *Il Tirreno*, 12 Settembre 2017.

INDEX

Note: Page numbers in italics refer to figures.

acacia trees (black locust, *Robinia pseudoacacia*), 78, 112, 114, 121, 207, 210, 232, 257n7, 266–67n8
Accademia Italiana di Scienze Forestali (Italian Academy of Forest Science), 194
afforestation, 59, 156–57, 191
agriculture: abandonment of, 18, 84, 87–88, 90, 95, 152; and greenhouse gas emissions, 151, 187; industrial, 67, 75, 85, 87, 119, 125, 171, 173, 197, 216, 225; lowland, 45; olive, 77, 231; peasant, 13, 18, 67, 74, 90–91, 123–24, 223, 227, 228, 251n24; on reclaimed lands, *135*; smallholder, 13, 123, 171; subsistence, 78, 98; terraced, 45
agronomical treatises, 14, 33, 132–33
agronomists/agronomy, 29, 33
agropastoral systems, 57
Agro Pontino, *134*
agrosilvopastoral systems, 44, 65
airscapes, 199, 200–201, 202
American chestnut (*Castanea dentata*), 79, 173
Anopheles mosquitos, 133–34
Anthropocene era, 3, 4, 55–56, 74, 111, 113, 147, 149, 151, 155, 196, 198, 210, 222, 227, 230
anthropology/anthropologists, 10–11, 30, 96, 97, 159, 171–72, 175; anthropological thinking, 173–74; cultural, 51; decolonization of, 226; systems models of, 151
Apennine mountains, 6, 13, 42, 117, 124, 131, 203, 220, 223, 247n11; chestnut trees in, 16–18; remote areas, 114; smallholder farmers in, 67; tectonic processes, 126–27; transhumance in, 57, 61. *See also* Monte Pisano
Apuan Alps, 6, 28, 117, 150, 203, 261n11
arbutus (*Arbutus unedo* L.), 69, 232
archaeology, 51
Arno River, 6, 101, 132, 136, 156
assemblages: biogeomorphological, 226; climate/landscape/plant, 11; fruit/olive trees/vines, 123; human/nonhuman, 248n3; multispecies, 63; plant/soil/animal, 48, 55; plant/soil/climate, 229; plant/soil/water, 9, 230; root/soil, 120; weather/landform/tree, 147

bacterial respiration, 171
Bagni di Lucca, 143, 182, 199, *201*, 204–5
bark: patterns on, 25; texture of, 14, 20, 26
Barnes, Jessica, 47

beech forests, 166, 170
Berlusconi, Silvio, 182
Bientina, Lake of, 136, 231
bioengineering, 139, *140*
biogeochemical cycles, 3
biogeomorphology/ies, 7–8, 34, 111, 128, 131, 226, 246n22; as cause of disaster, 129; and climate, 131; and climate change, 194–95; defined, 246n22, 257–58n2; and landscape politics, 148; of landscapes, 138; in New Orleans, 227; noticing, 9; and plant morphology, 142
biology, 11, 52, 56; evolutionary, 26; field, 51
biomass energy: as "carbon neutral," 186–89, 196, 220, 264–65n8; and climate change, 173, 186–90, 208; construction of plants, 168, 177–80, 182–83, *182*, 195, *201*, 215–17; controversy surrounding, 8, 149, 205–6, 220; and forests, 180–81, 183, 195, 228; and government policy, 183, 186; as infrastructural politics, 213–17; international discussions of, 189; as landscape care and welfare, 206–9; logging for, 184, *184*, 195; opposition to, 182–83, 198, 205, 209–13, 220; political opposition to, 217–19; promotion of, 189–90, 191, 193, 195–98, 205, 206–9, 267n10; sources of, 182–83; supply chain for, 69, 178–80, 193, 195, 205, 206, 208, 215, 216, 218, 219
BIOME-BGC model, 163, 165–66, 167, 169, 170, 233
Birch effect, 262n12
Borge, Jorge Luis, 32
Borgo a Mozzano, 26
botanical surveys, 61–62
bracken (*Pteridium aquilinum*), 69
Brown, Kate, 148

cadastral maps, 41, 62, 81, 250n19. *See also* tax maps
Caisse, Hannah, 10
Calci valley, 77, 80, 92
Campo di Croce, 61
canals, 28, 65, 122, 134, 135, 136
capitalism, 32, 45, 46, 54, 68, 149, 175, 186, 218; petro-, 227; salvage, 225
carbon cycle, global, 187–88, *187*
carbon dioxide absorption, 151–52, 153, 161
carbon emissions. *See* greenhouse gas emissions
carbon flux measurement, 150, 152–53, *154*, 155, 158, 159, 166–70, 176–77, 220
carbon flux towers. *See* eddy covariance towers
Cardoso, 128
Carse, Ashley, 47
Caruso, Girolamo, 33, 77
Casella, Fabio, 34, 88–91, *89*
Castelnuovo di Garfagnana, 109, 139, 203
Castro, Eduardo Viveiros de, 32
Cedrus libani, 68, 232
cementification, 118, 140
Centro Nazionale di Richerche (CNR), 163
Certosa di Calci, 91
charcoal, 58, 164, 187, 188, 252n2
check dams, 92, 93, 94, 118, *133*, *134*. *See also* dam building
Chernobyl, 148, 227
chestnut canker (*Cryphonectria parasitica*), 22, 23, 45, 47, 51, 54, 78, 79, 95, 161, 173, 210, 225, 245n11; virus as protection against, 78
chestnut drying sheds (*metati*), 44, 69, 78, 80, 81, *81–83*, 144
chestnut forests: and climate change, 170; destruction of, 172, 221; dying, 190; loss of, 83; in the Monte Pisano, 174, 175
chestnut groves/orchards (*castagneti*), 44, 49, 70; abandoned, 19, 44, 95, 126; destroyed, 77, 78, 207; near Fosciandora, 17–18, *17*; locations of former, 81; low-level elevation, 83–84; maintenance of, 18; on Monte Pisano, 42, 43, 44, 68, 232; owned by urban elites, 67. *See also* chestnut trees
chestnuts, drying and milling, 80
chestnut standards, 115, *116*
chestnut stools. *See* stumps (stools/*ceppi*)
chestnut trees: abandoned, 56, 68; ancient, 50, 56, 223, *224*; from Asia, 75; buds of, 71; and climate change, 195; coppices of, 95, 112; cultivation of, 7, 13, 15–19, 28, 29, 32, 34, 44, 45, 51, 61, 67, 85, 96, 120, 161, 194, 195, 243n1, 243–44n4; destruction

of, 70, 228; diversity among, 83; domestic vs. wild, 15–16, *16*; fire-killed, *106*; as food crop, 16–17, 29, 58; forms of, 55; grafted, 16, 19–20, *21*, 26, 50, 55, 95, 223, 224, 225; growing regions in the Mediterranean, 76; infected with canker, 22, 23, 45, 47, 51, 54, 78, 79, 95, 161, 173, 210, 225, 245n11; and ink disease, 45, 70, 74–78, 84, 85, 95, 210; landscape structures, *72*; Marrone di Pozzuolo, 19; removal of, 210; state policies regarding, 29–30; technical terms for, 55, *55*; and terraces, 38, 40, 41; traditional varieties of, 96; tree trunks, 115; used for firewood/timber, 17. *See also* American chestnut (*Castanea dentata*); chestnut groves/orchards (*castagneti*); Chinese chestnut (*Castanea mollissima*); Japanese chestnut (*Castanea crenata*); sweet chestnut (*Castanea sativa*)

Chiaro, Alessandra del, 19–21, 56, 60, 128

Chiaro, Giuseppe del, 19–22, 24, 47, 56, 78, 84

Chiesi, Marta, 163–67, 170, 174, 177, 233

Chinese chestnut (*Castanea mollissima*), 76, 79, 252n3

CHV-1 virus, 22, 23, 47, 78, 79, 173

Cinque Terre heritage landscape, 136

climate: intersecting variables of, 76; Mediterranean, 130; of the Monte Pisano, 231–32; official conceptions of, 176; predicting possible futures, 169–73; rainfall, 130; relationship to plants and soil, 8; relationship to trees and landforms, 113; responses to, 30; systems models of, 151; vernacular knowledge/models of, 98, 111, 119, 121, 130, 138, 145, 151, 176, 196, 222, 227; and weather, 111–12. *See also* weather

climate change: and agricultural history, 97–98; alternate response to, 97; and biomass energy production, 69, 208; blamed for disasters, 137; discussion of, 141–45; and drought, 2, 4; effects of, 2, 84, 87, 88, 139–40; and energy production, 181; and environmentalism, 205; and forest fires, 75, 76, 95, 99, 108, 162; framings of, 30, 52, 98–100, 137–39; and the future, 228; global, 138, 143, 227; global responses to, 196–97; and landscape history, 176; and the links between people, plants, and landscapes, 125; media coverage of, 139–40; in the Mediterranean, 35, 131, 138; models of, 190; overlooking of, 136–37; and plant disease, 96–97; politics of, 8, 98; popular view of, 15, 196–97, 221, 228–29; rainfall patterns, 97, 130; resistance to damage done by, 83; skepticism about, 146–47, 230; temperature patterns, 97; urgency of, 11; variables, 150–51; and weather, 98. *See also* ecological modeling

climate change policy/ies: critics of, 221–22; EU, 178; global, 187; official, 147–48, 173, 197, 212, 229–30; treaties, 190–91, 196

climate change science, 137, 149, 176; international, 147; Tuscan, 194–95

climate justice movement, 148, 190, 265n11

climate scientists, 131, 229

climatologists, 166

climax equilibrium, 164, 233, 262–63n18

coastal floodplains, 6, 135–36; swamp drainage in, 133–34

coastal live oaks (*Quercus agrifolia*), 5

coastal redwoods (*Sequoia sempervirens*), 5

colmata, 132

colonialism, 148–49

Comitato Alce (Alce Committee), 210

common land, 57; for grazing, 59, 68, 70

Comunità del Bosco (Forest Community), 255n23

conifers: abandoned plantations of, 60; on the Monte Pisano, 232; plantations, 57, 61, 68–69, 163, 232; planting of, 59; replacing chestnut trees, 79; shape of, 56. *See also* pine trees

conservation, 4, 5, 113, 256n2

consorzi di bonifica (improvement consortia), 132, 135

controlled burning, 85, 90–91, 254n13

cork oak (*Quercus suber* L.), 232

Corpo Forestale dello Stato. *See* forest service

corruption, 137, 139

COVID-19 pandemic, 161, 173
critical-zone scientists, 175
Crocus biflorus, 61
Cryphonectria hypovirus 1 (CHV-1), 22, 23, 47, 78, 79, 173
Cryphonectria parasitica (chestnut canker). *See* chestnut canker (*Cryphonectria parasitica*)

dam building, 157, 158, 191, 204, 248n4, 266n2. *See also* check dams
decolonizing practices, 15, 226
deforestation, 58, 59, 132, 133
desertification, 194
disease: malaria, 134. *See also* pathogen epidemics; plant disease
Douglas fir (*Pseudotsuga menziesii*), 60
drainage systems: abandonment of, 148; in agronomical treatises, 132; in Agro Pontino, 134; ancient, 44; biogeomorphologies of, 32; clogged, 89; crumbling, 97; in earthen terraces, 39; in Egypt, 47; and the landscape, 14, 15, 19; local responsibility for, 138, 143–44; maintenance of, 30, 33, 34–35, 92, 128, 132, 135–36, 138, 145, 146, 226; morphology/ies of, 9, 100, 135, 137, 175; names of different types, 34–35; in pine and chestnut forests, 44; and plant morphology, 7, 32, 33–34; repair/restoration of, 74, 144, 230; in San Rossore, 157; state-sponsored, 118; in stone wall terraces, 37, 40, 41; in *vite maritata*, 36. *See also* water management
Drax Power Station (UK), 216
drought, 75, 76, 99, 111, 171, 196; and climate change, 2, 4; and parametrization, 165–66
Dryocosmus kuriphilus (gall wasp), 55

E. arborea L., 232
earthquakes, 127, 141
ecological change, 85, 97, 169, 176
ecological climax, 164, 233, 262–63n18
ecological modeling, 162–65, 176; absence of history from, 171; BIOME-BGC model, 163, 165–66, 169, 170; C-Fix model, 163; HadCM3 global circulation model, 170; models as diagrams that capture uncertainty, 166–69; Net Ecosystem Exchange (NEE), 165; Net Primary Productivity equation, 164–65, 168; normalized actual volume equation, 164; simulation models, 169, 174–75, 190; using tree volume, 164
ecologists, 80, 97, 155, 159, 170, 175, 226; historical, 4, 228
ecology/ies, 11; historical, 6, 46, 61–62, 70, 97; of the Monte Pisano, 231–32; and morphology, 11, 32; political, 47–48, 98
economic change, 158; political, 151
ecotourism, 73, 84, 92
eddy covariance towers, 150, 152–53, 154, 155, 158, 159, 165, 261n4
Edwards, Paul, 150
embankments. *See* riverbanks; riverbeds
energy production: "carbon negative/neutral," 186, 188, 220; coal, 214; geothermal, *201*, 202; hydroelectric power, 191, 203–4, 248n4, 265n13, 266n2; kinds of, 180; national energy policies, 190–91; nuclear power, 227; oil-based, 214; and politics, 214; renewable, 181, 186, 188, 191, 214, 217, 265n13; solar and wind, 187–88, 214; sustainable, 178–79, 190, 194; wood pellets, 215. *See also* fossil fuels
environmental change, 3, 94, 97, 99–100, 142, 145, 147, 148, 162, 176, 197, 225n28; global, 3, 5, 6, 15, 44, 52, 60, 149, 159, 162, 171, 174, 193, 213, 222, 228; regional/national, 170–71, 174, 227; socio-, 175, 229; understandings of, 145
environmentalism/environmentalists, 4, 94, 205, 218
environmental justice movement, 214
epidemiology, 212
Erica arborea, 44, 232
erosion, 126, 132, 133, 194; and landslides, 136; prevention of, 15; reducing, 133
ethnography, 32, 81; landscape, 48, 62; multispecies, 244n8
Extinction Rebellion movement, 145, 221

Fazzi, Stefano, 26, 55, 78
Ferri, Aldo, 144
fertilization/fertilizers, 29, 35, 44, 45; chemical, 85; of forests, 152; of terraces, 30; using guano, 29; using leaf litter, 49, 59; using sheep manure, 59
fire management practices, 90–91; abandonment of, 84, 85; prescribed burning, 90–91
fire prevention, 57, 73–74
firewood cutting/gathering, 59, 74, 85–87, 109, 111, 113–15, 117, 121, 152, 155, 184, 185, 185, 188–89, 192, 211, 219, 264n11; histories of, 163; practical considerations, 113–15; as rural enterprise, 192–93, 214; traditional system of, 110, 120; by women, 254n14
fir trees, 152. *See also* conifers; pine trees
flood expansion basins, 137
floods, 4, 6, 8, 9, 89, 92, 94, 97, 110, 111, 112, 118, 122, 227; causes of, 120, 128–30, 145; changing patterns of, 98; and climate change, 137; in the coastal plains, 135–36; and concrete riverbanks, 139; and forest cover, 256n4; increases in, 141; and landscape stability, 146; media coverage of, 145; memories of, 135; prevention of, 15, 146; protection from, 28, 132; and rain, 136; on the Versilia plain, 130; vulnerability to, 136, 140, 193, 194; and water management, 131
flu pandemics, 172
FLUXNET network, 152
flux towers. *See* eddy covariance towers
folded sandstone, 127
forest cover, 135; actual (FC_A), 233
foresters, 113–15, 117, 120
forest fires: in California, 1–2, 199, 228, 229, 241n1; and climate change, 2, 75, 76, 95, 99, 108, 151, 162, 227; concern about, 229; as fast disasters, 84–91; firefighting, 90, 228; and forest management, 71, 74; impacts of, 4, 5–7, 9, 11, 14, 26, 31–32, 46, 49, 51, 52, 62, 68, 85, 89–90, 89; increases in, 142; linked to landslides, 94; media coverage of, 91, 255n20; in the Monte Pisano, 38, 48, 72, 74, 75, 85–86, 90, 91–100, 162; in pine forests, 73, 75; "post-litter raking/postgrazing," 89–90; prevention of, 57, 149; regrowth following, 44; smoke from, 199; surviving, 54; vulnerability to, 8, 45, 60, 69, 97
forest guards, 58
forestry laws, 132
forests: abandoned, 111, 118, 137, 208; Amazon, 171; of the American west, 164; beech, 166, 170; and biomass energy, 188, 195, 228; as carbon sink, 177; classification of, 166–67; and climate, 256n4; and climate change, 151–53, 155, 163, 167, 194; community, 57; coppiced, 109, 113, 114, 117, *121*; cutting of, 58; destruction of, 91, 212; diagramming ghost forests, 78, 80–81; drying of soil and leaf litter, 75; and energy, 180–81, 183, 191–92; evidence of human use in, 44–45; ghostly presences in, 49, 51–52; high forest, 56, 114–15, 152, 155; local responsibility for, 138, 143–44; management of, 19, 109; Mediterranean, 163–66, *168*, 233; of the Monte Pisano, 228; North American, 152, 163–64; overgrown, 119–20, 191, 205, 209, 221; reclamation of, 94; reforestation, 59, 163; regrowth of, 152; regulations regarding, 58; as stabilizing structures, 112–13; state presence in, 57–61; swamp, 157; technical terms for, 55; threats to, 161; Tuscan, 170, 177, 178–79; vulnerability to fires, 87–88. *See also* chestnut forests; pine forests (*pineta*); trees
forest service, 59–61, 85, 92, 110, 114, 129, 255–56n1, 266–67n8
Fornovolasco, 128
fossil fuels, 3, 152, 181, 186, 190, 204
fruit trees, 30, 34, 56, 63, 162
fungus/fungal disease, 46, 78; mycorrhizal, 26. *See also* chestnut canker (*Cryphonectria parasitica*)

gall wasp (*Dryocosmus kuriphilus*), 55
Garfagnana, 78, 109–10, *121*
geologists, 194
geology: and bedrock, 130; folded sandstone, 127; of the Monte Pisano, 231; rock formation, 131

geomorphologists, 136
geomorphology/ies, 109, 122, 130, 257–58n2; and chestnut cultivation, 194; concern over, 122; geomorphological potential, 141; as intersection of many factors, 157; in Italy, 148, 258–59n10; politics of, 122, 148; in San Rossore, 157; as slow process, 122; transformation of, 109
Giambastiani, Massimo, 56, 83, 96, 128
Giurlani, Oreste, 179
globalization, biological, 95
global trade, 45, 76, 174. *See also* international trade
gorse (*Ulex europaeus*), 44, 69, 85, 86, 90, 95, 108, 232
Gozzi, Michele, 114
grafting, 13, 18, 24–26, 96, 245n12; of chestnuts, 16, 19–20, 21, 26, 31, 50, 55, 95, 223, 224, 225; as deception, 26; diagrams of, 26, 27, 28; multiple grafts, 78; peasant knowledge of, 29; of plums, 25; present-day practices of, 30; relationship to terracing, 30; scars from, 22, 25; skill necessary for, 24; as symbiosis, 25–26
grapevines: cultivation of, 28–29, 30, 34; destroyed by fire, 91; with earthen terraces, 39; supported by trees, 35, 36, 65; trellised (*vigne a pergola*), 63
Grassiini, Alsio, 162
Grava, Massimiliano, 80
grazing, 49, 54, 85–86; abandonment of, 74, 75, 142; in common areas, 57–58, 59, 70; of goats, 44–45, 49, 59–60, 61; of sheep, 44–45, 49, 59–60, 61, 74, 85, 87, 89; state control of, 57; and transhumance, 57
greenhouse gas emissions, 145, 151, 191

HadCM3 global circulation model, 170
Hadley Center (UK), 170
Hallé, Francis, 9
Haraway, Donna, 22, 47
hazel trees, 195
heath (*Erica scoparia*), 69
heather (*Erica* species), 85
heat waves, 4, 140, 143
history/historians, 10–11, 30, 151, 159, 171–72, 175; decolonization of, 226; ecological, 229; environmental, 4; natural, 46, 51, 81; oral, 83, 88, 96; social, 57; socionatural, 212
holm oak (*Quercus ilex* L.), 85, 105, 107, 108, 157, 158, 232
hornbeam trees (*Ostrya carpinifolia* Scop.), 185, 185, 232
Hulme, Mike, 2–3, 111
human/nonhuman encounters, 30, 44–47, 51–52, 99, 110, 113, 125, 148, 155, 207, 228, 248n3
human/plant encounters, 30, 49, 51, 126, 128, 155, 160, 223
Hurricane Katrina, 227
hydrogeological instability, 119, 135, 136, 193, 211, 259–60n16
hydrologists/hydrology, 28, 136, 226, 257n10

Indigenous people, 5, 190; knowledge of, 30; landscape care by, 2, 4, 5, 88, 119, 241n1, 261n7
industrialization, 45, 75, 86, 204, 221, 227
infrared carbon dioxide detectors, 153, 154
infrastructure: energy, 267n12; flood management, 137; landscape as, 33, 47; maintenance of, 136; oil-based, 213–14; and politics, 213–17; and the state, 213
Ingold, Tim, 2, 48
ink disease (*Phytophthora cambivora [male del inchiostro]*), 45, 62, 70, 74–76, 84, 95, 161, 172, 210, 253n5; and chestnut landscapes, 76–78; and pine forests, 85; spread of, 77–78. *See also* oomycete water molds
insect infestation, 99, 158, 160, 161, 169, 172, 174; gall wasps, 55; mosquitos, 133–34; scale insects, 158, 162, 172
International Energy Agency, 188
international trade, 4, 60, 71, 75, 96, 161, 172, 228, 253n5, 255n27. *See also* global trade
iron industry, 58
Italy: chestnut cultivation in, 16–19; climate change in, 35; climate change politics in, 8, 11; environmental politics in, 15, 31; landscape in, 3–7; unification of, 58. *See also* Tuscany

Japanese chestnut (*Castanea crenata*), 76, 79, 252n3
Jasanoff, Sheila, 119, 168
job creation, 178, 181, 193, 194, 195, 196, 206, 209

knowledge(s): local, 119, 230; partial/situated, 22, 47; peasant/indigenous, 30, 56; popular, 119; specialized, 117; vernacular, 125

LaMMA, 194
land abandonment, 5, 11, 85, 110, 130–31, 194, 205, 209, 251n25
landowners: and ecotourism, 84; as grafters, 26; as landlords, 67–68; land use tax reports, 62–65, 250n19; leasing to sharecroppers, 67; organized into districts, 132; peasants as, 110; property rights of, 58–59; responsibilities of, 135, 138, 259–60n16; sale of wood by, 208, 219; tax boondoggles for, 60
land ownership, 244n6; inheritance laws, 68; privatization, 58; property rights, 58
land reclamation, 4, 118, 132; in coastal floodplains, 145; state involvement in, 132, 134; and swamp drainage, 132, 134
landscape: abandoned, 100, 110, 117, 125; abandonment of, 93–94, 97, 123–25, 147–48, 176, 196, 207, 229; *alberata* (polycultures), 65; anthropogenic, 149; bureaucratic classifications of, 61–62; care of, 74, 88, 91, 97, 99, 113, 118–19, 122, 131, 146, 221, 222, 230; changes to, 69, 171; chestnut, 76–78; Cinque Terre heritage, 136; descriptions of, 49; effect of ink disease on, 76–78; ethnography of, 62; history of, 76, 90–91, 155–58, 176; human-modified, 3, 4–5; human-shaped, 131; human use of, 49; as infrastructure, 33, 47, 194, 196–97; in Italy, 3–7; maintenance of, 98; mobile, 149; modification of, 155; of Monte Pisano, 61, 71, 72; overgrown, 112; patterns of, 47–49, 51, 61, 75, 96, 108; peasant traditions of care, 228; phenomenological experience of, 174; *piantata*, 65; pine as agent of transformation, 101–8; postpeasant, 117, 148, 155, 167, 195; reshaping, 30–31, 33, 67, 132; restoration of, 92, 95; shape of, 128; stability of, 74, 89, 94, 109, 111, 112, 114, 118–20, 122, 125, 128, 134, 136–41, 144, 146, 149, 194, 196, 218, 229; stabilization of, 28–29, 57, 92–93; structures of, 48–49, 70–72, 95–98, 111, 112, 122, 160, 171, 190; and weather, 136, 137, 112. *See also* landscape morphology
landscape architects, 226
landscape morphology: attention to, 198, 226–28; and biogeomorphology, 138; care of, 112, 119, 127, 131, 136, 137, 144, 149, 194, 195, 197; changing patterns of, 130, 145; management of, 112, 137; noticing, 9, 148, 203, 208–9, 243n2; politics of, 91, 98; questions about, 138; shaping of, 11, 34, 194; stable, 141; state maintenance of, 95, 146, 194; threats to, 91
landscape thinking and systems thinking, 158–62
landslides: causes of, 35, 58, 110, 112, 114, 115, 120, 145, 208–9, 211, 227; and climate change, 140, 146; concern about, 193; and erosion, 136; and floods, 146; and geomorphology, 109, 122, 126–27, 130; increases in, 141; inventory of, 141; maps predicting risk, 141; media coverage of, 145; memories of, 135; prevention of, 74, 109–10, 112, 117–18, 121, 149; and rain, 120–21, 128, 136, 138–39, 210; restoration of, 139; vulnerability to, 6, 94, 193, 194; and weather, 8, 98, 110, 120–21
land-use change, 74, 113, 151, 161, 162, 170, 172
Latour, Bruno, 175
Law, John, 46
leaf litter: accumulation of, 75–76, 87, 89, 95, 97; burning, 85, 244n5; and forest fires, 38, 75; measurement of, 153, 159; raking of, 85–86; used for fertilizer, 49, 59, 73, 75, 85, 86; used in sheep stalls, 73, 86. *See also* litter raking
Legambiente, 136
Lenzarini, Maria, 86–87
Leptoglossus occidentalis (western conifer-seed bug), 156, 172, 261n8

Lien, Marianne, 46
Liguria: flooding and mudflows, 136; terracing in, 14
litter raking, 45, 59, 71, 85, 86, 87, 88, 228, 254n15; abandonment of, 73–74, 75, 89; history of, 229; impacts of, 88–89; as women's work, 87. *See also* leaf litter
Livorno, 137, 218
loblolly pine plantations, 152
logging, 59, 109, 113–14, 152; for biomass energy, 184, 195; of chestnut trees, 225; clear-cutting, 121; for firewood, 184, 185, *185*, 195; industrial, 210; in San Rossore, *184*; small-scale, 219
Logli, Francesca, 155, 157, 159–60, 162
lopping. *See* pruning
Lucca, 6, 43; cadastral survey, 81; flood protection in, 28; history of, 57; map, *7*, *43*; Office of Chestnut Groves, 29; oligarchy in, 57; Republic of, 58; river maintenance in, 132; tax maps and registers, 62–63

Macchetti, Cristina, 211
macchia scrub, 85, 232
malaria control, 134
Malfatti, Fabio, 80
Manigrasso, Manuele, 149
manna ash (*Fraxinus ornus* L.), 69, 232
Maracchi, Giampiero, 137
maritime pines (*Pinus pinaster*, *Pinus pinaster* Aiton), 44, 68–69, 71, 74, 85, 86, 90, 101, 103, 105, *107*, 156, 157, 158, 162, 231, 247n2; diseases and pest attacks, 158, 161–62, 172
Masco, Joe, 226–27
Maselli, Fabio, 163–67, 170, 174, 177, 233
Massoni, Giovanni, 144
Matsucoccus feytaudi. *See* scale insects (*Matsucoccus feytaudi*)
Mela, Giuseppe (pseudonym), 109, 112, 119–20, 208, 216, 218
methane hydrates, 171
migrant labor, 57
Mitchell, Tim, 213
monocultures, 68
Montaigne, Michel de, 33, 204
Monte Pisano: biogeomorphological politics of, 8; chestnut drying sheds (*metati*), *82–83*; climate change politics in, 99; communal lands in, 58; community forests, 57; crest of (photo detail), *71*; ecology and climate, 75, 88, 231–32; forest fires, 38, 85–86, 91–95, 162; forests, 49, 59, 228; history of, 97; ink disease on, 70; landscape structures, 61, 174; panoramic view, 81, 83; pasture land, 59; people of, 229; pine and chestnut forests, 42, 43, 44, 72, 78, 80, 161, 174, 175; plant pathogens on, 45; study of, 6, 7, 32, 34, 47, 171; transect drawing, 68–70, *69*; trees of, 11, 19; weather events on, 126
Monte Serra, 43, 89, 94, 231
Montevarchi, 178, 180–81, *182*, 183, 188, 191, 193, 196
Moretti, Eugenio, 153, 155, 156, 159
morphology/ies: of air currents, 193, 199, 211; atmospheric, 199, 211; of drainage systems, 135, 137, 175; and ecology, 11, 32; of riverbeds, 129–30; of riverbeds and riverbanks, 122, 129, 135; of sandstone, 127; seed, 52; soil, 9; of terracing, 122, 175. *See also* biogeomorphology/ies; geomorphology/ies; landscape morphology; plant morphology; tree morphology
mountains: Alpine, 131; in the Italian peninsula, 131; slope stabilization, 133. *See also* Apennine mountains; Apuan Alps
mudflows/mudslides, 9, 74, 89, 92, 94, 97, 98, 111, 112, 118, 122, 136; in Cardoso and Fornovolasco, 128–31, *131*; in the coastal plains, 135–36; and concrete riverbanks, 139; plans to prevent, 129–30; and rain, 136; repairing damage from, 139; summary of events, 136; vulnerability to, 140
mulberry trees, 63
Mushroom at the End of the World, The (Tsing), 46
Mussolini, Benito, 59, 134, *134*
mycorrhizal fungi, 26
Myrtus communis L., 232

national forest law, 59
natural engineering techniques, 139
natural history, 46, 51, 81
natural resource extraction, 60, 148
natural scientists, 80, 176
Net Ecosystem Exchange (NEE), 153, 159, 165
Net Primary Productivity (NPP), 164–65, *168*; equation, 233–34
Nixon, Rob, 148
normalized actual volume (NV_A), 164, 233
nuclear testing, 3

oak trees (*Quercus pubescens* Willd.), 45, 49, 228; coppices of, 112, 185, *185*, 232; evergreen, 166; in the lowlands, 170; Mediterranean, 165. *See also* holm oak (*Quercus ilex* L.)
oligarchy, 57
olive oil, 58
olive trees, 29, 30, 34, 37, 38, 56, 58; attack by *Xyllela* bacteria, 172; cultivation of, 85, 120; destroyed by fire, 91; fertilizer for, 73; pruning, 199, *200*; replacing chestnut trees, 77; and stone wall terraces, 37
Olwig, Kenneth, 46
ontological anarchism, 32
ontology, 48, 51, 62, 69, 96, 161, 166, 169
oomycete water molds, 75, 76. *See also* ink disease (*Phytophthora cambivora [male del inchiostro]*)
orchards. *See* chestnut groves/orchards (*castagneti*)
overflow basins, 132

paper mills/factories, 210–11, 219
parametrization, 165–66
pastoralism, 11, 67; abandonment of, 84; and forest fires, 84; shaping the landscape, 67
pastoralists, 61, 73, 133
pastureland, 109; abandoned, 124; after fire, 90; on mountains, 59
pathogen epidemics, 45, 68, 71, 74, 76, 95–96, 97, 161, 169, 171, 172, 174, 176, 210, 228, 229; as slow disasters, 84. *See also* plant disease
peasants: as agriculturalists, 49; defined, 65, 67–68; displacement of, 190; and drainage systems, 34; as farmers, 45, 55; firewood management by, 110, 120; knowledge and practices of, 13–15, 18–19, 29–30, 33–34, 39, 55–56, 163; landscape care by, 88, 123, 163; as sharecroppers, 63, 67, 98; as smallholders, 57; and terracing, 34. *See also* agriculture: peasant; smallholder farmers
permafrost thawing, 171
pest epidemics. *See* insect infestation
Peter Leopold (Archduke of Tuscany), 58
Petri, Lionello, 79
phenomenology, 47, 48, 49, 151, 160, 162, 174
photographs, drawbacks of, 56
photosynthesis, 150, 165, 189
Phyllyrea angustifolia L., 232
Phytophthora cambivora. *See* ink disease (*Phytophthora cambivora*)
Phytophthora cinnamomi, 75
Phytophthora water molds, 253n5. *See also* ink disease (*Phytophthora cambivora*)
pine forests (*pineta*), 42, 43, 44, 68, 69, 73, 74, 80–81, 89, 95, 97, 150; coastal, 184; dying, 190; fire-prone, 75, 97; low-elevation, 85, 95; in the Monte Pisano, 175; replacing chestnut groves, 77; in San Rossore, 170, 174, 183; use for biomass energy, *184*. *See also* pine trees
pine nut gatherers, 101, 155–56, 158, 160, 162, 172
pine trees, 45, 49, 70, 152; cultivation of, 101–8; fire/pine/oak interactions, 105, 108; forked, 172; landscape structures, 72; in the lowlands, 170; Mediterranean, 165; on the Monte Pisano, 232; pine/fire/chestnut interactions, 103, 105, *105*, *106*; as prone to fire, 45; used for shipbuilding, 58. *See also* conifers; maritime pines (*Pinus pinaster*); pine forests (*pineta*); stone pines (*Pinus pinea*)
Pinus nigra, 68, 232
Pisa, 6; forest protection in, 59; map, 7, 43; medieval republic of, 58
Pistacia lentiscus L., 232
Pistoia, 58
Pizzorna, 28, 32, 60, 114, 143

Pizzorna mountains, 114, 143
plant disease, 6, 72, 73, 151, 174, 228; in chestnut forests, 78; effects of on landscape, 96–97; effects on trees, 52, 54; in ghost forests, 78, 80–81; and plant morphology, 22; resistance to, 55–56; surviving, 54. *See also* pathogen epidemics
plant morphology, 8, 11, 51, 61; as anthropological evidence, 31–32; and biogeomorphology, 142; as biography of encounter, 9; care for, 125, 127; in drawings and diagrams, 10, 70; growth patterns, 14; as historic record, 5, 14, 31–32; influences on, 30, 34; instability of, 22, 31; and landscape structures, 70–72; linked to drainage systems, 32; linked to terracing, 32; noticing, 7, 9, 13, 30, 31, 34, 60, 96; official responsibility for, 142; and plant disease, 22; and social history, 57
plants: adaptability of, 8; colonization of, 45; coordination with people, 3, 175; indeterminacy of, 51; international trade, 4, 60, 71, 75, 96, 161, 172, 228, 253n5, 255n27; non-native, 60–61; pasture flowers, 61; role in soil formation, 127; rootedness of, 9; sensing capacity of, 245n13; sensory experience of, 31–32; shape-shifting, 52; understory, 60–61. *See also* plant morphology
plate tectonics, 6, 126–27, 227
PM10 particles, 210–11, 217
political ecologies, 47–48, 98
politics: agrarian, 68; biogeomorphological, 11, 14, 111, 128, 131–36, 143, 145–48, 196, 206, 226; and biomass energy, 149; biomorphological, 111, 122; climate change, 99–100; energy, 222; environmental, 15, 31, 73, 99, 111, 149; geomorphological, 30, 94, 137, 138, 219; infrastructural, 213–17; in Italy, 212–13; landscape, 83–84, 148, 220–22, 230; of landscape stability, 109; morphological, 113–15, 117, 122
Polli, Simone, 142
pollution: air, 93, 142, 147, 193, 210–12, 214, 216–18, 220, 221; and the environment, 197; industrial, 219
polycultures, 68
Pontine Marshes, 132
poplar tree (Populus nigra), 35, 63, 65, 204; supporting grapevines (*vite maritata*), 65, 66
Pozzuolo, 78
pruning, 13, 18, 19, 35, 54, 65, 96, 199, 200; of pine nut trees, 156
pumping stations, 134

Rackham, Oliver, 9, 248n5
rainstorms, 75, 89, 94, 111, 122, 125, 136, 144, 194–95, 227; causing flooding and mudflows, 128–29, 136–37; increasing intensity of, 139; and landscape stability, 146; and landslides, 130, 138–39, 141. *See also* climate; weather
real estate development, 58, 119, 137, 138, 139, 140, 146, 147
REDD+ (Reducing Emissions from Deforestation Forest Degradation), 152
redwood trees, 5
reforestation, 59, 163
Representative Concentration Pathways (RCPs), 169
restoration practices, 74, 92, 95
riverbanks: and flooding, 146; morphology of, 122, 129, 135; repairing, 132, 139
riverbeds: channeling, 136, 139; clogged, 120, 128, 136–37; and flooding, 146; management of, 112, 117–22, 132, 139; morphologies of, 129, 130, 135
river canalization, 131
rivers: draining and moving, 132; in the Italian peninsula, 131
road maintenance, 119
Rocheleau, Diane, 47
rock formation, 131
Roma-Marzio, Francesco, 49, 52, 60–61, 69, 78
Rose, Deborah Bird, 31
Rossi, Ornella, 144
Royal Forest Service, 59

Sabbatini, Renzo, 57–58
Saminiati, Vincenzo, 28–29

San Rossore park, 101, *102*, *104*, 171; ecology of, 159; eddy covariance towers, 150, 152–53, *154*, 165, 167; forests, 172; insect pests in, 161; landscape history of, 155–58; logging in, *184*; pine forests, 170, 174, 183; plant disease and landscape transformation, *157*; tree morphology in, 158
scale insects (*Matsucoccus feytaudi*), 158, 162, 172, 262n11
scenario building, 169–70, 172, 186, 188–89, 263n24
scions, 20–22, *21*
scrub, 60, 74, 77, 94, 98, 128; fire-prone, 97–98; heath (*Erica scoparia*), 69; *macchia*, 85, 232; overgrown, 94; pine, 68; poplar and willow, 204; postfire, 89. *See also* gorse (*Ulex europaeus*)
seed morphology, 9, 52
Seravezza, 129, *140*
Serchio watershed, 129, 132, 136, 156, 203, 231, 248n4; reclaimed farmland, *135*
Sereni, Emilio, 65
Sesto, Lake of, 136
sharecroppers/sharecropping, 45, 67, 98, 251n24
Sistemazioni Idraulico-Forestali, 139
smallholder farmers, 56, 57, 60, 78, 123, 124, 128, 171; as agricultural laborers, 251n24; with chestnut groves, 13, 16; fire set by, 94–95; as firewood cutters, 115, 188; as industrial and service workers, 15; livelihoods of, 57–58; vs. peasants, 64, 67–68, 243n1
social change, 85, 119, 147, 158, 169, 173, 174, 227, 228, 229, 248n6
socioenvironmental change, 175, 229
soil(s): care of, 223; classification of, 33, 35; clay, 126; erosion of, 58, 133, 194; fertility of, 15; formation of, 11, 15, 30, 32, 46, 111, 120, 127, 131; improvement of, 29; management of, 65; morphology of, 9; movement of, 9; permeability of, 120; recognizing quality of, 29, 30; retention of, 139; sedimentary, 112, 227; thickness of, 130; unstable, 112, 227; and weather, 110–11
species extinctions, 138
state abandonment, 113, 119
state formation, 45, 47, 60
state power, and plant form, 57–61
stone buildings, 78
stone pines (*pino domestic, Pinus pinea*), 101, *102*, 103, *103*, *104*, 155–57, *157*, 158, 262n10; and conifer-seed bug, 172; with Y-shaped forks, 160, *161*
stone walls (*muretti a secco*), 37, *37*, 40, *41*, 44, 109; and chestnut trees, *40*, 41, *41*
stools. *See* stumps (stools/*ceppi*)
streams, cleaning out, 117–22
structural violence, 47
stumps (stools/*ceppi*), 44, 52, 53, 55, 71, 115, *116*, 242n6
suckers (*polloni*), 49, 50
swamp drainage, 4, 131, 132, 133–34, 145, 227
sweet chestnut (*Castanea sativa*), 13, 15–19, 44, 172
symbiosis, 25–26, 71
systems thinking, 158–62

tannin factories, 79, 206–7, *207*, 209–11, 225
tax assessment, 62–65, 223
tax maps, 61–63, *64*, 68, 80, 81, 250n19
tectonic processes, 6, 126–27, 227
terracing, 9, 13, 14, 18, 19, 29, 33, 135; abandonment of, 46, 69, 89, 95, 97; in agronomical treatises, 132; ancient systems of, 44, 49; banked terraces, 29; banks and hanging fields, 38, *38*; building of, 46; care of, 145; for chestnut farming, 28; and chestnut trees, 38, *40*, *41*; and climate change, 99; earthen, 39; and fertilization, 30; and grafting, 30; history of, 14–15; in Italy, 30; and the landscape, 48, 91, 94, 98; maintenance of, 35, 74, 92, 128, 225; in the Mediterranean, 30; morphologies of, 100, 175; names of different types, 34–35; and plant morphology, 32, 33–34; stone walls (*muretti a secco*), 37, 40, *41*; technical terms for, 55
Terra Uomini e Ambiente (TUA), 139
tourist economy, 204–5
toxicity, 52

transect drawing, 68–70, *69*
transhumance, 57, 61
tree morphology, 32, 44–45, 110, 111, 112, 117, 159; chestnut trees, 51; as historic record, 5, 18, 135, 155, 160, 223; human impact on, 25; indefinite, 51; maintenance of, 112; noticing, 9, 22, 47, 175, 208–9, 225; perception(s) of, 22; and weather, 110
trees: cambium layer, 20, 24, 54, 223, 245n12; care of, 127; coppiced, 55, 56, 57, 68, 69, 111, 242n6; cultivation of, 7, 13–14; fallen, 126, 143; as firewood, 31, 45, 49, 55, 56, 57, 68, 69; as fodder, 49; forms of, 117; as hedges, 29; ivy climbing on, 207, 209; management of, 256n6; multistemmed, 57; overgrown, 110, 111, 207, 211; ownership of, 58; relationship to soil and weather, 110–11; response to disaster by, 31–32; rhythm of growth of, 122; role of roots, 115, *116*; shaped by human encounters, 46; as shape shifters, 223, 225–30; shape-shifting, 31, 33, 54–55; shapes of, 113–14, 122; shaping, 262n13; single-stemmed (*ceduo affrancato*), 56; and slope stabilization, 110; as support for grapevines, 29, 35, 36, 65; supporting grapevines; as timber, 45, 49, 113, 152; trunk volume, 164; used to prevent erosion and flooding, 28. *See also* chestnut trees; forests; fruit trees; pine trees
Trillion Tree Campaign, 190
Trump, Donald, 190
Tsing, Anna, 46, 175
Tuscany: climate change policy in, 194–95; forestry in, 139, 264n2; forests in, 44, 58, 164, 165, 205, 233; landscape care in, 118, 139; plans for biomass plants in, 178–79, 183, 197, 205, 216, 217; property rights in, 58, 156; swamp drainage in, 143; tax maps, 250n19; unification of, 59

Uccelliera, 19
Ulex europaeus. See gorse (*Ulex europaeus*)
ultrasound gas anemometer, 153, *154*
United Nations Framework Convention on Climate Change (UNFCCC), 188, 190, 265n12
United Nations Intergovernmental Panel on Climate Change (IPCC), 169
urbanization, 60, 164, 173
urban sprawl, 140. *See also* real estate development

Val di Chiana, 132
Versilia region, 130, 143
Villa Minutoli-Tegrimi, 63
vineyards. *See* grapevines
viruses, 71, 173; CHV-1, 22, 47, 78, 79, 173
vite maritata, 35, *36*, 65, *66*
Vorno river and valley, 63, 65, *66*, 132, 231, 250n19

walled gardens (*chiuse*), 63
watercourses, 118; channelized, 140
water management, 65, 131. *See also* check dams; dam building; drainage systems
water masters (*maestri delle aque*), 132
weather: changing patterns of, 98, 142–43; and climate, 111–12; and climate change, 2–3, 75, 98; connected to plants and soils, 74; daily cycles of, 47; disastrous events, 110–11, 136–37; expectations of, 111; extreme, 144; forests' response to, 165–66; and landforms, 138; media coverage of, 137–40, 145; relationship to soil, 110–11; stability of, 136–41; vernacular model of, 141–42, 148; vulnerability to, 136. *See also* climate change
weather station data, 166
wildfires. *See* forest fires
willow trees, 204
wind/windstorms, 75, 76, 94–95, 110, 143
women: agricultural work done by, 85–86; as clothes washers, 67, 86; gathering firewood, 254n14; raking leaf litter, 87
woodlot management, 110
wood pellets, 215–16, 267n14

Xyllela bacteria, 172